ARCHAEOLOGY
OF THE SOUTHEASTERN
UNITED STATES

ARCHAEOLOGY OF THE SOUTHEASTERN UNITED STATES

PALEOINDIAN TO WORLD WAR I

JUDITH A. BENSE

Department of Sociology and Anthropology
The University of West Florida
Pensacola, Florida

Academic Press

San Diego   New York   Boston   London   Sydney   Tokyo   Toronto

Cover and interior illustration: A design stamped on pottery from the Swift Creek culture, approximately AD 200. This appears to be a stylized mask that was probably used in rituals. (Actual size of stamp was 2 X 3 inches.) From Snow, 1977, with permission.

Photograph of author: Photograph by Rosanne Mann taken during 1993 excavations for the Colonial Fort of Pensacola Archaeological Trail Project, Pensacola, Florida.

This book is printed on acid-free paper. ∞

Academic Press, Inc.
A Division of Harcourt Brace & Company
525 B Street, Suite 1900, San Diego, California 92101-4495

United Kingdom Edition published by
Academic Press Limited
24–28 Oval Road, London NW1 7DX

Library of Congress Cataloging-in-Publication Data

Bense, Judith Ann.
     Archaeology of the southeastern United States : Paleoindian to
World War I / Judith A. Bense.
         p.   cm.
     Includes index.
     ISBN 0-12-089060-7 (case) -- 0-12-089061-5 (paper)
     1. Indians ot North America--Southern States--Antiquities.
2. Excavations (Archaeology)--Southern States.   3. Southern States-
-History.   4. Southern States--Antiquities.   I. Title.
E78.S65B45   1994
975--dc20   93-46445
                                                                CIP

PRINTED IN THE UNITED STATES OF AMERICA
94 95 96 97 98 99   EB   9 8 7 6 5 4 3 2 1

Contents

3

HISTORY OF SOUTHEASTERN ARCHAEOLOGY

4

PALEOINDIAN STAGE: 13,000?–8000 B.C.

5

ARCHAIC STAGE: 8000–1000 B.C.

6

WOODLAND STAGE: 1000 B.C.– A.D. 1000

7

MISSISSIPPIAN STAGE: A.D. 1000–1500

8

EUROPEAN STAGE: A.D. 1500–1821

9

AMERICAN STAGE: A.D. 1821–1917

Judith A. Bense was born in New Jersey to a dairy farming family. In 1951, her family moved to Panama City, Florida to purchase a new farm. Growing up in rural northwest Florida, her interests in history and archaeology were nurtured by her parents and an exceptional high school history teacher. After earning her doctorate degree, Professor Bense began, at age 27, practicing archaeology in the Southeast. Professor Bense started the Anthropology–Archaeology program at the University of West Florida and founded the Archaeology Institute. Additionally, she has received several awards in archaeology, such as the National Public Service Award and the Distinguished Teaching Award, and she has been awarded nearly $5 million in grants and contracts for a variety of archaeology projects. Her research interests include the Archaic and Woodland prehistoric Indian cultures, which existed in the Southeast between 6000 B.C. and A.D. 1000, and the Colonial Period between 1513–1821. She has designed and conducted research from remote swamps of the Southeast to urban inner cities. Having published over a dozen articles, book chapters, and over 20 technical reports, Dr. Bense has also appeared on CNN and ABC's *Good Morning America,* and her projects are regularly covered by the media in the Southeast. Judy Bense continues to teach and do research in archaeology on a wide variety of topics in the Southeast.

Preface

This volume is a *summary,* not an encyclopedia, of archaeology in the southeastern United States. It is intended to be used as a text for undergraduate courses in southeastern archaeology and as a source for the educated amateur. This volume was written for people who have a limited background in archaeology but are curious enough about archaeology in the Southeast to read a book or take a course on the subject. The goals of this volume are to describe the archaeological remains of the Southeast and to explain the meaning and interpretation of these remains. The archaeological information summarized here represents the work of many people who have written thousands of publications.

Having established the target audience for this volume, I nonetheless want to enter a note of caution to my archaeological colleagues and advanced students of southeastern archaeology who may use this volume. Some things may trouble you, as they have troubled me. Primary sources of information are often not cited. The reason is that if citations were handled in the standard academic manner, the text would be cluttered with citations that would distract the reader, and over 100 pages of references would be required. To produce an easily read text and to summarize other people's work, I para-phrased and used the footnotes to guide readers to publications for more details or sources of further information about a particular subject or site. Page constraints also prohibited close citation of hundreds of publications. Profes-sionals and advanced students of southeastern archaeology will see their thoughts (and words) scattered throughout this book without direct citation; I ask their understanding of the nature of this book, which is to summarize other people's work into one document. Almost every statement in here could have been cited.

Another aspect of this volume that may bother my professional colleagues and advanced students is the omission of some interesting and significant research. Examples of "missing" research include that done on Plaquemine in the lower Mississippi Valley and the prehistoric Mississippian and historic Siouan research in North Carolina. Because of space limitations, I had to select representative research rather than summarize all the research done on a particular subject in the Southeast. The selection of examples was difficult to make, but there was not room for all of them. The examples used in the text had to be representative, to include different geographic areas, and to have a significant body of published information. Unfortunately, there were often several equally qualified bodies of research that met these criteria, and in those cases, I just had to choose one, which resulted in omissions of some perfectly good archaeology that has been done in the Southeast. The choices were difficult, and I ask those researchers who are not mentioned in this book to understand the situation and the constraints.

I have been studying southeastern archaeology since 1966, and for this entire period I have wanted a comprehensive summary as a guide to the complex archaeological record and publications of the Southeast. I waited for decades for someone else to write this summary, but no one did. People still struggle with the complexities of southeastern archaeology without a guide-book. A vast body of literature exists about the archaeology of the southeastern United States. However, information often is published in obscure journals or is out of print, and the rapidly growing but poorly distributed "gray" literature of cultural resource management reports is not easily accessible. I hope this book will help to alleviate this situation. I wrote it for those who are interested in the archaeology of the southeastern United States and who need an over-view to help understand it. The book is a structured presentation of the archaeological sites and artifacts and the theories explaining them. I hope it is useful for teaching. The illustrations are revisions of those I have used for 15 years of teaching this course without a text, and those that students have said are useful.

I also wrote this book for another reason—to gain a relatively comprehen-sive personal understanding of archaeology in the Southeast. It has been my favorite intellectual pursuit, and I immensely enjoyed sitting down for two years to read everything I ever wanted to read and to research detailed issues of southeastern archaeology. For example, how was the Mississippian way of life on the coast without significant maize agriculture different from the traditional maize-based agriculture in the river valleys? I can now at least deal with that issue. Simply making the chronological charts for the Archaic, Woodland, and Mississippian stage for the entire Southeast helped bring things into perspective. The proverbial "light bulb" came on many times as I finally saw threads that linked research together, and I began to understand the larger as well as the small views of an issue.

Last, but not least, I want to explain the scope of this summary. In my view, archaeology is archaeology, and regardless of the age of the deposits, this book should include the archaeology from all time periods. Therefore, the temporal scope is from the Paleoindian period, about 15,000 B.C., to the beginning of World War I, A.D. 1917. I did not include the period between World War I and II due to the small amount of research that has been done on this period, although there are several research projects underway at this writing. Nautical archaeology is not included, primarily due to space limitations. At this writing, our research program at the University of West Florida is participating in the excavation of a sixteenth-century Spanish galleon in Pensacola Bay, and I fully appreciate the importance of nautical archaeology. As the result of this and other research now being conducted, information about prehistoric and historic watercraft will grow by leaps and bounds in the next few years. Maybe I can do justice to post-1917 and nautical archaeology in the revision!

I hope readers will enjoy this summary of the archaeology of the southeastern United States. It is a fascinating field of knowledge, and perhaps now it will not be one of the South's best-kept secrets.

Judith A. Bense

Acknowledgments

I can say without hesitation that this book is the product of a team. I had the idea and did the research and writing, but this is only part of what it took to create this volume.

There is a very special group of archaeology colleagues I want to thank for providing an academic "safety net" for me and this book. In the planning process, I knew that the scope of this project was so broad that I would need the assistance of several respected colleagues whose knowledge and experience complemented my own to review the manuscript. This review committee was essential to the accuracy of this book. The members were James B. Griffin, David G. Anderson, Vernon J. Knight, Jr., Bennie C. Keel, Jefferson Chapman, and Joseph W. Joseph.

These archaeologists patiently reviewed every paragraph, table, drawing, and illustration at least twice. They personally researched information and wrote long discussions on topics difficult to summarize. Professor Griffin was always the first to send back his detailed, handwritten, long review, and he personally reviewed several chapters three times. Thanks to these colleagues, I felt that I was a member of a book "team," rather than a lone individual writing away in the basement of the library. I relied on this six-person review team as partners rather than reviewers in the traditional meaning of the term. I sincerely thank these colleagues, because they have made this book far better than I could have done alone. Each reviewer added accuracy and clarity, and although the contents have been agreed on by the seven of us, I am solely responsible.

When I had the idea for this book, the Anthropology teaching and research faculty at the University of West Florida consisted of four people. Over lunch at our favorite Asian restaurant, I asked Professors Terry J. Prewitt and Chung-ho Lee and Archaeology Institute Assistant Director John C. Phillips what they thought of the idea of my writing this book, and if they could shoulder my load, if I chose to do so. Not only did they agree to shoulder my burdens, but they promoted the idea, stressing that it would benefit our program in the long run. So while I was in the basement of the library for a year and a half, quietly reading and writing, they taught my courses, ran my projects, and handled all my administrative duties in addition to their own work, and they were my cheerleaders in the rough times. I am not only grateful for their help, but deeply touched by their supportive attitude. My department chairman, Professor Dallas A. Blanchard, eagerly agreed to support my writing this book and found the extra funding needed. Professor Blanchard also agreed to reduce my teaching load and to support a student assistant during the academic year before my sabbatical. This greatly helped me get started on the research. My dean, Professor Richard E. Doelker, Jr., was also a source of support by helping the Chairman with funding, supporting my full-year sabbatical request, and with personal encouragement. The Academic Provost, Douglas D. Friedrich, and President, Morris L. Marx, stressed to me many times that this book would be good for the College of Arts and Social Sciences and the University of West Florida.

Illustrations are a key aspect in a text book. For the last several years, the archaeology team at the University of West Florida has been fortunate to have the help of a retired computer graphics expert, Dr. Margret J. Smith, as a consultant and teacher. Dr. Smith generously taught the intricacies of computer mapping and drawing to several students and Institute staff members, especially Mr. Colby Lee McKenzie. Dr. Smith and Mr. McKenzie together produced over 40 computer-generated illustrations for this book. As we all know, the quality of illustrations in a publication is an index of its overall caliber, and their drawings clearly explain and illustrate many complex issues. Just before we went into high gear to complete the manuscript, Dr. Margret Smith fell seriously ill, and Mr. McKenzie took up the reins without the blink of an eye, and he added her load to his already full schedule by working nights and weekends. The computer drawings are very important to this book and they are very good, thanks to these two people.

I also thank the editors who have worked long, hard hours on the manuscript: John Hord from Fort Walton Beach, and Rick Roehrich, the former

Archaeology Acquisitions Editor for Academic Press. Debra Wells, one of our graduate students, also put in untold hours getting copyright permissions and straightening out the references.

An important ingredient of this project was being shielded from the interruption of phone calls and paperwork by the unflagging efforts of Archaeology Institute secretary, Mr. Steven R. Mitchell. He took my calls, returned calls, and kept my schedule as free as humanly possible so I could write. For the first time in decades, I could work without the interruptions of a phone or drop-in visitors. I also thank UWF Pac Library Special Collections Director W. Dean DeBolt and assistant Katrina King who constantly came to my aid in the library. They made my time there very pleasant.

I especially thank Alice F. Harris, who came on board in the home stretch. She devoted long days and evenings to such tedious tasks as finalizing every one of the hundreds of the references, placing copyright information in each caption, and editing the text for the last time. I sincerely thank her for her help in that fast-paced period, as well as during the two years when writing this book dominated my life.

1

INTRODUCTION

Most of the archaeology in the Southeast is not obvious to the nonarchaeologist living in or visiting the region. Most of the archaeological sites are hidden under dense vegetation or buried under layers of sediment that have washed into the river valleys. Unlike in the southwestern United States where many sites, such as pueblos, can be seen from miles away, and artifacts have laid on the ground in plain view for centuries, in the Southeast, one must usually dig to find archaeological sites. For the last 15,000 yr, this region of the United States has generally had abundant rainfall and moderate temperatures, which have fostered not only human populations, but animals and plants that consequently have covered human artifacts. Forty-feet tall mounds often cannot be seen from 100 ft away in the dense flood plain forest, and archaeologists regularly have to dig just to look for sites. Many archaeological sites have been reduced in height and size from repeated clearing and plowing. Due to these factors, the archaeology in the Southeast has been one of the better-kept secrets of the region.

Archaeologists of the Southeast realize that archaeological sites are abundant and hold important information about the people who have lived there for at least the last 12,000 yr. A wide range of archaeological sites and artifacts lie in the dense forests, in plowed fields, or under city parking lots. I have vivid memories of placing small test units on low knolls in the Tombigbee River flood plain, surrounded by swamps for miles, and finding they were mounds of human garbage 6 ft thick that had been accumulating for more than 6000 yr with deposits extending several feet into the modern water table. I also have walked to a complex of 13 mounds, some of which were 30 ft high, on an island in the delta of the Mobile River with vegetation so thick that I did not see these great mounds until we started walking uphill. I have watched backhoes pull up asphalt on the streets of Pensacola, Florida, and expose pristine British and Spanish Colonial cannons, building foundations, and 250-yr-old wells. Glen Doran found a 6,000-yr-old Indian cemetery at the bottom of a pond being drained for a development in central Florida. Many of the burials had preserved brain matter within. Biologists have cloned the DNA from these sources, the oldest human DNA ever recovered. Over and over archaeologists document the richness of southeastern archaeology.

The archaeological record in the Southeast contains many clues to how humans operate and learn to deal with the changing times. Unfortunately, the archaeological sites in the Southeast are being damaged at an unprecedented rate, partially due to the camouflage of vegetation and sediment, but also because most people do not know that archaeological sites are in their midst, or that they are important. As you read this book, or even look at the pictures, I think you will be surprised at the quality and information value of the archaeology in the Southeast. Two of my main purposes in writing this book are to describe the archaeology in the Southeast and what archaeologists have learned from studying it.

Another important purpose of this book is to describe the environmental changes that have occurred in the southeastern United States while humans have been living there. Significant environmental changes have influenced the development of Indian culture. The current natural environment and weather patterns of the Southeast have existed for only about 2000 to 3000 yr. When Indian people first arrived at least 2,000 yr ago, the Southeast was a much different place. Their ancestors had crossed the Bering Land Bridge from Asia during the last glacial period, walked down the corridor between the Canadian ice sheets, and followed the Mississippi and other river valleys into the Southeast. At that time, sea level was at least 300 ft lower than today, hardwood forests covered most of the region, and south Florida was a desert with sand dunes. Animals that are now extinct, such as the giant mastodons, saber-toothed tigers, and giant sloths, roamed the forests and savannahs. The change in climate from glacial conditions to the interglacial conditions of today caused many changes in the weather, plants, animals, and resources that are important to humans. Chapter 2 is devoted to explaining the evolution of the modern southeastern environment and landscape to provide a background for understanding the changes in the ways of life of people living there.

People of two distinct cultural traditions have lived in the Southeast: American Indian and European-American. This book contains a summary of the archaeology of the prehistoric (pre-Columbian) and historic (post-Columbian) societies that have lived in what is now called the southeastern United States. Because Indians have lived in this region for much longer than European-Americans (about 10,000 yr versus 400 yr) and, historically, archaeologists have studied prehistoric Indian cultures longer that European-American cultures, more is known about prehistoric than historic archaeology. Consequently, about 60% of this book is devoted to the archaeology of prehistoric Indian societies in the southeastern United States. Reflecting the shorter time span and research attention, only about 25% of the book is allocated to historic period archaeology. The remainder of the book is dedicated primarily to background information and references.

This book is a chronological summary of the archaeology in the southeastern United States. It begins with the earliest and least complex cultural stage, the Paleoindian (about 13,000–8000 B.C.), and ends with the latest and most complex cultural stage, the American (A.D. 1865–1917). As shown in the chronological chart in Fig. 1.1, there are four prehistoric Indian cultural stages. They are defined by changes in technology, material culture, and sociopolitical organization. The prehistoric cultural stages are the Paleoindian (13,000?–8000 B.C.), the Archaic (8000–1000 B.C.), the Woodland (1000 B.C.–A.D. 1000), and the Mississippian (A.D. 1000–1500). Each cultural stage is divided into two or three internal periods. During these 15 millennia, Indian culture evolved from small, mobile bands of hunters and gatherers to large groups of relatively sedentary agricultural societies with a chiefdom or "pre-state" level of sociopolitical organization.

PALEOINDIAN STAGE   13000? - 8000 BC

EARLY PALEOINDIAN   13000? - 9000 BC
MIDDLE PALEOINDIAN   9000 - 8500 BC
LATE PALEOINDIAN   8500 - 8000 BC

ARCHAIC STAGE   8000 - 1000 BC

EARLY ARCHAIC   8000 - 6000 BC
MIDDLE ARCHAIC   6000 - 4000 BC
LATE ARCHAIC   4000 - 1000 BC

WOODLAND STAGE   1000 BC - AD 1000

EARLY WOODLAND   1000 BC - AD 0
MIDDLE WOODLAND   AD 0 - AD 500
LATE WOODLAND   AD 500 - 1000

MISSISSIPPIAN STAGE   AD 1000 - 1500

EARLY MISSISSIPPIAN   AD 1000 - 1200
MIDDLE MISSISSIPPIAN   AD 1200 - 1400
LATE MISSISSIPPIAN   AD 1400 - 1500

EUROPEAN STAGE   AD 1500 - 1821

CONTACT   AD 1500 - 1670
COLONIAL   AD 1670 - 1821

AMERICAN STAGE   AD 1821 - 1917

EARLY AMERICAN   AD 1821 - 1865
VICTORIAN   AD 1865 - 1917

FIGURE 1.1   Chronology of the Southeast.

Paleoindian is the first recognized cultural stage in North America, as well as in the Southeast, and it is characterized by well-made lanceolate-shaped stone spear points that were used to hunt many animals, including some large Pleistocene animals such as elephants and bison, which are now extinct. The weather was cooler than at present, hardwoods covered the region, and sea level was rising relatively rapidly from 300 to 90 ft below the modern level. While there is a scarcity of firmly dated Paleoindian sites in the Southeast, there is no lack of sites, as they number in the hundreds. For most of the Paleoindian stage, people appear to have practiced a conservative, hunting-based, mobile way of life in a few major river valleys in the northern part of the Southeast. During the last 1000 yr of the Paleoindian stage, the population expanded outward and the first internal cultural distinctions developed. Societies adapted to different local conditions and became more isolated. Late Paleoindians had a generalized, flexible economy that enabled them to move around the region and take advantage of the scattered and diverse resources of the Southeast.

The next stage of cultural development in the Southeast was the Archaic stage, which lasted from 8000 to 1000 B.C. It was the longest stage of cultural development in the Southeast. During the middle of the Archaic stage, postglacial warming peaked and southeastern climate has been generally cooler ever since. Sea level rose about 90 ft to near its present position, and there was a change in weather patterns that changed the forests of the southern portion of the region from hardwoods to the fire-maintained pine forests of today. Key Archaic cultural developments included the use of notched and stemmed triangular stone spear points, containers of stone and pottery, and ground and polished stone artifacts. During this stage, the first mounds and earthworks were constructed and long-distance trade was established. People fully adapted to the different geographical areas of the Southeast, developing not only a distinctive southeastern way of life, but distinctive regional cultures in different environmental zones. The Archaic stage is important to archaeologists because of the increased number of archaeological sites and amount of materials.

The Woodland stage existed between 1000 B.C. and A.D. 1000. People concentrated in river valleys and along the coastal strip, pottery diffused throughout the region, earth mounds were built and used for burial at an unprecedented rate, elaborate mortuary rituals developed, long-distance trade increased, and many plants were cultivated and stored. While all of these characteristics originated in the Archaic stage, they were more common during the Woodland. In the early Woodland period, pottery technology rapidly advanced and spread throughout the Southeast. The technological improvements allowed pottery containers to be made in a variety of shapes and sizes that could be used for direct heat cooking, storing, and serving food. By the middle Woodland period, ornamental pottery vessels were made and ceramic art had reached a high level of development. Mound building first flourished during the middle Woodland in association with the spread of a ceremonial complex called Hopewellian. Some mounds were for human burials, often the local elite, while others were platforms for special activities. The tradition of placing personal items with special high-status burials was practiced in all periods.

During the late Woodland in the Mississippi Valley, the functions of mound centers in some areas expanded as they became sociopolitical centers for local societies. Platform mounds became the dominant type. The elite resided on many, and others were used for special activities. Platform mound centers in this region became the hub of social, political, and religious events, while the general population was dispersed in the countryside in relatively small settlements.

Sociopolitical organization of the middle and late Woodland periods was characterized by relatively equal, unranked kin groups that could rise to power through the ambitions of self-made leaders called Big Men and Big Women. This triggered sociopolitical advancement from the band to the tribal level of complexity. The high status earned by specific extended families was temporary, however, and power could shift when the leader died. In the Mississippi Valley during the late Woodland, it appears that the leaders of the ruling families had begun to centralize power and were able to pass social rank to descendant generations.

The Mississippian stage (A.D. 1000–1500) was the last prehistoric Indian stage of cultural development. Its hallmarks are the development and spread of the chiefdom level of sociopolitical organization, the florescence of a belief system called the Southeastern Ceremonial Complex, and the expansion of platform mound centers. During the Mississippian stage, agriculture was practiced in areas with good soil, especially in river valleys. Mississippian agricultural societies were composed of small family farms. Maize, beans, squash, sunflower, marsh elder, and gourd were grown in fields using crop rotation. Agricultural Mississippians were relatively sedentary, but also relied heavily on wild foods from flood plains near their farms. Along the coasts, farming played a much smaller role, if any, and hunting, gathering, and fishing continued to support the growing population. Cultivation was limited to scattered small plots that could be used for only a few seasons. People spent most of the year in small groups tending the scattered farm plots and harvesting wild marine and terrestrial foods.

During the Mississippian stage, most southeastern societies evolved to the chiefdom level of sociopolitical organization. A chiefdom is a political organization of several communities controlled by one extended family with centralized power. The most distinct characteristic of chiefdoms is the pervasive inequality of people. The most powerful positions are held by a small group of related people. People had to be born into the chiefly family to obtain the most powerful positions; this is one of the main differences between the tribal and chiefdom levels of sociopolitical organization. The mechanics of the spread of Mississippian culture are not well understood, but it is thought that defense, imitation, and migration were important.

The main themes of the Mississippian Southeastern Ceremonial Complex were ancestor worship, war, and fertility; these themes were expressed in a myriad of symbols and objects. This complex flourished in the middle Mississippian, between about A.D. 1200 and 1400, when rituals and mound building reached their peak. The roots of this belief system can be traced back to the Archaic and Woodland stages of southeastern Indian cultural development, and elements still survive today. It was during the middle Mississippian that more complex chiefdoms formed in many areas and the Southeastern Ceremonial Complex reached its peak. Sociopolitical centers of complex chiefdoms usually underwent a rapid expansion, and platform mound building reached its highest level in Southeastern prehistory, as did the use of the rituals and paraphernalia of the Southeastern Ceremonial Complex to establish power and authority. There were many similarities between the mound centers of complex chiefdoms across the Southeast, but there were also local differences in mounds, preferred iconography, and specific mortuary practices. Warfare began to replace ceremonialism as the primary means of political control during this period. The late Mississippian period was characterized in many areas by political turmoil and population relocations.

The next stage of culture in the Southeast began abruptly with the arrival in A.D. 1500 of Europeans, and it ended in 1821 with a change of ownership from European countries to the United States of America. The archaeological features of the European stage are the introduction of European and African materials and settlements, the incorporation of European items into Indian material culture, and Indian sociopolitical reorganization. Spain claimed all of the Southeast during the first portion of the European stage. There were several early Spanish explorations of the region in the 1500s, but because nothing as valuable as the gold and silver of Mexico and South America was discovered, the Southeast was used as a buffer zone to protect the rich area to the south. Despite several attempts, only one successful Spanish settlement was established in the Contact period. This was St. Augustine, founded in 1565. Archaeological research at Spanish exploration sites and the early settlements indicates that the Spaniards tried to establish a Spanish way of life in the Southeast, and that Indians were an important part of their households and community support.

One result of the early Spanish explorations and settlement attempts was a severe reduction in Indian population as a result of European and African diseases. Catholic missions became an important part of Spain's hold on the Southeast in the 1600s. After a series of mission failures, Indian groups along the Atlantic coast and north central Florida began to accept missionaries into their communities. Franciscan missions to the Apalachee in north Florida were particularly successful, and mission archaeology has shown that, at least on some Apalachee missions, a high standard of living in the Spanish style was maintained.

In 1670, England encroached on Spain's claim to the Southeast and established Charles Town and the Carolina colony on the Atlantic coast. The English Colonial economy in the Southeast thrived on the private deerskin trade and slave-labor plantations. The French established the colony of Louisiana. They also developed a deerskin trade business, but it was run by the government. The Spanish hold on the Southeast was limited to Florida during the end of the European stage, and it became a refuge for Creeks and Africans. The Seminole emerged from these immigrants.

The last stage of cultural development in the Southeast is the American stage (A.D. 1821–1917). The key archaeological features of this period are a severe reduction of Indian materials and sites, industrial mass production of European-American materials, and an increase in urban archaeological deposits. Most of the Indian population in the Southeast was forcibly removed from the Southeast between 1828 and 1835 and relocated on reservations west of the Mississippi River. Immediately afterward, European-Americans spread rapidly into the interior of the Southeast, establishing agricultural plantations and small farms. The Civil War resulted in serious social and economic changes and saw the destruction of most infrastructure in the region and the abolition of slavery. Most plantations were converted to tenancy or broken into small farms. African-American culture developed as their societies became more consolidated after emancipation.

Historical archaeology is beginning to unravel the cultural realities of the Antebellum period (pre-Civil War) of the American stage. The most frequent entity studied has been the plantation. Studies of African-American culture before the Civil War have focused on plantations, although a few studies of African-American urban communities, both free and slave, have been conducted. There has been growing archaeological interest in Indian culture during the Antebellum period, especially the Seminole, Creek, and Cherokee, and this research is beginning to document how these groups coped with the increasing European-American pressure of this period.

Archaeologists studying the Victorian period (Civil War to World War I) have focused on the development of rural European-American or "southern" culture. Studies of small farms are revealing how European-American farming families adapted to the effects of the Civil War and the Industrial Revolution. A few archaeological studies of small towns and cities also have been conducted. Industrial archaeology is revealing how towns and cities grew around railroad yards, steam-driven factories, and wharfs. Archaeological studies of African-American urban neighborhoods and segregated towns during the Victorian period reflect not only their social and economic conditions, but the coalescence of African and European influences into modern African-American culture. There is a significant gap in the documentary record of this culture, and historical archaeology is making an important contribution to filling the void.

The volume of archaeological sites and materials takes a great leap during the Victorian period, especially in towns and cities. The Industrial Revolution facilitated mass production of consumer goods, and there was a dramatic increase in the amount of materials in all but the poorest households. People purchased and used thousands of items of glass, pottery, and metal during this time, much of which went into the archaeological record of their individual house sites.

Over 15,000 yr of human residence in the southeastern United States has resulted in a tremendous archaeological record in the region, and much of it has been revealed and interpreted by archaeologists. The chapters that follow detail the sites and artifacts that have been studied and the theories that have been constructed to explain them. Remember that new information is constantly being produced. Undoubtedly most of the explanations given here will be modified in the future. Stay tuned!

2

GEOGRAPHY AND LANDSCAPE EVOLUTION

KEY GEOGRAPHIC FEATURES

Sandy Coastal Plain
Rocky Interior Highlands
Forest Belts

**KEY LANDSCAPE CHANGES IN LAST
20,000 YEARS**

Shift from Glacial to Interglacial Conditions
Sea Level Rose 300–390 ft
Warming Peak 6000–4000 B.C.
Modern Climate Established 1000–2000 B.C.

INTRODUCTION AND OVERVIEW

Archaeology is the study of humans through the material remains they leave behind. In the southeastern United States, humans have been leaving things behind them for up to 15,000 yr; these populations experienced many different environmental and social changes. To understand the progression of human culture in the Southeast as reflected in the archaeological record, it is important to understand at least the basics of the physical environment of the region today as well as the changes in the landscape that have occurred. This information is the subject of this chapter. The remaining chapters of this book are concerned with how humans adjusted to changes and their social consequences.

At present, the southeastern United States has two main physiographic regions: the Coastal Plain and the Interior Highlands. These two physiographic divisions of the Southeast are quite different in river patterns, soil, forest types, stone, and many other natural features. The Coastal Plain is a former seabed, composed of loose sand and gravel deposited on an ocean floor. The surface of the Coastal Plain slopes seaward, and it is cut by a series of rivers, most of which originate in the Interior Highlands. The vegetation of the Coastal Plain is dominated by pine forests; hardwood forests exist only in fire-protected areas, such as wetlands. The Fall Line separates the Coastal Plain from the Interior Highlands. This steep bluff line was the old beachhead of the primeval Atlantic Ocean during the Cretaceous period (the Dinosaur age). The Interior Highlands have been eroded not by the sea but by water and ice. The dominant feature of these highlands is the Blue Ridge Mountains, which are a series of southwest–northeast ridges. The vegetation of the Interior Highlands is dominated by hardwood forests, most of which are sprinkled with pines and conifers.

There have been two major climatic periods in the last 20 millennia: the glacial period and the postglacial period. During the height of the glacial period, sea level was greatly lowered, which exposed the continental shelf and extended the coastline seaward for many miles. The weather was cooler, and there were fewer seasonal differences than today. The vegetation in the northern part of the region was dominated by northern forest types with spruce and fir. The ice started melting about 16,000 B.C., and true postglacial conditions were established around 8000 B.C. With warmer weather and ice retreat, there was a northward migration of vegetation. Sea level rose as the ice melted, submerging part of the continental shelf. Postglacial temperatures peaked about 3000 B.C. when the weather in the Southeast was hotter and drier than today; it has been cooler ever since. Pine forests replaced hardwoods on the Coastal Plain about 4000 B.C., and modern weather conditions were established about 1000 B.C. Sea level stopped rising about this time, although there have been fluctuations of up to 10 ft since.

The remainder of this chapter is divided into two sections. The first section describes the modern environment and geography of the Southeast, and the second summarizes the landscape evolution changes that have occurred during the last 20,000 yr.

MODERN GEOGRAPHY

Coastal Plain

The Coastal Plain is formally defined as the part of the continental shelf that is now above sea level and that has not been substantially deformed.[1] The Coastal Plain was created by erosion of the continent during the Cretaceous period, 135–68 million yr ago, when the entire continental shelf was under water, and eroded sediments were deposited on the Atlantic Ocean floor. The inner border of the Coastal Plain is called the Fall Line because of the many waterfalls that form as rivers flow over this steep feature. In areas of soft sediments, the Fall Line is a slope between 5 and 10 mi wide, while in areas of hard rock it is narrow and steep. As shown in Figure 2.1, the Atlantic portion of the Coastal Plain is more narrow than that along the Gulf of Mexico.

The sediments of the Coastal Plain consist of mixed layers of sand, gravel, and clay that have been moved and redeposited by water. Some of the sandy sediments have cemented into hard formations of sandstone or limestone, but most are in their original loose condition. The main feature of Coastal Plain sediments is horizontal banding. Zones of different types of sediments are arranged in a series of belts that parallel the Fall Line. The composition of the sediment in the belts varies with the different rocks that were eroded. The surface of the parallel sediment belts on the Coastal Plain also varies with the hardness of the underlying rock. Where the rock is soft, like chalk, the surface is low and flat. Where the rocks are hard, like quartzite, the surface is hilly.

The Coastal Plain slopes seaward at a low and gradual rate, averaging only about 2 ft per mile. The surface of the Coastal Plain is terraced by a series of beachheads, called marine terraces, that were established during the long periods of different sea levels since the Cretaceous period. Geologists disagree about the number of marine terraces in the Southeast, but at least four and as many as seven have been proposed, organized in a stair-step fashion from the coastline to the Fall Line. Because the sea is level, the surface of each terrace is at the same elevation throughout the Southeast. Terrace edges are steep due to erosion by the sea during periods of lower sea level.

Figure 2.2 shows that most rivers originate in the Interior Highlands and flow across the Coastal Plain. The valleys through which these rivers flow

[1] For more details on the modern geography of the Southeast, see Fenneman, 1938, and Thornbury, 1965.

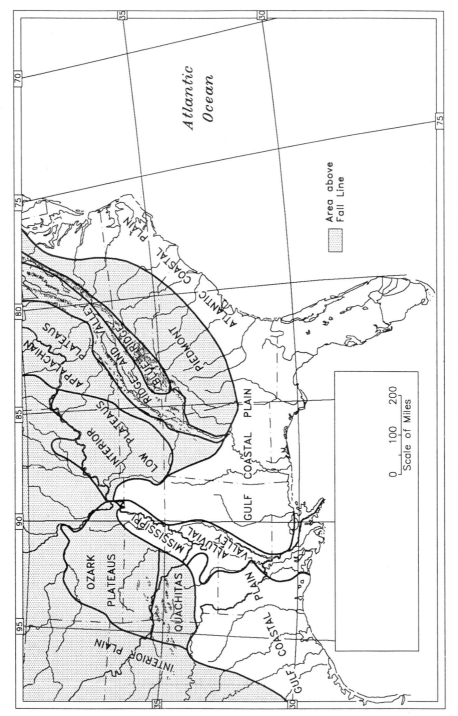

FIGURE 2.1 Physiographic regions of the southeastern United States.

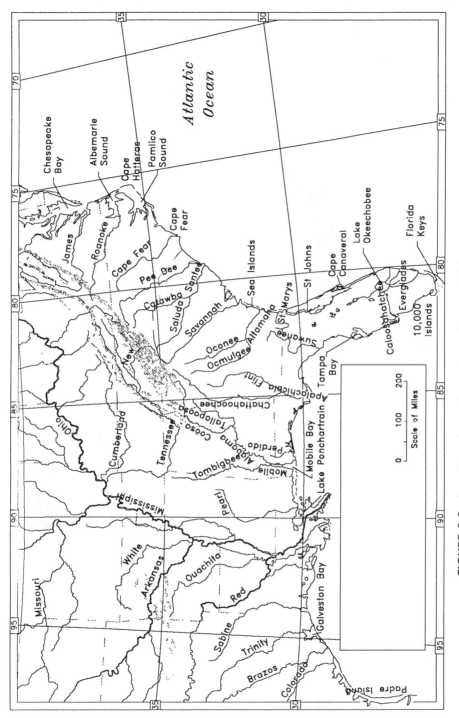

FIGURE 2.2 Location of some large rivers, bays, and lakes in the Southeast.

have a different ecosystem than the surrounding areas. They are linear strips of wetlands with mixed deciduous forests that cut across stretches of dry sandy soil and pine forests. The river gradient is steepest in the inner half of the Coastal Plain. As a consequence, upper river valleys are generally eroding and have narrow flood plains. In the lower half of each valley, the river gradient is less steep, and the river deposits the sediments eroded upstream. Lower valley flood plains are wide with deep deposits of fine sand and silt. The rise and fall of sea level during the Ice Age (formally named the Pleistocene epoch) caused a rise and fall in river gradients. During each glacial period, when sea level was lowered, the gradient of the rivers was greatly increased, and rivers scoured most of the sediments out of their valleys. Fragments of the former flood plain sediments remained on the walls of the valleys, however, as river terraces, as shown in Figure 2.3A. When sea level rose again, stream gradients were lowered, and flood plains were filled again with sediment. Near the coast, the river terraces merge with the marine terraces. At the mouth of each valley, where the river meets sea level, there is a plume of very fine silts and clays called a delta. These delta plumes have also moved up and down river valleys with changes in sea level, as indicated in Figure 2.3B. The weight of the wet, heavy, and thick delta deposits causes them to compress and sink below the water line. This sinking of land in deltas is called subsidence, and it is especially active at the mouths of larger rivers.

The Mississippi, Missouri, and Ohio rivers form the largest river system in North America. The Mississippi flows across the Coastal Plain for 600 mi from its confluence with the Ohio River. The valley is bordered by an almost continual line of bluffs up to 200 ft high. On the eastern side of the valley, the bluff line is interrupted by only a few small streams, while on the western side it is broken by several large river valleys that cross the Great Plains, such as the Arkansas and the Red rivers. The valley varies in width from 25 mi near Natchez, Mississippi, to 125 mi near Helena, Arkansas. The stair-stepped river terraces are well expressed in the Mississippi Valley, as shown in Figure 2.3A. The main channel of the Mississippi River has changed position many times, as have most rivers in the Coastal Plain. These changes are due to clogging of portions of the channel, which causes the river to cut a new course, usually during floods. The present channel of the Mississippi River was established about 800 B.C.[2] Since then there has been a tremendous buildup of sediments in the lower Mississippi Valley. Between Vicksburg, Mississippi, and Memphis, Tennessee, the sediments are 20 to 25 ft thick, and in the delta below Baton Rouge, Louisiana, they are between 75 to 80 ft thick. As illustrated in Figure 2.3B, sediment buildup and subsidence in the delta have caused many diversions of the mainstream.

---

[2] For details on the geomorphology of the Mississippi River valley see Saucier, 1974; and Fisk, 1944.

A

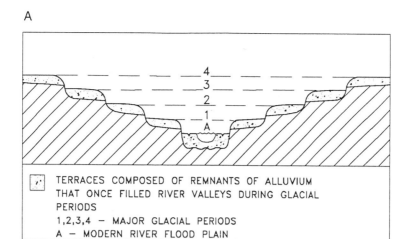

B

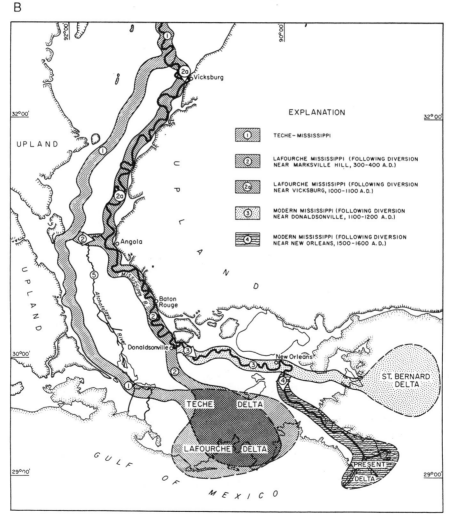

FIGURE 2.3 (A) Cross section of the Mississippi Valley showing idealized position of the river terraces. (B) Location of deltas of the Mississippi River (From Fisk, 1944.)

The Florida peninsula is a distinctive area of the Coastal Plain. Its low elevation and high water table have resulted in the largest wetland area in the Southeast, the Everglades. The Everglades is almost flat, less than 20 ft above sea level, and tilted toward the west. It is permanently wet in many areas. Water south of Lake Okeechobee runs southwest in large sheets and spills into the Gulf of Mexico. This infusion of nutrient-rich runoff supports extensive mangrove swamps along the shoreline below the Caloosahatchee River as well as unusually dense fish populations.

There are about 2500 mi of shoreline on the Coastal Plain from Louisiana through North Carolina. Most of the coast is dotted with lakes and bays that have formed at the mouth of each river, and there are long stretches with sandy barrier islands and smooth shorelines along the oceans, as shown in Figure 2.4. Between the barrier islands and the mainland are tidal lagoons and marshes. On the Atlantic coast from near Georgetown, South Carolina, to Jacksonville, Florida, is a chain of islands that rise 15–20 ft above the sea. These are thought to be fragments of the mainland that were cut off by erosion. The tides are especially high in this area, eroding the coast and backing up freshwater streams 10–20 mi inland, forming large swamps. There also are extensive coastal marshes on the Gulf shoreline between Tampa Bay, Florida, and the Apalachicola River and along the Louisiana coast.

Interior Highlands

The Interior Highlands are formally defined as the portion of the Southeast that was not eroded by the primeval Atlantic Ocean. It is characterized by rock formations, many of which are extremely old. Due to the great age of these rocks, many have been quite deformed by tilting, lifting, and folding. There are two main areas of the Interior Highlands, separated by the Mississippi Valley: the Appalachian Highlands and the Ozark-Ouachita Highlands.

The Appalachian Highlands include, moving west, the Piedmont, Blue Ridge Mountains, Ridge and Valley area, and the Appalachian Plateau, shown in Figure 2.1. The difference between these regions are in elevation, rock types, and geological characteristics. The Piedmont is a relatively level, broad belt of rocks that slopes toward the sea and is deeply dissected by stream valleys. The Blue Ridge Mountains rise abruptly to the west of the Piedmont, and they are a series of short chains of mountains with high peaks. The Ridge and Valley area has a series of long narrow valleys with smooth walls, separated by high narrow ridges that were formed by the folding of hard rock formations. Along the whole western border of the Ridge and Valley region, like a thousand-foot wall, stretch the Appalachian and Interior Low plateaus. These Appalachian and Interior Low plateaus are high, flat, uneroded plains of very hard rocks that are very distinct from the adjacent geologically deformed regions in the Ridge and Valley area and the Blue Ridge. There are two major drainage patterns in the Interior Highlands, divided by the Blue Ridge

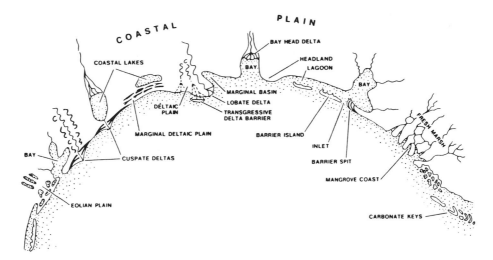

FIGURE 2.4 Typical features of the southeastern coastline. (From Gagliano, 1984. Reprinted with permission.)

Mountains. East of the Blue Ridge, streams flow east and south across the Piedmont and Coastal Plain. West of the Blue Ridge, streams flow west and south through deep valleys cut out of soft layers of rock. The Tennessee River system dominates the area immediately west of the Blue Ridge, and it follows a bedrock-controlled course through the mountains and valleys.

Across the Mississippi Valley and a few hundred miles away, the Ozark Plateau and the Ouachita Mountains are connected to, and part of, the Appalachian Highlands. They are both parts of the same geological formations that dip below the sandy sediments of the Coastal Plain and Mississippi Valley and rise on either side. Both these areas have the same geology and topography. The Ozark Plateau is like the Appalachian Plateau, with level surfaces and radiating drainage. River valleys on the edges of the plateau have exposed rich deposits of chert (flint), which was an important resource for Indians for stone tools for many millennia. The Ouachita Mountains are an extension of the folded Ridge and Valley region of the Appalachian Highlands. These east-west parallel ridges are distinct from the adjacent high plateau. The main rivers in this region flow along the edges of the Ouachita Mountains: the Arkansas on the northern edge and the Caddo-Ouachita on the south. The vegetation cover of the Ozark-Ouachita Highlands is different from that of the Appalachian Highlands. Due to dry conditions, the area is covered primarily with prairie grasses, with pine forests in the upper elevations.

In sum, the geography of the Southeast has two main regions: the Coastal Plain and the Interior Highlands. The Coastal Plain consists of loose sand and gravel once deposited on the ocean floor. The Interior Highlands have not been eroded by the sea, and it has extensively deformed rock formations. The Fall Line separates these two regions. The vegetation of the two regions is quite different. The Coastal Plain is covered with pine forests; the Interior Highlands are dominated by hardwood forests sprinkled with pines and conifers; and the dry Ozark-Ouachita Highlands have a prairie vegetation with some pine forests. The physiographic areas in the Southeast also have very different river patterns and natural resources.

LANDSCAPE EVOLUTION

The Southeast today is the result of the continual processes of formation, deformation, erosion, and weathering. Although the periods of rock formation and deformation are not covered in this section, be aware that the formations in the Interior Highlands are very old. Their great age has exposed them to much more erosion and pressure than the Rockies, which are much younger and less eroded. As the focus of this book is the archaeological remains of the human occupants of the Southeast, I cover only the climate and landscape changes that have occurred since human entry. While the earliest date of human occupation in the region is not yet firmly known, archaeologists are fairly confident that it was sometime between 20,000 and 10,000 B.C. There have been two geological epochs since the early date: the end of the Pleistocene and the Holocene.

The Pleistocene

The Pleistocene epoch is known informally as the Ice Age. It began between 2.5 and 1.5 million yr ago, for reasons not well understood by paleoclimatologists, and it is held to have ended with the last withdrawal of the ice sheets. This geological epoch is characterized by severe cold spasms, called glacial stages, separated by periods of warm weather, called interglacials. There have been four major glacial stages, but Pleistocene geologists disagree on the details. The four glacial stages were each named by geologists for the southernmost state that was reached by its ice: Iowan (or Nebraskan), Kansan, Illinoisan, and Wisconsin. The Pleistocene is divided into a period of full glacial conditions and a late glacial period of ice retreat.

During the full glacial period the Southeast was 21°–27°F cooler than today, especially during the summers, and there was less seasonal variation. Sea level was 330–390 ft lower, and much of the continental shelf was exposed, as shown in Figure 2.5A. Rivers draining into the Atlantic cut deep canyons into the continental shelf, scouring their valleys. On the Gulf continental shelf, rivers were less affected by the drop in sea level, due to the greater width of the continental shelf. Most of the Southeast was covered in thick spruce, pine, and hardwood forests, while the southern half of Florida was a desert. There also was a narrow belt of tundra in the upper Appalachians. There were many large animals such as the well-known mammoths and mastodons, as well as horses, camels, saber-toothed cats, and the full range of modern animals. In general, there was a richer diversity of plants and animals than in modern times.

The forests in the Southeast during the full Wisconsin glacial period were much different than they are today. Pollen specialists, such as Hazel Delcourt, Paul Delcourt, and William Watts, have mapped the former vegetation of the Southeast, shown in Figures 2.5A.[3] They determined that during the late Pleistocene, the Southeast had two major vegetation belts: spruce and jack pine forest in the northern half, and an oak-hickory-southern pine forest in the southern half. There was also a sand dune scrub on the Florida peninsula and alpine tundra along the crest of the Smoky Mountains.

The Wisconsin glaciation peaked between 26,000 and 16,000 B.C., after which temperatures began to increase, and the glaciers and ice sheets began gradually to melt and retreat from south to north. The late Pleistocene, 16,000–8000 B.C., was a time of transition from full glacial to interglacial conditions. Increasing summer and winter temperatures caused the breakup of the glacial forest belts and plant and animal communities. At this time, the Southeast was characterized by a patchwork of relatively small areas of different plant and animal communities. By the end of the period, about 8000 B.C., however, once again there were horizontal belts of plant/animal communities, as shown in Figure 2.5C.

For most of the Pleistocene epoch, the Mississippi River was very different than it is today. It carried most of the outwash (gravel, sand, and silt) from the melting Canadian ice sheet for the first half of this period. The water volume was so high that the surface salinity of the Gulf of Mexico was lowered by 10%.[4] The Mississippi Valley became clogged with outwash, forcing it into a "braided" pattern of small channels that crisscrossed the flood plain in many areas. Sometime before 10,000 B.C., the ice sheet retreated north of the Great Lakes, and meltwater outwash was diverted across Ontario into the St. Lawrence River, which carried it to the Atlantic Ocean.

The Holocene

The Holocene is the current interglacial stage.[5] The 8000 B.C. starting date is relatively arbitrary, but it signifies the end of glacial conditions and the beginning of interglacial conditions. There are three internal periods of the

[3] For details on fossil pollen studies see Delcourt and Delcourt, 1981, 1985; Watts, 1980, 1983; and Davis, 1983.

[4] For more information on the effect of ice melts on the Gulf see Emiliani, 1980.

[5] For an informative summary of the Holocene see the Introduction by Wright in Wright, 1983; and the chapters by Davis and Kutzbach.

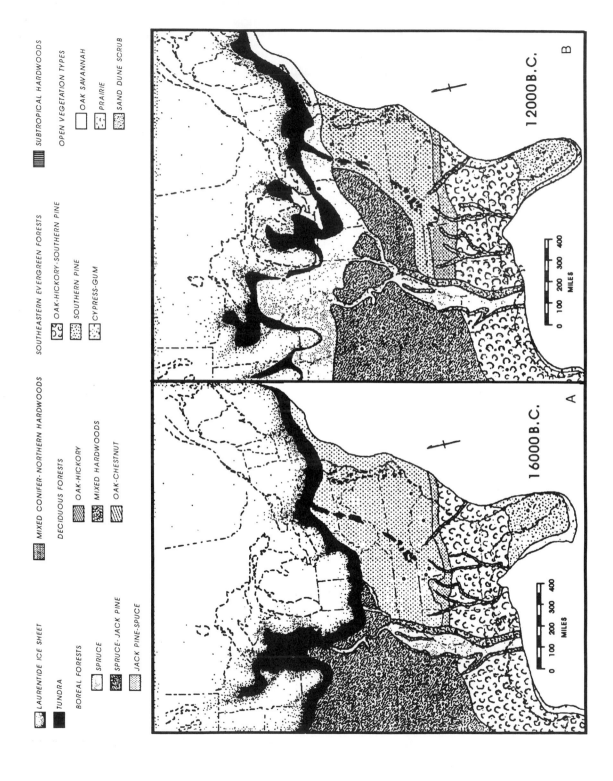

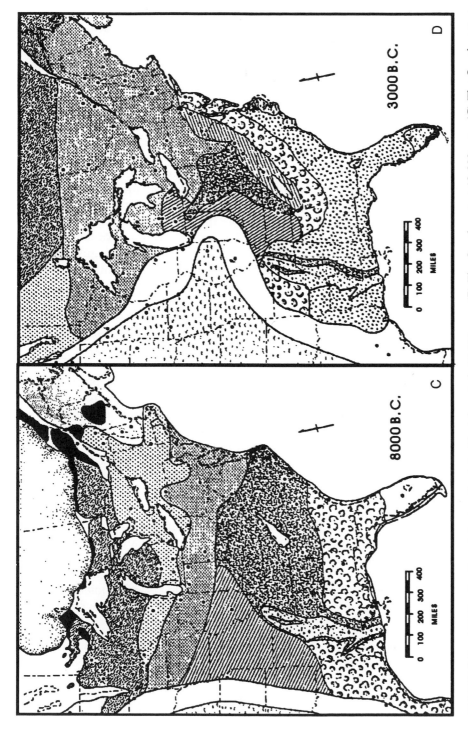

FIGURE 2.5 (A) The Southeast during the late Glacial period, 16,000 B.C.; (B) The Southeast at 12,000 B.C.; (C) The Southeast at the beginning of the Holocene, 8000 B.C.; (D) Modern vegetation of the Southeast, established at 3000 B.C. (From Delcourt and Delcourt, 1981).

Holocene: early, middle and late, each of which had different weather and environmental features.

During the early Holocene, 8000–6500 B.C., summers became increasingly warmer and drier.[6] By 7000 B.C., the weather was quite similar to that of today. Sea level rose rapidly during the early Holocene, as shown in Figure 2.6, so that by 6500 B.C. it was within about 65 ft of its present level. The flat continental shelf was characterized by drowning forests, flooded swamps, and backed-up streams as the shoreline receded. The forest belts were broken into a complex mosaic of biotic communities, especially in the northern half of the region. Compared to today, most of these communities had larger populations of plants and animals, individuals were larger, and there was more species diversity. Massive extinctions of many large species of verte-brates, including mammoths, mastodons, and their predators, took place between 9000 and 8000 B.C. Researchers theorize that the primary cause was the changes in vegetation. Hunting by humans also may have been cause for their demise. After all, while there had been several previous interglacial periods, massive extinctions of mammals occurred only once: shortly after humans entered North America.[7]

The middle Holocene, 6500–2000 B.C., also called the Altithermal or Hyp-sithermal period, was the peak of interglacial conditions. The rise of sea level slowed, and it was during this period that the Everglades developed in the Florida peninsula. The middle Holocene was significantly hotter and drier than any other Holocene period, and the weather pattern changed. Summer weather came to be dominated by the tropical maritime air mass from the Gulf of Mexico and the Caribbean, characterized by summer thunderstorms.[8] By 3000 B.C., this change in weather had caused major changes in Southeast vegetation, as shown in Figure 2.5D. Two of the greatest changes were the extension of the prairie across the central Mississippi Valley and the complete dominance of the Coastal Plain by pine. The prairie extension was due to the reduction of rainfall. The expansion of pine forests was due to chronic lightning-started forest fires. This new climatic regime literally burned the hardwood trees out of Coastal plain forests, leaving a fire-maintained forest of fire-tolerant pines. Without the fire factor on the Coastal Plain, the forest would not have changed. Remnants of the former hardwood forest survive only in areas protected from fire, such as river flood plains and swamps.

In the late Holocene, 2000 B.C. to present, the climate became cooler, and sea level stabilized within about 10 ft of its present position. Modern weather

---

[6] Example paleoenvironmental studies are Delcourt and Delcourt, 1981; Graham and Lundelius, 1984; and Watts, 1983.

[7] For more about Pleistocene extinctions see Kelly and Todd, 1988; Guthrie 1984; and Meltzer and Mead, 1983.

[8] For more information about the Altithermal see McMillan and Klippel, 1981; Wright, 1983; and Watts, 1980.

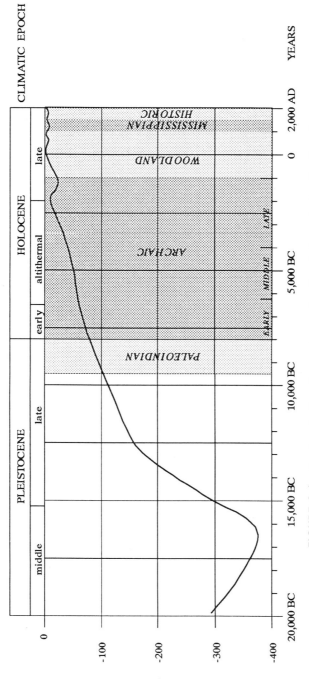

FIGURE 2.6 Sea level, climatic epochs, and cultural stages in the Southeast.

conditions were established between 2000 and 1000 B.C., and major modern plant and animal communities were in place soon afterward. With a more stable sea level, the current coastal ecosystems developed and matured. By 2000 B.C., barrier islands and spits were forming along the coast and across the mouths of bays, significantly reducing their current and backing up the rivers. This embayment reduced salinity and caused a rapid buildup of sediments in the bays and lagoons. These now-shallow estuaries soon developed extensive grass beds, which provided food and protection for new and dense populations of shellfish and fish. Early in the late Holocene, southeastern coasts had developed ecosystems rich in marine life.

SUMMARY

The geography of the Southeast has two main regions: the Coastal Plain and the Interior Highlands. The Coastal Plain consists of loose sand and gravel once deposited on the ocean floor. The Interior Highlands have not been eroded by the sea and have extensively deformed rock formations. The Fall Line separates these two regions. The vegetation of the two regions is quite different. The Coastal Plain is covered with pine forests; the Interior Highlands have mixed deciduous forests sprinkled with pines and conifers in the Appalachian Highlands and prairie vegetation with some pine forests in the Ozark-Ouachita Highlands. The physiographic areas in the Southeast also have very different river patterns and natural resources.

During the last 20,000 yr, the landscape of the Southeast has undergone many changes caused by the last glaciation and current interglacial global climatic stages. The most significant changes have been in sea level, vegetation, and drainage. During the Wisconsin glaciation, sea level was 330–390 ft lower than it is today, and forest belts were pushed southward. Global warming during the late Pleistocene and early Holocene flooded the continental shelf. Forest belts broke up as plant and associated animal communities migrated northward unevenly. Between 10,000 and 8000 B.C., there was a wave of extinctions of large mammals that left a much lower-level of diversity of large mammals in the Southeast. The peak of interglacial warmth was reached during the middle Holocene, about 3000 B.C., and afterward the climate cooled to present conditions. The influx of tropical weather during this period, with its associated summer thunderstorms and lightning fires, virtually burned out the hardwoods on the coastal plain, leaving fire-resistant pine forests. Sea level stabilized within about 10 ft of the present position at the beginning of the late Holocene. Modern coastal ecosystems that have dense marine plant and animal communities subsequently developed.

3

HISTORY OF SOUTHEASTERN ARCHAEOLOGY

KEY PERIODS

Speculative Period: 1492–1840

Descriptive Period: 1840–1914

Culture History Period: 1914–1960

Modern Period: 1960–Present

Modern archaeology developed in western Europe from interest in Greek and Roman monuments during the Italian Renaissance. By the eighteenth and nineteenth centuries, after western European scholars had discovered the principle of evolution, the perception of the past changed from a mysterious entity to a discoverable reality. This intellectual breakthrough led directly to the development of both history and archaeology as academic disciplines and professions.

Archaeology in the United States is a component of anthropology, which is the comparative study of human culture. There are four fields of American anthropology: cultural anthropology (or ethnology), linguistic anthropology, physical anthropology, and archaeology. The objective of archaeology is the comparative study of culture through material remains, especially artifacts. The primary contributions of archaeology to anthropology are to provide information about cultural development through time and the role of material culture in that development. Most archaeologists in the United States have academic degrees in anthropology, which means a graduate-level education in all four fields of anthropology, but significantly more in archaeology.

Archaeology in the United States, and the rest of the Americas, began and remains strongly tied to Indian culture. Other than some Viking remains in Canada, literally all of the archaeology older than A.D. 1492 in the Western Hemisphere is from American Indians. Archaeologists in the Americas initially were almost exclusively interested in prehistoric Indian archaeology (also called pre-Columbian), but in the past 50 yr, historic archaeology (post-Columbian) of Europeans, Americans, Africans, and Indians has become an important part of archaeology in the United States.

There are several well-written publications on the history of American archaeology in general as well as southeastern archaeology in particular. In this chapter, I will briefly summarize the major developments in southeastern archaeology to provide some background for the remainder of this book. For more details about the development of archaeology in the Southeast, please see the references in this footnote.[1]

SPECULATIVE PERIOD: 1492–1840

The first archaeologists in the southeastern United States were primarily interested in the earth mounds scattered through the region. Travelers in the early eighteenth century, such as William Bartram and Henry Brackenridge, had described the larger mound groups and some of the artifacts found at them in their popular publications. As Indians in the Southeast during the

[1] For a detailed history of American archaeology see Willey and Sabloff, 1974; see Dunnell, 1986 and 1990, for short summaries of the history of southeastern archaeology, and Johnson, 1993, for a detailed history of the development of the different subfields in southeastern archaeology.

nineteenth century did not use mounds nor know about them, the origin and function of mounds were a mystery. Most Europeans and Euro-Americans considered Indians incapable of building the complex earth architectural monuments, so they speculated that the mounds had been built by a lost race of civilized people they called the "Mound Builders" who had disappeared, leaving the mounds and primitive Indians behind.

Throughout this period, speculation was the primary method for explaining things, including the origin of the American Indian, the age of the earth, and abandoned mounds and pyramids. During this period, Judeo-Christian theology was the basis for explanations. It was thought that all human beings were descended from Adam and Eve, and more directly from Noah and his family, who were the only human survivors of the worldwide flood. Biblical scholars had determined that the earth was 6004 yr old and all the plants and animals were unchanged since creation. However, travelers continually discovered new groups of people in distant lands with different cultures and physical features, crude human tools were excavated which were no longer in use, and the principles of evolution and stratigraphy were discovered. New information such as this put increasing pressure on scholars for explanations within a biblical framework.

By the end of the eighteenth century there was a growing number of educated, intelligent, and wealthy men who did not accept the biblical-based speculative explanations of the theological establishment. Rather, they began to carefully gather their own information and generate natural, rather than supernatural, explanations for their observations. This group of scholars included Charles Lyell, Charles Darwin, Gregor Mendel, and Carolus Linnaeus who began a new form of information-gathering called the "scientific method" and who generated explanations called "theories," which offered alternative explanations based on controlled observations and record-keeping and which could be tested and refined.

In the Southeast, the first speculative theory to be tested by natural science was the mound builder theory; it was tested by none other than Thomas Jefferson, who thought that it was possible that the mounds had been built by the ancestors of the Indians, rather than by an extinct race of people. In 1784, he investigated a mound on his Monticello Plantation in Virginia to gather information about the nature of earth mounds. He carefully excavated a trench into the mound and recorded the distinct layers, human skeletons, and objects encountered. This excavation was very carefully done for that time, and information, not objects, was the goal of the work. Jefferson's excavation is considered the first scientific archaeological investigation in the United States, and because of it, Thomas Jefferson is often referred to as the "father of American archaeology." Although Thomas Jefferson's excavations did not prove which theory of the origin of the mounds was correct, it left the issue open and he called for further scientific investigations.

By the end of this period, field investigations such as Jefferson's were occurring in many disciplines, and it was becoming clear that many of the speculations of the "arm chair" scholars were not realistic and could not be verified. This situation sparked a period of unprecedented scientific field observations and descriptions by European and American scholars worldwide.

DESCRIPTIVE PERIOD: 1840–1914

During the Descriptive period, the public and their representatives in congress sponsored archaeological investigations to determine the origin of the mounds in the eastern United States. Several expeditions sponsored by museums, universities, and the government were conducted to locate and describe the mounds. Early expeditions were mainly in the Midwest, where land clearing had exposed many mounds. Attention was soon turned to the mounds in the Southeast by the mound expedition conducted by Squire and Davis reported in 1848. A more extensive mound expedition was directed by Cyrus Thomas between 1882 and 1894, along with several others that were conducted at the turn of the twentieth century. The documents containing detailed maps, drawings, and descriptions of mounds and mound centers made during these studies were one of the most important archaeological contributions of the Descriptive period. In the following 100–150 yr, most of the mound sites visited and described during the early mound explorations have been either completely destroyed or greatly altered. Consequently, the maps and descriptions made by the early studies are often the only record of the mounds and mound groups in their original, or near original, condition.

With funding from the federal government, the Smithsonian Institution was given the responsibility of identifying who built the mounds in the United States. The Smithsonian formed a Division of Mound Exploration within the Bureau of Ethnology dedicated to this task and hired Cyrus Thomas, an entomologist by training, to direct the research and report the findings to Congress. Thomas designed a classic natural science research project to gather systematic and comparable information on mounds. He developed a mound classification system and formulated excavations to determine how the mounds were constructed and to recover artifacts from the mounds.[2] The project was long and complex. There were three teams in the field year-round for 10 yr, and more than 2000 mounds were investigated in over 140 counties. The Cyrus Thomas mound exploration project is considered by most American archaeologists to have established the empirical foundations of modern archaeology through the use of the scientific method, research objectives, and systematic field methods.

---

[2] For the final report see C. Thomas, 1894; for more details see the Introduction of B. D. Smith, 1985d.

The reports of Thomas' Mound Exploration project were detailed and well illustrated.[3] For each of the mounds that were investigated, the report described each site, often with a scaled survey map, the field methods used, the stratigraphy, and materials recovered. Thomas extensively reviewed historical documents that described Indains using and building mounds in the sixteenth and seventeenth centuries in eastern North America, especially in the Southeast. His reports also contained early historical drawings of Indians using mounds both for burials and to elevate special buildings. His systematic comparison of documented historic Indian mound use and the recovery of Indian artifacts from mounds demonstrated that it was the ancestors of the living American Indians who made and used the mounds in the eastern United States. Cyrus Thomas put an end to the Mound Builder theory.

Thomas' Smithsonian Mound Exploration Project generated interest in Southeast archaeology. Expeditions were led primarily by men educated in other professions, but who had an interest in archaeology. For example, Jefferies Wyman, a natural scientist, was the first curator of the Peabody Museum of Harvard University, and he excavated several prehistoric Indian sites on the Florida Atlantic coast and the St. Johns River between 1868 and 1875.[4] Soon after, S. T. Walker excavated prehistoric sites along the Florida Gulf coast in 1883. The most extensive archaeology done in the Southeast during this period, however, was by the physician and socialite, C. B. Moore, from Philadelphia. At the age of 40, he became interested in archaeology and retired from medicine. He equipped a flat-bottomed steamboat named *The Gopher* for his expeditions, and made innumerable trips up and down the waterways and the coasts of the Southeast excavating hundreds of mounds between 1892 and 1916. He was accompanied by Milo Miller on his annual expeditions, a fellow physician who was both the secretary and skeletal specialist for the archaeology projects. The excavations were well organized and well documented through excellent field notes, drawings, photographs, and skeletal records. Importantly, Moore published detailed reports of his excavations complete with maps and illustrations of the mounds and artifacts that he had recovered.[5] He gave the more unusual artifacts to major institutions where they continue to be available for study.

C. B. Moore's publications are arguably one of the most important set of documents in southeastern archaeology. It was primarily through his publications that the archaeology in the Southeast was first extensively revealed. Moore's publications often contain the earliest, and often the only, documentation of mound groups that have long since been destroyed or greatly damaged.

---

[3] See Thomas, 1894, for the full final report.

[4] See Wyman, 1863, 1875, for details.

[5] Examples of C. B. Moore's reports were published in 1901, 1905, and 1908.

Another important aspect of C. B. Moore's publications was his emphasis on artifacts as well as mounds. His publications contain superb color illustrations of beautiful artifacts, especially pottery vessels. His publications sparked further interest in southeastern archaeology, and it became one of the centers of American archaeology for the next several decades. Even today, Moore's reports and artifact collections are used by archaeologists on a regular basis for information for modern research investigations.

CULTURE HISTORY PERIOD: 1914–1960

During the Culture History period, descriptive mound investigations and detailed publications continued, but a serious concern for the age of the materials and their chronological order developed. To deal with the question of age, four chronological principles had been developed in the field of archaeology and geology: stratigraphy, superposition, seriation, and classification.

The principle of stratigraphy was developed in the field of geology, and it states that materials in the same geological stratum or deposit are relatively the same age and contain similar materials. Closely related to stratigraphy is the principle of superposition, which states that in any buildup of strata which is undisturbed, the oldest stratum will be on the bottom, and the youngest will be on the top. With the discovery of these two geological principles, the relative age of archaeological strata and the artifacts contained in them can be determined.

In an effort to refine the relative dating method, archaeologists noticed that the shape and decorations on artifacts changed through time as materials accumulated on sites. Quantification of changes in artifacts through time led to the discovery of the principle of seriation: artifact styles gradually change through time. Subtle changes in artifact styles were identified and quantified by the development of a detailed system of artifact classification. Classification is the process by which artifacts are organized into groups called artifact types, based on the presence or absence of particular combinations of well-defined features or attributes. The first classification systems emphasized artifact types made up of attributes that change through time. With the development of seriation, archaeologists could relatively date artifacts from different archaeological sites and strata.

The four basic archaeological principles were developed early in this period, which enabled archaeologists to determine the relative age of archaeological strata and the artifacts within them. Determining the calendrical date of prehistoric artifacts and cultures in the eastern United States was a problem, until after World War II when radiocarbon dating was developed. With the advent and refinement of radioactive dating in the late 1940s, most archaeologists all over the world were suprised at the great antiquity of prehistoric cultures, and the Southeast was no exception. By 1950, dates as old as

3000 B.C. had been obtained in the southeastern United Staes, and there were still older, but undated, deposits. By the 1960s, it was established that Indians had lived in the Southeast for at least 10,000 yr.

During the middle portion of the Culture History period, the Southeast was selected for one of the largest archaeology efforts ever conducted in the United States. By 1930, the Great Depression had set in, and millions of people were out of work. One of the main programs sponsored by the federal government to combat unemployment was a series of "work relief" programs such as the Civilian Conservation Corps (CCC) and the Works Progress Administration (WPA). These "make-work" programs sponsored large-scale labor-intensive projects to provide jobs for the unemployed. In 1933 at the Marksville Site in Louisiana, a large-scale archaeological excavation was conducted to determine of it could be used as a source of public employment. Robert Seltzer and James Ford directed the excavations and demonstrated that large numbers of unskilled laborers could be effectively employed excavating prehistoric Indian mounds. As there were great numbers of unemployed people in the South as well as plenty of mounds, the success of the Marksville experiment opened the floodgates of federal relief funding for archaeology. Many federal programs sponsored large excavation projects, but after 1935, the WPA and the Tennessee Valley Authority (TVA) were the dominant agencies sponsoring federal excavations.[6] The work relief projects focused primarily on excavating large sites, especially those with mounds, so that large numbers of people could be employed for a long period of time. Hundreds of sites were investigated all over the Southeast (147 excavations were conducted in Tennessee alone) with crews averaging 150 people. Many prehistoric mounds and settlements were completely excavated, which exposed large portions or even complete prehistoric Indian community plans, architectural remains, burials, and cemeteries.

Prior to the Depression, there were only a few trained archaeologists in the United States who were associated either with the few original Anthropology departments, universities, or federal government agencies, such as the Smithsonian Instituiton. Archaeologists, who had been primarily conducting surveys or limited excavations, were thrust into large-scale excavation projects where they and their graduate students literally became the "fathers and mothers" of American archaeology. Many of my contemporaries and I were educated by Depression era archaeologists.

The sheer volume of everything associated with Depression work relief archaeology was large. Millions of artifacts, thousands of features and burials, miles of stratigraphic profiles, thousands of photographs, hundreds of filing cabinets full of field and laboratory documents, and even documentary films were produced. The information generated by these large excavations overloaded the existing archaeology management system and the archaeologists

---

[6] For further details about Depression era archaeology in the Southeast see Haag, 1985.

in charge of the projects. Whereas there were excellent reports written for several projects, many others were never written. One of the main reasons for the lack of reporting was the abrupt end of the work relief program due to the surprise beginning of World War II. For example, the excavation phase of many sites had been completed, but the massive laboratory analysis and long report preparation phases had not been performed. Consequently, many huge collections of carefully excavated and cataloged materials, detailed field notes, and photographs were placed in storage while the labor force and funding went to war. Many of these massive collections still sit in government warehouses. Even today, government archaeologists, graduate students, and professionals regularly study these stored materials and publish information from WPA excavations conducted over 60 yr ago.

The increase in archaeological excavation in the Southeast during the Depression concentrated most archaeologists in the United States into this region, and it created a great demand for archaeologists with formal training. The University of Chicago had provided many of the Depression archaeology supervisors, most of whom had been educated and trained under the department head, Fay-Cooper Cole. As a consequence, Cole and his students had a tremendous impact on southeastern archaeology. Because archaeology projects had to use large untrained labor forces, there was an immediate need to formalize field and laboratory procedures. This led directly to the codification of American archaeology field and laboratory methods by the "Cole School," which is the core of American archaeology today. The standardized procedures included field and laboratory methods and forms to assure comparable information-gathering, the use of grids to organize site collection units, isolation of features for excavation, photographic documentation procedures, artifact classification systems, artifact cataloging and sorting procedures, and basic organization principles of stored archaeological material. There have been many additions and refinements of the basic archaeology procedures established during the Depression in the Southeast, but they remain the nucleus of American archaeology. As Robert Dunnell writes, southeastern archaeology and archaeologists played a significant role in the professionalization of archaeology in the United States.[7]

The escalation of archaeology in the Southeast during the Depression also created communication problems among archaeologists working in the region with large labor forces. This situation led to the formation of the Southeastern Archaeological Conference in 1938, only 4 yr after the foundation of the national Society for American Archaeology.

After World War II, archaeology in the Southeast changed from labor-intensive mound excavations to smaller-scale excavations and surveys. Large-scale government projects, and associated archaeological work, were still conducted, but they were primarily in the West, where there was a flurry of

[7] For details of the theoretical history of southeastern archaeology see Dunnell, 1986, 1990.

construction of large reservoirs in river valleys. In the Southeast, the first comprehensive, though limited, site surveys were performed in many areas by universities, museums, and government agencies. A few large surveys were conducted, such as the Smithsonian survey of the Gulf coast in the mid-1940s by Gordon Willey and the Peabody Museum surveys of the lower Mississippi Valley and the lower Yazoo Valley survey by Phillip Phillips, James Ford, and James Griffin.[8]

The importance of the post-war surveys is that for the first time the full range of archaeological sites in the Southeast was revealed. The surveys documented deep, dry rockshelters, large shell midden rings and embankments, sites on isolated islands, in swamps, and buried under alluvium. Testing and dating the newly discovered sites refined the cultural chronology in many areas of the Southeast and provided a more comprehensive understanding of past southeastern societies. Patterns of settlement, subsistence, and sociopolitical organization were developed both for specific cultural periods and many internal regions. The more detailed and anthropological approach to prehistoric societies through archaeology signaled the beginning of the modern era of archaeology. The appeal of the mounds and large-scale excavations waned as archaeologists and their students realized that the cultures of the societies responsible for building the mound sites were not well understood; thus, archaeologists turned their attention to this broader focus in the 1960s.

MODERN PERIOD: 1960–PRESENT

In the 1960s and early 1970s, laws and regulations were enacted that required archaeological investigations prior to the initiation of construction or mining projects funded or permitted by the government. The cornerstone federal laws were the National Historic Preservation Act (NHPA) of 1966, the National Environmental Protection Act (NEPA) of 1969, and the Archaeological and Historic Preservation Act (Moss-Bennet) of 1974. NHPA required states to gather and maintain archaeological and architectural information in the state, and to review the federally required archaeological investigations being conducted in the state. An historic preservation office was established in each state, which had a staff and facilities to perform these tasks. NEPA required federally funded or permitted projects to determine the effects on archaeological sites and the Moss-Bennet Act ensured funding for the mandated archaeology. While the implementation of the laws and regulations were not immediate throughout the country, the directives and mandated funding brought another explosion of archaeology in the 1970s similar to the Depression era in the

---

[8] For the central Mississippi Valley surveys see Phillips, 1970, and Phillips *et al.*, 1951; for the Gulf coast survey see Willey, 1949.

Southeast. Once again, there was an immediate need for archaeologists with formal training to direct and supervise large-scale federally funded projects. This time, many of the students of the original WPA archaeologists answered the call. Many new anthropology programs had been started by former WPA archaeologists in the Southeast following World War II including Alabama, Georgia, North Carolina, Florida, and Tennessee.

Much of the "new" federal archaeology in the Southeast was and continues to be conducted through three primary agencies: the Tennessee Valley Authority (TVA), National Park Service (NPS), and the U.S. Army Corps of Engineers (COE). These agencies have jurisdiction over a significant amount of land in the Southeast, and the TVA and COE have had a series of large construction projects for the past 30 yr. With the large amounts of money involved in modern federal archaeology projects, the gentlemanly agreements of Depression archaeology projects between federal agencies and educational institutions became inadequate. Archaeology projects are now awarded through a competitive bidding process where a formal business contract is signed. Because of the importance of contracts, regulatory archaeology is often referred to as "contract archaeology." There have been several single federal contract projects for over a million dollars and thousands of smaller ones in the Southeast since the 1970s, which has produced an enormous amount of information about the archaeology in the Southeast.[9]

There are many differences between modern and Depression era federal archaeology. Depression archaeology had as its goal the employment of large groups of unskilled labor directed by very few supervisors with formal training in archaeology. Today, it is required that all senior supervisors have a graduate degree in anthropology, and in many states, even skilled laborers must have a bachelor's degree in anthropology. In Depression archaeology there was an emphasis on large site excavations to employ large crews. Today, modern federal archaeology requires comprehensive surveys to locate all archaeological sites, structures, bridges, cemeteries, and even landscaping features 50 or more yr old in proposed project areas. The suite of properties included in federal and state surveys are called "cultural resources" today, and regulatory-driven archaeology today is called cultural resource management (CRM).

Most CRM projects have three phases: survey, testing, and mitigation. The survey must locate all cultural resources in specified areas over 50 yr old, regardless of how small or large. The second phase consists of evaluating the cultural resources that could be significant according to criteria stipulated in federal regulations and which will be impacted by the proposed construction. The third phase, if necessary, involves mitigating the impact on significant sites that will be damaged by the proposed construction. The most frequent types of mitigation include redesigning construction to avoid impact, pro-

---

[9] See Steponaitis, 1986, for the location and publications of most major contract archaeology projects; see Keel, 1988, for a state-by-state summary of federal archaeology in the Southeast.

tecting the resource from impact, or excavating a representative sample prior to destruction. Unlike Depression archaeology, time and funds must be allocated for fieldwork, laboratory work, and report preparation in each phase of CRM projects. Submission of approved final reports are required, and if they are not completed satisfactorily and on time, serious legal repercussions and fines take place.

When federal cultural resource laws and regulations were first enacted, almost all archaeologists were located in academic departments and museums. Therefore, most contracts for federal archaeology were between federal agencies and these institutions. Over time, the business of contract archaeology became ill-suited for cumbersome state university bureaucracies and the high number of regulatory archaeology projects encouraged archaeologists to leave educational institutions and start private contract archaeology businesses. Today, most contract archaeology is performed by archaeologists in private businesses, not in academic institutions or museums. Private contract archaeology businesses can make good profits, and it is a growing field of archaeology in the United States today. There are firms in most major cities, and there is a brisk competition for contracts.

The ever-increasing contract archaeology done by an ever-increasing number of archaeologists has produced a staggering amount of information in the last 30 yr. Not surprisingly, this has caused communication problems, not only owing to the number of people doing archaeology in the Southeast, but the low circulation of the reports. These problems are being worked on by both state and regional professional societies as well as the National Park Service, which has recently created a computerized annotated bibliography of reports in the United States, the National Archaeological Database (NADB). In the Southeast alone, about 30,000 reports have been entered into the database, and federal archaeologists estimate that there are upwards of 75,000 publications. Through NADB, archaeologists can research contract reports (called the "gray" literature) in a manner similar to that of most library computerized card catalogs and find where they can obtain a copy of each report.

Modern archaeology in the Southeast is much more complex than in the previous periods. Academic research and contract projects include the entire range of archaeological sites, including historic period sites, wet sites, drowned sites, and shipwrecks. Improved dating methods and a reduction in costs have resulted in thousands of new dates, and chronologies are being continually refined. New recovery techniques have also added new sources of information such as plant seeds, phytoliths, pollen, charcoal, animal bones, soil chemistry, and mineralogy. With this wealth of information, archaeologists are able to research higher-level questions about previous societies and the environment in the Southeast than ever before. There has been growing interest in settlement and subsistence patterns in many areas of the Southeast. Researchers are beginning to understand how prehistoric and historic cultures evolved and developed in the Southeast. For example, we now know that native gourds and hard-rind squash plants were grown as early as 5000 B.C. for containers, not food. It was not until A.D. 800 at the earliest, A.D. 1000 in most areas, that agriculture was practiced in some parts of the Southeast. Apparently, the food resources of the region were sufficient for societies to grow and flourish by hunting, gathering, and fishing. As another example, we now know that mound-building was not imported to the Southeast from Mesoamerica or anywhere else. In fact, mounds were built in Louisiana as early as 4000 B.C., long before they were constructed in Mesoamerica or anywhere else in the Americas.

SUMMARY

Archaeology in the southeastern United States began with Thomas Jefferson in the late eighteenth century. The first formal archaeological studies were the mound surveys of the late nineteenth century. The mound studies put to rest the speculation that a lost race of Mound Builders had constructed the mounds, and the studies documented that the mounds had been built and used by prehistoric and early historic Indians. Gentlemen archaeologists, such as C. B. Moore, explored the Southeast, excavating mounds for the next 50 yr. The descriptions of the excavations and the artifacts during the Descriptive period revealed a great number of mounds in the Southeast and many contained exquisite objects. During the Culture History period, the Southeast was the center of activity of American archaeology with massive Depression era work-relief excavations. It was during this period in the Southeast that the core of field and laboratory methods of American archaeology were codified, and archaeology became professionalized. Mounds and large-scale excavations were the focus of Depression archaeology, as well as chronology. Afterwards, research interest became broader, and comprehensive surveys were conducted to identify the full range of site types throughout the region. With the passage of federal laws and regulations requiring archaeology prior to federally funded or permitted construction projects, archaeology in the Southeast mushroomed once again in the 1970s and 1980s, and it continues to increase to the present day. Archaeology research and development continues to be conducted in academic institutions and museums, but most contract projects are done by archaeologists in the private business sector. With a vastly increased information base, archaeologists are now studying complex questions about cultural development and change in southeastern societies.

4

PALEOINDIAN STAGE:
13,000?–8000 B.C.

KEY FEATURE
Lanceolate Stone Points

IMPORTANT DEVELOPMENTS
Colonization and Expansion throughout the Southeast
Development of First Culture Areas

INTRODUCTION AND OVERVIEW

Paleoindian is the first recognized cultural stage in the Southeast. It began sometime during the late Pleistocene, and it ended about 8000 B.C. The key archaeological feature of this stage is the Lanceolate-Shaped Stone Point. The Paleoindian stage has long intrigued archaeologists as well as the public because of the association of Paleoindian material with extinct large Pleistocene animals, such as elephants and bison, and the high quality of stone tool craftsmanship. Almost every natural history museum in the United States and Canada has an exhibit showing "Early Man" hunting huge mammoths and mastodons with spears tipped with lanceolate stone points. This image has been promoted by the media and has captured the imagination of the public. Prior to the 1930s, many scholars had doubts that the American Indians had been in the Americas more than a few thousand years. However, radiocarbon dating and the association of Paleoindian points with now-extinct animals have documented that the American Indians arrived over 10,000 yr ago.

All the accepted evidence indicates that the first human occupants of the Western Hemisphere came from northeast Asia during the last glacial period via the Bering Land Bridge, which connected Alaska and Siberia during glacial periods. Most archaeologists agree that people migrated from Alaska southward through Canada in an "ice-free corridor" located between the two parts of the Canadian ice sheet, the Laurentide on the east and the Cordilleran to the west, as shown in Figure 2.5A. There are two schools of thought about when this southward migration took place. Some researchers hold that people migrated southward during the Wisconsin glaciation, sometime prior to 30,000 B.C.[1] But most American archaeologists think that people migrated southward sometime after 13,000 B.C., probably closer to 10,000 B.C. By this time the ice sheets had begun to recede and the environment in the corridor was much more habitable for people.

There are a few sites in the Americas south of the ice sheets with radiocarbon dates earlier than 10,000 B.C. However, at each of these sites, there are problems with either the dates or the artifacts or both, and the sites are not generally accepted as evidence of pre-10,000 B.C. occupation. In fact, the questions of when people first arrived, how and when they dispersed, and how Paleoindian culture developed are some of the biggest issues in American archaeology. A number of sites throughout the Americas have been claimed as evidence of pre-Paleoindian culture. Two of the most widely discussed claims are in South America, and another is in Pennsylvania. At the Toca do Boqueirão da Pedra Furada rockshelter in Brazil, the lowest levels date as early as 40,000 yr ago.[2] At the Monte Verde site in Chile, dates of 11,000 B.C. have been associated with features that are interpreted as dwellings and

[1] See Bryan, 1986, Dillehay, 1988, and Dillehay and Meltzer, 1991, for readings on this position.
[2] For details see Guidon and Delibras, 1986, and Lynch, 1990.

hearths and with crude artifacts. While Monte Verde is probably the most plausible of the South American pre-10,000 B.C. sites, neither the artifacts nor the dates from either site are well accepted. Closer to the Southeast, Meadowcroft Rockshelter in Pennsylvania, excavated by James Adovasio, has produced 13 dates older than 10,800 B.C. as well as stone points, artifacts, and features. However, there are problems with the proposed pre-Paleoindian culture radiocarbon dates at Meadowcroft. The point of contention is the possibility of contamination of the dated samples with "old" carbon from the ground water in nearby coal deposits.[3] This type of contamination could cause the samples to date older than they actually are. The controversy over the Meadowcroft dates is not resolved, and no similar site has been found in the 15 yr since its discovery that can offer corroboration.

The oldest securely dated and accepted human settlements in North America are between 10,000 and 8000 B.C., and at the present time there is no compelling evidence for a pre-13,000 B.C. immigration theory. Despite this situation, there is no conclusive evidence to deny it either, and it is possible that people did arrive earlier. What we do know is that by 9500 B.C. or shortly thereafter, people were here and occupied, if sparsely, most of the area south of the ice sheets to the tip of South America.

The most distinctive Paleoindian artifact is the lanceolate-shaped chipped stone point. This was a relatively long, thin, and parallel-sided point, usually made of fine-grained chert, which often had a shallow depression called a "flute" down each face running from the base towards the tip, as shown in Figure 4.1. There is a strong similarity of these very complex and difficult-to-make points across large portions of North America during this stage, which suggests to archaeologists that Paleoindian people must have kept in touch with each other, probably to maintain mate exchange and information networks, both of which would have been critically important given the low population levels.

Chipped stone tools are made from rocks that can be worked into thin pieces with sharp edges. The best rock in the Southeast for chipped stone tools is chert (also known as flint), although other types of rock were used. Chert is formed from sand deposits which, through great pressure and heat, were changed into a natural glasslike material, and it usually occurs in veins or pockets in limestone. The best quality cherts for chipped stone tools are those that were made from deposits of pure, very fine-grained sand. The technique of making chipped stone tools is illustrated in Figure 4.2. The first step is the preparation of a large piece of chert (either a chunk from a natural outcrop or a cobble from a riverbed) into a core or rough biface using a round, rough hammerstone. Cores are prepared so that long thin flakes can be struck

[3] For Meadowcroft archaeology details see Carlisle and Adovasio, 1982; for details on the radiocarbon dating controversy see Adovasio *et al.*, 1992, Tankersley, *et al.*, 1987, and Tankersley and Munson, 1992.

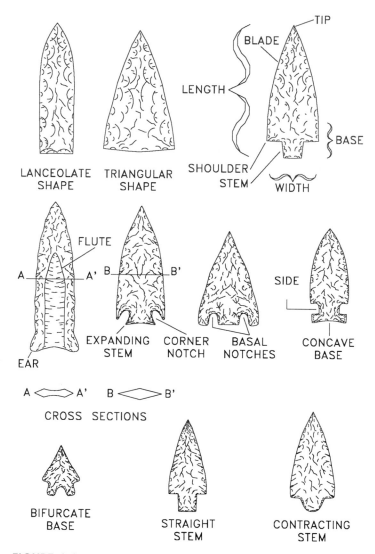

FIGURE 4.1   Chipped stone point morphology and attributes.

off with a hammerstone. The next stage is to thin and shape the core or biface by removing flakes from both edges, using a softer hammer such as a piece of antler to avoid shattering. Finally, the long biface is sharpened by the removal of tiny flakes, by pressing a small soft pointed tool, such as an antler tine, along the edge. Most chipped stone bifaces were then cemented into a wood or bone handle with sinew and adhesive (resin or asphalt).

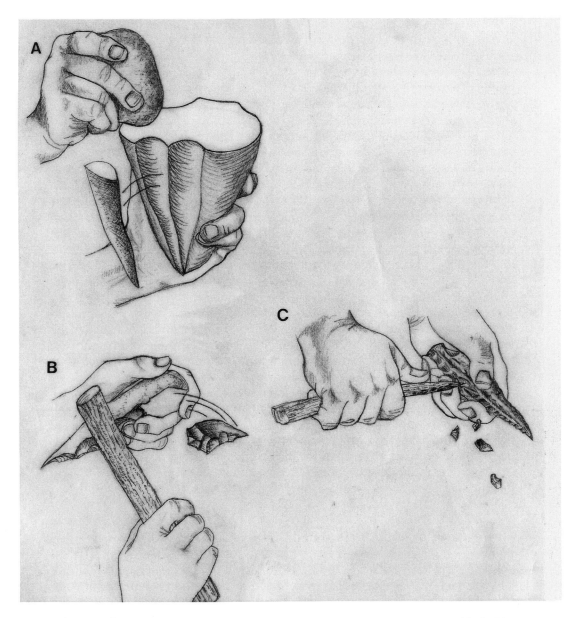

FIGURE 4.2 Steps in manufacturing chipped stone tools: (A) removing blade like flakes from a prepared core; (B) thinning a biface by percussion with an antler hammer; (C) sharpening a biface by pressure flaking with an antler tine.

There is a scarcity of firmly dated Paleoindian sites in the Southeast, but there is no lack of sites with Paleoindian-style points. On the contrary, thousands of sites have been recorded in the Southeast, and more stone points have been found there (over 5000) than in any other region of the United States. There are two problems with Paleoindian sites in the Southeast. The first is that many of the known sites are very shallow and consist of no more than surface scatters of artifacts. There is no doubt that there are many buried sites, but we have not developed an efficient way to find them. The second problem is that many Paleoindian sites were continually reoccupied for thousands of years, so that the Paleoindian artifacts are so mixed with later materials as not to be very useful sources of information. These problems have continually frustrated archaeologists throughout the Southeast. Despite the fact that there are more early Paleoindian sites and points in the Southeast than anywhere else in North America, there is a severe lack of clear archaeological information.

The Paleoindian stage is divided into three periods: early, middle, and late, as shown in Figure 1.1. The periods are differentiated primarily on changes in chipped stone points, shown in Figure 4.3. While this three-part division is generally accepted, it has not been completely confirmed through stratigraphic excavations and absolute dating. There is a consensus that the large, fluted parallel-sided Clovis point style preceded the more constricted or non fluted forms, but the exact timing of the different styles has yet to be worked out.

Most information about the Paleoindian periods in the Southeast has come from studies of the distribution of Paleoindian points collected from the surface. An example study is that of David Anderson, who for many years has been compiling the numbers, locations, and stone types of early Paleoindian points on a county-by-county basis in eastern North America.[4] From studies such as this, archaeologists are beginning to understand how early Paleoindian groups colonized eastern North America.

EARLY PALEOINDIAN PERIOD: 13,000?–8000 B.C.

The early Paleoindian period is distinguished by the Clovis style of lanceolate chipped stone point and the extinction of more than 30 species of large mammals. The people who migrated south through Canada by way of the ice-free corridor arrived on the high plains of Montana. From the distribution pattern of Clovis points and the drainage pattern of the Plains, archaeologists generally agree that early Paleoindian people spread into eastern North America by following the eastward-flowing rivers, such as the Missouri and

---

[4] For details on Anderson's study and colonization model see Anderson, 1990c, and Anderson *et al.*, 1992.

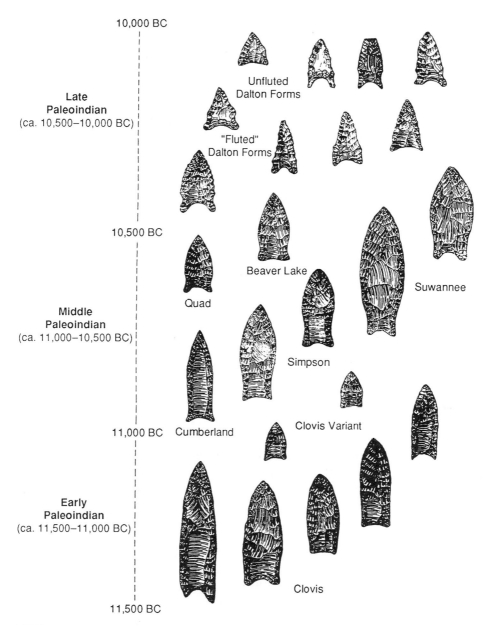

FIGURE 4.3 Changes in Paleoindian lanceolate chipped stone point styles in the southeastern United States. (From Anderson *et al.*, 1992).

the Platte, which originated near the mouth of the ice-free corridor. Once people reached the central Mississippi Valley, they probably spread into the East via the Ohio, Tennessee, and Cumberland river valleys, where some of the largest concentrations of Clovis points in eastern North America are found.

Subsistence

The subsistence strategy of early Paleoindians has been the subject of much discussion in the past 60 yr. At first, archaeologists theorized that Paleoindians specialized in hunting large mammals such as mammoths and mastodons, and these early people were called the Big Game Hunters. This theory was based on the early findings of Paleoindian mammoth kill sites in the Plains and Southwest. The theory has since been refined, but scholars continue to think that reliance on hunting and fishing played an important part in the initial immigration of people into North America and their rapid spread throughout the hemisphere.[5]

The extinction of Pleistocene megafauna appears to have been going on throughout the early Paleoindian period. Paleontologists and archaeologists agree that the continent-wide extinctions were complete no later than 8000 B.C., and possibly by 8800 B.C.[6] Although archaeologists suspect that the large animals were hunted by early Paleoindians in the Southeast, there is little evidence for it. It is also suspected that the impact of the extinctions on the early Paleoindian people in the Southeast was much less than in other areas of North America, such as the Plains and Canada. The reason behind this suspicion is the abundance and diversification of food resources that were present in the Southeast during that time. Archaeologists think that early Paleoindian people in the Southeast probably easily made the switch to alternative food sources, such as the white-tailed deer, and therefore they escaped any serious effects from the mass extinctions at the end of the Pleistocene.

The archaeological record in Siberia and Alaska confirms that the subsistence of the immediate ancestors of the early Paleoindians was based on hunting and fishing.[7] We also know that the few plants that can live in the cold northern latitudes are not generally edible by humans, yet they support large numbers of grazing animals and their predators. People who live in these cold climates, such as the Eskimos, traditionally subsist by hunting land and sea animals. As a result, Eskimos had a very mobile settlement pattern and a set of efficient and portable tools made of chipped stone and bones. Based on observations of traditional people who live in the Arctic, many archaeologists think that when humans first arrived in southern Canada from

---

[5] For a recent summary of early Paleoindian economics see Tankersley and Isaac, 1990.

[6] For more about Pleistocene extinctions see Mead and Meltzer, 1984, and Martin and Klein, 1984.

[7] See Meltzer, 1989, for further information about early Siberian-Alaskan cultures.

the cold north they had a mobile hunting and fishing way of life much like the Eskimo. Since there were no resident human populations south of the ice sheets who had knowledge about the resources, archaeologists suspect that early Paleoindians at least initially used their northern-derived mobile hunting- and fishing-based economy and portable technology to spread rapidly into new and unfamiliar areas.[8] This theory does not imply that people ignored easily acquired foods when they were available, such as berries, seeds, roots, nuts, or small animals. In fact, several early Paleoindian sites have the remains of these foods, such as Shawnee-Minisink in Pennsylvania and Little Salt Spring in Florida.

Material Culture

Supporting this hunting mobility theory is the fact that throughout North America we find essentially the same Clovis point and tool kit that has been demonstrated to be designed specifically for killing animals, butchering meat, processing hides, and working bone. Their hunting weapon was the Clovis stone point. Meat butchering tools, shown in Figure 4.4, included bifacial knives and on-the-spot tools made from flakes. Small end scrapers were common and were used to scrape and process hides into leather. Bone tools were made by splitting bones with small wedge-shaped stone flakes called *pièces esquillées,* which were placed in grooves made with small stone chisels called burins. Bone splinters were made into needles, awls, and other hide-working implements by rubbing them on rough stones (abraders). Rounding out the early Paleoindian Clovis tool kit found across North America are well-shaped cores of high-quality chert from which long blades were struck.

Exactly how the Clovis points were mounted is not known, because we have never found one still in its shaft. Archaeologists suggest that points probably were mounted on short bone or wooden shafts (called foreshafts) that were then placed into the hollowed-out end of a long wooden spear, as shown in Figure 4.5, and thrust into game animals. The point and short foreshaft would stay in the animal and the long spear shaft was worked loose quickly and rearmed with a new point on a foreshaft. In this way, a person only had to carry one long spear shaft that could be rearmed quickly and on the spot.

Clovis points have been found all over eastern North America; however, two concentrations have been identified in the Southeast by David Anderson, shown in Figure 4.6. These areas all have exposures of some of the best fine-grained chert in the Southeast, and they were environmentally diverse in the late Pleistocene. David Anderson calls these "staging areas" in which early Paleoindian groups familiarized themselves with the environment during the colonization process and from which groups spread into the rest of the region.

[8] For more information about this theory see Kelly and Todd, 1988, and Meltzer, 1989.

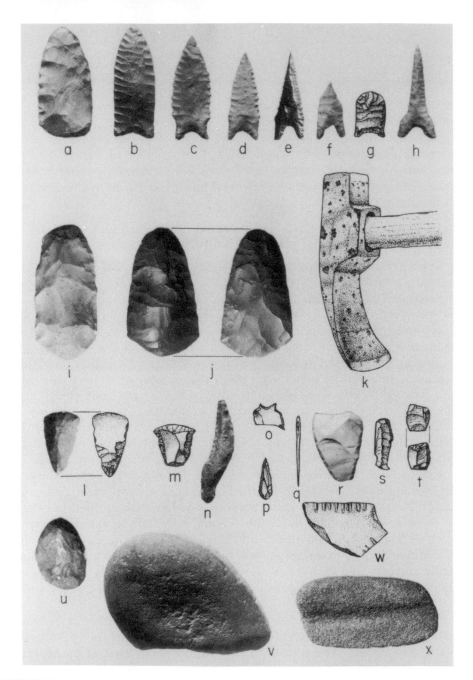

FIGURE 4.4   Paleoindian tool kit from the central Mississippi Valley. (a and b) bifaces; (c) unsharpened Dalton point; (d and e) resharpened Dalton points; (f) burin; (g) end scraper; (h) awl; (i) adz preform; (j) adz); (k) historic metal adz; (l) end scraper; (m) end scraper with graver points; (n) backed blades; (o) graver; (p) microlith; (q) bone needle, (r) utilized flake with scraper retouch; (s) bladelike flake; (t) *pièce esquillée;* (u) discoidal hammerstone; (v) edge-ground cobble; (w) notched abrader; and (x) grooved sandstone abrader (from Morse and Morse, 1983.)

FIGURE 4.5   Artist's depiction of how Paleoindian points could have been mounted on a foreshaft that was inserted in the hollow end of a spear.

Dates

Only a few early Paleoindian dates have been determined in the Southeast. Three dates, between 10,150 and 9750 B.C., were recently obtained at the Johnson site, near Nashville, Tennessee, (located in Figure 4.7) excavated by John Broster. Two currently submerged sites in Florida—Little Salt Spring and the Wascissa River—also have early Paleoindian dates. In Little Salt Spring, near Sarasota, Carl Clausen and his colleagues found the shell of a now-extinct species of tortoise pierced by a bipointed wooden stake on a once-dry ledge that is now about 85 ft below the surface, shown in Figure 4.8.[9] The stake was dated at 10,080 B.C. The tortoise shell had indications that it had been burned. Also present in the same layer on the ledge were the remains of other now-extinct fauna such as mammoth (*Mammuth* or *Mammut sp.*) and bison (*Bison antiquus*). The second Florida underwater early Paleoindian site is in the Wacissa River in north Florida, where paleontologist David Webb and his colleagues found the skull of an extinct form of bison with the tip of a stone point embedded in its forehead. A humerus found within 3 ft of the skull was radiocarbon dated at 9220 B.C.[10]

Summary

In sum, the Early Paleoindian period was marked by the initial immigration of people into eastern North America. The origin of this culture is still not known, but it is very likely a North American development from a Siberian prototype. The people appear to have had a mobile hunting- and fishing-based way of life that was well suited for moving through the new and unfamiliar environments. Their archaeological remains are distinguished by the Clovis stone point and a small, portable, efficient tool kit tailored to hunting and processing animals. Clovis points are found all over the Southeast, but the largest concentrations are in the lower Cumberland, central Tennessee, and central Ohio valleys. The actual dates associated with Clovis points are between 9250 and 8950 B.C.

[9] Clausen *et al.*, 1979.

[10] Webb *et al.*, 1984.

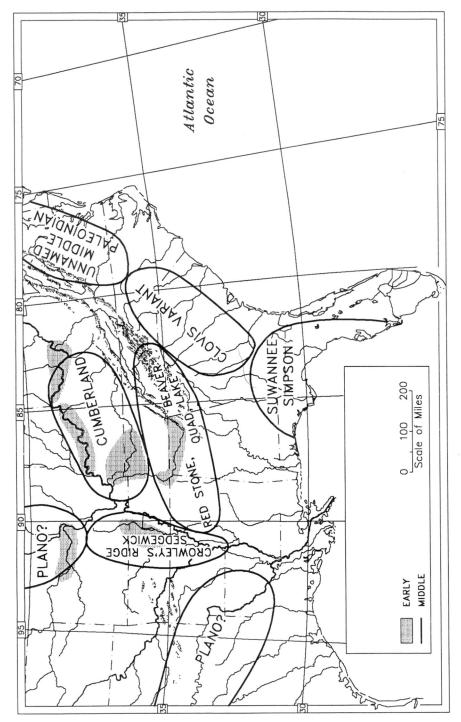

FIGURE 4.6 Early and middle Paleoindian culture areas.

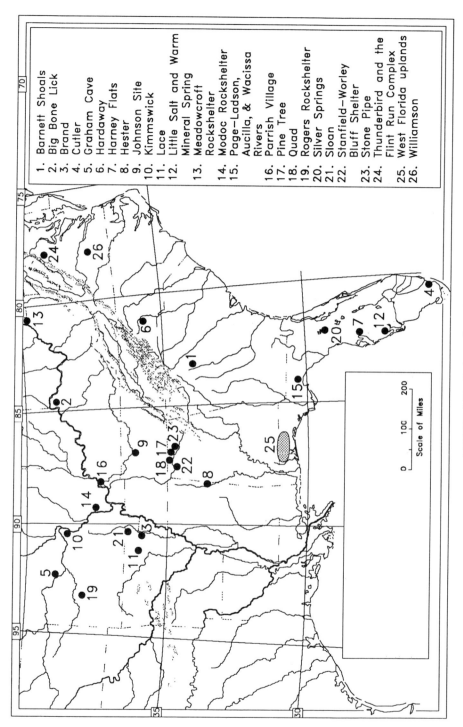

1. Barnett Shoals
2. Big Bone Lick
3. Brand
4. Cutler
5. Graham Cave
6. Hardaway
7. Harney Flats
8. Hester
9. Johnson Site
10. Kimmswick
11. Lace
12. Little Salt and Warm Mineral Spring
13. Meadowcroft Rockshelter
14. Modoc Rockshelter
15. Page-Ladson, Aucilla, & Wacissa Rivers
16. Parrish Village
17. Pine Tree
18. Quad
19. Rogers Rockshelter
20. Silver Springs
21. Sloan
22. Stanfield–Worley Bluff Shelter
23. Stone Pipe
24. Thunderbird and the Flint Run Complex
25. West Florida uplands
26. Williamson

Scale of Miles

0   100   200

FIGURE 4.7 Paleoindian sites.

49

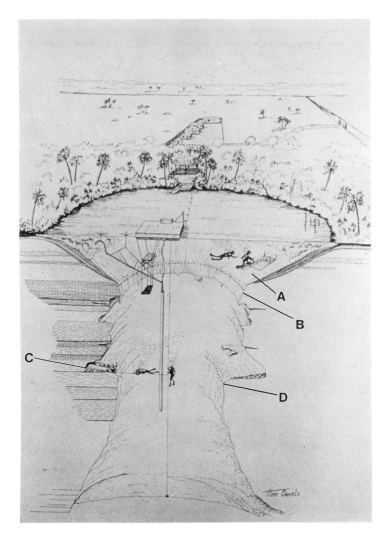

FIGURE 4.8   Artist's conception of the cross section of Little Salt Spring near Sarasota, Florida. (A) underwater Early Archaic excavation unit; (B) upper row of wooden stakes dated to an average of 7622 B.C.; (C) ledge on which the burned tortoise shell was recovered and dated 10,080 B.C.; (D) wooden lower row of wooden stakes. (From Purdy, 1991).

MIDDLE PALEOINDIAN PERIOD: 9000–8500 B.C.

The middle Paleoindian period is marked by the development of regional Paleoindian cultures in the Southeast that are identified by different chipped stone point styles. Archaeologists theorize that the regional cultures developed due to migration into different environments in the Southeast as well as increased social and reproductive isolation.[11] Groups that migrated north, following the cold steppe-tundra plains of the receding ice sheet, maintained a mobile hunting- and fishing-based economy and technology. Paleoindian groups that remained in the forested Southeast adapted to the new environments and began to diversify.

Material Culture

One of the main archaeological indicators of the middle Paleoindian period is the appearance of new styles of lanceolate stone points, which are shown in Figure 4.3. Tool kits that had once been composed primarily of specialized tools for hunting and processing animals, now contained few such tools and many more general tools that could be used for a variety of tasks. Crude cores and simple flake tools, made with little bifacial preparation or finishing, dominated middle Paleoindian tool kits. Microscopic studies of the edges of pointed bifaces have consistently revealed that they had been used for cutting, and only a low percentage had impact fractures common to points used as projectiles. This use pattern of middle Paleoindian pointed bifaces has been interpreted as indicative of a decrease in hunting and an increase in diversification of subsistence

Culture Areas

While the new styles of lanceolate chipped stone points that characterize the middle Paleoindian period are similar, as shown in Figure 4.3, they are distinct enough to be classified as separate types, such as Cumberland, Suwannee, and Simpson. The different point types also have been recovered from relatively distinct areas in the Southeast. In archaeology, differential distribution of similar yet different artifact styles is an important clue in tracking population movements and in identifying prehistoric culture areas. Seven culture areas have been suggested for the middle Paleoindian period, which are identified primarily by differences in styles of lanceolate chipped stone points. The culture areas are shown on the map in Figure 4.6.

Another line of evidence that reinforces the proposed culture areas is the increase in use of local stone resources during the middle Paleoindian period. In the early Paleoindian period, only a few select varities of high-quality chert in the Southeast were used to make chipped stone tools. While the favored cherts were available only in a few restricted areas, such as the lower Tennessee Valley, tools made from them were found throughout the region. The wide distribution of specific cherts indicates that intergroup contact was frequent. In middle Paleoindian period assemblages there is a much wider range of

---

[11] For details about this theory see Meltzer and Smith, 1986.

stone used to make tools and a preference for locally available, often moderate-quality cherts.

The cultural material in each middle Paleoindian culture area is slightly different, as are the kinds of sites and their distribution. The key aspects of the culture areas in the Southeast are summarized below.

Redstone-Quad-Beaver Lake Culture Area

Of all the middle Paleoindian regional culture areas, more chipped stone points have been found in the Redstone-Quad-Beaver Lake area. In Alabama alone, 1546 fluted points have been recorded, primarily from sites along the Tennessee River.[12] Anderson's Paleoindian point survey has documented that the density of points and implied density of population in this area are unique to the eastern Woodlands during this period. Judging from the large numbers of other types of artifacts from several of these sites, there likely were quite large settlements with high populations that served as bases of activities (base camps) for wide areas of the valley. Examples of these large middle Paleoindian settlements are the Quad, Stone Pipe, and Pine Tree sites in northwest Alabama where scores of Paleoindian points have been collected from each.

Middle Paleoindian Culture Area

The middle Paleoindian culture area in the southern Atlantic Coastal Plain and Piedmont is characacterized by small fluted and unfluted points called Clovis variants. While the overall distribution of Paleoindian points is low, sites appear to be concentrated around outcrops of good local stone. One of these middle Paleoindian site clusters is in the Piedmont of northern North Carolina and southern Virginia, where up to 200 points have been reported in a two-county area. Anderson has suggested that this cluster of sites, along or near the headwaters of several major rivers, may be one of the first areas of the Atlantic Slope to be occupied.[13]

Flint Run Culture Area

Farther north, in the Shenandoah Valley of Virginia near Washington, D.C., is another concentration of Paleoindian settlements known as Flint Run.[14] There, William Gardner has located at least 50 Paleoindian sites clustered around chert quarries. He interpreted these sites to be either quarry- or hunting-related. There are three large settlements within 0.75 mi of this area. One of the large sites is the well-known Thunderbird site, which appears to have been a base camp for the resident Paleoindian population. The artifacts recovered in the excavations indicate that one of the main activities conducted at the Thunderbird site was refurbishing stone tool kits from the nearby

[12] For more information about the Paleoindian points in Alabama see Futato, 1982.

[13] See Anderson, 1990c, for details.

[14] See Gardner, 1974 and 1977, for details about the Flint Run Complex.

FIGURE 4.9   Reconstruction of a middle Paleoindian shelter at the Thunderbird Site in Virginia. (Reprinted with permission of Joan Walker, Thunderbird Research Corporation).

quarry. Gardner also found large, oval-shaped patterns of postholes that probably were structures that resembled the one shown in Figure 4.9. These structural remains are the oldest yet identified in the Southeast.

Suwannee–Simpson Culture Area

In the Suwannee–Simpson culture area, several middle Paleoindian sites have been investigated that had intact deposits. Two are land sites, Silver Springs and Harney Flats, and the others are underwater. The Silver Springs site in central Florida was located along the river that flows from the well-known spring. As the site was being destroyed in the early 1950s, William Neil documented an 8-in. thick undisturbed middle Paleoindian deposit that was over 7 ft below the surface.[15] The artifacts consisted of fluted and unfluted Suwannee points, a chopper, graver, scrapers, sandstone abraders, and utilized flakes.

Much more time and effort was put into the excavation of the Harney Flats site, near Tampa, prior to its destruction for an interstate highway. This site, excavated by Randy Daniel and Michael Weisenbaker, was almost completely undisturbed.[16] The settlement had been situated in a low gap in the divide ridge between the Hillsborough and Palm river valleys, overlooking an open savannah that would have had grazing animals. Excavations at the site recovered thousands of Paleoindian artifacts. Unfortunately, there was

[15] For details about the Silver Spring Paleoindian site see Neil, 1958.

[16] For details about the Harney Flats excavation see Daniel and Weisenbaker, 1987.

no datable material recovered, but the stone points were middle Paleoindian Suwannee and Simpson types. From the distribution of the artifacts at Harney Flats, it appears that this settlement was used to renew stone tool kits with chert from nearby outcrops. Worn and exhausted tools were brought to the site, resharpened or thrown away, and replaced with new ones. By carefully plotting artifacts, archaeologists were able to identify specific stoneworking activity areas and separate living areas.

A promising underwater middle Paleoindian site is the Page-Ladson site in the limestone area of the panhandle of Florida. There, in the spring-fed Aucilla River, archaeologists and paleontologists have discovered a drowned rockshelter with stratified deposits that date older than 8000 B.C.[17] While the investigations at this site are still underway, remains of both extinct and modern animals with artifacts (including bone tools) have been found. There appear to be several Paleoindian strata that have well-preserved bone deposits, which promise good information in the future.

Central Mississippi Valley Culture Area

In the central Mississippi Valley, northeastern Arkansas, and southeastern Missouri, over 120 fluted points have been found on both sides of the 200-mile-long Crowley's Ridge (described in Chapter 2). This high ridge provides an excellent view of the flood plain. Archaeologists Dan Morse and Phyllis Morse suggest these sites were hunting camps.[18] The distribution of points is interpreted by the Morses as indicative of two populations that lived on either side of Crowley's Ridge.

Summary

In sum, the middle Paleoindian period in the Southeast was a time when distinct culture areas emerged. The change from Pleistocene to Holocene animal populations had occurred, and humans had adapted to this change. Four regional culture areas have been proposed as emerging in the Southeast, with the largest population in the central Tennessee Valley. The most important socioeconomic change that took place during this period was the development of a more generalized economy that focused on local resources.

LATE PALEOINDIAN PERIOD: 8500–8000 B.C.

The late Paleoindian period, also called the Dalton period, was distinguished by continued population expansion and the establishment of many new settlements. Middle Paleoindian period migrations had established at

---

[17] For more about the Page-Ladson site see Dunbar *et al.*, 1988, and Purdy, 1991, 1992.

[18] For details about central Mississippi Valley Paleoindians see Morse and Morse, 1983.

least low populations in most parts of the Southeast, as shown in Figure 4.6. During the late Paleoindian period these populations appear to have grown rapidly, because there are many more Dalton sites. Archaeologists literally have found thousands of late Paleoindian (Dalton) sites in the Southeast. The sites are not only in river flood plains, where almost all earlier settlements were located, but they are also regularly found on higher terraces and upland areas. As a result of the increase in late Paleoindian archaeological sites, researchers know much more about this period than the previous ones.

Material Culture

The late Paleoindian tool kit had two distinctive artifacts: the Dalton point and the Dalton adz. Despite regional differences, the Dalton point (shown in Figures 4.3 and 4.4) is quite similar throughout the Southeast and Midwest. The Dalton point is significant for reasons other than its use as a temporal marker. First, this is the first chipped stone point to be consistently and extensively resharpened and recycled. Previous Paleoindian points had been only slightly or moderately retouched. The Dalton point's sequence of use has been reconstructed by Dan Morse and is shown in Figure 4.4, and most points went through many shapes and functions. Experiments and microscopic studies of different stages of the Dalton recycling sequence have revealed that they were used less as projectiles and more for cutting and sawing. Initially, the blade was convex and serrated to facilitate sawing through meat and hide. The later uses of the original point were as a scraper, drill, or bone-engraving tool (burin). The second significant aspect of the Dalton point is that it was often made from poorer-quality cherts than were points from previous periods, even when good chert was nearby. This is especially true on the Atlantic Coastal Plain. In the eastern portion of the Southeast, another style of chipped stone point with side notches near the base, which is called a Big Sandy point (shown in Figure 4.1), was manufactured along with the Dalton point type.

The Dalton adz marks the first appearance of a heavy woodworking stone tool in the Southeast Indian tool kit. Replication experiments and microscopic studies of the use marks on the artifacts have revealed that it was used in the same manner as modern adzes, as shown in Figure 4.4. It was mounted on a handle and used to shape wood. Almost certainly, the adz was used to make wooden bowls and dugouts, and to shape timbers and other wooden artifacts.

Despite a change in point styles, the initiation of extensive resharpening and recycling, and the addition of woodworking tools, late Paleoindian stone tool technology shows strong continuity with previous periods. Other stone tools that continued to be made and used were end scrapers, flake scrapers, gravers, burins, and knives. A variety of knives, scrapers, choppers, and abraders were also made and used. Small wedge-shaped flakes, or *pièces esquillées,* continue to be made and used for splitting bone, along with small microliths and burins. Larger cores were also used to make true blades.

Subsistence and Settlement Patterns

The diet of the Dalton population, wherever food remains have been found, consisted exclusively of modern plants and animals. Dalton sites with the best preserved food remains have been in and near rockshelters in the Missouri Ozarks. Rogers Rockshelter, for example, had a pure Dalton deposit on the terrace outside a shelter, with buried hearths containing the remains of fish, turtle, rabbit, squirrel, raccoon, beaver or muskrat, and other terrestrial rodents, as well as deer, bison, elk, and turkey.[19] Plant foods found at the site included hickory nuts and black walnuts. Other important rockshelters with Dalton components include Graham Cave, Modoc Rockshelter, and Stanfield-Worley Bluff Shelter.

Examples of Late Paleoindian Cultures

Central Mississippi Valley

One of the areas of the Southeast where significant long-term archaeological research on the Dalton culture has been conducted is the Arkansas portion of the central Mississippi Valley, where Dan Morse, his colleagues, and interested amateurs have recorded almost 1000 Dalton sites and excavated several key locations.[20]

Three types of Dalton sites have been identified in the central Mississippi valley: base camps, hunting camps, and cemeteries.[21] An example of a Dalton base camp is the Lace site, located near Wynne, Arkansas, which was in the center of a cluster of smaller sites on a knoll surrounded by sloughs and shallow lakes. The main portion of the settlement was about 1.5 acres in size, and it had a dark, organically stained midden. This midden contained thousands of artifacts, and included the entire Dalton assemblage. The nearby Brand site, excavated by Albert Goodyear, is an example of a smaller, more temporary site. It was much smaller (0.25 acre), and five clusters of artifacts were identified, which averaged about 125 square ft.[22] Morse and Goodyear interpreted this site as a hunting camp, with the artifact clusters resulting from individual field butchering stations. Another interpretation of this site, by Michael Schiffer, is that it was a base camp occupied by several families that engaged in a wide range of domestic activities.[23] Regardless of which

---

[19] For more on Rogers Rockshelter see Wood and McMillan, 1976.

[20] See Morse and Morse, 1983, for a summary.

[21] For a summary of this model and site types see Morse and Morse, 1983.

[22] For details on the Brand site see Goodyear, 1974.

[23] For details on this interpretation see Schiffer, 1975.

interpretation is correct, this site was much smaller than the larger Lace site, it contained fewer artifacts, and there were only limited areas of organic midden with artifact concentrations.

One Dalton cemetery has been located, the Sloan site in Arkansas.[24] People were buried with several complete, unused artifacts, which appeared to archaeologist Dan Morse to have originally been in containers, such as bags. The grave goods were different from artifacts found at Dalton campsites. Most items placed in the graves were complete and unused. The artifacts in the grave good clusters were mainly chipped stone adzes and points. One point was 7.5 in. long, which Morse suggests is too large to be practical; based on these factors, he infers that it was purposefully made to be a special grave gift, not a tool destined for everyday use. Morse thinks that the Sloan site was set aside as a cemetery, and it had at least 12 graves. If this is the case, the Sloan site is one of the earliest known cemeteries in the Americas.

Based on the distribution of these three types of Dalton sites, as well as artifact patterns in the central Mississippi Valley, the Morses have suggested that the late Paleoindian period social organization consisted of bands of related families that occupied discrete territories. The territory of each band is thought to have been the watershed of a specific stream and included uplands, lowlands, and terraces. Due to the presence of clusters of large sites in a small area of each flood plain, each band is thought to have had a central area, like a base of operations, where their largest settlement, a base camp, was located. From the distribution pattern of large and small sites, Morse has suggested that the Dalton bands practiced a base camp–satellite camp subsistence and settlement pattern. He suggests that their largest settlement was possibly inhabited year-round by the entire group. From this central base, smaller groups went out during the year to hunt, fish, and gather other food and supplies, as well as to bury their dead. Morse interprets the high number of Dalton sites in the central Mississippi Valley as evidence of stable territories. He estimates that there were about eight Dalton bands in the central Mississippi Valley, each of which had 20–50 people.

Georgia Piedmont

Another area of the Southeast in which the Dalton period has been researched is the upper Oconee River Valley, near Athens, in the Georgia Piedmont.[25] Although Lisa O'Steen and her colleagues found Paleoindian remains from all periods there, they also documented that most early and middle Paleoindian sites were located only on the flood plain, near outcrops of fine-grained chert. Late Paleoindian Dalton sites were also found on the flood plain, but there were also many sites in the uplands. This regular use of the uplands is interpreted by O'Steen as an indication of not only population

---

[24] For details on the Sloan site see Morse, 1975, and Morse and Morse, 1983.

[25] For details, about Dalton in this area see O'Steen et al., 1986, and Anderson et al., 1992.

growth but the development of a more diversified economy. At Barnett Shoals on the Fall Line of the Oconee River, O'Steen found a cluster of 10 Dalton sites. Two of these sites appear to have been base camps due to the wide range of formal and expedient tools. This cluster of sites may be similar to the central base camp area proposed for Dalton band territories in the central Mississippi Valley. The Oconee Dalton tool kit was similar to that in the central Mississippi Valley, both in content and in the pattern of reworking and recycling of Dalton points.

Coastal Plain

Use of the uplands on the Coastal Plain during the Dalton period has also been corroborated. Scores of Dalton sites in the well-drained sandy uplands in northwest Florida and south-central Alabama have been identified.[26] These Dalton sites are located primarily on or near the headwaters of almost all small tributaries and along divides between the watersheds of major streams. As in the Oconee Drainage, upland Dalton sites are numerous, but they are smaller and have fewer artifacts than sites on the flood plains and low terraces of major streams and tributaries. This research supports O'Steen's theory that the interior uplands were first utilized on a regular basis during the Dalton period.

A good example of a Dalton flood plain base campsite on the inner Coastal Plain is the Hester Site, which is located on a sandy knoll in the Tombigbee River valley in east central Mississippi, near Amory.[27] Excavated by Sam Brookes, the Dalton assemblage was similar to the tool kit defined in the central Mississippi Valley, except there were no chipped stone adzes. The Hester tool kit had a wide variety of tools, including pitted anvil stones, wedge-shaped flakes (*pièces esquillées*), and bladelike flakes, which indicated to Brookes that this site was repeatedly occupied by small groups performing a wide range of domestic activities.

Summary

More is known about the Dalton period than any other Paleoindian period. The number of sites is much higher and new environmental zones, especially the uplands, were occupied regularly for the first time. A general population increase and the development of a flexible, broad-based economy, geared to utilizing local resources, were probably the driving forces behind the Dalton expansion. This was a particularly important period in the development of southeastern Indian culture, because it was the time during which it became advanced enough to enable populations to thrive in almost every environmen-

[26] For information about Dalton in northwest Florida see Bense, 1983b, and Thomas and Campbell, 1992.

[27] For details on the Hester site excavation see Brookes, 1979.

tal zone. As Albert Goodyear has pointed out, practically all major caves excavated in the Midwest and Southeast have substantial Dalton deposits,[28] and their sites are found in substantial numbers in the Piedmont as well as the coast, as far south as Miami on the Florida peninsula.

SUMMARY OF THE PALEOINDIAN STAGE

The early Paleoindian period was marked by the initial colonization of the Southeast by people. The diagnostic artifact of this period is the Clovis stone point. The tool kit contained well-made portable and efficient tools made from high-quality chert designed primarily for hunting and processing animals. Early Paleoindians appear to have been organized into highly mobile bands with a hunting- and fishing-based economy. This socioeconomic system enabled people to move easily and successfully into new environmental areas. While Clovis points are found almost all over the Southeast, there appear to have been three main areas of population concentration in the area: the flood plains of the lower Cumberland, central Tennessee, and central Ohio rivers.

The middle Paleoindian period was distinguished by the expansion of significant numbers of people into new areas of the Southeast. This led to the development of the first distinct subregional cultural traditions, or culture areas, during this period as each population adapted to its local area and had less interarea contacts. The stone tool kits in all areas became less specialized and more generalized in both manufacturing techniques and function. Local stone was used for making tools, and different styles of lanceolate stone points evolved in the culture areas. During the middle Paleoindian period, the economy appears to have been changing from one that had been based on hunting and fishing of a limited range of food sources to a more diversified system that used a wide variety of plants and animals.

During the late Paleoindian period, population increased and people regularly used many new environmental areas. The late Paleoindian (Dalton) culture had a generalized, flexible economy that was adapted to almost any local environment. It is thought that at least in some areas, distinct band territories within a specific watershed had developed. Interriverine uplands of the Coastal Plain and Piedmont, as well as caves and rockshelters in the Interior Highlands were regularly used for the first time by Dalton groups. This successful expansion into new environments is interpreted as a reflection of the flexible economy.

By the end of the Dalton period, Indians were well adjusted to the postglacial Southeast. They appear to have acquired a depth of knowledge about the environment and its resources that enabled them to move around successfully at will. The great achievement of the Paleoindian stage was the attainment

---

[28] For details about Dalton site distribution see Goodyear, 1982.

of this high level of cultural adjustment. Starting from the original Clovis groups with a conservative hunting-based, mobile way of life and a specialized technology, Paleoindians developed distinct culture areas with a detailed knowledge of each home area and a generalized economy that could take advantage of the scattered diverse resources of the Southeast.

5

ARCHAIC STAGE:
8000–1000 B.C.

KEY ARCHAEOLOGICAL FEATURES
Notched and Stemmed Stone Points
Containers of Stone and Pottery
Ground and Polished Stone Artifacts

IMPORTANT DEVELOPMENTS
Increased Sedentism
First Mound and Earthwork Construction
Large Base Camp Settlements

INTRODUCTION AND OVERVIEW

The Archaic stage existed between 8000 and 1000 B.C., and it was the longest stage of cultural development in the Southeast. The key archaeological traits of the Archaic stage are (1) Notched and Stemmed Triangular Stone Points, (2) Containers of Stone and Pottery, and (3) Ground and Polished Stone Artifacts. Important cultural developments during this stage include the first construction of mounds and earthworks, the formation of large settlements and sites, and establishment of long-distance trade.

The initiation of the Archaic stage in the Southeast generally coincided with the beginning of the Holocene climatic epoch, and its end generally coincided with the onset of modern climatic conditions. Global warming peaked at the midpoint of this stage, during 4000–3000 B.C., and southeastern climate has been generally cooler ever since. During the Archaic stage, there was a steady rise in sea level of about 90 ft to near its present position as shown in Figure 2.6. It was also during the Archaic stage that the forests of the Coastal Plain changed from hardwood deciduous tree communities to the fire-maintained pine forests of today.

There was sharp increase in the number and variety of artifacts made and used during the Archaic stage in comparison to the Paleoindian stage, and chipped stone points continue to be the most sensitive temporal marker. Millions of Archaic chipped stone points have been found in the Southeast, and their utility as time markers was effectively demonstrated in the early 1960s by Joffre Coe in the North Carolina Piedmont and Bettye Broyles in the Appalachians of West Virginia.[1] The general sequence of changes in chipped stone points during the Archaic stage is illustrated in Figure 5.1. The basic differences between Archaic and Paleoindian chipped stone points are in their overall shape and the treatment of the base. Paleoindian points are generally lanceolate shaped with straight or concave sides and bases, as shown in Figure 4.1. Archaic points are generally triangular shaped with notched or stemmed bases. While these changes in chipped stone points occurred in a relatively uniform manner across the Southeast, local versions of the basic forms were made in each area.

Southeastern Indian artifact assemblages expanded during the Archaic stage.[2] While there were fewer additions in chipped stone tools, significant advancements were made in ground and polished stonework. New tools made by this method include axes, celts, and spear-thrower weights, along with finely made ornamental items such as beads, effigies, pendants, and plummets. The use of shell as a medium for ornaments and tools developed also during this stage. A trade network for personal ornaments and special

---

[1] For details on these classic studies see Coe, 1964, and Broyles, 1971.

[2] See Griffin, 1952, 1967, for culture histories of eastern North America.

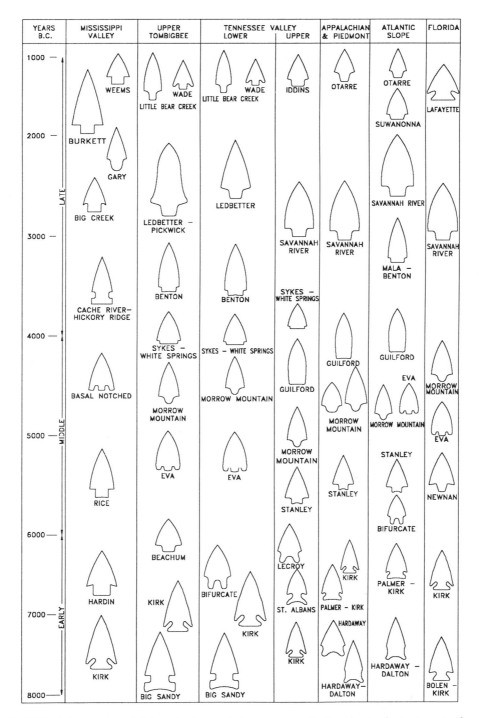

FIGURE 5.1 Regional chipped stone point sequences during the Archaic stage in the Southeast.

raw materials, especially colorful stone and marine shells, developed during the Archaic stage, and some special personal items became high-status markers. Hard containers made of wood, stone, and pottery first appeared in the Archaic stage. As techniques of pottery manufacture improved, pottery became the dominant medium for hard containers. Earth ovens, pits in which food was baked by previously heated hot stones or fired clay balls, were also developed.

Organic artifacts from the Archaic stage have been found in wet sites and sites enriched with calcium from shells (called shell middens). Archaeologists have documented Archaic textiles such bags, nets, baskets, and clothing, as well as wooden sculpture and artifacts, dugouts, tools, and ornaments. A wide range of bone artifacts have been recovered from wet sites and shell middens, including points, beautifully decorated pins, needles, awls, and tool handles. Human remains from some wet sites have preserved brain matter as well as undigested food. Archaic wet and shell midden sites have provided some of the first glimpses of the multitude of items made of perishable materials during the Archaic stage, as well as information about the health and physical condition of some of the people.

Plant and animal food remains indicate that by the beginning of the Archaic stage, southeastern Indians had begun to develop a diversified economy, and during this stage people settled into almost all areas of the region. One of the best indications of success of the Archaic population is the increase in the number and size of archaeological sites. The Archaic stage food base expanded to include many plant foods, and there is evidence that some plants were purposefully planted by 5000 B.C. The first cultivated plants in the Southeast were bottle gourds and hard-rind squash, which are thought to have been used for containers. Food plants were grown late in the Archaic stage, but only in the northern part of the region.

The settlement pattern of the Archaic stage was similar to the preceding Dalton populations in the central Mississippi Valley: seasonal base camps and short-term, special-purpose camps. During the middle Holocene or Altithermal, base camps became the focal point of the settlement pattern and were probably occupied year-round by at least part of the group. The increased use of base camps produced large archaeological sites, especially those that contained shellfish remains, some of which are up to 40 ft thick. Features are abundant at Arachaic base campsites and include houses, hearth complexes, pits, artifact concentrations, and burials.

As early as 4000 B.C., the first earth mounds were built in the Southeast in the lower Mississippi Valley, and they became popular in this area during the last millennium of this stage. Earth was used to build mounds, and midden was used to build earthworks in the shape of doughnuts, crescents, and horseshoes. Large rings of shell midden were constructed by 2000 B.C. along the Atlantic coast, and two Archaic shell midden earthworks have been found on the Florida Gulf coast.

The Archaic stage is divided into three periods: early (8000–6000 B.C.), middle (6000–4000 B.C.), and late (4000–1000 B.C.). Each period is summarized as follows.

EARLY ARCHAIC PERIOD: 8000–6000 B.C.

Environment

It is important to understand that the environment of the Southeast was significantly different during the early Archaic period than it is today. The most important differences were vegetation and sea level. At the onset of the early Archaic period, sea level was about 90 ft lower than today, and most of the Southeast was covered with an oak-hickory forest, as shown in Figure 2.5C.[3] Some Southern pines were mixed in the hardwood forest in the southern half of the region, and some cold-loving conifers were in the northern forests east of the Appalachians. The Florida peninsula was an oak savannah. By the end of the early Archaic period global warming was changing the vegetation pattern. The Coastal Plain and Piedmont regions became drier, and lightning fires began to remove the oak-hickory hardwood forests. Rising sea levels perpetuated an unstable coastline, and shoreline erosion was common as the mainland was directly battered by the rising sea.

Material Culture

In the early Archaic period, chipped stone points were smaller than during the Paleoindian stage, triangular in outline, and had notched bases. Archaeologists think that the change in size was related to the invention of the spear thrower (atlatl), shown in Figure 5.2. Spear throwers use the principle of leverage to increase the accuracy, velocity, and distance of a projectile's course, which enabled hunters to kill more efficiently the small, quick-moving game, especially deer, that inhabited the postglacial Southeast.

Chipped stone artifacts used during the early Archaic period were similar to those made and used in the preceding Dalton period. The change in shape from lanceolate to triangular points occurred during the early Archaic period. The hallmark of this period is the triangular-shaped, corner-notched Kirk point, which probably developed from the preceding Dalton shape. In many areas of the Southeast a side-notched type of point, called Big Sandy, preceded the corner-notched Kirk style. The sequence of chipped stone point changes and cultures in several areas during the early Archaic are shown in Figure 5.1 and 5.3.

The rest of the early Archaic chipped stone tools, some of which are shown in Figure 5.4, include knives, end scrapers, adzes, and a variety of

[3] For details on the past vegetation of the Southeast see Delcourt and Delcourt, 1981 and 1985.

FIGURE 5.2   The atlatl (spear thrower) in use.

cutting and scraping tools made from blades and flakes struck from prepared cores. The bipolar technique of producing chert flakes was developed during the early Archaic period. The technique consists of placing a small chert cobble on a flat stone (the anvil) and hitting it from above with a hammerstone. The force of the blow penetrates the chert nodule, bounces back to the hammerstone, and forces flakes off the core that look like they have been struck from both ends or poles, hence the term "bipolar." The flakes produced by the bipolar method, called *pièces esquilées,* are distinctively small, square in outline, and wedge-shaped in cross section. An example of a *pièce esquilée* is shown in Figure 5.4E. Early Archaic assemblages also contain many exhausted tools and debitage (waste flakes) from the toolmaking process. Waste flakes were commonly used for many expedient tools for cutting, scraping, and boring holes, shown in Figure 5.4D. Well-made ground and chipped stone celts were made for the first time during the early Archaic period. As shown in Figure 5.5, celts were made from local river cobbles. Other large stones show evidence of grinding and abrading on their edges and flat surfaces.

At the Icehouse Bottom site in the Tellico Reservoir (see Figure 5.6) in Tennessee near Knoxville, Jefferson Chapman found impressions of basketry and netting in clay used to make prepared campfire hearths, shown in Figure 5.7.[4] Fortunately, 29 clay hearths had impressions of simple twined basketry

---

[4] For details on the textiles at Icehouse Bottom, see Chapman and Adavasio, 1977, and Chapman, 1973.

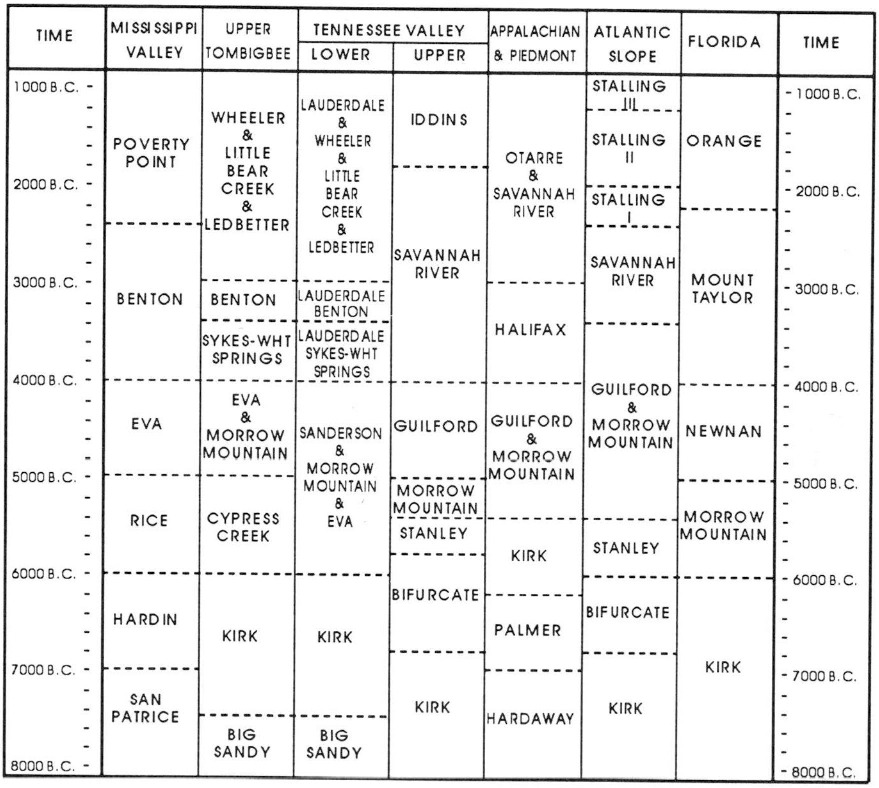

TIME	MISSISSIPPI VALLEY	UPPER TOMBIGBEE	TENNESSEE VALLEY LOWER	TENNESSEE VALLEY UPPER	APPALACHIAN & PIEDMONT	ATLANTIC SLOPE	FLORIDA	TIME
1000 B.C.	POVERTY POINT	WHEELER & LITTLE BEAR CREEK & LEDBETTER	LAUDERDALE & WHEELER & LITTLE BEAR CREEK & LEDBETTER	IDDINS	OTARRE & SAVANNAH RIVER	STALLING III / STALLING II / STALLING I	ORANGE	1000 B.C.
2000 B.C.				SAVANNAH RIVER				2000 B.C.
3000 B.C.	BENTON	BENTON	LAUDERDALE BENTON		HALIFAX	SAVANNAH RIVER	MOUNT TAYLOR	3000 B.C.
4000 B.C.		SYKES-WHT SPRINGS	LAUDERDALE SYKES-WHT SPRINGS			GUILFORD & MORROW MOUNTAIN		4000 B.C.
5000 B.C.	EVA	EVA & MORROW MOUNTAIN	SANDERSON & MORROW MOUNTAIN & EVA	GUILFORD / MORROW MOUNTAIN	GUILFORD & MORROW MOUNTAIN		NEWNAN	5000 B.C.
6000 B.C.	RICE	CYPRESS CREEK		STANLEY	KIRK	STANLEY	MORROW MOUNTAIN	6000 B.C.
7000 B.C.	HARDIN	KIRK	KIRK	BIFURCATE	PALMER	BIFURCATE	KIRK	7000 B.C.
8000 B.C.	SAN PATRICE	BIG SANDY	BIG SANDY	KIRK	HARDAWAY	KIRK		8000 B.C.

FIGURE 5.3 Archaic stage chronological chart.

and netting, which were made when the clay was moist. Specialists have determined that the items that made the impressions were rectangular mats and globular net bags. The impressions are the oldest evidence of textiles yet found in Eastern North America, and date between 8000 and 7300 B.C.

Early Archaic wooden artifacts have been recovered from underwater at Little Salt Spring, near Sarasota, Florida, and they are among the oldest wooden artifacts yet found in the Southeast.[5] As shown in Figure 4.8 stakes had been driven into the wall at systematic intervals just below the former edges of the spring hole. These stakes likely could have functioned to secure ropes for hauling water from the water below. The upper row of stakes have

[5] For details about Warm Mineral Spring excavation and Little Salt Spring see Clausen *et al.*, 1975; for information on the wooden tools see Purdy, 1991, 1992.

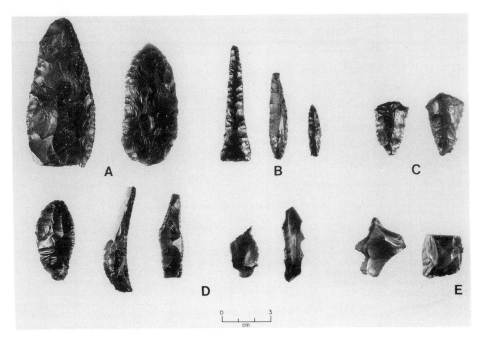

FIGURE 5.4   Some Early Archaic chipped stone tools from the Tellico Reservoir near Knoxville: (A) knives; (B) drills; (C) end scrapers; (D) utilized flakes partially sharpened for cutting, shredding, and perforating; (E) wedge or slotting tool for working bone. (From Chapman, 1985.)

been dated to an average of 7622 B.C. Underwater excavations near the upper row of stakes, also shown in Figure 4.8, recovered more early Archaic wooden items including an antler point still attached to the shaft, a carved oak mortar, and a boomerang.

Mortuary Patterns

Early Archaic burials have been found only at the Icehouse Bottom site, and they were both cremated remains that had been buried in shallow pits.[6] While you might think that nothing is left after a human is cremated, there actually is considerable residue, such as chunks of calcined burned bone, teeth, and ashes. The bone fragments are often large enough so that specialists can determine the age, sex, and some of the life history of the cremated individuals. Forensic archaeologists were able to determine that both of the Icehouse Bottom cremations were of women who had been cremated soon after death.

---

[6] For details about the Icehouse Bottom excavation see Chapman, 1973.

FIGURE 5.5 Some early Archaic ground stone tools from the Tellico Reservoir near Knoxville: (A) chipped and ground stone celt or chisel fragment; (B) ground hematite used for red pigment; (C) broken hand-held milling stone; (D) hammerstone; (E) chopper or scraper; (F) mortar (metate); (G) pitted cobble anvil stone. (From Chapman, 1985.)

Settlement Pattern

Most early Archaic sites appear to have been short-term campsites at which people reconditioned their tool kits and prepared food. Several base camps have been found, and these sites have many features and abundant artifacts. The features found at base campsites include prepared clay fire

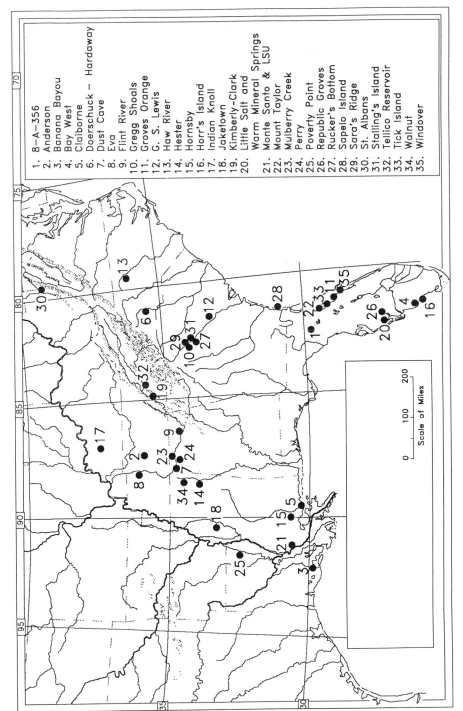

1. 8–A–356
2. Anderson
3. Banana Bayou
4. Bay West
5. Claiborne
6. Doerschuck – Hardaway
7. Dust Cave
8. Eva
9. Flint River
10. Gregg Shoals
11. Groves Orange
12. G. S. Lewis
13. Haw River
14. Hester
15. Hornsby
16. Horr's Island
17. Indian Knoll
18. Jaketown
19. Kimberly–Clark
20. Little Salt and
    Warm Mineral Springs
21. Monte Santo & LSU
22. Mount Taylor
23. Mulberry Creek
24. Perry
25. Poverty Point
26. Republic Groves
27. Rucker's Bottom
28. Sapelo Island
29. Sara's Ridge
30. St. Albans
31. Stalling's Island
32. Tellico Reservoir
33. Tick Island
34. Walnut
35. Windover

FIGURE 5.6   Archaic sites.

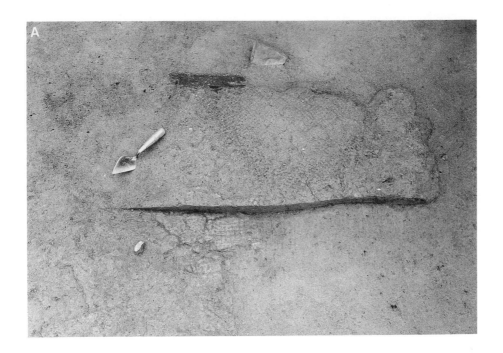

FIGURE 5.7   (A) Early Archaic period clay hearth at the Icehouse Bottom site showing textile and basketry impressions. Note that upper hearth overlies an earlier hearth. (B) Schematic drawing of simple twined basketry similar to the impressions observed on the early Archaic clay hearth surfaces. (From Chapman, 1985).

hearths, fired hearth areas, refuse pits, and artifact concentrations from specialized activities, especially hide preparation and chipped stone tool manufacture. Examples of base camps are the G. S. Lewis-East Site on the Savannah River, the Haw River sites, Icehouse Bottom on the Little Tennessee River, and the Hardaway site in the Pee Dee River drainage.

The settlement pattern of early Archaic populations in the Southeast has been the subject of considerable research in the last decade.[7] Several patterns have been proposed for early Archaic populations starting with James B. Griffin in 1952, who theorized that there were seasonal population movements by relatively mobile bands of people to obtain food and other resources and periodic gatherings of people for socializing, information sharing, and ceremonial events.[8] David Anderson and Glen Hanson have performed extensive research and review of early Archaic settlement patterns on the Atlantic Slope, and they have proposed a refined version of the Griffin theory which they call the band-macroband model, illustrated in Figure 5.8.[9] They propose that groups of related families (macrobands) were organized within river valleys, but most of the year people lived in scattered small extended family groups (bands) in their valley, obtaining the relatively evenly distributed food resources. During the fall, when food was more plentiful, they postulate that larger groups congregated for a short time near the Fall Line. From the artifacts and features found at the large camps, they interpret that the activities included hide preparation, heavy-duty woodworking, tool manufacturing, and building structures. These annual congregations were also thought to have included people from neighboring river valley macrobands. Anderson emphasized Griffin's earlier proposal that the annual congregations were very important social events. In fact, he thinks that with the low population density and need for small mobile residential groups, the need to find and exchange mates might have been the critical and primary reason for annual congregations at the Fall Line. Other theories of early Archaic settlement pattern place more emphasis on quarries and the need for stone to make tools, while others place more emphasis on the environment.

Summary

The early Archaic environment was different from today. Sea level was 90 ft lower than present and hardwood forests covered most of the area. The coastline continued to advance landward as sea level rose about 20 ft. The changes in the chipped stone points that identify this period are side, corner, and basal notching. An important addition to the stone tool kit was the ground and chipped stone celt. Most sites are small and have few features, but there are some large base camps that have frequent features such as prepared clay hearths, shallow pits, and abundant artifact concentrations from chipped stone tool manufacturing and use, especially hide processing. The only human

---

[7] See Anderson et al., 1992 for a detailed overview of early Archaic settlement patterns in the Southeast.

[8] See James B. Griffin, 1952, for details on this theory.

[9] For details see Anderson and Hanson, 1988, and Anderson et al., 1992.

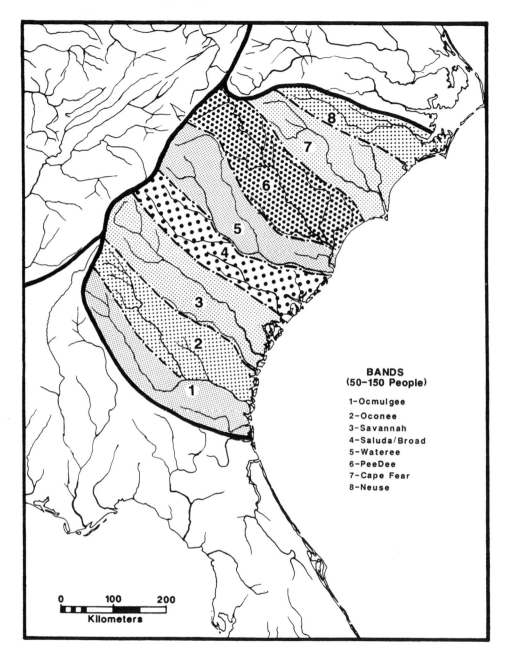

FIGURE 5.8 Theorized band-macroband early Archaic settlement pattern on the Atlantic Slope. (From Anderson *et al.*, 1988. Reproduced by permission of the Society for American Archaeology from *American Antiquity*, Vol 53:2).

burials yet recovered were cremated. The early Archaic settlement pattern and social organization appear to have been characterized by river valley-based family bands dispersed in small family groups for most of the year, except for temporary large settlements during brief periods in the fall.

MIDDLE ARCHAIC PERIOD: 6000–4000 B.C.

Environment

The middle Archaic period coincided with the climatic episode known as the Altithermal or middle Holocene, during which the postglacial global warming trend peaked. The Altithermal was a worldwide climatic event, but local conditions varied with differences in latitude, geography, and weather patterns. In the Southeast, the hot, dry weather caused a shift in the weather pattern, a change in the composition of the forests, and a change in the hydrology of river valley floodplains. The weather pattern change was a northward shift of tropical weather from the Caribbean, and for the first time in this postglacial period, summer thunderstorms became a regular event. Lightning fires caused by these thunderstorms literally burned away the hardwood forest in the southern half of the region except those in permanently wet (fire-protected) areas such as flood plains and marsh islands. On the Florida peninsula, the decreased rainfall lowered water levels in sinkholes, vegetation became sparse, and dune fields formed in some areas. In the northern portion of the Southeast, lightning fires were less of a problem, but the warmer temperatures caused the once homogeneous hardwood forest in the Appalachian Highlands to break up by the end of the period. The Piedmont hardwood forest was infiltrated with pines, and in the Blue Ridge Mountains, the oak-chestnut forest had spruce only in the very uppermost elevations. Continuous hardwood forests remained only in the very northern edge of the Southeast as shown in Figure 2.5D. West of Mississippi, the oak-savannah prairie expanded eastward into parts of Arkansas and Missouri, and pines invaded the oak-hickory forest of the Ozarks and Interior Highlands.

The hot, dry Altithermal also affected the river systems in the upper portion of the Southeast. Decreased rainfall resulted in reduced runoff, which slowed stream velocity and stabilized the river channels in the northern part of the region (above 34° north latitude).[10] Stabilization of river channels resulted in expansion of wetland areas of the flood plains. Low areas on the flood plain such as back swamps and oxbow lakes were bypassed by the channelized mainstream, but remained wet much of the year due to water retention from rains and floods. Rivers near the Fall Line became quite shallow, creating shoals and rapids.

---

[10] For information on paleoenvironment see Carbone *et al.*, 1983; for stream change see Stein, 1982.

Material Culture

During the middle Archaic period there was general change in the shape of chipped stone points to a basally notched form (Eva type) or a variety of stemmed forms such as contacting (Morrow Mountain type), short and straight (Sykes-White Springs type), and expanding (Stanly), as shown in Figure 5.1. Points were often extensively resharpened and recycled into drills and end scrapers. The remainder of the chipped stone tools and biface and bipolar technology used to make them remain essentially unchanged from the early Archaic. The technique of heating stone to improve the manufacture of chipped stone tools became widespread during this period. Heat was slowly applied to cobbles or crude bifaces of chert and other types of rock probably in a closed pit with hot coals or in the hot ashes and coals of open fires. Slowly heating and cooling chert in this manner makes it more glasslike and easier to work into thin, bifacial tools. Heat treatment can usually be detected on chert by a color change from the unheated state and a glossy surface.

Significant technological advancements in stone tool manufacture were made in ground and polished stone technology during the middle Archaic period. Grooved axes for felling large trees and for other heavy woodworking were added to the tool kit, as illustrated in Figure 5.9. The earlier type of ax, the celt, continued to be made. Another important advancement was the development of the ground and polished stone atlatl weight. This device, shown in Figures 5.2 and 5.9, is thought to have improved the atlatl's effect, enabling spears to be thrown harder and farther. Stone atlatl weights were usually rectangular- or wing-shaped with a hole drilled through them for the atlatl shaft, which was about 2–3 ft long. As shown in Figure 5.9 the atlatl weight was placed on the shaft between the handle and a hook for the spear. The workmanship on many of the atlatl weights is so outstanding that some archaeologists suggest that perhaps these objects were more than utilitarian items, but had some ceremonial or spiritual meaning. Atlatl handles and hooks were made of a variety of materials including ground stone, antler, shell, and probably wood. Other new ground stone items made in the middle Archaic period are notched weights and sinkers, which were probably tied to fish nets, traps, and lines to keep them underwater.

Ornaments became increasingly popular during the middle Archaic, as shown in Figures 5.9 and 5.10. Shell, bone, and stone were cut and polished into a variety of beads and pendants. Stone beads were usually small (1 × 0.25 in.) and tubular in shape, but some delicate animal effigy beads were made, such as the one shown in Figure 5.9F. Shell was also a popular medium for beads, and disk-shaped shell beads were prevalent, which are illustrated in Figure 5.10B. Bar pendants and gorgets of stone were also popular, and they were made of colorful ground and polished stone and cut shell. The most common pendants and gorgets were made into thin geometric shapes with holes drilled for suspension, such as the example shown in Figure 5.9.

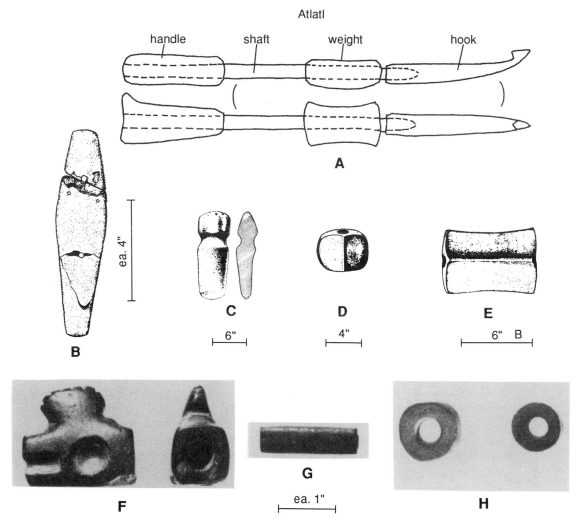

FIGURE 5.9   Middle Archaic ground stone artifacts: (A) reconstructed composite atlatl; (B) bar gorget; (C) full grooved ax; (D, E) atlatl weights; (F) bird effigy bead; (G, H) tubular beads. (A, reproduced with permission from Jesse D. Jennings, Distinguished Professor Emeritus, University of Utah and Adjunct Professor, University of Oregon; B–E from Griffin, 1952, with permission of the University of Chicago Press, copyright © 1952 by The University of Chicago. All rights reserved. F, G, H, from Bense, 1983a.)

Long-distance trade in beads and gorgets increased during this period. Stone beads from the Interior Highlands have been found as far south as Florida, and shell beads from the Gulf have been found as far north as Tennessee.

Shell midden sites formed in several parts of the Southeast during the middle Archaic. The low soil acidity in these calcium-enriched sites preserved

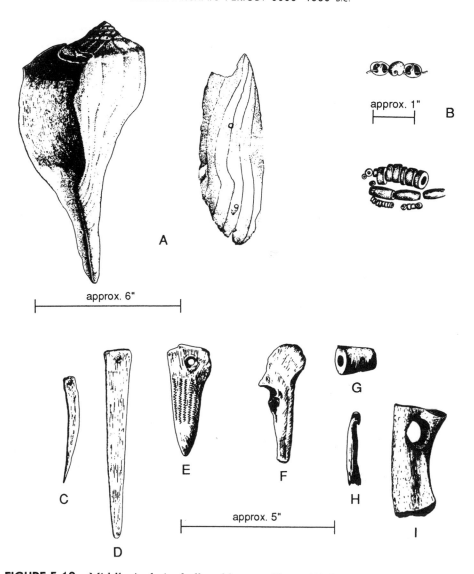

FIGURE 5.10 Middle Archaic shell and bone artifacts. (A) *Busycon* shell on left, shell gorget made from outer whorl on right; (B) shell beads; (C) bone needle; (D) bone pin; (E) decorated bone awl; (F) bone punch; (G) bone bead; (H) bone atlatl hook; (I) antler wrench. (From Griffin, 1952, with permission of the University of Chicago Press, copyright © 1952 by The University of Chicago. All rights reserved.)

large numbers of bone and antler artifacts, providing archaeologists the first detailed view of how important bone and antler were to the southeastern Indians as a raw material and the wide range of items made. Utilitarian artifacts made from deer antlers include pressure flakers, shaft straighteners or wrenches (pieces of antler with a large hole), hammers, atlatl hooks, and weights, some of which are illustrated in Figure 5.10. Splinters of deer and turkey bones were made into a variety of awls, pins, and needles. Gouges and chisels were made from sections of deer long bones. Harpoons and fishhooks were made from deer and turkey bones. Bone and antler also were used for projectile points. Teeth of rodents, dogs, and sharks were used to carve wood and bone. Animal teeth were drilled and used as personal ornaments. Other ornaments made from bone were beads, long, flat, decorated pins, and decorated shafts of long bone.

Wooden artifacts from the middle Archaic period have been found at wet sites in the Florida peninsula. From Little Salt Spring, an oak digging stick and a carved wooden table or plaque have been recovered along with portions of what probably are grave litters made from limbs of wax myrtle (*Myrica cerifera*). From the Windover wet cemetery near Cape Canaveral, Glen Doran and David Dickel recovered wooden stakes, tool handles, points, and shafts.[11] Of the seven wooden tool handles found, one was decorated, and two handles still had bone points inserted. Wooden atlatl shafts with the weights still attached were also found at Windover. Other wooden artifacts included a complete double-end pestle, a spring trap with a strand of cord still attached, a paddlelike object, and a small wooden bowl. Most wooden items were made from the hard inner portion of pine, hickory, or oak, which is dense, strong, fine grained, and more resilient to decay. Pointed stakes were also used as markers in Florida wet cemeteries.

Middle Archaic wet cemeteries have also preserved textiles. At the Windover mortuary pond near Cape Canaveral, Florida, five types of textiles were found in 37 graves, including a finely made plain weave (up to 25 strands per inch) for a tuniclike inner garment, which is currently the oldest cloth in the Western Hemisphere. More durable, heavier textiles were used for bags, mats, shrouds and blankets, and cords. Twined and plaited materials were made with a three-strand twining method. A few pieces of textiles were also found in the Republic Groves wet cemetery, but they included only a few pieces of cordage and a mat impression under one of the burials.

Mortuary Patterns

Human burials were found for the first time in any quantity in middle Archaic sites in the Southeast. Burials provide a new source of information about people that is different from the information gathered from artifacts and features. Burials reveal information about individual people and the social organization of their society. How a person is buried generally reflects his or her specific role and status in life, and many social values of their society.

---

[11] For more on Windover items see Dickel, 1992, Doran, 1992, Doran and Dickel, 1988, and Purdy, 1988 and 1991.

Paleobiologists and forensic archaeologists can extract from human burials information about population size, health, nutrition, and the genetics of extinct populations. Archaeologists study patterns of grave placement, age, preparation of corpses, and the distribution of items placed in graves. The information gathered from the study of human burials is used to deduce past systems of status, wealth, and social organization.

Patterns of grave placement and items placed in graves have been documented at several middle Archaic sites. At the Walnut site in northeast Mississippi, burials were placed in rows in several areas of the settlement, and more than one individual had been placed in several graves.[12] While we do not know exactly what this means, it at least reflects the existence of distinct burial areas in the settlement and some method of marking grave locations within the areas. Formal cemeteries were used in Florida, often isolated from settlements, both on dry land and in shallow-water "mortuary ponds." At the Gauthier cemetery in Florida, graves were organized into clusters that are interpreted as possible extended family groups.[13] Most middle Archaic burials in the Southeast, though, were scattered throughout the living area of the settlement in no discernible pattern. Archaeologists speculate that what the scattered burials may originally have been placed in or adjacent to houses that have left no traces, but there is yet no firm evidence of this.

The typical middle Archaic mortuary process was to bury people in a fetal position (called the flexed position) within a few days after death in a round or oval pit about 3 ft deep. In most sites there usually are a few extended burials as well as cremations. In mortuary pond burials in Florida, about one-third of the people were buried in clothes or wrapped in a shroudlike cloth and laid on mats or litters. Many of the Windover burials had been covered with a cone-shaped stack of wood and pointed stakes consistently had been driven into the bottom in the vicinity of burials. The top of the stakes indicate that they projected above the surface, and it is theorized that the stakes marked either the general cemetery area, or specific groups of burials (family plots?) within the cemetery. At Little Salt Spring, the remains of a possible collapsed structure was found on top of one burial.

People buried during the middle Archaic period often wore or had placed with them utilitarian items and personal ornaments. For example, at the Anderson site in central Tennessee, 41% of the 73 burials had grave goods.[14] There, the most frequent items found in graves were strings of shell beads, shell pendants, chipped stone points, atlatl weights, bone pins, and red ocher. There were only three cremations at Anderson, but each had significantly more and unusual grave goods than the full-flesh burials. Children often had

---

[12] For details about the burials at the Walnut site see Bense, 1983a and 1987.

[13] For details on the Gauthier site see B. C. Jones, 1981.

[14] For details about the Anderson Site excavations see Dowd, 1989.

many items buried with them. In mortuary ponds, most people were buried with baskets and tools of bone and wood. One burial had a complete bottle gourd (*Lagenaria siceraria*) which dated 5340 B.C. It is the oldest known specimen in eastern North America.[15]

Archaeologists have studied the patterns of grave items by gender at a few middle Archaic sites in an effort to determine the nature of gender-based roles within the societies in which the people lived. For example, in the Windover mortuary pond, only females were buried with polished simple bone pins, antler punches, and bird bone tubes, and only males were buried with awls made from the radius of carnivores, antler atlatl hooks and weights, and particular types of awls.[16] Adult males generally were buried with more bone and antler tools than females. This differential distribution of tools by gender in the windover graves indicates to David Dickel that there was a sexual division of labor, but because the functions of some artifacts are not known, interpretation is limited. However, it is clear that hunting with spears and atlatls was a male activity in middle Archaic Windover society.

Middle Archaic burials also reflect violent death. For example, at the Mulberry Creek shell mound on the Tennessee River, one grave contained three individuals who had been shot or stabbed with stone points that were still imbedded in their bodies when they were buried.[17] The bodies also were not buried in the usual flexed position as the rest of the population at this settlement, but appear to have been flung into a pit. At Windover, one adult male had an antler point embedded in his hip, and three adults and two subadults died from blows to the head.

Bone and demographic studies have been conducted on many skeletons from the Anderson, Windover, Republic Groves, and Little Salt Spring sites.[18] The studies indicated that the burials at each site included the full range of ages from infants to over 65. The infant mortality rate was about 20%. Those who survived infancy could expect to live into their 30s, and about 20% lived to their 40s. People were generally healthy and did not suffer from malnutrition or major chronic diseases that we can detect from their skeletons. There was a significant difference between the size and build of males and females. Males averaged 5 ft 7 in. tall with a muscular build, while females were 5 ft 3 in. tall with a light build. Many adults showed signs of arthritis in their joints, and their teeth were very worn. There were many instances of broken arms and legs, and it appears that the middle Archaic Indians regularly set

[15] For details about the bottle gourd see Doran *et al.*, 1990.

[16] For details on the gender study at Windover see Dickel, 1992.

[17] See Walthall, 1980, and Webb and DeJarnette, 1942, for more information on the Mulberry Creek burials.

[18] For details see Saunders, 1972, and Wharton *et al.*, 1981, for Republic Groves site; Dowd, 1989, for the Anderson site; Doran and Dickel, 1988, for the Windover site; and Purdy, 1991, for the Little Salt Spring site.

their broken bones in splints for better healing. The congenital defect known as spina bifida is documented at several sites. Iron-deficiency anemia was chronic. But the cases were not severe. Kidney stones were also found in a few burials.

Brain tissue was preserved at all three Florida wet cemeteries. More than 80 individual brains were recovered from Windover, and they have received intense study, some still ongoing.[19] When archaeologists Glen Doran and David Dickel discovered the preserved brains at Windover, they realized the significance of these remains, and took great care to ensure their survival for study. They removed the brain from the skull in the field, and immediately placed it in a nitrogen-flooded container at −20°C. Within 24 hr, the brains were transferred to a permanent storage facility and kept at −70°C. The preservation procedures made it possible to extract the nucleic acids, nuclear DNA, and mitochondrial DNA (mtdna) from the tissue. DNA samples have been replicated (cloned) in the laboratory. The brain tissue at Windover is the oldest human tissue studied on a molecular level in the world. Studies of this DNA are being used to investigate gene flow and population divergence of the early populations in the Southeast. In addition, mtdna is being used to identify the genetic families of the people buried in the mortuary pond, trace genetic diseases, discover new versions of known genes, and describe genes not found in modern populations.

Some of the people buried at Windover had undigested food in their gastrointestinal tract. A study of some of the undigested food from the stomach of several individuals has been made by Lee Newsom.[20] She concluded that most people probably were buried in the late summer and early fall, due to the presence of fall fruit seeds and lack of spring fruit seeds in their stomachs. The most common plants in the stomach samples were elderberry, grape, persimmon, and prickly pear. Her studies also documented that plants were used as grave goods, as in the case of a 40-yr-old female who was buried with cactus pads on her leg, over the right thigh, and beneath the right hand, and another person who was buried with a large shelf fungus.

Overall, the graves of middle Archaic communities in the Southeast share several common characteristics. Burials were made soon after death, and people were usually buried in the flexed position. There usually are a few other types of burial treatments, such as cremations and extended burials. Usually a significant percentage of the graves have items buried with the deceased, and there are different local preferences in grave items. The distribution of items buried with people was not homogeneous (i.e., people were buried with different numbers and kinds of items, and some graves had none). These burial patterns are interpreted by archaeologists as the reflection of an

---

[19] For details about studies of Windover brain tissue see Doran *et al.*, 1986, and Dickel *et al.*, 1988.

[20] For details about the plant study from the Windover burials see Newsom, 1988.

egalitarian type of social organization. This is an equal opportunity system that allows people of ability to achieve status and wealth regardless of the position of their parents. Therefore, the individuals singled out for special burial treatment and the highest number of grave goods are thought to have been the people with the highest status in the community. Children also were often given special treatment, and archaeologists speculate that they could have been the offspring of people with high status.

Settlement Pattern

In most areas of the Southeast, middle Archaic settlement and subsistence patterns were similar to those in the early Archaic period. Archaeologists theorize that people continued to live in macrobands of extended families whose territories consisted of all or part of a river valley. The macroband was usually broken into smaller family groups who moved through the valley, periodically shifting their campsites throughout the year. The archaeological remains of the small band sites are relatively uniform and similar to early Archaic sites. In most valleys studied, there are a few large middle Archaic sites with abundant artifacts and features near the Fall Line or shoals, which are interpreted as base camps similar to the early Archaic.

About 5000 B.C. there was a change in this traditional settlement pattern in at least three areas: the lower Tennessee River Valley, the upper Tombigbee Valley, and the eastern Florida Peninsula. In these valleys segments, exceptionally large sites developed consisting of thick deposits of midden (8 to 15 ft) and hundreds of domestic-related features. The larger of the sites are called "midden mounds" because of their size. Excavations in some of the large midden mounds and shell middens have revealed dense concentrations of artifacts ecofacts (plant and animal remains), and features.[21] The most common features are pits and hearths, and burials are often present. Some fired clay hearths were quite complex, carefully prepared, and reused. Several complex hearths were found in the upper Tombigbee Valley midden mounds, such as the one shown in Figure 5.11, and they appear to have been built inside structures that were repeatedly reoccupied and refurbished. Hundreds of pits filled with refuse were scattered throughout the large middens, such as the one shown in Figure 5.12. Excavations in the large shell middens in Tennessee, such as the Eva and Anderson sites, have documented that shell midden began accumulating about 5200 B.C.[22] In addition to the abundant artifacts, food remains, and burials, several shell middens had thick lenses of heat-treated chert flakes. At the Anderson site, John Dowd found mussel-

[21] Some midden mound excavations in the upper Tombigbee Valley are Atkinson *et al.*, 1980, Bense, 1983a and 1987, Dye and Watrin, 1985, and Rafferty *et al.*, 1980.

[22] See Dowd, 1989, for further information on the Anderson site and Lewis and Kneberg, 1961, for the Eva site.

FIGURE 5.11 Cross section of a middle Archaic complex fired clay hearth area found in the Walnut site midden mound in northeast Mississippi. Approximate diameter of the hearth area is 10 ft. Note that there are three internal fired clay hearths within the general hearth area. (From Bense, 1983a.)

processing pits filled with ash, and some were lined with slabs of local limestone. He also identified several circular areas of flat limestone slabs that could have been floors of structures.

In the Florida Peninsula, the rise in sea level raised the water level nearly to the ground surface, forming extensive swamps and wet prairies. With the reduced rainfall and increased dryness of the Altithermal, the food resources in these wetlands drew the population, and large settlements developed adjacent to many of them. The large middle Archaic settlement 8-A-356 near Gainesville, for example, was situated on high ground between a lake and a wet prairie.[23] The site is over 6 acres, and hundreds of the broad-bladed Newnan points were found, as well as many other stone tools. The presence of hundreds of blades, flakes, and cores at this settlement indicates that cutting

[23] For details about the 8-A-356 site see Clausen, 1964; for a summary see Milanich and Fairbanks, 1980.

FIGURE 5.12 Cross section of a middle Archaic refuse filled pit at the Walnut site midden mound in northeast Mississippi. Pit is approximately 5 ft in diameter, and it was filled with many layers of burned hickory nut shells. (From Bense, 1983a.)

was a dominant activity, probably associated with meat processing. The developing coastal wetlands also attracted people on the Florida peninsula. For example, on Horr's Island off the southwest coast, Michael Russo has recently documented that people were well adapted to coastal resources and living year-round in large settlements on some islands between 5419 to 5119 B.C.[24] The subsistence of these coastal populations was based on aquatic resources, especially fish and shellfish.

Summary

There is much more information from the middle Archaic than from any previous period in the Southeast. During this time, weather conditions became increasingly warm and dry, and lightning fires were changing the forest composition in the southern half of the region from hardwood to pines.

[24] For details on southwest Florida coastal Archaic see Russo, 1991.

Sea level continued to rise, and shorelines were being eroded and flooded. Important advancements were made in stone technology. The process of heat treating chert was developed, and the techniques of grinding and polishing stone were significantly improved. Long-distance trade in personal ornaments developed during the middle Archaic period. New types of sites also appeared in the middle Archaic: large mounds of midden and shell and cemeteries. Studies of burial practices and skeletons indicate that middle Archaic people lived healthy, normal lives at least into their 30s, and had an egalitarian social system.

LATE ARCHAIC PERIOD: 4000–1000 B.C.

The late Archaic period was a time of several key developments that eventually boosted southeastern Indian culture to a new stage of cultural development. These new developments consisted of the first containers of stone and fired clay, plant food cultivation, and mound building. All of these developments were somewhat isolated and only in their first stage of formation during the late Archaic. The Southeastern Indian population continued to grow. Thousands of archaeological sites from this period have been identified, and hundreds have been excavated.

Environment

The hot, dry weather of the Altithermal reached its peak at the beginning of the late Archaic period, and weather conditions then became cooler and more moist. Modern vegetation and weather conditions were reached about 2000 B.C. Sea level rise slowed, stabilized near the present level about 3000 B.C., and began to drop again about 1500 B.C. As sea level stabilized, modern barrier islands emerged along much of the coastline, and by about 1000 B.C. modern coastal ecosystems developed in many areas. Embayed river mouths rapidly filled with sediments, forming mud flats and marshes along bay and lagoon shores, which developed dense populations of marine life.

Material Culture

The chipped stone point styles that mark the beginning of the late Archaic period in most of the Southeast are the broad-bladed, long-stemmed "Savannah River" type and the narrower-bladed, short-stemmed "Benton" types, shown in Figure 5.1. In the Mississippi Valley, a smaller side-notched type was made. During this 3000-yr period, chipped stone points generally became smaller, but kept the same triangular blade shape and stemmed base. The rest of the chipped stone tool assemblage remained as before. Stone points and bifaces are the most common chipped stone tools, and they were used for a variety of functions such as sawing, cutting, piercing, scraping, and drilling. Retouched flakes were also used for a variety of tasks. In fact, there were only a few specialized chipped stone tools, such as end scrapers and microliths. Large chipped stone tools included notched river cobbles used as weights on fish nets and traps, and crudely flaked chisels.

Ground and polished stone tools and ornaments continued to be developed during the late Archaic, as shown in Figure 5.13. A new type of ground and polished stone atlatl weight was developed called a boatstone because of its boatlike shape. Another new ground stone artifact was a teardrop-shaped stone object about 2 to 4 in. long, with a groove or hole for suspension, which was often decorated. These items are called plummets, and they probably were used as weights for nets and bolas, to capture birds on the wing. Ground and polished stone ornaments reached an all-time high in popularity in several areas during the late Archaic period. Tiny carefully crafted ornaments, often less than an inch in size, were made into the shapes of animals from brightly colored chert and sandstone pebbles. This lapidary industry flourished particularly in the lower Mississippi Valley, and it is unique in the Southeast.

Another new advance in stone utensils during this period was the manufacture of bowls from steatite (soapstone) and occasionally sandstone. Stone bowls were more frequent in the Interior Highlands where soapstone occurs, especially in the Carolinas, northern Georgia and Alabama, and eastern Tennessee. Steatite is soft, can be easily carved by hand, and it can withstand rapid heating and cooling without cracking. Several prehistoric steatite quarries have been found in the Southeast in northern Georgia and Alabama. A good example of a quarry is Soapstone Ridge near Atlanta, where boulders of steatite are concentrated on the surface, and there is massive debris from quarrying and manufacturing of stone bowls.[25]

Steatite was also carved into flat pieces about $8 \times 4 \times 1$ in. in size with a perforation near one end, as shown in Figure 5.13. Until recently, these items were thought by many archaeologists to have been used as net weights. Recently, though, Kenneth Sassaman has suggested that they were used primarily in cooking.[26] In the Savannah River Valley, the flat "slabs" have been consistently found in and around hearths, and they are often discolored

---

[25] For details about the Soapstone Ridge Quarry see Dickens and Carnes, 1983.

[26] For details on steatite use see Sassaman, 1993; for a summary see Anderson and Joseph, 1988.

FIGURE 5.13 Late Archaic artifacts. Ground stone (A) boatstone, (B) plummet and (C) beads; Fired clay (D) cooking balls and (E) figurine; (F) decorated bone pin; (G) steatite slab and (H) bowl; (I) fiber-tempered clay bowls. (A–E, H From Webb, 1982. F, from Williams, 1977, copyright © 1977 by the President and Fellows of Harvard College. G, from Anderson and Joseph, 1988. I, from Jenkins and Krause, 1986.)

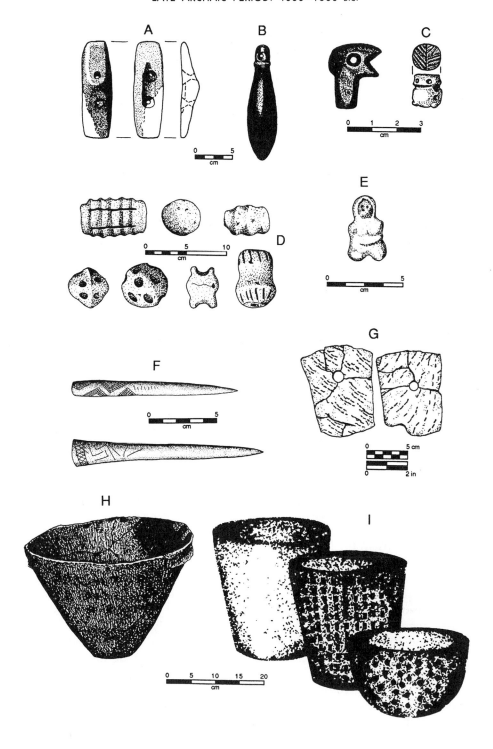

from heating. Sassaman proposes that steatite slabs would have been superior to other types of cooking stones because they are more resistant to thermal shock and more easily repaired, handled, and transported.

It was during the late Archaic that the process of making pottery was developed. The first items made from fired clay during this period were containers, cooking balls, and figurines, illustrated in Figure 5.13. The very first pottery containers in the Southeast were made on the Atlantic Coastal Plain in Georgia and South Carolina about 2500 B.C., and by 2100 B.C., they were made in peninsular Florida. By 1300 B.C., pottery containers had spread along the Atlantic coast as far as Virginia, westward along the Gulf coast as far as the Mississippi, up some of the rivers flowing into the Gulf, and to the Tennessee River. At first, clay was initially mixed with plant fibers, such as grass, palmettos, and Spanish moss, to "temper" the clay and prevent cracking during firing. The fibers burned during firing, leaving a distinctive porous pattern in the ceramics. Later, sand was used to temper the clay, or no tempering was added. Fiber tempered pottery vessels were shaped by molding the clay mixture into simple bowls and shallow, flat-based circular and rectangular pans. Soon after their appearance, people began to decorate their pottery vessels, and archaeologists have been able to isolate four geographical areas in which people decorated their pottery differently. These areas are shown in Figure 5.14 and include Stallings Island-Thom's Creek on the Georgia and South Carolina Atlantic Coastal Plain, Orange in east Florida, Norwood on the eastern Gulf Coastal Plain, and Wheeler in the upper Tombigbee and central Tennessee Valleys.

Fired clay cooking balls, shown in Figure 5.13, were used to bake food in earth ovens. The clay balls were heated in an open fire and then placed in the base of a small pit; food was then placed over them and the pit was covered while the food slowly cooked. Clay cooking balls are generally considered to have been a substitue for cooking stones in areas that had little rock, especially in the Mississippi Valley and the outer Coastal Plain. Earth ovens and cooking stones are regular features on late Archaic sites in rocky areas of the Southeast, especially the inner Coastal Plain and Interior Highlands. Clay figurines were made primarily in the lower Mississippi Valley during this period. As shown in Figure 5.13E, they are usually of females, 2 to 4 in. high, with reasonably lifelike torsos, abdomens, and buttocks. Facial features usually crude, but hairstyles are visible on some figurines. Several torsos suggest pregnancy.

Long-distance trade increased during the late Archaic. The most traded items were personal ornaments, which are usually found buried with the dead, and they likely were valuable exchange items as well as social-status markers. Steatite bowls and slabs were also frequent trade items along with native copper, greenstone, slate, colorful cherts, and marine shells. Both raw materials and finished products were traded; and it appears that manufacture could take place at the raw material source, along the way, or at the final destination.

Mortuary Patterns

Burial customs during the late Archaic were similar to those of the previous period. In the Interior Shell Mound Archaic culture area, there was a moderate increase in variety and quality of local and imported burial goods, but no increase in the labor investment or social organization has been detected. The practice of cremation also continued, and Jefferson Chapman and his colleagues have found that cremation apparently was the preferred mortuary method in the upper Tennessee Valley. Four formal cremation cemeteries have been located in this area, which were away from settlements, as at the Kimberly-Clark site in east Tennessee, which had 28 cremation interments.[27] Cremation was also practiced in the Mississippi Valley.

Mounds and Earthworks

Earth architecture was initiated at the very beginning during the late Archaic in the lower Mississippi Valley, consisting of mound and earthwork building. Mounds were usually dome- or conical-shaped, but one flat-topped mound has recently been documented.[28] Earthworks were constructed of midden refuse and earth piled and shaped into rings, crescents, or horseshoes. At least four mounds and two earthworks from the Archaic stage have been dated between 5180 and 1000 B.C. in the lower Mississippi Valley. The earliest dated mound is Monte Santo near Baton Rouge, Louisiana, which produced a single date of 5180 ± 140 B.C. Other early mounds include the LSU mound (4160–3310 B.C.), Banana Bayou Mound (3380 B.C.), Hornsby Mound (3150 B.C.), and the Poverty Point Mound (1080–410 B.C.). Researchers have found scores of other mounds in the lower Mississippi Valley, that contain late Archaic artifacts, but they have not been dated.

While only a few of these early mounds have been excavated, the results have been relatively consistent. Several mounds covered low platforms that appear to have been cremation areas or crematoria, judging from the presence of burning, charred bone, and surrounding structure postmolds. Other mounds covered burned areas and fire pits, some of which contain burned human bones, but without platforms. Artifacts are very scarce in late Archaic mounds; they usually consist of a few small ground and polished stone animal effigies and beads, chipped stone points and bifaces, microliths, or chipping debris. Mounds were built by piling baskets of soil that had usually been excavated from a nearby borrow pit. The earliest mounds range in size from 100 to 120 ft in basal diameter and between 4 and 15 ft high. One exceptionally large mound at Poverty Point is over 60 ft tall. Mounds were constructed to cover special areas, and they usually were adjacent to settlements. Mounds occurred singly or in groups of two or three. It is generally thought by archaeol-

[27] For details see Chapman, 1990.
[28] See Gibson and Shenkel, 1988, for details on early mounds.

ogists that the late Archaic mounds in the lower Mississippi Valley were associated with mortuary activities, and served as special mortuary markers or symbols.

Earthworks of midden were constructed primarily in the lower Mississippi Valley and along the Georgia and South Carolina coast. They were between 5 and 10 ft high and constructed primarily of midden, but layers of earth were sometimes used. The most common shapes of the late Archaic earthworks in the lower Mississippi Valley were horseshoes and crescents, while closed rings were most frequent on the Atlantic. The arrangement of midden earthworks varied; they occur singly as well as in overlapping and adjacent groups of two or three and a few are concentrically arranged. Most archaeologists agree that most midden earthworks were lived on, and that their purpose was a practical one of providing an elevated dry living platform in generally wet environments. However, the explanation for the regularity of their shapes is much more debated. Some archaeologists suggest that the earthworks built up over time as refuse accumulated around structures arranged in a circular or horseshoe-shaped pattern. Others think that the earthworks were carefully planned, and at least some were aligned with solar events.

Settlement and Subsistence Patterns

During the late Archaic period many populations targeted only a few specific base camps in their valleys, at which some of the population lived most of the year. This sedentism trend is explained by archaeologists as a response to the aridity in many upland areas and the development of food-rich wetland habitats in the flood plains and coastal strips. The number of large base camps increased during the late Archaic as populations were more concentrated on the flood plains and along the coastal strip. The archaeological sites formed by the late Archaic base camps were similar to those of the previous period. They contain thick midden deposits with abundant artifacts and domestic features, such as large prepared hearths, earth ovens with cooking rocks or fired clay cooking balls, refuse pits, artifact concentrations, and burials.

In the late Archaic period, there is strong evidence that the use of plant foods was increasing.[29] Plant cultivation, as detailed in the preceding section, actually began in the middle Archaic when the Indians grew the bottle gourd (*Lagenaria siceraria*) for containers. In the late Archaic, another container plant was added: hard-rind squash (*Curcurbita pepo*). The earliest squash has been found at the Anderson site in central Tennessee from which a seed was accelerator dated at 4040 B.C. by Crites. In the Tellico Reservoir Jefferson Chapman also dated squash at 2500 B.C. Archaeologist Bruce Smith views these "container crops" as marking the beginning of plant husbandry in

---

[29] For details on late Archaic plants see Crites, 1991, Chapman and Shea, 1981, and B. D. Smith, 1985a, b, and 1986, and Yarnell and Black, 1985.

eastern North America. Seeds of wild fleshy fruits, such as persimmon and grapes, also reached an all-time high percentage in relation to all other seeds during this period. Small-grain plant seeds other than greens (pokeweed and purslane) are relatively scarce in the archaeological record until the last portion of the late Archaic, when seeds of maygrass, sunflower, knotweed, cheno-pods, amaranth, and grasses begin to appear in river valley base camp sites in the Interior Highlands. These fruits and seeds are presumed to have been gathered from the general vicinity of base camps during this period, although later, these plants were all cultivated to some extent.

Examples of Late Archaic Cultures

As shown in Figure 5.14 several late Archaic regional areas have been identified. These are not necessarily all the regional cultures that existed during these three millennia; realistically, these are only the areas in which enough research has been conducted to define the late Archaic culture. To date, archaeologists have defined a mosaic of culture areas in the Southeast. The information of some of these culture areas is summarized as follows to serve as examples of the archaeology and theories that archaeologists have generated to explain the ways of life that existed in the Southeast during the late Archaic period.

Interior Shell Mound Archaic

This large culture area includes much of the Midwest as well as the northwestern portion of the Southeast. There has been extensive research in this area, much of which took place in the 1930s, when many large flood plain base camps were excavated. These base camps were located along or near major streams situated near wetlands and river shoals in which mussel beds were present.

The Lauderdale culture in the lower Tennessee Valley is a good example of an Interior Shell Mound Archaic cultural complex. Prominent excavated shell midden sites include Eva, Mulberry Creek, Perry, and Flint River. Most sites are very large, with deposits between 20 and 40 ft thick, such as the Mulberry Creek site, shown in Figure 5.15. The shell middens contained abundant artifacts, residential domestic features, and burials. Fire hearths, prepared clay areas, and large concentrations of fire-cracked rock are the most frequent features. Prepared clay areas consisted of several inches of clean clay brought to the site, which was smoothed in an area 6–10 ft in diameter. Fires were built on the clay surfaces, which hardened and turned brick red. Often there were several superimposed fire-hardened clay layers, and postmolds in and around them suggest that they likely were the floors of houses.[30] These clay areas were surrounded by midden containing ashes, charcoal, animal

---

[30] For details on these fired clay features see Webb and DeJarnette, 1942, DeJarnette, 1952, and Walthall, 1980.

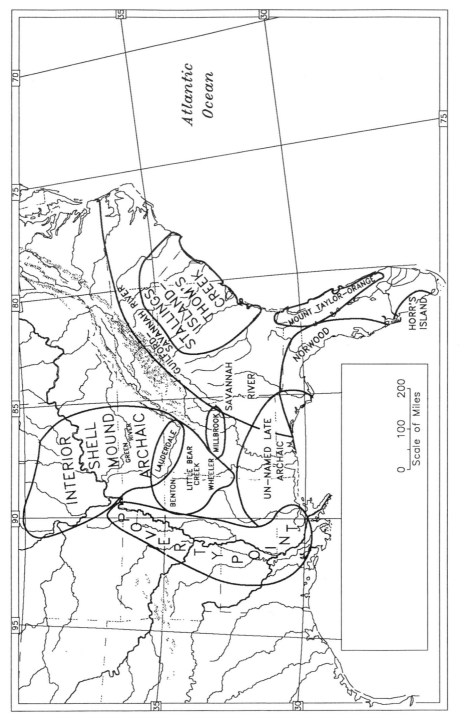

FIGURE 5.14 Late Archaic culture areas.

FIGURE 5.15   Photograph of the profile of the Mulberry Creek shell midden on the central Tennessee River in northern Alabama during WPA excavations in the 1930s. (From Webb and DeJarnette, 1942).

bones, and artifacts. Smaller hearths are also common in the Lauderdale shell mounds, and they are usually lined with stones.

The stone and bone artifact assemblage of the Lauderdale culture was typical of the late Archaic. Midway through the late Archaic period, steatite containers appeared and became an important item thereafter. One source area for some of this steatite has been identified in an east-central Alabama, and those sites that are nearer these deposits in the eastern portion of the middle Tennessee Valley contain more steatite. About 1300 B.C. fiber tempered pottery containers, known as Wheeler, appeared in the Tennessee Valley.[31] The vessels were typical late Archaic shapes: round, flat-based pans and bowls. Surfaces were plain or decorated by punctations. Wheeler ceramics also appear about the same time in the upper Tombigbee Valley of Mississippi and Alabama, but not elsewhere in the Interior Shell Mound Archaic culture area.

The burial customs of the southern portion of the Interior Shell Mound Archaic have been labeled the "Pickwick Burial Complex." In addition to the traditional late Archaic burial customs described in the summary above, caches of large, well-made triangular bifaces, red ocher, and boatstones or gorgets

[31] See Walthall, 1980, and Walthall and Jenkins, 1976, for details.

were placed in isolated deposits or with the dead. The thin bifaces were usually large (5 to 10 in. long), and made of grey flint. Some of the grey bifaces were bipointed, and some had angular notches at one end. Other bifaces have short stems, like the Benton points shown in Figure 5.1. In many instances, the artifacts were intentionally burned and destroyed during cremations. Another distinction of Lauderdale burials is that, occasionally, there are unusual individuals, such as a dwarf or a decapitated person. These unusual people were also buried with out-of-the-ordinary grave goods, such as long thin awls and necklaces of human teeth. These rare burials are thought to have been of spiritual leaders or shamans who were buried with their "medicine bundles" of special fetishes used to perform rituals.

There are sand and silt layers in the shell middens throughout the Interior Shell Mound Archaic area that indicate that the settlements were periodically inundated. Flooding occurs regularly between November and March in this region. During these months, the annual late autumn nut crop draws numbers of deer and turkeys to nut the acorn and hickory groves in the upper valley terraces and uplands. Based on these factors, a model of settlement and subsistence pattern has been proposed for the Lauderdale area, which can also be extended to most of the larger culture area.[32] This settlement pattern projects that late Archaic flood plain base camps, located by mussel beds, were used from early spring until early fall, and relatively large groups of extended families harvested fish, shellfish, and plants and hunted nearby. In the late fall and winter, the large group broke up into small family bands that went up to the valley terraces and uplands to harvest, process, and store nuts and hunt deer and a variety of small game.

Stallings Island–Thom's Creek

Across the Appalachians on the Atlantic Coastal Plain, the Stallings Island–Thom's creek culture was similar in several ways to the Interior Shell Mound Archaic.[33] From the Fall Line downstream, large base camps were established by mussel shoals, and large shell middens were formed. The Stallings Island site at the Fall Line, for example, was 260 ft long and 25 ft high. There were large base camps above the Fall Line, but they did not contain shell, due to the lack of mussel beds in this section of the river. Shell middens also formed at large base camps along the coast that were established adjacent to the extensive coastal marshes.

The stone tool assemblage of the Stallings Island–Thom's Creek culture was typical of the late Archaic. However, stone tools are generally scarce on coastal sites, probably because stone is scarce in this area. Steatite was used, and several steatite quarries have been found in the Piedmont. The distribution

---

[32] For details see Jenkins, 1974, and Morrison, 1942.

[33] For a summary see Anderson and Joseph, 1988, Sassaman et al., 1990, Sassaman, 1993, and White, 1982.

of steatite, however, is uneven in the Savannah Valley. For example, at the Stallings Island site near the Fall Line, over 2500 steatite slabs were recovered, while at Rabbit Mount site, only 75 mi downstream, only 86 were present. Steatite bowls are also surprisingly scarce in the Savannah Valley, and have been found at only a few sites.

Bone and antler artifacts were abundant and very similar to the assemblage described in the summary above. However, a distinctive bone pin was made by the Stallings Island–Thom's Creek societies, which was polished and often decorated, as shown in Figure 5.13F.

Pottery containers were also used in the Stallings Island–Thom's Creek area. Archaeologists have been aware of Stallings Island fiber tempered pottery since William Clafin's publication in 1931 of Cosgrove's excavations in 1929 at the Stallings Island site. However, it was not until the mid-1960s that archaeologists realized the chronological significance of this pottery, when James Stoltman dated it at 2500 B.C.[34] This early date for the pottery has been consistently substantiated, making Stallings Island the oldest fiber tempered pottery in North America. The earliest pottery containers were flat-based bowls and pans, but one shape that appears to be unique to this area is a bowl with a prominent, angular shoulder and sharply in-curving rim.

Something else is different about the pottery in this culture area. Soon after the development of fiber tempered pottery, a sand tempered pottery appeared, called Thom's Creek. Both types had similar decorative patterns of rows of punctations and pinches in geometric patterns. Both types of pottery temper were used until 1000 B.C., when fiber tempering stopped and only sand tempering was continued.[35] The distribution of the two ceramic types does overlap somewhat, but not completely. Stallings Island fiber tempered pottery is most common on the coast and in river valleys to the Fall Line in the Georgia–South Carolina area. The Savannah River Valley was at or near the center of its distribution. Thom's Creek sand tempered pottery is most common on the South Carolina Coastal Plain, particularly in the Santee and Edisto Valleys. Thom's Creek pottery is low in frequency away from this area, and is not found on the Georgia coast.

The settlement and subsistence pattern for the Stallings Island-Thom's Creek culture was typical of the late Archaic in the Southeast. Sedentism increased as areas were selected for base camps in strategic locations. In the river valleys, from the Fall Line downstream, flood plain base camps were located near shoals and mussel beds. Upstream from the Fall Line, however, shellfish were not gathered, and researchers suspect that anadromous (migrating) fish were the target food. In the coastal zone, settlements were located both on the mainland and on sea islands, next to marshes and estuaries with

---

[34] For details on dating Stalling Island pottery see Stoltman, 1966, 1974.

[35] For details on Stallings Island–Thom's Creek pottery see Phelps, 1968, and Sassaman, 1993.

shellfish beds. Coastal shell middens appeared about 2200 B.C. These coastal base camps were quite large and were occupied year-round.

Over 30 shell rings dot the coastal landscape from Cape Fear, North Carolina, to northeast Florida, and they are all located adjacent to tidal creeks, many of them surrounded by marsh.[36] Most earthworks are doughnut- or horseshoe-shaped. The shell midden earthworks, called "shell rings," are usually 30–50 ft wide at the base and 2–10 ft high. The rings are between 130 and 200 ft in diameter and their interior is distinctively clean of artifacts or features.

Why did the Stallings Island–Thom's Creek people make these shell rings? We really do not know. Michael Trinkely suggests they were started by initially arranging houses at a new settlement in a circular or horseshoe pattern facing the center. In front of the houses were earth ovens and seafood steaming pits, and trash pits were dug in the back. These trash pits were quickly filled, and then piled over with refuse forming the basic shape of the midden ring. Shell midden continued to be thrown on top of the full refuse pits and the shell ring began to grow in size. There have been enough postmolds and hearths found in the shell midden ridges to substantiate the presence of houses, lean-tos and tanning racks. Based on this information, Trinkely suggests that people lived on the inside portion of the shell midden rings, which grew in height and width from dumping refuse on and over the outside edge of the ridge. Other researchers have theorized that the shell rings were special settlements that served communal functions, perhaps as social and ceremonial centers. Fragmentary human remains have been found at most shell rings, and Cheryl Claassen suggests that these could have been special burial sites.[37] Realistically, however, we simply do not know why midden was carefully arranged in circles or horseshoes.

A few late Archaic structures have been found in Georgia and South Carolina. At the Sara's Ridge site in the upper Savannah Valley, Dean Wood found a subrectangular (i.e., rounded corners) structure with a central hearth that opened to the river.[38] Jerald Ledbetter also recently found a well-preserved semisubterranean pit house in eastern Georgia that was subrectangular in shape, 18 ft wide, and over 1 ft deep. In the house pit were over 100 Savannah River points, as well as steatite disks or slabs, three stone tool caches, and an interior hearth dated to 1900 B.C.[39] This is the earliest pit house so far discovered in the Southeast.

[36] For details about shell rings see Marrinan, 1975, and Trinkley, 1980 and 1985.

[37] For details on this interpretation see Claassen, 1986.

[38] See Wood *et al.*, 1986, for details on the structure and Anderson and Joseph, 1988, for a summary.

[39] See a summary by Jefferies, 1992, for more details.

Mount Taylor–Orange

Immediately to the south of the Stallings Island–Thom's Creek culture area was the Mount Taylor–Orange culture. This region is dominated by the sluggish St. Johns River and coastal lagoons. The St. Johns Valley is unusual because it is actually a long, flat, wide trough of fresh water. The gradient of this sluggish river is so low (less than 0.1 ft per mile) that the river is affected by the tides for over 150 mi, causing the river to flow backwards.[40]

Fiber tempered pottery was made and used in the St. Johns Valley by about 2000 B.C. This pottery, called Orange, was often decorated with geometric designs made with incised lines and punctations. The most frequent vessel shape was a rectangular, flat pan with lug handles (much like a casserole dish). Unlike other late Archaic sites in other areas, Mount Taylor–Orange sites characteristically have few artifacts. One of the suspected reasons for this artifact scarcity is the chronic lack of stone for tools, which likely necessitated that most things had to be made from organic material, especially wood, or shell. The shell of the lightning whelk (*Busycon contrarium*) was extensively used to make chisels, hammers, gouges (scrapers), and celts (axes). Steatite was regularly imported into this area and used for atlatl weights and containers.

Wooden items have been recovered from wet sites in the St. Johns Valley.[41] These include wooden bowls and dugouts. Four dugouts from this period have been found, dated between 3190 B.C. and 1090 B.C., and all were made from pine logs by a combination of burning and chopping with adzes. The oldest of these watercraft is in fact the oldest known dugout in the Western Hemisphere. The oldest type of dugout is quite primitive with blunt ends, and these are 1000 yr older than any other type of dugout thus far discovered. Dugouts had either blunt ends, beveled ends, or an overhanging bow, and they averaged between 15 and 18 ft long and 16 in. wide. As James Miller describes, the use of the dugout in the late Archaic period in the St. Johns Valley and coastal lagoons provided access to large areas that were virtually inaccessible by foot. Dugouts also improved the efficiency of travel for people, and allowed them to transport much larger loads than could be carried by hand. With the dugout, people could exploit larger areas and new sources of food and stay in better communication than on foot.

The Mount Taylor culture had distinctive mortuary customs, which included mass burials of prepared skeletons. At the Tick Island shell midden, for example, Ripley Bullen excavated 175 flexed burials that had been interred in separate groups at different times.[42] A shallow depression was initially

---

[40] See Miller, 1992, for a detailed description of the St. Johns Valley.

[41] See Purdy, 1991, and Newsom and Purdy, 1990, for details.

[42] For details on the Mount Taylor burial customs see Bullen, 1962, and Jahn and Bullen, 1978; for a summary see Milanich and Fairbanks, 1980.

made in the surface of the settlement, and over time, several mass graves of secondary burials wrapped in matting were placed in this spot and covered with sand. The presence of cleaned and individually wrapped human skeletons implies that the bodies had been prepared by removing the flesh from the bones, bundling them in a special wrapping, and storing them until their final burial. This activity usually takes place in or near a charnel house (similar to our funeral homes). The Mount Taylor–Orange practice of secondary mass burials, and the implication of charnel houses by about 3500–3000 B.C. is the earliest in the Southeast, and it is unique to late Archaic cultures. Burial goods found in the mass graves were similar to those in other contemporaneous culture areas and consisted of utilitarian and ornamental objects, including stemmed chipped stone points, beautifully decorated and polished bone pins, and shall hammers or picks. One burial clearly showed violent death, as there were three stone points imbedded in the skeleton.

In the flat and wide St. Johns Valley, an extensive wetland with rich food resources developed during the late Archaic period. Not so coincidentally, there was an immigration of people into this area, where they established base camps in the wetlands, often adjacent to large colonies of pond snails (*Viviparus georgianus*) and mussel beds. The new base camps formed huge shell middens, such as Mount Royal and Tick Island, some of which are over 10 acres in size and 20 ft high and are the highest points in this vast wetland. Archaeologists suspect that the base camps were occupied year-round, but this lacks theory documentation. Other smaller, nonshell midden sites are scattered on most low elevations throughout the valley, and they represent short-term special-use sites similar to upland sites in the interior river valleys.

About 2000 B.C., the coastal lagoons behind the barrier islands along the Atlantic were occupied. Jerald Milanich and Charles Fairbanks have suggested that the St. Johns Valley population was beginning to deplete some of the snail colonies, and the people began to move seasonally to the coastal wetlands to compensate for this problem.[43] Milanich, Fairbanks, and others have suggested that the Orange period settlement and subsistence pattern consisted of spending the winter months on the coast and the spring and summer months in the St. Johns Valley. Michael Russo and his colleagues have suggested another theory, which proposes that there were separate populations in the St. Johns Valley and the coast, rather than one population that moved seasonally.[44] Studies of animal bones in shell middens in the St. Johns Valley have documented that small fish were the primary food source (87%). However, a variety of other food sources were used. For example, at the Groves Orange Midden, the residents used 20 species of snails and bivalves, 3 species of snake, 3 species of bird, 5 species of mammals, and 31 types of plants, including bottle gourd and squash, between 4843 and 1265 B.C.

[43] For a summary see Milanich and Fairbanks, 1980.
[44] For details see Purdy, 1991, Russo, 1986, Russo *et al.*, 1993, and Sigler-Eisenberg, 1988.

Horr's Island

Recent late Archaic research on the southwest coast of Florida has revealed that at least portions of the 10,000 islands were permanently occupied by coastal dwellers during this period.[45] At least one shell midden site on Horr's Island was permanently occupied. The midden had been made into the shape of a large horseshoe with arms over 1100 ft long, and had four associated shell and sand mounds. This site is the largest known permanently occupied coastal late Archaic settlement, and dates from 3000 B.C. Michael Russo has found evidence of small, circular structures directly on the shell midden. There also were areas of crushed shell and many hearths and pits, which are interpreted as large living areas. Artifacts were low in frequency, as in the St. Johns Valley, and shell was the most frequent raw material for tools.

Three of the mounds at this site were built directly on the horseshoe-shaped shell midden. Two of the four mounds have special construction features and so are thought to be garbage dumps. However, two mounds are interpreted by Russo to have been ceremonial. The largest mound, Mound A, was conical in shape, 16 ft high, and over 100 ft wide at the base. The mound was built on a naturally high dune and it towered almost 30 ft over the surrounding area. The ground initially had been leveled and intentionally burned about 2320 B.C. and covered with a low 3–4 ft-high sand mound. This was gradually covered with about 5 ft of shell midden. A second, thinner layer of special sand was then placed over the mound and it was again covered with shell midden. There were no living floors or other evidence of domestic activity, such as pits or hearths, in this mound. Russo suggests that the internal sand mounds were symbolic, and the caps of shell midden may have reaffirmed their importance over a long period of time. The other mound was much smaller but built in the same manner.

While research has just started in this area of the Gulf coast, the results thus far have added important new information. It has documented that by 3000 B.C. there were permanent, large coastal settlements in some parts of the coast. Subsistence was focused on aquatic resources, especially small fish, and the interior was not an important source of resources.

Poverty Point

Near the midpoint of the late Archaic period, about 2200 B.C., the Poverty Point culture emerged in the lower Mississippi Valley, and is one of the most well-known late Archaic cultures in the Southeast.[46] It is renowned for the construction of mounds and earthworks, an advanced stone lapidary industry, microliths, stylized baked clay cooking balls, and a far-flung, long-distance trade network. Ironically, while these characteristics of the Poverty Point culture are very well known, archaeologists are only now beginning to under-

---

[45] For more information see Marquardt, 1988 and 1992, and Russo, 1991.

[46] For details see Gibson, 1974, 1980, and Webb, 1982.

stand the details of its internal development, chronology, and social organization.

Stone lapidary work is one of the most distinctive aspects of the Poverty Point artifact assemblage. The tiny, well-crafted ground and polished stone beads, effigies, pendants, and plummets were made in great numbers and exhibit attainment of a high level of skill in stoneworking. Experiments have shown that these small ornaments probably were perforated and shaped using bow drills of hollow cane and placing loose sand in the drill hole. Small (2–3 in. long) sandstone saws have also been found and are presumed to have been used to cut up the small pebbles. Other stoneworking tools in Poverty Point assemblages include whetstones, reamers, pumice polishers, pallets, and anvils.

Another trademark of the Poverty Point artifact assemblage is fired clay balls. Not only are they far more abundant in this culture area than anywhere else, but they were made in several specific styles with distinctive shapes and decorations. A few examples of the different styles are shown in Figure 5.13D. Thousands of these fired clay balls have been found on Poverty Point sites, and concentrations of fired clay balls are consistently found in cooking pits and in middens. The pits were then sealed, and the food was baked by heat from the clay balls. Thus the fired clay balls performed the same function in the rock-free lower Mississippi Valley as cooking stones and steatite slabs did elsewhere.

Microliths (also called microflints) are another distinctive artifact in Poverty Point assemblages, and they exist in enormous quantities on larger sites. Microliths were made from a small pebble core of chert or quartzite, which had one end struck off to leave a flat surface from which an average of about 15 tiny flakes could be removed. The flakes were about 1–2 in. long and one-quarter of an inch wide. These small blades were used for a variety of tasks, such as perforating, scraping, drilling, sawing, and engraving. The most frequent type of microlith is the "Jaketown perforator," which has an unworked broad end and a well-used pointed (distal) end.

Containers made of steatite, sandstone, and fiber tempered pottery are also a consistent part of Poverty Point assemblages, although they are generally low in frequency. Stone containers are used well before pottery containers, which appeared in this area only about 1100–1000 B.C. Pottery vessels were deep bowls and jars with disk, ring, or podal-supported (small feet) bases. They were decorated with punctated and incised designs as well as nodes punched around the rim. Solid clay figurines were also made, which were 2–3 in. tall. Although they are rare, they are found consistently at larger Poverty Point sites. They were usually female figures, and they were relatively crudely made, as shown in Figure 5.13E. Tubular pipes, plummets, beads, and pendants were also made of pottery.

Archaeologists theorize that Poverty Point societies had an extensive long-distance trade network centered on stoneworking. The trade network moved the raw materials necessary for the ground and polished ornaments into the lower Mississippi Valley and moved the finished products around the region. Mineralogical studies of some of the raw materials of Poverty Point stone ornaments and items have been performed, and the sources have been traced to the Appalachian Mountains, Piedmont, Rocky Mountains, Ouachita Mountains, Illinois, and the Great Lakes. Some of the imported raw materials were argilite, slate, copper, galena, jasper, quartz, and steatite. This material probably was transported down the Red, Arkansas, Mississippi, Tennessee, and Ohio rivers. At some sites, imported raw material makes up a significant part of the craft items. For example, at the Poverty Point site itself, 40% of all chipped stone points were made from stone that had been imported from over 100 mi away. Many archaeologists think that the Poverty Point acquisition and delivery system of raw materials and finished products included traditional down-the-line trading as well as specific trade between local centers and with neighboring culture areas.

Poverty Point societies extended throughout the lower Mississippi Valley from St. Louis to New Orleans. Within this long valley, several individual societies have been identified in different geographical areas or territories.[47] Archaeologists theorize that each sociopolitical area had a central large settlement with semicircular and horseshoe-shaped earthworks and one or more mounds. Other settlements were smaller and amorphous in shape, and there were numerous short-term campsites as well. Whereas there are enough similarities between the regional Poverty Point societies to tie them together into a relatively cohesive culture area, archaeologists have documented that each society was characterized by specific artifact assemblages, site distribution patterns, and earthworks.

Poverty Point was originally thought by many archaeologists to have been an agricultural society, but it has now been documented that the traditional Archaic hunting, gathering, and fishing subsistence was practiced. The huge flood plain of the Missisisppi River developed into one of the richest and largest wetland habitats in North America during the late Archaic period and, coupled with the arid conditions just to the west, it attracted and supported large numbers of people. In addition to fishing, gathering, and hunting, they also grew the late Archaic "container crops" of bottle gourds and squash.[48]

One of the best known archaeological sites in the Southeast is the Poverty Point type site. Shown in Figure 5.16 it lies on a ridge next to a bayou overlooking the Mississippi flood plain near the confluence of six major rivers. The site consists of two large mounds and six concentric midden ridges arranged in a semicircle covering about 500 acres. The midden ridges are divided into five segments about 82 ft wide, and they once were up to 10 ft tall. The ridges are about 130 ft apart, and recent studies by Jon Gibson have documented

---

[47] For projected location of the societies see Webb, 1982.

[48] See Jackson, 1981, and Shea, 1979, for details on Poverty Point cultigens.

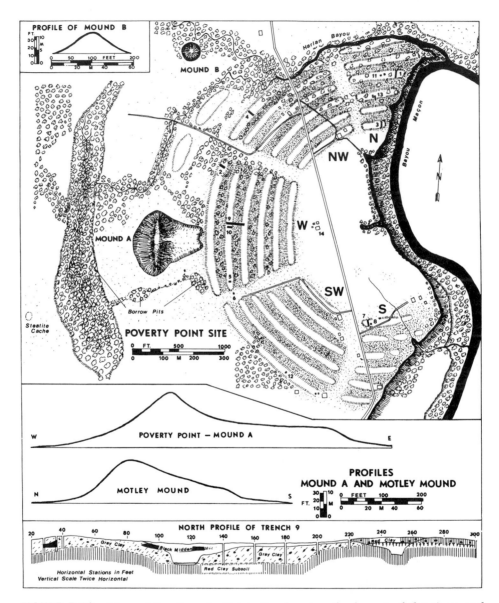

FIGURE 5.16 Map of the Poverty Point site showing the layout of the rings and mounds. (From Webb, 1982.)

that they are composed of a series of flat linear clay platforms on which structures and hearths were built.[49] Gibson suggests that these linear platforms were built fairly rapidly, by throwing kitchen refuse down the sides of the ridges, which added to the width of the base each. The ridges nearest the center were highest, and had the most occupation debris and features. Gibson hypothesizes that the function of the clay platforms or ridges appears to have been to elevate living areas above the naturally low, wet surface.

There are two mounds at the Poverty Point site, Mounds A and B. Mound A is T-shaped, oriented to the cardinal directions, about 70 ft high, and measures 640 × 710 ft at the base.[50] It has a small flat summit about 15 ft in diameter at the very top, and a lower larger platform 240 × 300 ft in size about 40 ft from its base. There is a ramp on the east side of the mound from the summit, which points directly at the center of the arc of midden ridges. Mound B lies 740 ft north of Mound A, also outside the midden ridges. It is conical in shape, about 20 ft high, and 180 ft in diameter at its base. A third mound, the Motley Mound, also appears to have been associated with the site. It lies 1.5 mi north of Mound A, and is oriented toward the midden ridges. It is oval in shape, 500 ft in diameter at the base, and about 21 ft high. The summit has a narrow platform about 20 ft long and probably a ramp was present on the south flank.

James Ford excavated Mounds A and B at Poverty Point and the Motley Mound in 1955.[51] In the single trench he excavated in the lower platform of Mound A, there was no evidence of structures or that other activities were conducted there. However, in profiles of the gullies cut into the lower platform, there were clear indications that the mound had been built by individually carried and dumped baskets of soil. He found that both mounds had been built in this manner. Mound B was initially built over a small fire pit, 2 ft wide and 10 in. deep, which had been excavated into the original, premound surface. In this pit, there were 32 baked clay objects, charcoal, and ash. Around this pit on the premound ground surface was a 6-in.-thick layer of burned cane and ashes in which at least one burned human bone was found. Ford speculated that this ash layer could be the remains of a large, burned crematory area. Over this ash bed a 4-ft-high platform of compact yellow clay was built, which had a clean surface. This was capped by another, larger, 4-ft-high clay platform, which had evidence of burning on its surface. A third 4-ft-high platform of soil was built over the second, which also had scattered ash and charcoal on the surface. The last platform was covered with a 7.5-ft-high conical mound. A final mantel of soil was placed over the entire mound and it was then abandoned.

---

[49] For a summary of the work see Jefferies, 1992.

[50] See Ford and Webb, 1956, for a description of the mounds at Poverty Point and the nearby Motley Mound.

[51] For details on this excavation see Ford and Webb, 1956.

Thousands of artifacts have been recovered from the midden ridges at the Poverty Point site, and they are well known by Southeastern archaeologists and their students because of the publications of Clarence Webb and Jon Gibson, both of whom have spent much of their lives studying this site and culture. At Poverty Point, the artifact assemblage includes high numbers of baked clay cooking objects, stone points, microliths and cores, and ground stone lapidary items. Steatite was present in large amounts, including a cache of almost 3000 pieces of broken vessels in a pit 8 ft wide and 2 ft deep, about 400 ft southwest of Mound A, as shown in Figure 5.16. Some of the steatite vessels were decorated with geometric designs, and one had a bird with spread wings and talons engraved on the side. Very few pottery vessels have been found at Poverty Point, and those found have been identified as Wheeler fiber tempered. Studies of the distribution of artifacts have shown that cooking tools, domestic tools, ornamental items, and raw materials were unevenly distributed in the different sections of the midden ridges. For example, most fired clay objects came from the northern sector, whereas most of the copper, lapidary items, and pipes were in the southern sector.

The sociopolitical organization of the Poverty Point society has been the subject of much debate. Due to the size, organization, and earth architecture at Poverty Point, the presence of mounds and earthworks at other large settlements, and a consistent series of settlement sizes, some archaeologists theorize that some Poverty Point societies had evolved beyond the egalitarian band level of social organization into a ranked society called a chiefdom. Other archaeologists think some Poverty Point societies were just on the verge of becoming a ranked society. Most archaeologists, though, agree with Vincas Steponaitis, who contends that it is quite possible that Poverty Point society was simply an elaborate version of the egalitarian social systems typical of late Archaic groups elsewhere. Accordingly, Poverty Point base camp settlements are only larger, and some are more planned, than elsewhere in the Southeast at the time.

Summary

During the late Archaic there was a shift in settlement and subsistence as a result of increased use of wetland food resources. This shift was related to the peak of the xeric climate at the beginning of the period, and the natural development of food-rich wetland habitats in river valleys and along the coastal strip. During the late Archaic period, most of the population spent most of their time either in river valleys or coastal base camps. Population increased as sedentism and the food supply increased. Technical advances were made in ground and polished stoneworking as new axes, atlatl weights, plummets, and ornamental items were developed. The first stone containers were developed, but they were soon replaced by pottery containers. Fired clay was also used for a variety of new items such as cooking balls, pipes, and figurines. Long-distance trade in raw materials and ground and polished stone ornaments significantly increased, especially in the Poverty Point culture area, and it was this society that built the first planned settlement and mound centers in the Southeast. Burial ritual expanded and included the use of red ocher, mass graves, caches of special objects, and mound building.

SUMMARY OF THE ARCHAIC STAGE

The initiation of the Archaic stage in the Southeast generally coincided with the onset of the Holocene stage and ended with the onset of modern climatic conditions. Global warming continued through the early Holocene and Altithermal and peaked early in this period between 4000 and 3000 B.C. Sea level rose from about 90 ft to its present position about 2500 B.C., but soon began dropping once more.

During the Archaic stage, Southeastern Indians greatly expanded their knowledge of the resources in the region and became experts in tapping the wealth of resources in the forests, river valleys, and coastal areas. The population had steadily risen in previous periods and it increased significantly during the late Archaic period. Settlements became more numerous with houses, large hearths, pits, and sizable formal cemeteries. Through time, there was a steady increase in the number of artifacts and the thickness of midden deposits. Skilled craftsmanship in ornamental items developed in the Archaic stage, especially in ground stone and polished stoneworking, and a trading network developed for these items and raw materials. During this stage, the social organization remained egalitarian, and the individuals who achieved higher status during their lifetimes were often treated differently in death, by special treatment of their bodies and by placing well-crafted items in their graves.

The Archaic stage was marked by a series of subsistence, technological, and social advances. In subsistence, the major developments included the inclusion of aquatic resources in the diet, the cultivation of bottle gourds and squash for containers, and the use of fired clay. Technological advances were made in the invention and improvement of the atlatl, ground and polished stone artifacts, and the use of shell for tools and ornaments. Social conflict and violence is first documented in the middle and continued into the late period.

The Archaic stage is divided into three periods: early (8000–6000 B.C.), middle (6000–4000 B.C.) and late (4000–1000 B.C.). The differences between the periods mark the evolution of southeastern Indian culture during this period.

In the early Archaic, the environment was different than today, with hardwood forests covering most of the area. The change in the chipped stone points that identify this period are side, corner, and basal notching. The most important additions to the stone tool kit were plant-processing tools made from ground stone. Most sites are small and have few features, but some larger sites have clay hearths, shallow pits, and surface concentrations of artifacts from chipped stone tool manufacturing and hide processing. The only human burials yet recovered were cremated. Early Archaic settlement pattern and social organization appear to have been characterized by river valley-based family bands that moved through their valley with the seasons in small family groups. It is probable that temporary large settlements occurred during brief periods in which important social activities took place, such as marriage and resource information exchange.

During the middle Archaic period, the weather was becoming increasingly warmer and drier, and the forests in the southern half of the region were changing from hardwood to pines because of chronic forest fires started by summer lightning. Sea level continued to rise, and shorelines continued to erode. Technological advancements were made in ground and polished stone tools including grooved axes, atlatl weights, and stone net weights. Ornaments of ground and polished stone, shell, and bone increased in popularity, craftsmanship improved, and long-distance trade in these items developed during this period. New types of sites appeared, with large midden mounds and cemeteries. From the studies of their burial practices and skeletons, we have indications that the middle Archaic people lived at least to their 30s, and they had an egalitarian social system.

During the late Archaic period, there were important developments in pottery, plant food cultivation, and mound building. The late Archaic chipped stone point styles were the broad-bladed, long-stemmed Savannah River type and the narrower-bladed, short-stemmed Benton types. Advances were made in ground and polished stone technology with a new form of atlatl weight, plummets for net weights and bolas, and tiny carefully crafted beads, pendants, and effigies. Another new development in stone artifacts during this period was the manufacture of stone bowls from steatite (soapstone) and occasionally sandstone. It was during the late Archaic that the process of making pottery was developed. The first items made from fired clay during this period were containers, cooking balls, and figurines. The very first pottery containers appeared on the Atlantic Coastal Plain in Georgia and South Carolina about 2500 B.C., and by 2100 B.C. they were made in peninsular Florida. Pottery spread westward along the Coastal Plain during the late Archaic, reaching the Mississippi Valley by 1300 B.C. Long-distance trade increased during the late Archaic. The most traded items were personal ornaments, which we usually find buried with the dead, and they likely were valuable exchange items as well as social-status markers. Earth mounds and midden earthworks were initiated at the very beginning of the late Archaic period, and perhaps even during the latter part of the middle Archaic, in the lower Mississippi Valley. While mounds were restricted to this area, midden earthworks were also constructed on the Atlantic coast of Georgia and South Carolina.

Sedentism increased in the late Archaic period as more populations targeted only a few specific base camps in their valleys at which some of the population lived most of the year. Base camps were strategically located near the developing wetlands, but several nearby environmental zones were exploited. These settlements were occupied for much or all of the year, and often formed large archaeological sites. Population increased with the growing sedentism and the new aquatic food supply. The archaeological sites formed by the late Archaic base camps contain thick midden deposits with abundant artifacts and domestic features, such as large prepared hearths, earth ovens with cooking rocks or fired clay cooking balls, refuse pits, artifact concentrations, and burials. There is strong evidence that the use of wild plant foods was increasing during this period, and the container crops cultivated included both bottle gourds and a hard-rind squash.

The Archaic was a very important stage of southeastern Indian cultural development. During the Paleoindian stage, people expanded to most parts of the region, but population levels were low. It was during the Archaic stage that the Indians fully adapted to the different geographical areas of the Southeast, and they developed not only a distinctive southeastern way of life, but internal cultures were more distinct than ever before as the populations adjusted to their particular environments. The Archaic is also an important stage to archaeologists because of the increased amount of archaeological materials. There are more sites, artifacts, features, and human remains preserved than ever before, and, consequently, we are able to understand the people and their culture better than in the Paleoindian stage.

6

WOODLAND STAGE:
1000 B.C.–A.D.1000

KEY WOODLAND TRAITS
Mound Building
Spread of Pottery throughout the Region
Hopewellian Ceremonial Complex

IMPORTANT CULTURAL DEVELOPMENTS
Increase in Sociopolitical Complexity
Ceremonial and Mortuary Centers
Bow and Arrow

INTRODUCTION AND OVERVIEW

The Woodland is the third major stage of Indian cultural development in eastern North America. This stage is best characterized with the adjective "more." There were more people concentrated in river valleys and along the coastal strip, more pottery was used throughout the region, more earth mounds were built and used for burial, more elaborate mortuary rituals were conducted, more trade developed and more plants were cultivated and stored. No one of these characteristics originated in the Woodland stage, but they were more common and they had more complex relationships during this stage; this is the hallmark of the Woodland.

By convention, the Woodland stage is divided into three periods. The early Woodland began in 1000 B.C. and ended in A.D. 0. The middle Woodland lasted from A.D. 0 until A.D. 500, and the late Woodland from then until about A.D. 1000. But, as you might guess from the lack of strikingly original widespread developments, the timing of the periods varied. Most southeastern societies passed through the Woodland stage within this period, but, as shown in the Woodland chronological chart in Figure 6.1, they did not do so simultaneously. The duration of the internal periods also varied locally. The dates used in this book are conveniences arrived at by a general consensus within the profession, and they encompass most of the period of time when prehistoric Indian societies passed through the Woodland way of life.

The climate during the Woodland stage was generally the same as that of today. The forest zones established during the late Archaic remain essentially the same today, as shown in Figure 2.5D. Sea level fluctuated somewhat and reached its present position by about 400 B.C.[1]

The beginning of the Woodland stage is best marked by the spread of pottery manufacturing throughout the Southeast. Pottery was employed for a wider range of purposes in the Woodland than during the Archaic stage, when it was used primarily for hot rock or hot slab cooking. During the Woodland stage, pottery technology rapidly advanced through innovations including the use of temper other than fiber, development of the coiling technique to build container walls, welding of coils and raising vessel walls with the paddle and anvil technique, and rounding or pointing of vessel bases, as illustrated in Figure 6.2. These innovations allowed people to make pottery containers in a wide variety of shapes and sizes so that they could better be used for direct-heat cooking and for storing and serving food. By the middle Woodland period, about A.D. 0, some exceptionally well-made ornamental pottery vessels were made. Examples of the expanded variety and range of pottery vessels in the Woodland stage are shown in Figure 6.3.

The earliest advancements in pottery technology were made on the South Carolina–Georgia Coastal Plain at the close of the late Archaic period between

[1] See DePratter and Howard, 1981, 1983 for details.

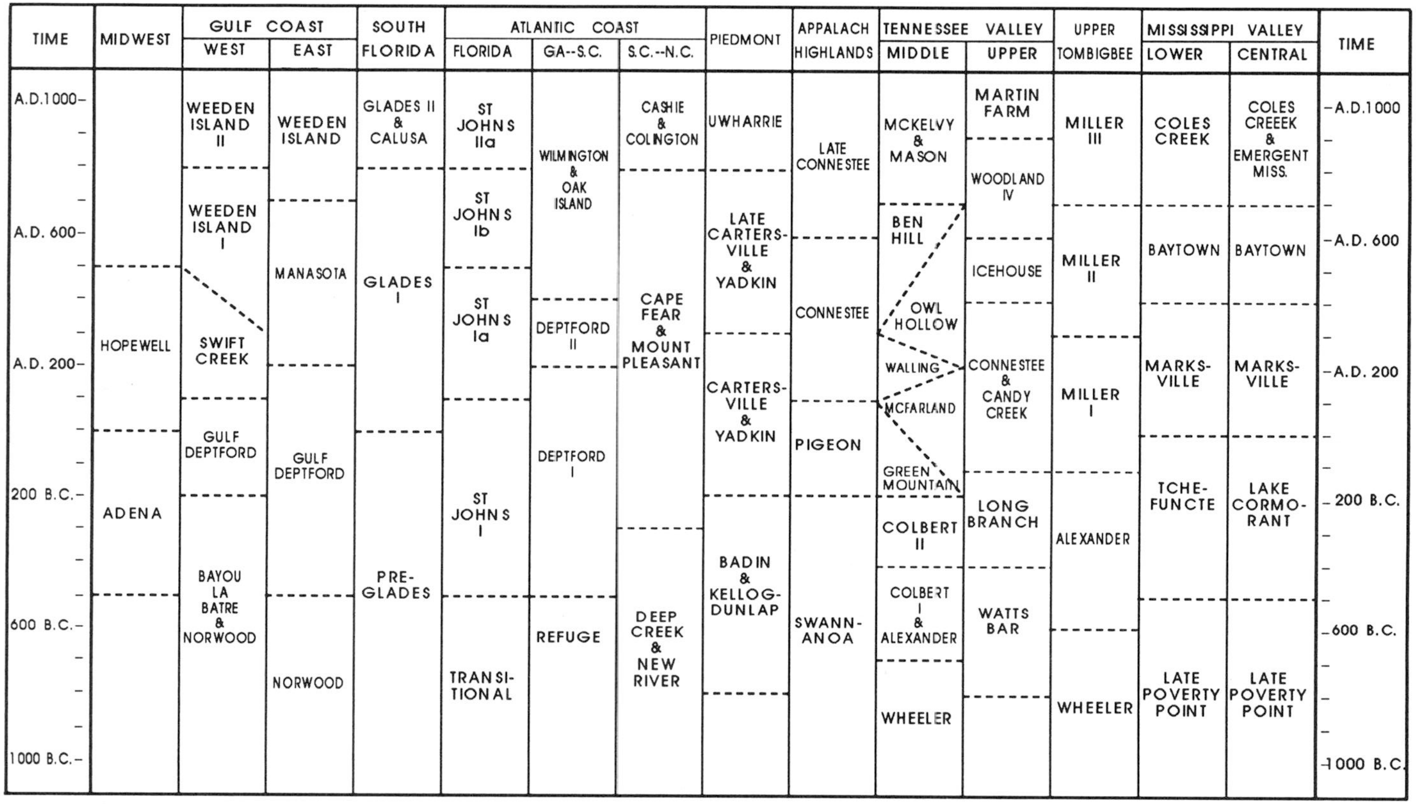

| TIME | MIDWEST | GULF COAST | | SOUTH FLORIDA | ATLANTIC COAST | | | PIEDMONT | APPALACH HIGHLANDS | TENNESSEE VALLEY | | UPPER TOMBIGBEE | MISSISSIPPI VALLEY | | TIME |
		WEST	EAST		FLORIDA	GA--S.C.	S.C.--N.C.			MIDDLE	UPPER		LOWER	CENTRAL	
A.D.1000–		WEEDEN ISLAND II	WEEDEN ISLAND	GLADES II & CALUSA	ST JOHNS IIa	WILMINGTON & OAK ISLAND	CASHIE & COLINGTON	UWHARRIE	LATE CONNESTEE	MCKELVY & MASON	MARTIN FARM	MILLER III	COLES CREEK	COLES CREEEK & EMERGENT MISS.	–A.D.1000
–											WOODLAND IV				–
A.D. 600–		WEEDEN ISLAND I	MANASOTA	GLADES I	ST JOHNS Ib		LATE CARTERS-VILLE & YADKIN			BEN HILL	ICEHOUSE	MILLER II	BAYTOWN	BAYTOWN	–A.D. 600
–	HOPEWELL	SWIFT CREEK			ST JOHNS Ia	DEPTFORD II	CAPE FEAR & MOUNT PLEASANT		CONNESTEE	OWL HOLLOW					–
A.D. 200–								CARTERS-VILLE & YADKIN		WALLING	CONNESTEE & CANDY CREEK	MILLER I	MARKS-VILLE	MARKS-VILLE	–A.D. 200
–		GULF DEPTFORD	GULF DEPTFORD			DEPTFORD I			PIGEON	MCFARLAND					–
200 B.C.–	ADENA				ST JOHNS I					GREEN MOUNTAIN	LONG BRANCH	ALEXANDER	TCHE-FUNCTE	LAKE CORMO-RANT	–200 B.C.
–								BADIN & KELLOG-DUNLAP		COLBERT II					–
–		BAYOU LA BATRE & NORWOOD		PRE-GLADES			DEEP CREEK & NEW RIVER		SWANN-ANOA	COLBERT I & ALEXANDER	WATTS BAR				–
600 B.C.–						REFUGE							LATE POVERTY POINT	LATE POVERTY POINT	–600 B.C.
–			NORWOOD		TRAN-SI-TION-AL					WHEELER	WHEELER	WHEELER			–
1000 B.C.–															–1000 B.C.

FIGURE 6.1   Woodland Stage chronological chart.

FIGURE 6.2 Steps in making pottery containers using coils and the paddle and anvil technique: (A) kneading and mixing clay with tempering agent; (B) making coils; (C) stacking and pinching coils; (D) welding the coils with the paddle and anvil method; (E) preheating pots near open kiln; and (F) firing pots in open kiln.

1500 and 1000 B.C., and it was here that sand tempering coiling, and the paddle-and-anvil method of welding clay coils were first developed. Most early Woodland vessels were shallow bowls with round bases, decorated with designs made by punctating and incising. Thick pottery tempered with grit (tiny pebbles) was made by 500 B.C. in the North and Midwest. These vessels were wide-mouthed jars and bowls with flat-to-round bases, and their surfaces

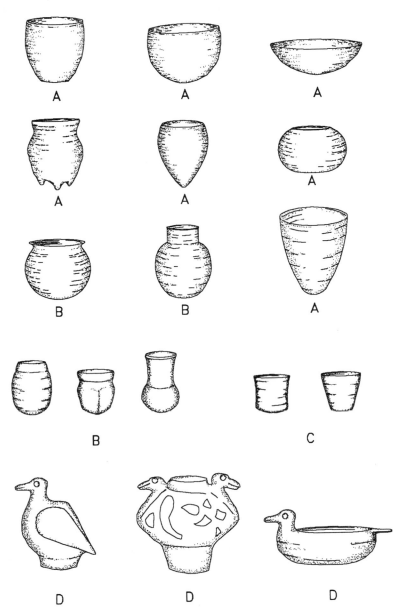

FIGURE 6.3 Woodland pottery vessel shapes: (A) bowls, (B) jars, (C) beakers, (D) animal effigies.

were covered with the impressions of fabric and cord that had been wrapped around a dowel, paddle, or stamp and then impressed into the wet surfaces of the clay containers. By about A.D. 0, there were four pottery traditions in the Southeast. Joseph Caldwell identified these as the Gulf, Northern, Middle Eastern, and South Appalachian.[2] Each tradition had distinct decorations and shapes, and was made in a particular geographic area as illustrated in Figures 6.4 through 6.7. In some cases, both the decorations and the geographical areas of the pottery traditions changed and overlapped through time.

Because most pottery decorating and manufacturing techniques change relatively rapidly through time, pottery is an excellent time marker in archaeology. While it is clear that the decorations had symbolic meanings, we do not know for certain what those meanings were or why a society changed from one pottery tradition to another or changed decorations within a tradition. We do infer cultural continuity when a society continued to make and decorate pottery in a traditional manner in an area for a long time.

The Gulf pottery tradition was characterized by designs made by incising, punctating, pinching, rocker stamping, and brushing with a variety of tools, including shells and human fingers. The designs were geometric, zoomorphic, and anthropomorphic. In the South Appalachian pottery tradition, vessel surfaces were covered with impressions of stamps from 2 to 6 in. in length with designs incised on them. There were several types of stamps. A simple stamp design consisted of parallel lines. Linear check stamping had rows of ladderlike designs, and bold check stamping had a checkerboard or "waffle" pattern. In the Northern pottery tradition, vessel surfaces were covered with impressions made by cordage wrapped around a paddle or stamp. Middle Eastern pottery containers had surfaces covered with impressions from a fibrous material that had been wrapped around a dowel, paddle, or stamp, which left a wickerlike pattern.

There were three additional important developments that occurred late in the Woodland stage: the bow and arrow; shell-tempered pottery; and maize horticulture. The latter two were established late in the period and were limited to the southeast corner of Missouri. A surge in population growth also seems to have occurred in many areas during this period, and much of the population was dispersed into the uplands and smaller tributary valleys in many culture areas.

Mounds are another hallmark of the Woodland stage, although only about 1% of Woodland sites have an associated mound. The phenomenon of mound building began in the late Archaic period in the lower Mississippi Valley, where some mounds were constructed as early as 4000 B.C. Mounds were present along the southwest Florida coast by 3000 B.C. The purpose of these early mounds is unclear, but a few in the lower Mississippi Valley contained human cremations. Outside the Southeast, there were two other mound-

---

[2] For details about the pottery traditions see Caldwell, 1958.

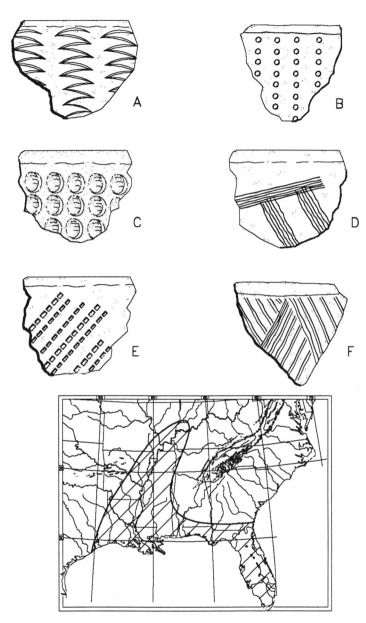

FIGURE 6.4 Gulf pottery tradition area and designs: (A) rocker stamped, (B) punctated, (C) pinched, (D) brushed, (E) dentate stamped, (F) incised.

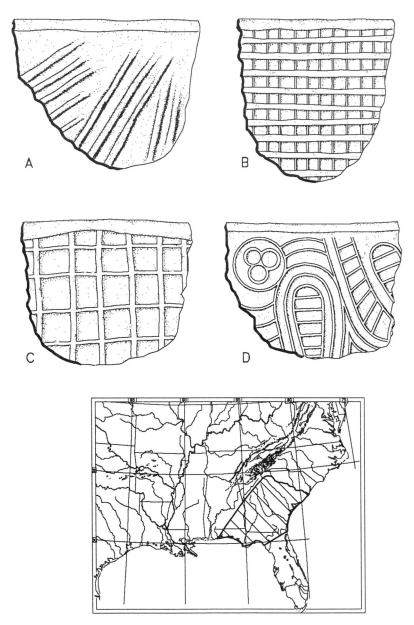

FIGURE 6.5 South Appalachian pottery tradition area and surface treatments: (A) simple stamped, (B) linear check stamped, (C) bold check stamped, (D) complicated stamped.

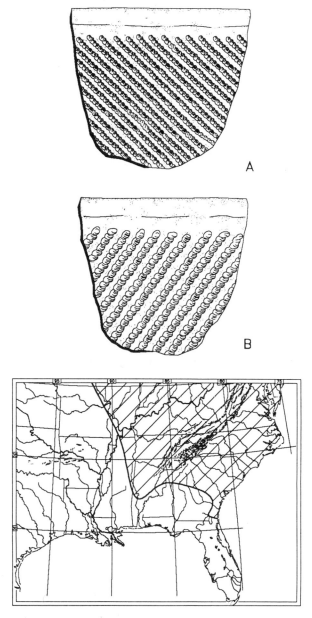

FIGURE 6.6 Northern pottery tradition area and surface treatments: (A) fine cord marked, (B) heavy cord marked.

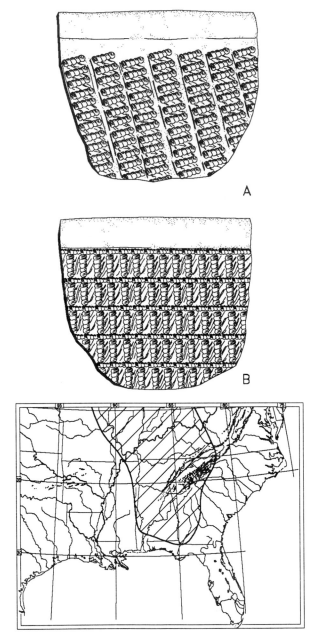

FIGURE 6.7   Middle Eastern pottery tradition area and surface treatments: (A) fabric-wrapped dowel, (B) fabric-wrapped paddle.

building late Archaic cultures. The earliest known mounds used exclusively for human burial were built in Labrador about 3500 B.C. By ca. 1500 to 1000 B.C., the Glacial Kame culture in the Midwest buried their dead in the natural summits of low hills with utilitarian and ornamental items of copper and shell. Archaeologists surmise that these early mounds inspired the development of the Woodland practice of burial mounds.

During the Woodland stage, mounds were used for human burial and for the performance of special events, such as feasting. Burial mounds were usually conical or dome-shaped and built to cover subsurface burial pits or tombs. Most burial mounds were small and dome-shaped, 2–5 ft high and 30–60 ft in diameter at the base. Human remains were sometimes accompanied by ornamental and prestigious grave goods, and occasionally they included caches of special items. Platform mounds were usually rectangular in shape with flat summits. In most of the Woodland stage, the function of mound centers was primarily mortuary and ceremonial, although some elaborate mound centers were built. After ca. A.D. 500, Mississippi Valley mound centers became civic-ceremonial centers and residences for a small number of elite.

Although the cultivation of plants increased during the Woodland stage, crops made up an important part of the diet only in the northern part of the Southeast during this period. The most important plants cultivated during the Woodland stage are listed in Table 6.1.[3] Many of these plants, known as the Eastern Agricultural Complex, had been used in the Archaic stage. For example, the bottle gourd was cultivated as early as 5200 B.C., and the gourdlike squash was grown by 3000 B.C. Both these early cultigens were probably used as containers in this early period rather than as food. By 4000 B.C. marsh elder was heavily harvested in the Illinois Valley and in Kentucky, and paleobotanists suggest that it was cultivated by 2000 B.C.[4] Sunflower, sumpweed, chenopod, and maygrass were cultivated somewhat later, between 2000 and 1500 B.C., and a small amount of maize appears much later, around A.D. 175. Paleobotanists determine whether a plant was deliberately cultivated by comparing the fruits and seeds found in archaeological sites with those growing wild. They apply the principle that plants consistently cultivated will have larger seeds and fruits and thinner seed husks than those that grow in the wild. Studies have shown that maize was not important to the diet of societies in the Southeast during the Woodland stage except in some northern parts of the central Mississippi Valley. There, maize was very important in the diet by about A.D. 800.

Recent research has shown that the Eastern Agricultural Complex spread unevenly, and it did not always lead to increases in population and cultural complexity, as was once believed.[5] For example, plant cultivation was prac-

[3] See Yarnell and Black, 1985, and R. Ford, 1985, for details and further reading.

[4] For more details about these studies, see Asch and Asch, 1985

[5] See Watson, 1985, for comparative information.

TABLE 6.1 Eastern Agricultural Complex Plants

	Harvest season
Native starchy seed annuals	
Maygrass (canary grass)	Spring
Knotweed	Fall
Goosefoot (lamb's quarter or pigweed)	Fall
Little barley	Spring
Native oily seed annuals	
Sunflower	Fall
Sumpweed (marsh elder)	Fall
Tropical starchy seed annuals	
Maize	Fall
Tropical oily seed annuals	
Squash	Summer?
Bottle gourd	Summer?

ticed in the Tellico Reservoir by 500 B.C., but is not known to be important elsewhere in the Southeast at that time. Although poor preservation of tiny plant materials and inconsistent recovery techniques make analysis difficult, it seems that substantial cultivation was very limited in the Southeast during the Woodland stage.

There was also an increase in the use of pits to store and conceal plant foods during the Woodland stage. The cooler temperatures and the fermentation process that occurred in pits helped to preserve food. Dried seeds or nuts were placed inside cylindrical or bell-shaped pits, and the opening was sealed with a tight hard cover, such as fired clay mixed with grass or moss. Nuts were preserved by the cool temperature in the earth. Seed preservation, however, worked on a different principle. Soon after closing, the wall of the pit developed a natural shell of fermented seeds, as illustrated in Figure 6.8. This shell sealed the pit sides, and the fermenting grain created an oxygen-free interior environment in which neither bacteria nor pests could survive.[6] Storage pits could be used several times, but they gradually changed shape from repeated emptying. After their shape had changed so much that they could not be sealed effectively, they were usually reused as trash pits, burial pits, and smudge pits for insect control and hide preparation.

Adena and Hopewell Ceremonial Complexes

During the early and middle Woodland stage, the center of cultural development in eastern North America was not in the Southeast but in the Midwest. The Adena and Hopewellian ceremonial and mortuary complexes developed

[6] See Morse and Morse, 1983, and DeBoer, 1988, for summaries.

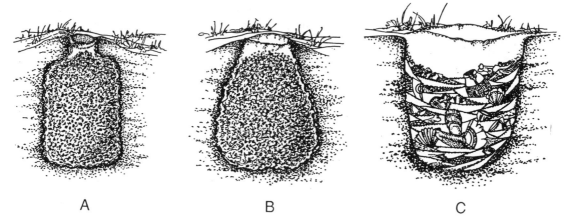

A   B   C

FIGURE 6.8   Life cycle of a storage pit: (A) new sealed storage pit, (B) reused sealed storage pit, (C) storage pit reused as a refuse pit.

in the central Ohio and Illinois valleys between about 500 B.C. and A.D. 300. These complexes affected the sociopolitical development of Woodland societies in much of the Southeast, and, because of their influence, they are briefly described here.

Adena

The Adena mortuary complex developed in the central Ohio Valley about 500 B.C., and it lasted until about A.D. 100.[7] Adena was a ceremonial and mortuary complex that was shared by many different local and regional cultures. As James B. Griffin describes it, Adena is a convenient term that includes dozens of different early Woodland societies in the central Ohio Valley that were quite diverse, sharing only a ceremonial system.[8]

Adena burial ceremonialism began with simple mounds covering shallow grave pits lined with bark, each containing the body of one person with utilitarian grave goods. By about 200 B.C., mortuary buildings were constructed in which a few individuals with both utilitarian and ornamental grave goods were placed on the floor or in shallow pits just prior to burning. A mound was then built over the burned mortuary building. New mortuaries were often built on top of the mound, and the cycle was repeated several times. As a result, some mounds became quite tall and contained many tombs and construction layers. Over 67 ft high, the Grave Creek mound in Moundsville, West Virginia, is the largest Adena burial mound ever discovered. Late in the Adena period, circular earthen ridges were sometimes built around or near mounds. The purpose of these circles is unknown. Late Adena log tomb

[7] For more information in Adena see Griffin, 1978a,b, Jennings, 1974, and Muller, 1986.
[8] For more details on Adena as a concept see Griffin, 1978b.

burials became very elaborate. Bodies were prepared by temporary burial to remove flesh from the bones, which, after exhumation, were often painted with bright pigments. Grave offerings included food and utilitarian artifacts, such as flint blades and awls, as well as distinctive Adena prestige ornaments. These included copper bracelets, finger rings, adzes, celts, marine shells, crescents and sheets of mica, many forms of ground and polished stone gorgets, zoomorphic pipes, and stone tablets with very carefully inscribed geometric designs and bird images. These items were the core of the Adena mortuary complex and were made, traded, and accumulated by participating societies.

Hopewell

Mortuary ceremonialism in the Midwest continued to increase in complexity. By ca. A.D. 1, mortuary ceremonialism was sufficiently different and a separate label, Hopewellian, is applied to it. The name comes from the Hopewell family who owned a farm in Ross County, Ohio, on which was located a ceremonial site with large geometric earthworks enclosing a village and burial mounds. The base name "Hopewell" applies specifically to the type culture in Ohio, whereas the term "Hopewellian" refers to the mortuary complex of which the Hopewell culture provides the most elaborate example. These terms have very different meanings. The Hopewellian ceremonial complex overlapped with Adena in many areas in the Midwest. As with Adena, Hopewellian societies maintained their own identity but shared a belief system, mortuary ceremonialism, and special artifacts and materials. The group of cultures that participated in this ceremonial complex was designated the "Hopewell Interaction Sphere" by Joseph Caldwell.[9]

Hopewellian ceremonialism was most elaborate in its Midwest heartland, where mound centers of an enormous scale were constructed. These centers had scores of mounds, often enclosed by geometric earthworks in the shape of octagons, parallel lines, and circles up to 50 acres in size. Elaborate tombs with great numbers of grave offerings, mortuary processing pits, fire pits, large caches of exotic artifacts, and burned charnel houses were found beneath the mounds. Tombs were rectangular pits surrounded by a low earth embankment and lined with logs, bark, and stone. Inside the tombs, flesh burials were laid out and covered with mats staked to the floor. Mortuary processing pits were used for temporary burials to decompose soft tissue, after which the bones were removed, bundled, and stored. The pits were then reused. The artifacts found in Hopewell mounds in the Ohio heartland were a rather distinctive set of elaborate items, many of which were made from exotic materials such as copper, marine shells, mica, obsidian, shark and alligator teeth, and meteorites. Finished artifacts included copper earspools, shell cups and beads, panpipes covered with copper or silver, effigy pipes, and pottery jars of distinctive shape and decoration.

---

[9] For the original definition of the Hopewell Interaction Sphere see Caldwell and Hall, 1964.

Many societies in the eastern Woodlands participated in the Hopewellian ceremonial complex, and some became more sociopolitically complex than others. Those people selected for special burial treatment must have acquired significant power, as evidenced by the accumulation of Hopewellian items signifying wealth and status, and by the construction of mortuary mound centers apparently dedicated to a few individual leaders and their kin groups. There is little agreement, though, on details of the sociopolitics within the Hopewellian Ceremonial Complex. The focus on status may have been due to increased competition for resources, but it is also possible that those buried in the mounds were exceptional traders and negotiators with easy access to special items and who were able to build a power base. Proximity to the major trade routes may have been a key factor in the emergence of powerful individuals because of the access to Hopewellian wealth and status items such proximity afforded. Regardless of how the powerful leaders emerged, studies have shown that Woodland societies were basically egalitarian in nature, and positions of power were very temporary. There appears to have been a constant competition for power and status, especially when a powerful leader died, and it appears that rank and power were not automatically transferred from one generation to the next generation. The middle Woodland period was a volatile period, and power shifts occurred frequently. These shifts fostered the continuous construction and abandonment of mound centers that were temporary seats of power.

Decline of Hopewell

Hopewellian ceremonialism declined in the late Woodland period. However, ceremonial and mortuary complexes continued during the late Woodland stage on the southeastern Gulf Coastal Plain, especially the Mississippi Valley, although they changed in many ways. The tradition of elaborate grave offerings essentially came to an end, and long-distance trade was dramatically reduced compared to earlier periods. Mound building, however, continued unabated in the central Mississippi Valley. Increasingly complex centers were constructed, civic-ceremonial mound centers were developed, and platform mounds became more popular than conical mounds.

Summary

The Woodland stage grew out of the Archaic stage beginning about 1000 B.C. and lasted until around A.D. 1000 in some parts of the Southeast. In general, the Woodland stage was not distinguished by great breakthroughs in technology or sociopolitics; rather, it was characterized by the growth and development of several traditions that began during the Archaic stage: pottery, mound building, mound centers, mortuary ceremonialism, sociopolitical complexity, and trade.

EARLY WOODLAND PERIOD: 1000 B.C.—A.D. 0

The early Woodland period was marked by the spread of pottery through-out the Southeast. Before this time, pottery was generally confined to the Atlantic Coastal Plain. Because pottery reflects cultural differences, it is one of the main criteria by which culture areas and historical periods are defined by archaeologists. Cultural anthropologists and ethnoarchaeologists have shown that there is a strong link between societies and their preferences for individual designs and symbols. Based on this information and the differential distribution of pottery traits through time, they are used to reconstruct the social and political territories of extinct societies.

Environment

Around 1000 B.C., the relative position of sea level dropped between 6 and 12 ft, but by 400 B.C. sea level had risen to its present position. This pattern is well documented along the Atlantic coast, and less so along the Gulf of Mexico.[10]

Material Culture

Four pottery traditions developed during the early Woodland period, as shown in Figure 6.9. Gulf tradition pottery was made throughout most of the Coastal Plain by the Transitional, Norwood, Late Poverty Point, Wheeler, Bayou La Batre, and Refuge cultures, located in Figure 6.10. The use of fiber tempering continued for a few centuries in the Norwood, Transitional, Late Poverty Point, and Wheeler culture areas. In the last half of the early Woodland period, Gulf tradition pottery was restricted to the western Gulf Coastal Plain, including the Tchefuncte, Alexander, and Bayou La Batre cultures, located in Figure 6.11. The pottery made by the Alexander societies is especially intricate, with complex incised designs. The use of podal supports on vessels, as shown

[10] See DePratter and Howard, 1981, for details about the Atlantic; for the Gulf see Milanich and Fairbanks, 1980, Dunbar *et al.*, 1992, and Garrison, 1992.

FIGURE 6.9   Early Woodland artifacts: (A) Tchefuncte rocker stamped and incised; (B) Alexander incised; (C) Bayou La Batre rocker stamped and punctate; (D) Mossy Oak simple stamped; (E) Dunlap fabric marked; (F) Deptford check and linear check stamped; (G) Otarre-Swannanoa point; (H) Weems point; (I) Flint Creek point. (A and C reproduced [with modification] from Jenkins and Krause, 1986, with permission of The University of Alabama Presses, copyright © 1986. D, E, and F reproduced [with modification] from Caldwell, 1958, by permission of the American Anthropological Association from MEMOIR No. 88 of the American Anthropological Association. Not for further reproduction. H modified from Morse and Morse, 1983.)

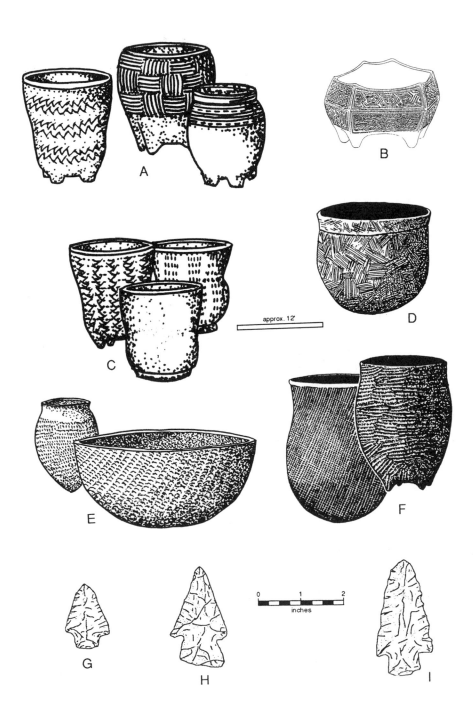

approx. 12"

0 1 2
inches

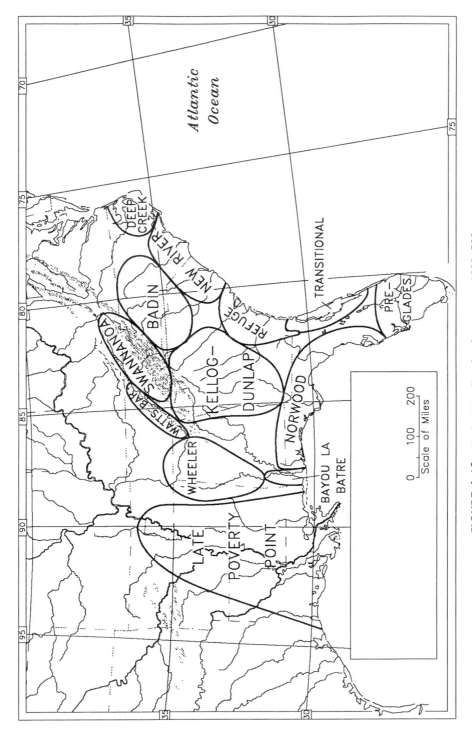

FIGURE 6.10 Early Woodland culture areas 1000–500 B.C.

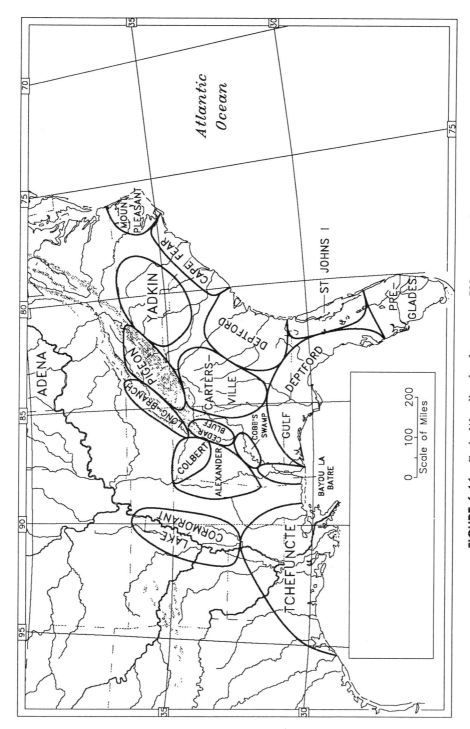

FIGURE 6.11 Early Woodland culture areas 500 B.C.–A.D. 0.

in Figure 6.9, was common in most areas. This attribute is used as a temporal marker for the early Woodland period.

Northern tradition pottery is found mainly on the mid-Atlantic Coastal Plain of the Southeast. This pottery was tempered with crushed steatite, coarse sand, crushed shell, and grit, and surfaces were covered with the impressions of cord-wrapped paddles. Vessels included jars and bowls. Middle Eastern tradition pottery first appeared in the Southeast in the Piedmont and Appalachian Highlands, in the Watts Bar, Swannanoa, Badin, and Kellogg-Dunlap culture areas, located in Figure 6.10. The ceramics were tempered with coarse sand, grit, crushed quartz, and limestone. Vessels were made into jars and simple bowls, and the exteriors were covered with impressions of a fabric-wrapped paddle or dowel. This ceramic tradition was continued by the Colbert, Long Branch, Pigeon, and Yadkin cultures, located in Figure 6.11, in the latter half of the late Woodland.

By about 500 B.C., the South Appalachian tradition of stamped pottery developed in the Cartersville and Deptford culture areas on the Atlantic coast and east Gulf Coastal Plain. Evidence suggests that this tradition developed out of the Refuge culture pottery decoration technique of dentate stamping made with small, notched implements. The early Appalachian stamped designs include simple, linear check, and bold check. Vessel shapes and sizes were similar to those found elsewhere in the region; small to large open-mouthed jars and bowls and large podal supports were common.

The early Woodland chipped stone tool assemblage was similar to that of the Archaic period with some stylistic changes, as shown in Figure 6.9. Stemmed points were made throughout the area, but there was a general reduction in size. In the eastern portion of the region, there was 50–75% reduction in the size of the former large, broad-bladed point style of the late Archaic period, and stems and shoulders continued to be well defined.[11] Several regional differences in shape are seen. A new stemless point type was developed in the north, and side notching was revived in the Carolinas. In central Tennessee and the Piedmont of North Carolina, a stemless, triangular-blade chipped stone point known as the McFarland or Badin type was adopted during this period. This style may have diffused from the Northeast where it developed earlier. In the western portion of the Southeast, stone points retained a fairly well-defined stem, and were about 50% smaller than previous late Archaic points. Point blades in this region were both triangular (Wade, Weems types) and lanceolate (Flint Creek type).

The raw material used for chipped stone tools changed along the Coastal Plain of Georgia and South Carolina between 1000 and 500 B.C. (especially in the Refuge culture). During the Archaic stage, the primary raw materials were imported, but during the early Woodland period local stone was used almost exclusively.

---

[11] See Oliver, 1985, for a summary of projectile point style evolution in North Carolina.

Containers of steatite and sandstone were used in the western part of the Southeast only during the very early portion of this period. Ornamental items such as two-hole gorgets and beads of stone and shell continued to be popular in the western portion of the region, particularly in the Mississippi, Tombigbee, and central Tennessee valleys. A new ground and polished stone item was the tubular "pipe." Tobacco (*Nicotiana rustica*) was apparently a very late introduction into the eastern Woodlands. Paleoethnobotanist Richard Yarnell has identified 27 native plants that were used for smoking by Indians in the historic period in the upper Great Lakes. These included willow and dogwood bark, sumac leaves, and goldenrod flowers.[12] During the historic period, Indians in the East smoked in a symbolic and ritual manner, rather than as a daily habit, and it is inferred that this practice was followed by prehistoric Indians. Because smoke is associated with fire, which had great symbolic importance, smoking pipes were used to produce puffs of smoke at rituals, ceremonies, and political meetings (e.g., the "peace pipe" ceremony). Shamans also used smoke in medicinal treatments.

Mortuary Patterns

Burial customs of early Woodland societies were similar to those of the late Archaic. Graves were usually scattered throughout the larger villages in round pits 3 to 4 ft in diameter, with the body placed on its side in a tightly flexed position. People were also buried in extended or sitting positions. In the middle Tennessee Valley large stones were sometimes placed over the top of burial pits. Grave goods were uncommon and consisted of utilitarian items and such ornaments as gorgets and beads for the most part.

A few southeastern cultures, including St. Johns, Deptford, Tchefuncte, and perhaps the Gulf Deptford, incorporated some elements of the Adena Ceremonial Complex in their burials between about 500 B.C. and A.D. 0, but the mounds in these areas did not contain Adena-type prestige items. The mounds contained flesh burials and secondary burials that had been processed and stored as bone bundles until final burial. Deptford burial mounds were built over subterranean tombs (often containing several people) with other burials placed in mound fill. Deptford grave goods included ceramic vessels, a few chipped stone points from imported stone, and some mica. Because St. Johns burial mounds in Florida usually contained more people, more than 25 bodies on average, they appear to have been general community cemeteries.[13]

[12] For details about this study see Yarnell, 1964.

[13] For more information about the St. Johns mortuary practices see Milanich and Fairbanks, 1980.

Settlement Pattern

For the most part, the settlement pattern of the early Woodland societies in the Southeast remained unchanged from the late Archaic period. Societies were composed of related families who were firmly tied to specific areas of the coast or a river valley. These kin groups had one or two base camps where they remained for much of the year. The camps were positioned at strategically located sites providing access to a wide range of resources. Smaller, special-purpose satellite camps were used for short-term stays by small groups procuring food and other supplies. Base camps developed thick middens and features such as pits and postholes, and human burials resulted from the concentration of people and domestic activity. In shellfish areas, such as along the Gulf coast and the St. Johns and central Tennessee rivers, large shell middens formed.

Summary

The early Woodland period was characterized by the widespread distribution of pottery throughout the Southeast, and by a reduction in the size of chipped stone points. The use of stone containers faded away, and the ground stone pipe was added to the artifact assemblage. Hunting, gathering, and fishing continued as the primary subsistence strategies, as did the base camp–satellite camp settlement pattern. Sociopolitical organization remained an egalitarian one, as evidenced by the burial pattern.

Examples of Early Woodland Cultures

Many early Woodland cultures have been identified in the Southeast, as indicated in Figure 6.1 and Figures 6.10 and 6.11. Because it is impossible to present all the archaeological information known about each of these cultures, only representative culture areas for each period are covered in this section. This necessarily excludes many archaeological cultures and sites. The example cultures that follow are those about which there is considerable published information and which were located in different geographical areas.

Refuge Culture

The Refuge culture existed on the Atlantic coast of Georgia and South Carolina between 1100 and 400 B.C.[14] Whereas aquatic resources of the coast continued to be exploited, they were not nearly as important as during the earlier late Archaic period. Refuge settlements in the coastal zone consisted mainly of small sites on well-drained soils and large sites along rivers and bays. By about 1000 B.C., the large shell middens and rings on the coast and

---

[14] For details on the Refuge culture see DePratter, 1976, Sassaman, 1993, Sassaman *et al.*, 1990, and Williams, 1977.

flood plain were abandoned, and Refuge sites became smaller and were more widely dispersed both in the coastal zone and in the uplands.

The fluctuation in sea level and consequent degradation of the coastal and lower riverine habitats may have caused the Refuge subsistence and settlement pattern changes. However, this does not appear to have caused major problems in Refuge societies. Rochelle Marrinan's study of the animal bones from the drowned Refuge midden on St. Simons Island showed a shift in subsistence strategy to include more reptiles (such as alligators and turtles) and mammals (such as deer and small mammals) to replace fish and shellfish.[15] The same shift is assumed to have occurred in Refuge groups living in the river valleys. Here subsistence emphasis shifted to hunting to make up for the loss of shellfish and fish. In the river valleys, increased hunting led to a settlement pattern shift to the uplands, where animals are more plentiful and more easily hunted. Refuge societies appear to have adjusted their subsistence strategy to meet the slowly changing conditions while maintaining the same standard of living.

The artifact assemblage of the Refuge culture reflects the adjustments made in subsistence primarily through the increased use of stone tools. This shift is interpreted as reflecting an increased importance of hunting. Another distinguishing characteristic of Refuge assemblages is the presence of pieces of pottery (sherds) used as abraders. In a study of the 150 sherd abraders found on St. Catherines Island, David Hurst Thomas and Clark Spencer Larsen found that most had rounded or flat edges, which was probably caused by rubbing them over soft animal skin during hide preparation, or in processing plant fibers.

The pottery made by Refuge societies indicates that it evolved directly from late Archaic pottery.[16] Pottery clay that had been tempered with coarse sand was now tempered with fine sand. Early in the period, pottery surfaces were decorated in typical Gulf pottery tradition styles, with incised and punctated designs often restricted to a band parallel to the rim. Later, the South Appalachian tradition stamping technique developed in this area, likely from dentate stamping, and it soon dominated pottery surfaces. Early check stamping consisted of small, rhomboid or diamond-shaped checks, line-filled triangles, nested diamonds, and other motifs that were applied very carefully.

Late Poverty Point Culture

In the lower and central Mississippi Valley, the florescence of Poverty Point culture occurred between 1200 and 800 B.C.[17] During this period there was substantial interaction between Poverty Point societies at regional centers such as the Claiborne, Teoc Creek, and the Poverty Point site. Most regional

[15] See Marrinan, 1975, for details on the St. Simon's Island shell ring investigations.

[16] For details on Refuge pottery see DePratter, 1976, 1979, and Phelps, 1968.

[17] For details about Poverty Point culture see C. Webb, 1982.

centers consisted of horseshoe-shaped ring middens with mounds that appear to have been laid out according to specific astrological orientations. Long-distance trade in lapidary items, marine shells, steatite vessels, and copper continued. The Poverty Point culture declined between about 800 and 500 B.C. While the causes of this decline are not understood, it is apparent that mound construction ceased, population shrank at the regional centers, and new smaller sites were established along main waterways. Steatite vessels were no longer imported, but were replaced by ceramic containers made from local clays, and the use of clay baking balls declined. The use of imported red jasper for lapidary items almost disappeared, as did the rest of the trade network. What caused the decline of this extraordinary culture remains a mystery.

Tchefuncte Culture

Tchefuncte culture emerged from the late Poverty Point between 600 and 500 B.C. in the lower Mississippi Valley and lasted until about A.D. 200. Originally identified by James Ford and George Quimby in 1945, the Tchefuncte culture was named for a shell midden by that name on Lake Ponchartrain, located in Figure 6.12.[18]

The Tchefuncte culture area extended between east Texas and the Mississippi Coast, as shown in Figure 6.10, and is dominated by the mouth of the Mississippi River. This 500-mi belt of marshy wetlands is crossed by a series of river mouths and dotted with large, shallow lakes such as Lake Ponchartrain near New Orleans, Louisiana. This belt of wetlands is one of the largest biomass areas in North America. Because it is low and wet, locations suitable for human settlements were restricted. The area slowly sinks from the weight of the muds deposited by the Mississippi River; this process is called subsidence.

The most distinctive material trait of this culture is Tchefuncte pottery, which is soft, unskillfully fired and finished, and made from poorly prepared inferior clays. The pottery is of such poor quality that no intact vessels have been found. Experiments have shown that the problems are related to the inferior quality of the local clay. Surfaces were decorated in Gulf pottery tradition styles by incising, pinching, rocker stamping, and punctating. Red painting and cord marking were occasionally used. Typical open-mouthed jars or tubby pots with podal supports or ring bases are shown in Figure 6.9. Ceramic tubular pipes about 6 in. long and 2 in. in diameter were also made. Clay baking balls continued to be made in the same styles as during the previous Poverty Point period.

Based on the distribution of different ceramic traits, seven Tchefuncte phases or societies have been defined.[19] The type-variety method of ceramic

---

[18] For a summary and further reading on Tchefuncte see Aten, 1984, Shenkel, 1984, and Weinstein, 1986.

[19] See Weinstein, 1986, for details on Tchefuncte pottery.

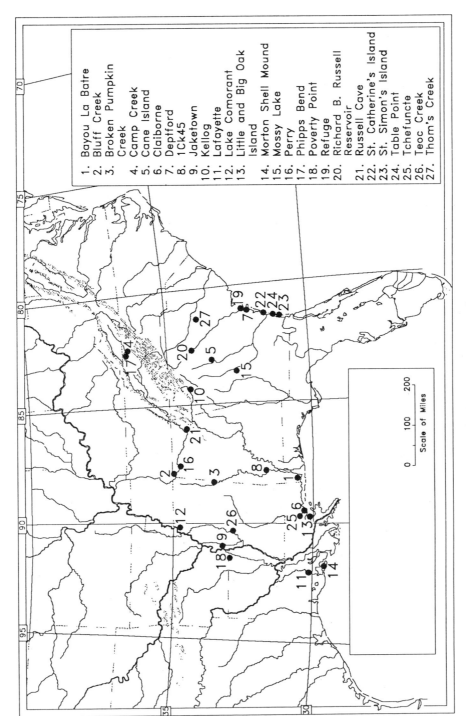

1. Bayou La Batre
2. Bluff Creek
3. Broken Pumpkin
   Creek
4. Camp Creek
5. Cane Island
6. Claiborne
7. Deptford
8. 1Ck45
9. Jaketown
10. Kellog
11. Lafayette
12. Lake Comorant
13. Little and Big Oak
    Island
14. Morton Shell Mound
15. Mossy Lake
16. Perry
17. Phipps Bend
18. Poverty Point
19. Refuge
20. Richard B. Russell
    Reservoir
21. Russell Cave
22. St. Catherine's Island
23. St. Simon's Island
24. Table Point
25. Tchefuncte
26. Teoc Creek
27. Thom's Creek

Scale of Miles

0   100   200

FIGURE 6.12 Early Woodland sites.

classification was used to identify, organize, and map the different phases. This system is similar to the genus-species classification system of plants and animals. For example, one *genus* of animals usually includes several *species* that have slightly different physical traits. In ceramic analysis, one *type* of pottery usually includes several *varieties* that have slightly different physical traits. This pottery classification system, which is also used in many other areas, was pioneered by Mississippi Valley archaeologists, especially Phillip Phillips.[20] Scores of individual phases or societies have been defined by this method in the Woodland and Mississippian periods throughout the central and lower Mississippi Valley.

Tchefuncte subsistence has been studied in a few large shell midden base campsites, such as Big and Little Oak Island on lake Ponchartrain and the Morton Shell Mound near Weeks Island.[21] Animal bones were well preserved in these sites, and the Morton Shell Mound had a peat layer below the shell midden that was full of well-preserved plant and animal remains. Studies indicate that a wide variety of plants and animals were consumed and that the primary meats were deer, alligator, turtle, fish, gar, and catfish. Common wild plant foods included acorns, hickory nuts, plums, grapes, and persimmons. Cultigens included squash, bottle gourd, and pumpkin. Tchefuncte subsistence was based on hunting, gathering, and fishing in the wetlands and nearby uplands. It is presumed that squash and bottle gourds were grown for use as containers rather than as food, as was the case in earlier periods. Surprisingly, there are no Tchefuncte sites along the Mississippi River or its major tributaries; this may reflect an economic focus on backwater swamps and marshes.

Tchefuncte sites include both shell and earth middens. The settlement pattern was the familiar base camp–satellite camp system used throughout the Southeast. Base camps were situated on the highest local elevations close to a wide variety of ecosystems, with smaller short-term extraction sites nearby. "Midden mounds" similar to ones that formed in the Archaic in the upper Tombigbee and St. Johns valleys developed at Tchefuncte base camps. Other than hearths, only a few features have been found at Tchefuncte base camps and no complete structures have been found.

Most people were buried without grave goods in shallow pits in their settlements. About half of the burials were primary and in the extended position, while the rest were bundles of bones. One cemetery with at least 29 individuals was encountered at Big Oak Island on Lake Ponchartrain.

There has been some debate over the existence of Tchefuncte burial mounds at near Lafayette, Louisiana.[22] Most agree that at least one of the

---

[20] See P. Phillips, 1970, for details about the type-variety in pottery classification.

[21] For details about the Morton Shell Mound see Byrd, 1974, 1976; for Oak Island see Shenkel, 1980.

[22] For more about Tchefuncte burial mounds see Gibson, 1974, Gibson and Shenkel, 1988, and Weinstein, 1986.

four mounds at the Lafayette site was built during the Tchefuncte period. Excavated by Edwin Doran and Robert Neitzel in 1941, it was 5 ft high, 60 ft wide at the base, and it covered a prepared surface from which the humus had been removed, and on which several structures were built. Thirty burials, both primary and secondary, had been placed without grave goods on the prepared surface and on the floor of the structures. The mound was then built over the structures and burials. Because Tchefuncte pottery was recovered from the submound midden and the mound fill, the mound and burials are associated with the Tchefuncte culture.

Three other multiple mound sites near Lafayette are tentatively attributed to the Tchefuncte culture. Jon Gibson interprets these low conical mound centers as communal burial places for a generally dispersed population. The absence of Adena ceremonial items indicates that there was little, if any, interaction with the Midwest. The presence of primary and bundle burials in the Tchefuncte mounds was a new development. Archaic mounds had contained only a few cremations and prestige items, such as carved stone effigy beads.

Kellog-Dunlap and Swannanoa Cultures

The Kellog-Dunlap culture in the Piedmont of Georgia existed between about 800 and 200 B.C. Early in this period, pottery surface finishes were dominated by fabric marking, but by 500 B.C. simple stamping and check stamping were more popular. Chipped stone point styles included both stemmed and unstemmed types with triangular blades, although the unstemmed triangular McFarland type was more numerous. Biconvex mortars and slate hoes have also been found in Kellog-Dunlap sites in northwest Georgia.

It appears that the Kellog-Dunlap population was concentrated in northwest Georgia. Research has revealed low numbers of sites with meager artifacts elsewhere. These include many base camps with abundant features and artifacts. The Kellog base campsite near Rome, Georgia, excavated by Joseph Caldwell, contained at least 10 cooking hearths and ovens, 60 storage pits, and a cluster of postholes suggesting a structure.[23] Nearly all the pits contained carbonized acorns. Hickory nuts and walnuts were also found. In several pits, the carbonized nutshells formed thick layers at the bottom, and one pit contained a complete pot with carbonized acorns. Unfortunately, few animal bones were preserved at this (or any other) Kellog-Dunlap site. The pits were cylindrical in shape (occasionally bell-shaped) and averaged about 3 ft in depth and width. Some pits appear to have been lined with vegetable material, and some show evidence of having had a fire in them.

Kellog-Dunlap societies continued the hunting, gathering, and fishing subsistence pattern established during the Archaic stage, with perhaps more emphasis placed on plant foods. In northwest Georgia, Kellog-Dunlap settle-

---

[23] For more details about the Kellog site excavation see Caldwell, 1958.

ments were concentrated on the narrow flood plains adjacent streams. These base camps covered about 1 acre, and some had middens several feet thick.

Fabric-marked pottery of the nearby Swannanoa culture in the Appalachian Mountains was very similar to that made during the early Kellog-Dunlap area.[24] Cord marking and simple and check stamping were used and vessel shapes were large wide-mouthed jars and simple bowls. The remainder of the Swannanoa artifact assemblage is similar to other nearby early Woodland cultures: small stemmed and stemless chipped stone points, bar gorgets, bone awls, pitted and pebble hammerstones, ground stone celts, net weights, and bone fishhooks. An atlatl with antler handles and bone hooks, along with a cane spear shaft with replaceable foreshaft tips, was found in the Swannanoa deposit at the Phipps Bend site in northeast Tennessee.

Dispersed small sites characterized the settlement pattern in the mountainous area. According to Bennie Keel, this pattern reflects a continuation of the broad-based economic strategy developed in the previous Archaic stage. In the Phipps Bend area of the Tennessee Valley flood plain, Robert Lafferty documented a settlement pattern similar to that of the Kellog-Dunlap culture.[25] Base camps were large with thick, rich middens and abundant cylindrical pits. Subsistence studies revealed a wide range of land animals such as deer, elk, beaver, turkey, and squirrel were eaten. Shellfish and nuts were also a part of the diet. A wide variety of plants including goosefoot or lamb's-quarter, persimmons, grapes, honey locusts, and grass seeds were also gathered. Base camps were occupied year-round and temporary upland sites were used largely for gathering nuts. Phipps Bend Swannanoa burials were found only at base camps, and individuals were flexed, placed in round pits, and accompanied by both utilitarian and ornamental items. One male burial had a necklace of perforated bear teeth, an antler handle, bifaces, points, and 146 pieces of pottery.

Summary of the Early Woodland Period

The early Woodland period was marked by the spread of pottery throughout the Southeast and the emergence of the four pottery traditions. Clay was tempered with sand, crushed stone, shell, or grog. Containers were made by coiling, and the paddle and anvil technique was used to weld the coils into thin, high-walled containers. Chipped stone points smaller than those made in the Archaic stage were usually stemmed with triangular blades. A stemless, triangular, concave base point type developed inside the Fall Line. Early Woodland societies remained reliant on hunting, gathering, and fishing. However, as in the Refuge culture area on the Atlantic coast, adjustments were made to adapt to changing conditions. Elements of the Adena Ceremonial

---

[24] For more about Kellog-Dunlap pottery see Keel, 1976, and Lafferty, 1981.

[25] For details on the archaeology at Phipps Bend, see Lafferty, 1981.

Complex were practiced in a few cultural areas in the Southeast during this period and some burial mounds were built. Some people were buried with imported prestige items, but interaction between groups was limited to intermittent trade.

MIDDLE WOODLAND PERIOD: A.D. 0–500

The middle Woodland period is marked by the spread of the Hopewellian ceremonial complex and the associated construction of mounds by many societies in the region. The diagnostic indicators of the middle Woodland period are shifts in local pottery types and the spread of Hopewellian traits. Long-distance trade in prestige goods escalated as the ceremonial complex spread south from the Midwest. New prehistoric periods have been documented throughout the region (see Table 6.1 and Figure 6.13). The transition from the early to middle Woodland was smooth, and by about A.D. 0, the progression was almost complete. The acceleration of plant cultivation in the central Tennessee Valley was another important, though more limited, middle Woodland development.

Environment

The climate and environment of the Southeast were stable during this millennium. Environmental conditions in the Southeast were similar to those of today and sea levels appear to have stabilized to within 10 ft of the modern position.

Material Culture

During the middle Woodland period, South Appalachian pottery dominated the area east of the Tombigbee Valley. Pottery designs changed significantly, with complex curvilinear designs (complicated stamping) becoming popular as shown in Figures 6.5 and 6.14. Check stamping was continued in some areas.

In the western part of the Southeast, pottery continued to be decorated in the Gulf tradition style. In the lower Mississippi Valley, a better-quality pottery tempered with grog (crushed pottery) replaced the low-quality Tchefuncte pottery. As elsewhere in the Southeast, podal supports became less popular and smaller.

The Middle Eastern and Northern pottery traditions continued to be popular in the northern portions of the Southeast. While surfaces marked with cord and fabric remained the rule, a new surface treatment, brushing, was initiated. Tempering agents also changed. In the Tennessee Valley, sand was

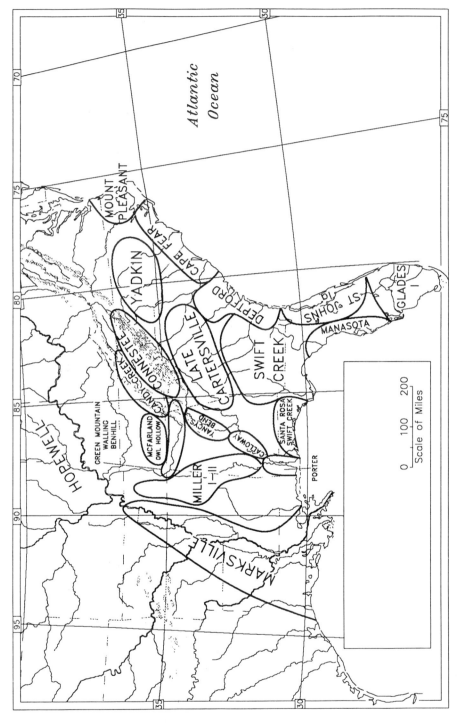

FIGURE 6.13 Middle Woodland culture areas.

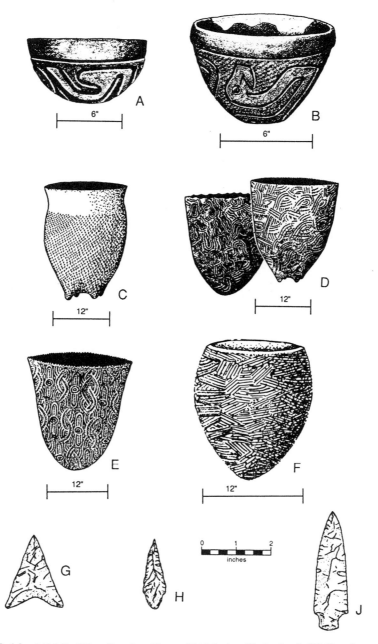

FIGURE 6.14 Middle Woodland artifacts: (A) Marksville incised; (B) Crooks stamped; (C) Cartersville check stamped; (D, E) Swift Creek complicated stamped; (F) Furrs cord marked; (G) Yadkin triangular; (H) Bradley spike, (I)Tchefuncte point. (A and B from Griffin, 1952, with permission of the University of Chicago Press, copyright © 1952, by The University of Chicago. All rights reserved; C–E reproduced by permission of the American Anthropological Association from MEMOIR NO. 88 of the American Anthropological Association. Not for further reproduction.)

replaced by limestone, and in the Carolinas, tempering agents included sand, grit, grog, and some crushed shell.

Chipped stone point styles during the middle Woodland period varied in the Southeast, as shown in Figure 6.14. In Tennessee and the Carolinas, the small square-stemmed points were no longer made, and triangular, concave base points (Yadkin and McFarland) became popular. In the southern part of the region, stemmed triangular-blade points, similar to the Tombigbee stemmed type, continued to be popular along with the expanded-stemmed, lanceolate-blade Flint Creek types. In the upper Tombigbee Valley, small thick points called "spikes" developed.

Hopewellian Ceremonial Complex and Sociopolitical Organization

Burial practices during the middle Woodland changed in many areas with the advent of the Hopewellian ceremonial complex in the Midwest and its subsequent diffusion into the Southeast. The Hopewellian ceremonial complex was a belief system shared by various local and regional cultures which otherwise were quite independent. Local pottery, chipped stone point styles, and subsistence methods persisted. Societies participating in the Hopewellian ceremonial complex shared a system of beliefs, status symbols, mortuary rituals, and ceremonial earthwork construction.

The Hopewellian ceremonial complex and its mortuary practices allows archaeologists to better understand changes in middle Woodland sociopolitical organization. Burial practices are one of the clearest expressions of the social organization of a community. The way people are treated in death is closely related to their status and role in life. Details of the mortuary customs of an extinct society are used to understand their social structure. The mortuary ceremonialism of Hopewellian cultures indicates that their sociopolitical organization was becoming more complex and that cultural evolution was taking place.

In most Hopewellian societies, prepared human remains, both fresh and stored, were placed in and under dome-shaped mounds at periodic intervals. The switch from scattered individual burials in settlements to a system of formal, planned, periodic burials in mounds means more than just a new way to bury people. This is an indication that the people buried in the mounds shared something, possibly descent from a common ancestor. The practice of initial processing of corpses and storage of human remains in a charnel house was fairly common throughout the Southeast during this period. What triggered mass burial events is not well understood. It may have been the death of a lineage leader or a special religious or celestial event such as a solstice. When such an event occurred, it appears that the charnel house was emptied, and often burned, and a mass burial took place.

Sociopolitical organization had advanced to the multicommunity level in some Hopewellian societies. This is most evident at the Hopewellian mound centers that had different burial treatment and locations for particular groups of people. It is apparent that some people had attained more power and wealth than the people interred in local community burial mounds. At mound centers, there is clear segregation of burials, differences in corpse treatment, and an unequal distribution of grave goods. These factors reflect a new and more complex sociopolitical organization in which a particular type of leader, called a "Big Man" or "Big Woman" emerged.[26] This type of sociopolitical organization is classified as a segmented lineage or tribe. It was first recognized in Melanesia and since has been documented in many other aboriginal cultures around the world. It is a step in cultural evolution between the band and chiefdom levels of social complexity. Ambitious and clever individuals can obtain enough wealth and power to elevate their lineage above others. However, the power of the lineage is not permanent and is not necessarily inherited by the descendants of the leader.

During the middle Woodland period in the Southeast, Big Men and Big Women seem to have risen to positions of wealth and power by acquiring Hopewellian prestige items through shrewd trading and political maneuvering. As a consequence, these individuals were able to dominate the local trade in such items. According to Bruce Smith, a rich assortment of raw materials and finished products entered and moved through a complex and ever-changing web of Big Men and Big Women who rose to power through the generations. Mound centers appear to have been the ritual centers for Big Men and Big Women, and they are usually located along the major rivers and trail systems at critical points connecting Hopewellian raw material source areas. The Hopewellian status and ritual system provided a mechanism for cultural evolution, and mortuary rituals preserved the steps in this evolution.

The Hopewellian ceremonial complex was centered in the Midwest. Differences in its expression increased with geographic distance. Cultures along the Atlantic Coastal Plain participated very little, if at all, in Hopewellian ceremonialism, while those located in major north-south river valleys participated more extensively. Cultures in the Southeast never reached the level of complexity of Ohio Hopewell. All Hopewellian cultures shared three basic features: mound building, Hopewellian ceramics, and a suite of personal ornaments and raw materials.

Hopewellian societies built more mounds than any preceding culture. The most mounds were low domes and cones about 5 ft high and 50 ft in diameter at the base. Dome- and conical-shaped mounds covered the remains of high-status people buried in the flesh in tombs and burial pits. Secondary burials of bone bundles and cremations are usually found near the central interments and in the mound fill covering them.

A new type of mound, the platform mound, was developed during the middle Woodland period. They were generally under 10 ft tall, rectangular,

---

[26] For details on Big Man and Big Woman see Sahlins, 1963, 1968, 1972, and Smith, 1986.

with dimensions between 50 and 75 ft. Once thought to be exclusively a Mississippian period construction, it is now apparent that platform mounds were built from the middle Woodland period onward. The largest and oldest of the southeastern middle Woodland platform mounds are at the Pinson mound center in southwestern Tennessee. Other middle Woodland platform mounds include a 25 ft-high ramped platform mound at the Ingomar mound center in northeastern Mississippi, the Marksville mound center in southeastern Louisiana, the Leake site in northwestern Georgia, the Mandeville site in southwest Georgia, and the Walling site in northern Alabama. The summits of these platform mounds usually have kitchen midden deposits, cooking features, and remains of large posts. Special studies of the artifacts, features, and food remains from the platform mounds reveal important clues about their use.

The Walling platform mound, excavated most recently by Vernon J. Knight, was a low mound approximately 4.5 ft high with a series of buried summits that had midden accumulations and hearths, pits, and postmolds.[27] Three large posts had been erected in a line and removed prior to surface repair of one of the summits. The mound contained a more diverse range of artifacts and foods than did the adjacent settlement. Animal bones consisted primarily of meat-bearing portions of older deer. Plant foods consisted of small seeds from grasses and greens, oily seeds, fleshy fruits, and a small quantity of maize and squash. Knight suggests the mound summits were used for communal food preparation and feasting. The platform mound may have been used by elite individuals who were supplied with special foods and who made and used special objects. Other middle Woodland platform mounds contained similar archaeological remains, and it appears they shared common functions.

The suite of special Hopewellian items includes panpipes, earspools, mica cutouts, shell cups, greenstone celts, ornaments of shell and stone, special pottery, and lumps of galena and ocher. Special pottery was common in Hopewellian mounds. Vessels included beakers, bowls, jars, and "tubby" pots. These small pots had flat bases, folded rims decorated with cross-hatched lines or punctations, and bodies decorated with incised and rocker-stamped geometric patterns and bird motifs. Hopewellian items were often placed as grave goods with the primary burials, although caches have also been found in mounds. The distribution of Hopewellian items was quite uneven, and most have been found at the larger mound centers.

There has been considerable research on the origins and distribution patterns of Hopewellian items in the Southeast.[28] It appears that Hopewellian items and raw materials from the Midwest and Great Lakes initially entered the Southeast at mound centers in the Tennessee Valley and northwest Geor-

[27] For details of the Walling Mound excavation see Knight, 1990.

[28] For studies on Hopewellian trade see Caldwell and Hall, 1964, Goad, 1979, and Walthall, 1973.

gia. Some of these imports were traded down the Chattahoochee River and into Florida where they are found in mound centers. After A.D. 150, imports decreased and copies were made from local materials and exchanged within the Southeast. As Sharon Goad states, late middle Woodland exchange in the Southeast appears to have been more intraregional than interregional.

The wide distribution of Hopewellian items, mortuary practices, and mound centers indicates a strong similarity in belief systems in the Midwest and Southeast during this period. There were direct connections between Ohio and Florida down the west side of the Appalachians, and from Illinois down the Mississippi River and up the Tennessee River. James B. Griffin suggests that Ohio and Illinois societies in the Hopewell heartland were the dominant exchange partners.

There probably were well over a thousand Hopewellian mounds built in the Southeast, but fewer than 50 multiple-mound centers were built, some of which are located in Figure 6.15. Multiple-mound centers are the best-known and most-visited archaeological sites in the Southeast, and this book would not be complete without descriptions of some of the most outstanding. Other prominent Hopewellian mound centers will be included in the representative culture area descriptions that follow.

Marksville Mound Center

One of the best known Hopewellian ceremonial centers is in Marksville, Louisiana, center of the classic Hopewellian culture in the lower Mississippi Valley for which most Hopewellian pottery in the Southeast is named.[29] The ceremonial area includes three earth enclosures along a bluff on a former channel of the Mississippi, shown in Figure 6.16. The largest earthwork is a C-shaped embankment enclosing an area about 1500 ft in diameter, which has three conical and two rectangular platform mounds. Just to the south is a small, circular earth enclosure about 300 ft in diameter lacking mounds. A northern embankment encloses a point of land with one rectangular platform mound. A number of small conical mounds are scattered along the edge of the bluff to the north, but of these only Mound 8, a Marksville burial mound, has been investigated. Several small circular embankments outside the main enclosures are believed to be house locations.

Mound 4, excavated in the federal work relief experiment in 1933, began as a rectangular hard clay platform 5 ft high and at least 25 ft on a side. A structure, probably a crematory, was built on this platform, and a burial vault was excavated into it. A number of flesh burials were placed in this vault, which was then covered with a log roof and sealed with seven alternating layers of cane mats and clay. Many cremations were placed on the clay platform surface, which was then covered with two layers of earth in which a few burials were scattered. This mound is conical, 25 ft tall, and 100 ft in diameter

[29] See Toth, 1974, for details on the Marksville excavations.

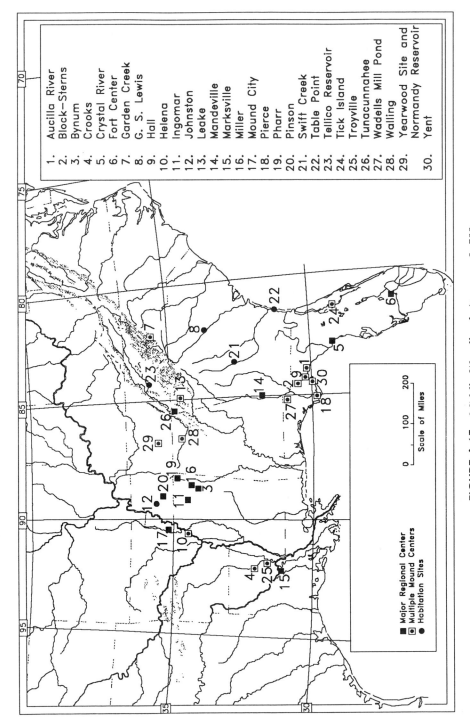

1. Aucilla River
2. Block–Sterns
3. Bynum
4. Crooks
5. Crystal River
6. Fort Center
7. Garden Creek
8. G. S. Lewis
9. Hall
10. Helena
11. Ingomar
12. Johnston
13. Leake
14. Mandeville
15. Marksville
16. Miller
17. Mound City
18. Pierce
19. Pharr
20. Pinson
21. Swift Creek
22. Table Point
23. Tellico Reservoir
24. Tick Island
25. Troyville
26. Tunacunnahee
27. Wadells Mill Pond
28. Walling
29. Yearwood Site and
    Normandy Reservoir
30. Yent

■ Major Regional Center
▣ Multiple Mound Centers
● Habitation Sites

Scale of Miles
0   100   200

FIGURE 6.15 Middle Woodland sites A.D. 0–500.

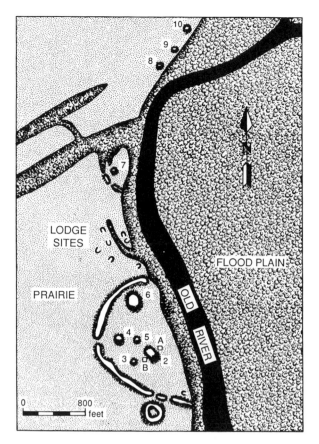

FIGURE 6.16 Map of the Marksville site, a Hopewellian mound center near Marksville, Louisiana. (From Toth, 1974.)

at the base. Later, additional burials were placed in the mound surface along with Hopewellian pottery vessels and clay platform pipes. A total of 12 people were buried in Mound 4, including males, females, infants, and children.

Mound 5 is also a conical mound, 70 ft in basal diameter and only 3.5 ft high. It too covered a clay platform. Mound 8, to the north on the bluff, was 80 ft in diameter and 15 ft tall. It did not cover a clay platform; rather, it covered burial pits lined with cane mats. Mound 6 is a platform mound that has an oval to circular base about 300 ft in diameter. It is 13 ft high. Early reports indicate it may have had a conical mound on its summit. Little is known about the platform mounds.

Within the enclosure, just east of Mound 2, were the remains of a rectangular structure, 20 × 25 ft, lined on two sides by posts. Inside, there was a large central pit 8 × 15 ft with posts at each corner, with a layer of burned cane fragments, logs, and charcoal on the bottom. There was also a clay hearth and an artifact cache. This structure may have been a crematorium, and the pit was likely used for cremations.

Helena Mound Center

About 225 mi up the Mississippi Valley from Marksville is the Helena mound center, near Memphis, Tennessee. It had five conical burial mounds, each about 100 ft in basal diameter and 15–20 ft high. Excavated by James Ford in 1960, Mound C covered five log-roofed tombs, four of which had been excavated into the original ground surface and buried under a mound of earth.[30] A fifth tomb was excavated through the first mound layer. At a later time, five groups of burials and an isolated skull had been placed on the surface of the first mound. These were covered with a second and final mantle of earth. Mound B covered only one log tomb and was built in a single episode.

The Mound C tombs contained from one and four people in both the extended and flexed positions. Many of the extended burials had bands of shell beads on their wrists, upper arms, ankles, and necks, and one wore a belt made of perforated wolf canines. These items, plus the recovery of several pieces of fabric, indicate that the bodies had been elaborately dressed when they were buried. Many exceptional Hopewellian items accompanied the individuals buried in this mound, some of which are shown in Figure 6.17. For example, the person in Tomb A had on his chest a musical instrument called a panpipe made from cane tubes covered with copper and which still contained the wooden plugs used to set the pitch in two of the tubes. A copper earspool was in each of his hands. On top of a bundle burial of a female in the center of Tomb E was a thin cylinder of copper, 10 × 2 in. in size, which apparently had been a ferrule or band placed over the end of a wooden staff. It was decorated with a cutout design. Other prestige items in burials included conch cups, a sheet of mica, and prismatic blades. Hopewellian pottery was also placed with burials, and there were caches of intentionally broken pots found in the fill of both mounds. The tombs were usually rectangular in shape, lined with logs, and covered by a log roof. The largest tomb was 11 × 7 ft. It had large logs along two sides and the roof and had been intensely burned, leaving a 2-ft-thick layer of fired earth above it.

The tombs and grave goods at Helena are the richest and most extensive Hopewellian assemblage yet excavated in the Mississippi Valley, and the materials more closely parallel Illinois Hopewellian tombs and their contents than those of any other site in the Southeast. The radiocarbon dates from the two excavated mounds were between 140 B.C. and A.D. 335. However, Alan Toth, a Marksville specialist, estimates that the burials probably took place about A.D. 100 to 200.

---

[30] See Ford, 1963, for details on the excavation at the Helena Mounds.

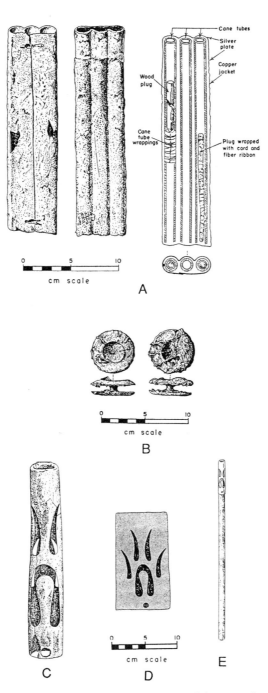

Cane tubes

Silver plate

Wood plug

Copper jacket

Cane tube wrappings

Plug wrapped with cord and fiber ribbon

0 5 10

cm scale

A

0 5 10

cm scale

B

0 5 10

cm scale

C

D

E

FIGURE 6.17 Hopewellian prestige items recovered from tombs at the Helena site, a Hopewellian mound center in Helena, Arkansas: (A) copper-covered panpipe, (B) copper earspools, (C) copper tube, probably a staff ferrule, (D) cutout design on the ferrule, (E) probable use of copper ferrule. (From Ford, 1963.)

Tunacunnahee Mound Center

A different version of a Hopewellian burial mound center is Tunacunnahee in northwest Georgia. This group of four low mounds and an adjacent settlement were investigated by Richard Jefferies in 1973.[31] The mounds were small, 12–45 ft in basal diameter and only 3–5 ft tall. Each mound covered a single tomb containing a single extended burial and a wide variety of Hopewellian items. For example, on the floor of the tomb below Mound C, dated at A.D. 150 ± 95, was what appears to be a baglike container with a rectangular copper plate, two sets of copper earspools, a copper pin, and a string of bone beads. Other artifacts on the floor of the tomb included a concentration of shark vertebrae and teeth, two human mandibles, a drilled bear canine, and a prismatic chert blade. The burial below Mound D had silver- and copper-covered panpipes, four platform pipes, a tubular pipe, a mica cutout, drilled bear canines, a copper breastplate, a quartz crystal biface, and a polished stone gorget. Three of the tombs were covered with a mound of earth capped with a layer of limestone rocks from the local area. One mound was built completely of limestone rocks and had a stone "apron" on one side. Thirty-six burials were recovered from the mounds. Jefferies identified three different groups of burials that shared burial treatment and offerings which may correlate with different social ranks.

Non-Hopewellian Societies

The culture areas that were relatively minor participants in the Hopewellian Interaction Sphere did not experience growth during the middle Woodland period. Some, like the Cartersville and Yancy's Bend culture areas, experienced a reduction in settlement size, site facilities (pits and structures), and midden accumulation during this period. Because the preceding Kellog-Dunlap culture had large base camps with abundant pits and thick deposits of midden, there has been much speculation concerning this decrease, especially in the Cartersville culture. What really happened is not known. Cartersville settlements were more numerous in the upper Savannah River and researchers attribute this to a high seasonal population.[32] Both the Cartersville and Yancy's Bend cultures built stone burial mounds, and they also placed their dead in natural cave tombs. Hopewellian items such as greenstone celts, copper breastplates, beads, and reels were placed with the dead in mounds and caves. People were also buried in villages, usually with sparse grave goods.

---

[31] See Jefferies, 1976 and 1979, for details about the Tunachunnee mound center excavations.

[32] For a summary see Anderson and Joseph, 1988, and Garrow, 1975.

Subsistence and Settlement Patterns

The middle Woodland cultures in the Southeast continued to subsist via hunting, gathering, and fishing. The settlement pattern also remained unchanged with a base camp–satellite camp pattern. In many culture areas base camps had more structures, pits, hearths, ovens, and other domestic features than before. In the river valleys inside and near the Fall Line, there was a general shift of base camps into less flood-prone areas and into secondary drainage flood plains. This settlement shift may reflect an increased population and perhaps a reliance on horticulture.[33] Squash and bottle gourds continued to be grown throughout the Southeast. Oily starchy seeds were domesticated in the Tennessee River drainage during this period and were also important in many areas. Sunflower was domesticated in eastern Tennessee by 900 B.C., during the early Woodland. There was a continual increase in the number of cultivated plants throughout the middle Woodland in the Tennessee drainage. Maize has been found at a few sites, but it did not make up a significant part of the diet. The best evidence for middle Woodland maize is in the Tellico Reservoir at the Icehouse Bottom site, where Jefferson Chapman obtained eight radiocarbon dates from maize averaging A.D. 439 ± 75. Researchers have found a general increase in the use of fleshy fruits, such as persimmon and grape, throughout the Southeast during the middle Woodland period. It is surprising that the developing horticulture in Tennessee has not been documented in other areas of the Southeast. However, many researchers have not used the time-consuming flotation method of recovery or performed enough of the expensive paleobotanical analyses to address adequately the question of middle Woodland plant harvesting and cultivation.

Summary

The middle Woodland period is best known for the spread of the Hopewellian ceremonial complex throughout most of the Southeast. This phenomenon instigated an unprecedented era of mound construction for both burial and ritual activities. The Hopewellian ceremonial complex also facilitated sociopolitical evolution, which transformed most southeastern Indian societies from a series of independent extended families into a more complex form of extended family-based social organization, the segmented lineage or tribe. Each society had its particular version of the Hopewellian ceremonial complex, which facilitated the formation of intra- and intercommunity organizations held together, if only temporarily, through the power of clever, self-made leaders. These Big Women and Big Men were buried with considerable ceremony in mound centers located in major north–south river valleys or along

---

[33] For details about the subsistence-settlement shift of interior cultures see Smith, 1985a, and Ford, 1985.

natural trading paths. The frequent rise and fall of new leaders led to great demand for prestige goods and fueled the growth of long-distance trade during this period. The subsistence and settlement patterns remained essentially the same as before. Intensified plant use and cultivation is documented only in the Tennessee Valley.

Examples of Middle Woodland Cultures and Ceremonial Complexes

McFarland Culture

The McFarland culture existed between about 200 B.C. and A.D. 200 in south central Tennessee. This culture has been studied for several years by Charles Faulkner and Major McCullough and their students at the University of Tennessee in association with Tennessee Valley Authority (TVA) reservoir construction in the upper Elk and Duck river valleys and supplemented with additional research grants.[34]

The McFarland culture area in Tennessee is steep and rocky with deep river valleys and narrow flood plains. The forest is dominated by hardwoods with scattered evergreens. Middle Woodland pottery was limestone-tempered, and most containers had four podal supports (tetrapods). Surface finishes included fabric marking, cord marking, check stamping, and simple stamping. Chipped stone points were primarily the stemless, concave-based triangular McFarland type, but a few small stemmed points were made. Hopewellian items included greenstone celts, sandstone elbow pipes, and expanded center and insect effigy gorgets.

Much is known about the details of McFarland community organization and activity area due to the use of heavy machinery in excavations to expose all or large parts of settlements. Pioneered during WPA archaeology in the 1930s, the use of earth-moving machines, such as backhoes, scraper pans, road graders and bulldozers, greatly facilitates preparation of sites for pinpoint excavation. Backhoe trenches reveal the stratigraphy of the site, and scraping machines expose the top of undisturbed features and midden areas by quickly stripping off overburden. The scraped areas are then cleaned by hand and all features are mapped and photographed. Stripping was particularly effective in central Tennessee where most sites were located in open fields with a shallow plow zone. There is a significant difference in the information that can be gathered from this approach and that gathered from small scattered excavation units. Heavy equipment is used on a regular basis throughout the United States, greatly reducing the time and expense of such investigations. Six complete McFarland settlements, such as that shown in Figure 6.18, were investigated in this manner.

The general McFarland community plan included separate areas for food

[34] For a summary of the McFarland culture and references to further reading see Faulkner, 1988.

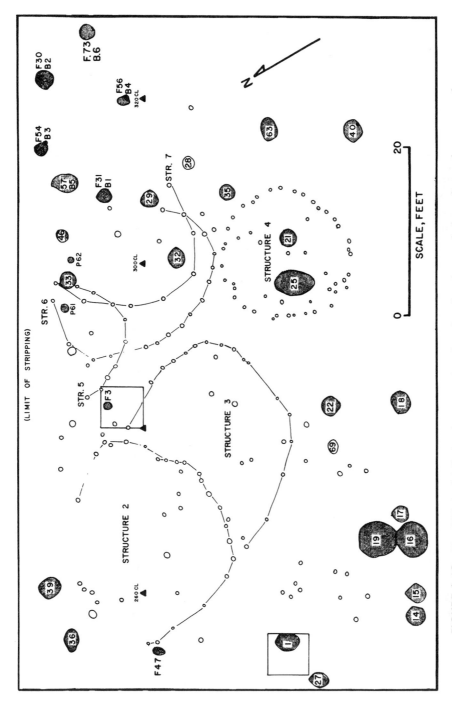

FIGURE 6.18 Ewell II site McFarland community plan showing the posthole outlines of warm weather (structures 2 and 3) and cool weather structures (structure 4) and food preparation features (top right) in the Normandy Reservoir in eastern Tennessee.

preparation, residence, and burial. Outdoor food preparation areas were located at the edge of settlements, well away from the residential area. Food preparation areas had clusters of cylindrical storage pits and shallow basins centered around earth ovens. Two types of domestic structures have been found, one a small, substantial structure interpreted as a cool season dwelling, and the second an open, less substantial structure interpreted as a warm season shelter, shown in Figure 6.18. The larger warm weather structures were round to slightly oval in outline and about 20 to 30 ft in diameter. The walls were built of widely spaced, deeply set poles held together at the top. The warm weather structures had an open side, like a cabana, and no associated inside or outside features. Cool weather structures were small and circular with walls of closely spaced small posts with both inside and outside hearths and pit features.

Settlements were concentrated on the rich, narrow valley flood plains during the McFarland period. Communities grew larger, and structures became more substantial. Large quantities of seeds from wild goosefoot, maygrass, and knotweed, and domesticated sunflower, marsh elder, squash, and maize have been recovered at several late McFarland base camps. The same suite of botanical remains and the same settlement pattern shift have been documented in other cultures inside the Fall Line. This pattern suggests a growing population and that the increasing food requirements were met by greater cultivation of plants. Evidence also suggests that large areas of the flood plain in the nearby Little Tennessee Valley were cleared by fire and that a series of plant crops were raised in rotation.[35]

During the 400 yr of the McFarland culture, mortuary practices shifted from flesh and cremation burials that were scattered through the residential area of a community to formal isolated cremation cemeteries. There was at least one specialized mortuary settlement, the Yearwood site, as well as an isolated, fortified ceremonial site. An isolated mortuary preparation area was found at one of the base camps. The Yearwood site had a community plan and structures different from residential base camps. It had a cluster of lightly built, open-sided rectangular structure, similar to arbors or ramadas, between 20 and 30 ft long located in the center of the settlement.[36] At each end of the settlement was a cluster of structures with substantial walls. One structure in each cluster was significantly larger than the others and it had an internal hearth. A smaller, circular structure was attached to each of these large structures. There were four redeposited cremations at the Yearwood site along with three extended flesh burials, a disarticulated infant burial, and a possible bundle burial. Hopewellian artifacts were found at this site, including copper and ceramic earspools, imported minerals (mica, galena, serpentine), imported flint blades, quartz crystals, and Hopewellian ceramics. A 6- × -9-ft

[35] For more information about this theory, see Smith, 1985a.
[36] See Butler, 1979, for details about the Yearwood excavations.

basin adjacent to this site had a heavily fired interior and a compact layer of charcoal and ash on the bottom. This appears to have been a crematory basin. The Yearwood settlement appears to have been used for a only short period of time during the warm season, as there was no evidence of rebuilding or superposition of buildings.

The Parks residential campsite had a separate mortuary area consisting of a cluster of open-sided, rectangular, arborlike structures with hearths, earth ovens, and cache pits at the corners as well as Hopewellian prestige items. Near this cluster of arborlike structures were four cremations, two flesh burials, and a crematory basin.

The other McFarland ceremonial site was a "stone fort" located on a narrow, high plateau. This site features a series of walls of stone and earth and seems to have been vacant most of the time. It was used periodically for ceremonies and refurbished as necessary; there is no habitation debris within the enclosure. Other similar "stone forts" are found in contemporaneous culture areas in the surrounding region.

Miller I and II Culture

The Miller culture area is found in the upper Tombigbee Valley and in southwestern Tennessee, as shown in Figure 6.13[37] The early pottery of the Miller culture was sand tempered with fabric and cord marking (shown in Figure 6.14), but about A.D. 300, this changed to grog-tempered cord-marked pottery. Miller chipped stone points were small, stemmed lanceolates and stubby spikes characteristic of the western Coastal Plain, as shown in Figure 6.14.

Miller I–II settlements were organized into the typical base camp–satellite camp pattern, and a hunting, gathering, and fishing subsistence strategy was practiced. Base camps, located on the flood plains, slope forest, and upland prairie, contained houses that were large and circular to oval in shape. The houses had single post walls covered with bark, thatch, or hide, and interior central hearths, earth ovens, and a covered entryway. Many storage pits and thick middens with abundant artifacts are found at these base camps and they appear to have been used during the warm months. During the cool season, communities broke into smaller groups for hunting and gathering of more dispersed food sources.

Hopewellian burial mounds were constructed throughout the Miller culture area. In the northern portion of the culture area, along the Indian trail known as the Natchez Trace, five mound centers have been found and investigated, including the Bynum mound center and the Pinson mound center.

---

[37] See Jenkins, 1981, Jenkins and Krause, 1986, and Johnson, 1988, for details on the Miller culture.

Bynum Mound Center   The Bynum mound center, located near Tupelo, Mississippi, consisted of six conical burial mounds adjacent to a settlement.[38] The mounds, excavated in 1951, were built to cover cremation facilities. Mound B is 20 ft tall and it covers a burned crematorium building lined with logs and built inside a 46- × -38-ft pit 4 ft deep, shown in Figure 6.19. The structure was made of large posts and had a small, hard-fired circular crematory basin containing the remains of several people. Three cremations were also found in a bed of ashes on the floor of the burned crematorium. After burning, a flesh burial had been placed on the crematory floor along with an L-shaped row of 29 greenstone celts and a cluster of nine chipped stone points. The points were Snyders Corner notched points imported from the lower Illinois Valley area. Two pairs of copper earspools, a lump of galena, and two fragments of marine shell were found in the ashes on the floor of the crematorium.

Another mound 6 ft tall had been built over another crematory. The second structure was similar to the first, but only a single greenstone celt was found in the burned building, and only one copper earspool and one bead were in the crematory pit.

The third mound excavated was 10 ft tall, and it was built over a burned clay burial platform, similar to those found at the contemporaneous Marksville mound center. On this clay platform were two extended and three flexed burials lying between two logs. Three of these burials had been cremated in place.

Pinson Mound Center   Of all the Hopewellian mound centers in the southeast, Pinson, in southwestern Tennessee, was the largest and most complex.[39] It has at least 12 mounds, as shown in the site map, Figure 6.20. Five are rectangular platform mounds, some with ramps, and one is enclosed with a large circular embankment. There are also several habitation areas. The mounds in this 400-acre complex appear to have been geometrically arranged, centering on the large flat-topped mound in the center. This mound, known as Sauls Mound, is 75 ft tall with a square base 330 ft on a side. This is the second largest mound ever discovered in the United States.

Two of the platform mounds at Pinson have been investigated. Mound 5, the Ozier Mound, is 32 ft high, and 240 × 230 ft at the base. It was built in six construction stages, each capped with yellow sand. As at other middle Woodland platform mounds that have been studied, the summits have features related to cooking. Mound 10 is much smaller (4.3 ft tall, 200 × 131 ft at the base), and the only feature encountered during its study is a large central hearth on the summit. Both platform mounds appear to have been used for communal cooking and feasting like the Walling Mound in northern Alabama. The largest platform mound, Sauls Mound, has been penetrated only with a small core, and little is known about it.

---

[38] For details about the Bynum excavations see Cotter and Corbett, 1951.

[39] For more information about the Pinson mound center see Mainfort, 1986 and 1988.

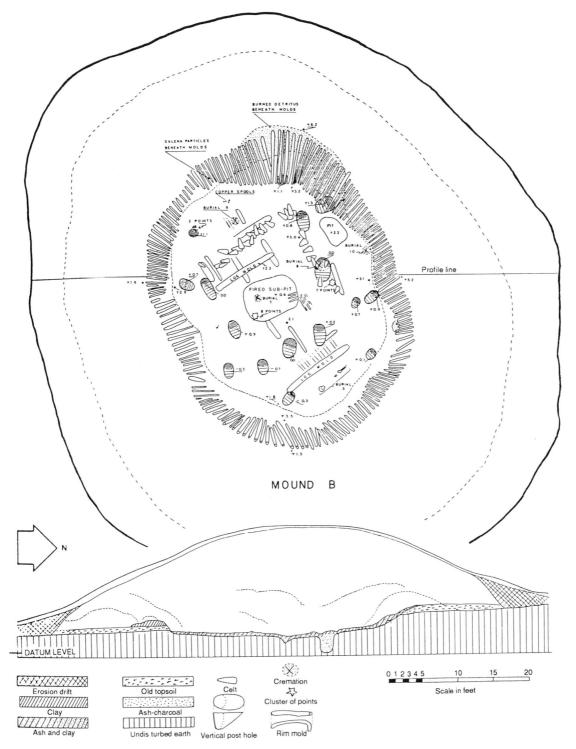

MOUND B

FIGURE 6.19 Mound B at the Bynum site, a Hopewellian mound center near Tupelo, Mississippi, showing crematorium and burials.

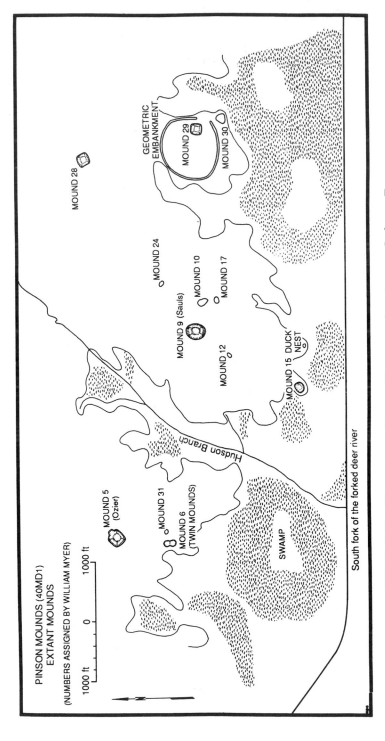

FIGURE 6.20 Pinson site, a Hopewellian mound center near Jackson, Tennessee.

Investigations in the area known as the "Duck's Nest" encountered a large central fire basin with redeposited cremations surrounded by a small circular earthwork. Excavations about 500 ft north of the Duck's Nest revealed 10 broken pottery vessels, which are associated with distant culture areas of the Southeast, as well as scattered burned human bones. Robert Mainfort, who conducted the most recent research at Pinson, suggests that the vessels contained cremations brought from distant societies for burial at the center.

The Twin Mounds, located in the western part of the complex, consist of two conical burial mounds joined at the base. Each is 23 ft tall with basal diameters of 85 and 100 ft. One of the Twin Mounds has been investigated. It was constructed by a brief series of events to cover several tombs. The first step was to remove the humus in a 75-ft-wide area. Six tombs, six small cremation basins, and six narrow deep pits were excavated into this prepared surface. Burials were placed in the tombs and cremations in the narrow pits, and the area was covered with a 6-in. layer of sand and sealed with puddled (wet) gray clay. Sandstone slabs were placed on the clay over three of the tombs, and two large fires were built. A small clay platform, about 2 ft high and 6 ft wide, was then built over the sandstone slabs. Two rows of posts were set into this platform. The interior row was made up of larger posts. These were later pulled up and the remaining holes were filled with light-colored sand, which was also used to cover the platform. Three layers of fill and a light-colored sand cap were placed over the small platform. Cremated animal remains were placed in each of the fill layers. In one layer, the animal remains were still hot when buried. Sandstone boulders were placed over two new burials in the last layer.

Each of the four tombs that were excavated contained several adults of the same sex and general age. For example, one tomb contained eight females between the ages of 20 and 30, each wearing a fiber headdress and copper ornaments. Each woman had been covered with a blanket decorated with shell beads and wore personal ornaments such as shell beads and pearl necklaces, pieces of copper, and earspools. The female burials were placed on a low clay platform made of fabric-covered logs. The tomb was roofed with cane matting suspended from two logs just below the top of the pit. The matting was sealed with layers of gray clay and mats, and sandstone boulders lined the pit walls. The tombs differed slightly in grave goods and ornaments. Of particular interest was a tomb containing four elderly males, one of whom had rattles made of human skulls with pebbles inside tied to each knee. One set of rattles, shown in Figure 6.21, was engraved with geometric designs similar to the designs on Hopewellian pottery. Another unusual feature in the mounds was the presence of what appeared to be animal cremations. But, as Mainfort points out, very few of the cremated bones were identifiable, and many could be human.

Pinson was used for about 500 yr, from 50 B.C. to A.D. 450. The main building episode appears to have been between about 50 B.C. and A.D. 150

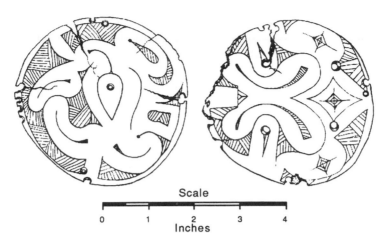

Scale

0   1   2   3   4
          Inches

FIGURE 6.21   Engraved human skull rattle found with the burial of an older man at the Pinson site, a Hopewellian mound center near Jackson, Tennessee.

or 250, when eight of the largest mounds were constructed, including the Ozier and Twin Mounds. The mounds constructed after A.D. 150 or 250 appear to have been built individually as part of separate mortuary ceremonial events. Robert Mainfort speculates that, after about A.D. 300, the center was used only by local groups, and it ceased to function as a ceremonial center for outside groups.

Swift Creek Culture

Swift Creek Culture evolved smoothly out of the Deptford and Cartersville cultures in south Georgia and northwest Florida.[40] Its key trait is complicated stamped pottery. It is believed that complicated stamping developed from check stamping during a relatively short transition period when both forms of stamping were practiced in the South Appalachian tradition. Swift Creek pottery is quite distinctive, as shown in Figure 6.14 and on the cover of this book. Researchers such as Betty Broyles, Frankie Snow, and Betty Smith in Georgia have studied the stamped designs on Swift Creek pottery for almost 50 yr.[41] The designs consist mainly of curvilinear elements such as scrolls, concentric circles, teardrops, and spirals. Some straight line designs, such as nested diamonds and chevrons, were used less frequently. Snow has identified many complete stamps from pottery in the Ocmulgee drainage in Georgia. The motifs appear to be carvings of human masks, special animals such as the spoonbill bird, and specific designs such as crosses and concentric circles.

[40] For details on Swift Creek culture see Bense, 1993, Penton, 1974a,b, and Phelps, 1969.

[41] For further information about Swift Creek design analyses see Broyles, 1968, B. Smith, 1975a,b, Snow, 1993, and Snow and Stephenson, 1993.

Some of these design motifs are similar to the cosmology and symbols of the Muskogean Indians who lived in this area in historic times. Some vessels were also decorated with the Gulf tradition techniques of incising, punctating, and rocker stamping, especially in the Santa Rosa–Swift Creek culture area in northwest Florida. Vessel shapes throughout the Swift Creek area included open jars and bowls with podal supports and notched and scalloped rims. Female figurines of baked clay are also found in Swift Creek middens and mounds.

The settlement pattern and subsistence pattern throughout most of the Swift Creek area remained consistent with that of the previous early Woodland period. Flood plain base camps and upland temporary camps were found along streams in river valleys, and there were large shell midden base camps and scattered smaller sites in coastal areas. On the Gulf of Mexico coast of northwest Florida, shell rings continued to be made in the shape of horseshoes and circles. These were similar to the late Archaic ring middens on the Georgia Atlantic and Gulf coasts and the Tchefuncte ring middens in the lower Mississippi Valley. There are indications of settlement clusters consisting of several small sites and a single large site in the Santa Rosa–Swift Creek area in northwest Florida. The large site is commonly a ring midden with an associated burial mound. This organization of settlements, if substantiated, likely reflects the extended family or lineage of a specific Big Woman or Big Man.

Much is known about Swift Creek ceremonialism, which is called the Yent–Green Point ceremonial complex. Mounds and mound centers were built by Swift Creek societies, and they actively participated in the Hopewellian ceremonial complex. C. B. Moore excavated many Swift Creek burial mounds at the turn of the twentieth century, which were used to initially define the Yent–Green Point ceremonial complex, described later in this chapter.

The largest and best-known ceremonial Swift Creek site is Mandeville, on the lower Chattahoochee River, near Fort Gaines, Georgia.[42] This site consists of a large rectangular platform mound, a conical burial mound, and a settlement. The platform mound is 270×170 ft at the base and 14 ft tall, and the conical mound is about 100 ft in basal diameter and 6 ft tall. Like other platform mounds, it had a series of summits covered with thick midden separated by construction layers of fill, shown in Figure 6.22. The first stage of Mound A (Layer 1) was built on top of a midden (protomound village). The construction layers consisted of stiff yellow clay capped with brightly colored sand. Each successive summit contained midden and features that indicate extensive areas of burning and deposits of animal bone; these reflect communal cooking and feasting activities. No traces of any structures were found on the platform summits.

Mound B began as a cone-shaped, 12-ft-high mound of compact clay and sand capped with a thin layer of orange sand. Later, at least 11 burial pits

---

[42] For details about Mandeville excavations see Kellar *et al.*, 1962, and B. A. Smith, 1975a, b.

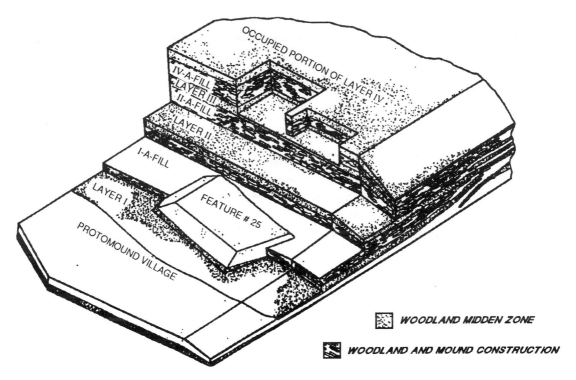

FIGURE 6.22 Block diagram of Mound A, the platform mound at Mandeville, a Hopewellian mound center near Fort Gaines, Georgia.

containing primary and secondary burials and Hopewellian grave goods were placed around one edge of the mound. The most common burial items were copper-covered panpipes and earspools. Others included clay platform pipes, pottery vessels and sherds, ceramic figurines, prismatic blades, greenstone celts, and mica. The last pit burial was especially elaborate. It was a cremated child, 11 yr old, who was buried with nine greenstone celts, 13 bicymbal earspools, and 2 kg of galena. A 12-ft-high mound consisting of four layers of different colored earth was built over the burial pits next to the original mound and both mounds were covered with a layer of sand and clay.

Hopewellian Ceremonial Complexes

The Yent–Green Point ceremonial complex was shared by Swift Creek societies.[43] It is divided into an earlier Yent period and a later Green Point period, based on differences in burial mound construction and use. Yent

[43] For details see Sears, 1962, and Milanich and Fairbanks, 1980.

mounds were conical or dome-shaped. They were initially built over a few burials that were placed on the ground with Hopewellian items. Mounds were often reused, with new burials placed on the surface of the mound and covered with a new layer of fill, and sometimes capped with clay. Mounds were located adjacent to settlements and were both circular and oval, averaging about 5 ft in height. Green Point mounds were constructed for a single burial event and were not reused. A wide variety of Hopewellian items were placed with the burials and in the mounds in both periods. These items included panpipes, rectangular plates, earspools, plummets, bar gorgets, cut teeth and jaws from bear, puma, and wolf, shell cups, and sheets and cutouts of mica. Particularly elaborate mortuary pottery was also placed in Yent–Green Point mounds. This pottery was very well made and included animal effigies with multiple spouts, cutout pedestal effigies, compound vessels, miniature vessels, and figurines. The pottery, both whole and broken, was often cached in the east side of the burial mounds, and many pots had holes knocked out of the bottom.

The only other well-defined Hopewellian ceremonial complex in the Southeast is called Copena, which was a mortuary complex shared by neighboring groups in the central Tennessee Valley.[44] Burial mounds were conical and averaged about 6 ft in height and 50 ft in basal diameter. They were built over clustered burial pits that were often lined with foreign clays, logs, or bark and filled with imported sand and clay. Some burials were placed into dugout logs, or bark troughs, or wrapped in bark matting. Mounds often contained several interments other than the primary burial, such as flexed burials, cremations, lone skulls, or disarticulated body members or bones. Burial caves in which bodies were cremated along with their associated grave goods were also used. Occasionally, bodies were placed in canoes or troughs in caves.

Copena is known for its distinctive copper items, especially reel-shaped gorgets. Other Hopewellian items include earspools, bracelets, celts and beads of copper, marine shell cups and beads, long stemless chipped stone points, ground galena modules, greenstone celts and digging implements, and large steatite elbow pipes. Pottery vessels were not part of the Copena ceremonial complex. Platform mounds, such as the Walling mound described above, were also built.

The Copena and Yent–Green Point ceremonial complexes are good examples of how the Hopewellian ceremonial complex was accepted and modified by southeastern societies. Each complex was shared by nearby groups, which often had very different domestic material cultures and appear to have shared little else. The two ceremonial complexes differed in specific practices and items, but they shared many practices with other Hopewellian cultures.

[44] For details on Copena see Cole, 1981, and Walthall, 1973, 1980.

Summary of the Middle Woodland Period

The most significant development during the middle Woodland period was the participation of most southeastern cultures in the Hopewellian ceremonial complex. The similarity of belief systems between the Midwest and Southeast during this period was exceptional, and it facilitated the evolution of sociopolitical organization from the extended family household to the segmented lineage or tribe.

In some Hopewellian societies, a more complex, if temporary, sociopolitical organization developed through the emergence of self-made leaders, called Big Men and Big Women, who gained power over several communities. These individuals controlled the local trade network, accumulated Hopewellian prestige items, and built complex mound centers. These center were the scene of rituals and feasts held on platform mounds. Big Women and Men were buried under and in the mounds along with elaborate imported Hopewellian items.

Plant cultivation was intensified in the northern portion of the Southeast inside the Fall Line. It is believed that plots on the Tennessee Valley flood plain were cleared for fields during this period. Cultivation of plants remained minimal outside this more northern area.

LATE WOODLAND PERIOD: A.D. 500–1000

The late Woodland period is associated with the decline of Hopewellian ceremonialism and the strong Midwest–Southeast interaction. The Hopewellian ceremonial complex ended by A.D. 300–350 in the Midwest, but it lingered until about A.D. 400–500 in parts of the Southeast. This was a time of considerable cultural variation with distinct differences within the Southeast. The highly variable nature of cultures in the Southeast is the most distinguishing characteristic of this period. Neighboring cultures differed in such basic activities as subsistence, settlement patterns, and mortuary customs.

Since the mid-1970s, the transition from the late Woodland to the Mississippian stage has been the focus of considerable research.[45] As this research has shown, the key traits once used to define the Mississippian stage, such as maize agriculture, shell-tempered pottery, residential platform mounds, and wall trench houses, developed quite early, by A.D. 700–800, prior to the full-blown Mississippian stage. Consequently, researchers in the north central Mississippi Valley (northern Arkansas, southeast Missouri, southwest Illinois) call the period between A.D. 700 and 1000 "Emergent Mississippian" rather than late Woodland, to reflect the early, though limited, developments of what

[45] For more information on the late Woodland see Nassaney and Cobb, 1991, and B. D. Smith, 1990.

later are very widespread Mississippian stage characteristics.[46] The earliest transition from the Woodland to the Mississippian stage took place in this region.

Material Culture

The bow and arrow arrived during the late Woodland period between A.D. 700–800, and eventually it spread throughout the Southeast. Shell-tempered pottery and chipped stone hoes were also developed about A.D. 700–800. However, these innovations were restricted to the north central Mississippi Valley and are related to the increased use of maize.

The introduction and spread of the bow and arrow is detected by the reduction in size and thickness of chipped stone points.[47] The most common arrow point in the Southeast during this period was a small (1 in. or less in size), thin (maximum $\frac{3}{16}$ inch), stemless, triangular type shown in Figure 6.23G. An equally small, thin, stemmed point with a lanceolate triangular blade was made in the Mississippi Valley. Both point types are well suited for use as arrow or dart tips. It appears that the bow and arrow diffused from the Northwest and West and spread rapidly across the southeast, cross-cutting environmental and cultural boundaries. John Blitz's study of the development of the bow and arrow has led him to propose that this technological change is related primarily to contact and competition between sociopolitical groups rather than pressure to increase hunting capability. As Blitz sees it, the increasingly competitive sociopolitical landscape in the Southeast fostered the development of the bow and arrow as a weapon and gave an advantage to those who used it. This situation in turn pressured the "have-nots" to adopt the new weapon system. Blitz theorizes that it was primarily through imitation that the bow and arrow developed and spread in the Southeast.

For more than a millennium, crushed shell had been used sporadically as a tempering agent for pottery in the Southeast; however the technological advantages were developed in the north central Mississippi Valley about A.D. 850. The addition of burned, finely crushed shell to pottery clay greatly improves its working quality and makes it less likely to shrink and crack when fired.[48] Vessels could be made larger, with much thinner walls, and they could be made into more shapes than ever before. While sand, grog, and limestone tempering were technologically advanced over fiber tempering, the use of crushed, burned shell was an important breakthrough in ceramic technology during the closing centuries of the Woodland stage in the central Mississippi Valley. Most archaeologists associate the initial improvement in ceramic tech-

---

[46] For further information about the Emergent Mississippi see B. D. Smith, 1990.

[47] See Blitz, 1988, for details about the bow and arrow in North America.

[48] See Morse and Morse, 1983, and Steponaitis, 1983, for details on shell-tempered pottery.

A

B

C

approx. 12'

D

F

0 ___ 10
cm

G   H

0 ___ 5
cm

E

nology with the increasing importance of maize. A good example of the improvement in ceramics is the appearance of the "hooded" bottle (a ceramic copy of a bottle gourd) with a clay stopper, that could be used to store seed maize more securely than organic gourds. Another example is the appearance of large flat pans and funnels that were used in making salt and lime, which are ingredients in processing maize. Also, new large globular jars that could take advantage of the high-storability feature of maize appeared for the first time. While the relationship between the appearance of shell-tempered pottery and maize is based on inference, the simultaneous appearance of both is at least a very auspicious coincidence.

Subsistence and Settlement Pattern

Subsistence during the late Woodland period outside the northern Mississippi Valley followed the traditional pattern of hunting, gathering, and fishing. Gardening was important only in the very northern part of the region, inside the Fall Line. Maize cultivation was important only on the northern fringe of the Southeast, specifically in northern Arkansas, the American Bottom near St. Louis, and in the lower Ohio and Illinois river valleys. The American Bottom appears to have supported some of the earliest maize-dependent societies in eastern North America, including the later part of the Patrick phase or the early Dohak culture, where maize appeared in significant quantities by A.D. 750–800.

Maize formed the foundation for complex cultural development throughout Central and North America. It provided the basis for the great civilizations in Mesoamerica, the Pueblo societies in the Southwest, and the complex chiefdoms in the Southeast. Because of the cultural importance of maize, its origins and development have been the subject of considerable research. Studies have shown that wild maize, or *teocentli*, originated in Mexico, where people gathered it as early as 7000 B.C.[49] All forms of maize, including the varieties grown today, are derived from that wild source. Most researchers who have studied the physical changes and spread of maize into North

[49] See Galinat, 1985, for a good summary of the domestication and diffusion of maize.

FIGURE 6.23   Examples of late Woodland artifacts: (A) Coles Creek incised bowl; (B) French Fork incised jar; (C) Tucker Ridge pinched bowl; (D) Late Swift Creek complicated stamped bowl; (E) Weeden Island effigy vessel with cutouts; (F) Mill Creek chert chipped stone hoe; (G) Sequoyah point; (H) Hamilton point. (A–B from Phillips, 1970; C, E, and F from Griffin, 1952, with permission of the University of Chicago Press, copyright © 1952 by The University of Chicago. All rights reserved; D from Caldwell, 1958, reproduced by permission of the American Anthropological Association from MEMOIR NO. 88 of the American Anthropological Association, not for further reproduction; G from Morse and Morse, 1983.)

America agree with James B. Griffin, who theorized in 1946 that maize spread to eastern North America via the Southwest or the Plains.[50] There is evidence that maize had spread to eastern Tennessee by 200 A.D., but only small amounts have been found in a few sites from the late Woodland period, such as the Miller and Martin Farm cultures (see Figure 6.24 and Figure 6.1). Maize played a very minor role in their diet.

The basic pattern of base camps with affiliated satellite camps continued, but there were many local variations on this theme. Late in the period many areas saw an increase in the number of new, small settlements along smaller tributaries and in the upper portions of estuary systems.[51] These settlements usually consisted of a few structures that were probably occupied by a family or a few extended families. Whether occupied on a seasonal or a permanent basis, the spread of these small settlements across a wide variety of landforms throughout the Southeast is an indication of a population increase during the late Woodland period. This population expansion is described as one that "filled up" much of the landscape in the Southeast.

Late Woodland culture in the Appalachian Highlands, the Piedmont, and the Atlantic Coastal Plain was different than that of the Mississippi Valley and Gulf Coastal Plain. A surprisingly small number of late Woodland sites are present in the former regions, even in large river valleys. Some researchers think that portions of the Atlantic Coastal Plain and Piedmont may not even have been occupied, but were used as buffer zones or hunting territories by groups based in northwest Georgia and on the coast.[52] In fact, so little is known about the late Woodland culture in the Appalachian Mountains that archaeologists are unsure about the diagnostic artifacts. It is thought that the middle Woodland Connestee culture likely continued until A.D. 1000 without the earlier practices of mound building and importing grave goods.[53]

On the Coastal Plain of the Carolinas, the late Woodland period began late, around A.D. 800, and lasted until historic times.[54] Although subsistence in this period included some maize cultivation, and ceramics were tempered with shell and grit, the culture was more similar to that of the Northeast than it was to the rest of the Southeast. Burial practices changed from typical Hopewellian burial mounds to the use of ossuaries. Ossuaries were large circular or rectangluar pits in which primary and secondary burials were placed. Ossuaries have been found with between 38 and 58 burials, including men and women ranging in age from infants to elderly. Ossuaries were used by both the Colington and Cashie cultures, but those in the interior of the

---

[50] See Keegan, 1987, and for details on the spread of maize and B. D. Smith, 1986, for a summary.

[51] For details on late Woodland see Kelly, 1990, and B. D. Smith, 1986.

[52] For more about the late Woodland problem on the Atlantic Slope, see Trinkley, 1989.

[53] See Anderson, 1985, and Purrington, 1983, for more details about the late Woodland problem in the Appalachians.

[54] For details about the late Woodland on the Carolina coast, see Phelps, 1983.

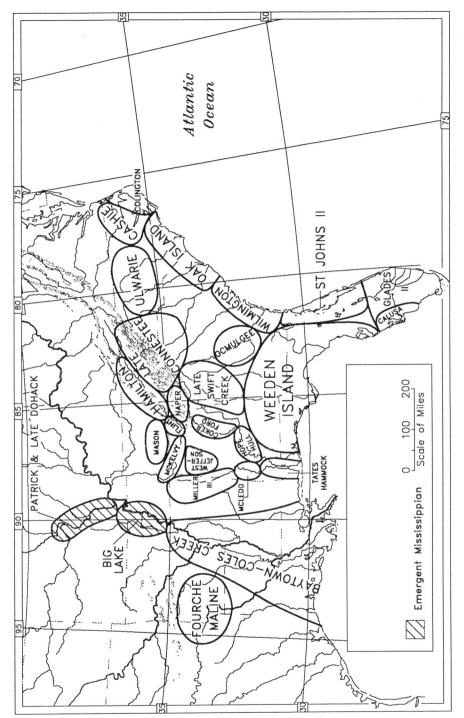

FIGURE 6.24 Late Woodland culture areas.

Cashie culture, were smaller and usually contained only a few bundle settlements, and suggests that they may be family graves. Strings of *marginella* shell beads were common grave goods. Status may be reflected by the number of strings buried with a person. Additional grave goods include disk and barrel-shaped beads and bone awls. Ossuaries are a northern cultural trait and Phelps suggests that the practice diffused into North Carolina from that direction.

Mortuary Practices and Ceremonialism

Even as the Hopewellian ceremonial complex declined, mound building and mortuary ceremonialism continued across much of the Gulf Coastal Plain. More large mound centers were built in the Mississippi Valley than ever before. In culture areas that did not build mounds, the dead were buried in scattered locations in the settlements or in separate cemetery areas. In the mound-building culture areas on the Gulf Coastal Plain, such as the Weeden Island culture, burial mounds were similar to those of earlier periods. Flesh burials were placed in pits or log tombs over which a mound was constructed. Secondary burials were often placed in the mound fill and included bone bundles, single skulls, and cremations. Mortuary items included caches of elaborate pottery, both broken and complete in the east sides of burial mounds. In the upper Tennessee Valley, ornate shell pendants and shell beads, often in great quantities, were placed with the dead. As the late Woodland progressed, mortuary treatments became simpler. Primary burials became more common, cremations almost ceased, and mounds were not elaborate. Mounds were often reused, with the different layers sealed with a clay cap or by burning. Grave goods were still placed with some mound burials or cached in the mounds, but generally the mortuary items were less elaborate than during the previous period.

Multiple-mound centers were still being built on the Gulf of Mexico Coastal Plain, and most were built in the Mississippi Valley. These centers usually contained several platform mounds and conical or dome-shaped burial mounds. In the Mississippi Valley, the function of mound centers expanded from the earlier primary mortuary focus to that of a civic-ceremonial center. Here, the elite resided in special residences on top of platform mounds and led a privileged existence, eating only the best food, conducting important events, and receiving the most elaborate mortuary treatment. Mounds were usually less than 20 ft tall and were arranged around a rectangular open space called a plaza. Mound placement at some of the civic-ceremonial centers has been correlated with solar alignments (such as the winter and summer solstices), the cardinal directions, and standardized distances.[55] In both the Mississippi Valley and the Weeden Island culture area only a small number

---

[55] For more on late Woodland mound center celestial alignments see Sherrod and Rollingson, 1987.

of special people resided at mound centers and the general population lived in settlements scattered across the landscape.

Platform mounds continued to be used for cooking and feasting, but they also were used for burials, residences, and special structures, such as ceremonial buildings and charnel houses in the late Woodland. Substantial mounds were built in stages with alternating layers of earth and destroyed buildings. New buildings were erected on top of these mounds. Sometimes, the construction did not raise the summit but expanded the mound laterally to increase the area rather than the height. This was the case at the Thornton and Gold Mine mound centers in Louisiana.

Sociopolitical Organization

The sociopolitical organization of late Woodland groups outside the Mississippi Valley remained like that of middle Woodland groups. Relatively egalitarian kin groups were the basic social unit. Status was earned through individual achievement and was conferred on members of a successful individual's family. Status was not inherited. Power shifts between kin groups were common through the generations.

There were strong indications of sociopolitical advancement in the Mississippi Valley. Mound construction at individual sites and mound centers increased, as did the population. The increase in mound construction is a convincing sign that elite members of society were accumulating power. Mound building programs appear to have been undertaken as a display of high status. T. R. Kidder suggests that Coles Creek lineages were achieving hereditary ranking, and that a hierarchy of communities developed based on the rank of the resident lineages.[56] Other strong signs of the development of community-level sociopolitical organization are seen in places such as the Emergent Mississippian settlement of Zebree, in northeast Arkansas, where residences were organized into discrete clusters (probably by lineage) around a plaza containing a tall central pole with community food storage pits around its base.

Summary

The late Woodland period was marked by the introduction and widespread diffusion of the bow and arrow, and, in some northern areas, the cultivation of maize and the development of shell-tempered pottery. Subsistence patterns were generally characterized by hunting, gathering, and fishing, supplemented in northern areas by gardening. The settlement pattern was the traditional seasonal base camp–satellite camp organization, with greater complexity in some areas. Population increased in many areas, and expanded

---

[56] See Kidder, 1992, for more details on Coles Creek sociopolitical organization.

into small tributaries and the uplands. The Hopewellian ceremonial complex declined in the late Woodland, although less elaborate mortuary ceremonialism and mound building continued in the Mississippi Valley and Gulf Coastal Plain. Civic-ceremonial centers emerged in the Coles Creek and Weeden Island cultures, some of which were quite large, complex, and well planned. The sociopolitical organization of the late Woodland period continued to be based on unranked kin groups that could rise to power through the ambition of self-made leaders. Such achieved rank was temporary, and power shifted when the Big Man or Big Woman died. In the Mississippi Valley, it appears that power became centralized in the leaders of the ruling lineage, and that power was beginning to be inherited. The rise of social inequality set the stage for the development of powerful chiefdoms in the Mississippian stage.

Examples of Late Woodland Cultures

Weeden Island Culture

The Weeden Island culture, located on the western Gulf Coastal Plain (see Figure 6.25), is one of the best-known late Woodland cultures.[57] It was one of the few to continue the tradition of placing elaborate grave goods in burial mounds. Early research concentrated on the burial mounds and their ornate burial goods. Only recently have studies been made of the daily life and organization of the Weeden Island societies that constructed the burial mounds.

The Weeden Island period began between A.D. 300 to 600 in the western Gulf Coastal Plain. The beginning of the period is marked by new pottery decorations quite different from the previous complicated stamping preference. The end of the Weeden Island period is much less clear in the archaeological materials. Weeden Island culture may have actually continued to around A.D. 1200, as did the contemporary Baytown–Coles Creek culture in the lower Mississippi Valley.

The Weeden Island culture is named after a site on an island of that name in Florida's Tampa Bay. It is identified by the appearance of Gulf tradition ceramics, shown in Figure 6.23. The popularity of Gulf tradition pottery gradually increased and eventually supplanted Swift Creek complicated stamped pottery (Figure 6.23D). During the first half of this period, about A.D. 350–600, pottery was decorated by both complicated stamping and Gulf tradition punctating, incising, and rocker stamping. The Gulf tradition types are very similar to pottery types made by the contemporaneous Baytown–Coles Creek cultures in the lower Mississippi Valley. The custom of making special mortuary pottery continued in the Weeden Island culture (Figure 6.23E,F). Mortuary pottery was very well made and had distinctive shapes, such as cutout animals,

---

[57] For further information on Weeden Island see Milanich *et al.,* 1984, and Milanich and Fairbanks, 1980.

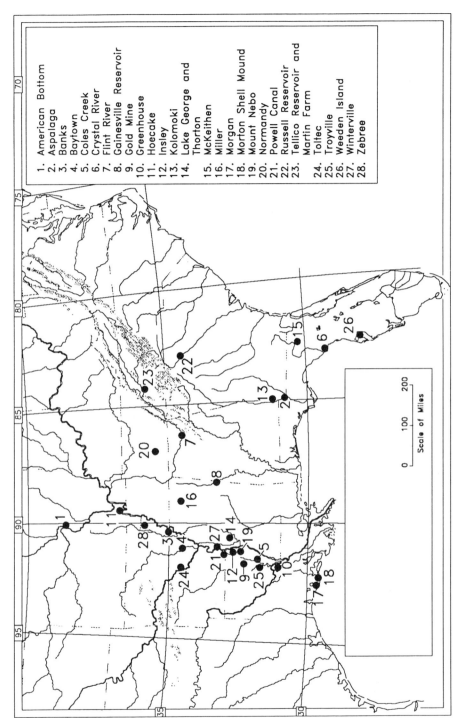

1. American Bottom
2. Aspalaga
3. Banks
4. Baytown
5. Coles Creek
6. Crystal River
7. Flint River
8. Gainesville Reservoir
9. Gold Mine
10. Greenhouse
11. Hoecake
12. Insley
13. Kolomoki
14. Lake George and Thorton
15. McKeithen
16. Miller
17. Morgan
18. Morton Shell Mound
19. Mount Nebo
20. Normandy
21. Powell Canal
22. Russell Reservoir
23. Tellico Reservoir and Martin Farm
24. Toltec
25. Troyville
26. Weeden Island
27. Winterville
28. Zebree

Scale of Miles

0   100   200

FIGURE 6.25 Late Woodland sites.

double and triple bowls, animal and human effigy bowls, and animal and human rim effigies. Such Weeden Island pottery represents the peak of prehistoric Indian ceramic achievement in Eastern North America.

The Weeden Island stone tool assemblage included a small triangular point and a larger stemmed point with an expanded stem. Otherwise, Weeden Island material culture is very similar to that of the previous Swift Creek period.

Weeden Island subsistence practices appear to have remained relatively unchanged from the preceding Swift Creek period. Coastal societies continued to harvest marine resources while inland groups focused on wetland and upland food sources. Whereas it has long been proposed that gardening and maize agriculture were an important part of Weeden Island subsistence, especially late in the period, evidence of cultigens has not been forthcoming.

The Weeden Island settlement pattern also was unchanged from the previous Swift Creek culture, with typical base camps and satellite camps. Forest hammocks with easy access to permanent fresh water and a diversity of environments were preferred base camp locations. Shell rings shaped into rings and rectangles with clean interior plazas continued to be constructed at some coastal base camps on the northern Gulf coast.

Along the coast of northwest Florida, a settlement pattern shift occurred during the Weeden Island culture. New base camps were often established near, but not exactly on, former Swift Creek base camps.[58] In noncoastal areas, Weeden Island base camps were located on river flood plains in areas of diverse environments. Base camps were also established at new locations, including lake shores near wetland areas.

In the western portion of the Weeden Island culture area, an additional settlement pattern change occurred after about A.D. 800. Numerous small settlements were established for the first time along small tributaries, at springheads, and on upper bay shorelines.[59] David Brose and George Percy have suggested that the small settlements were probably used by a single extended family. Base camps and satellite camps on the lower bay and river flood plains were not abandoned, nor were their populations reduced. Current thinking is that population at the older base camp settlements had grown beyond what the surrounding environment could support, and small groups broke away to relieve the pressure on food resources. Many of the new settlements were abandoned after only a relatively small amount of midden had accumulated, which indicates that the resources in these new areas were likely not abundant.

Weeden Island mortuary customs were similar to and therefore probably directly related to the previous Hopewellian Yent–Green Point ceremonial complex.[60] During the Weeden Island culture, a single burial mound was

---

[58] For details about this settlement pattern shift see Penton, 1974b, and Phelps, 1969.

[59] For more information about this settlement pattern change see Percy and Brose, 1974.

[60] See Milanich *et al.*, 1984, for a summary of Weeden Island mortuary customs.

usually built adjacent to larger settlements, but as before, some settlements had more than one mound, and there was at least one multiple-mound civic-ceremonial center. Burial mounds were usually dome-shaped and constructed of several layers of sand. Many variations in burial mounds exist, but there was usually a primary mound built over log-lined burial pits, some of which had stone caps. A cache of special mortuary vessels, and often human cremations, was often placed on the surface of the east side of the primary mound. The mound might then be burned and covered with a cap of stones. A second layer of earth, which could contain secondary bundle and single skull burials, was then placed over the primary mound. Some mounds were reused, with new tombs or burial pits placed in earlier layers. Platform mounds supported special residences or channel houses where mortuary activities, such as burial processing, were conducted.

Scores of Weeden Island burial mounds were excavated by Clarence Moore at the turn of the twentieth century. While his publications remain an invaluable source of information, his excavation techniques were crude compared to modern methods.[61] Most of the mounds Moore excavated were single burial mounds adjacent to settlements; however, he did excavate three mounds at the Aspalaga mound center on the Apalachicola River near the Florida–Georgia border. Since Moore's excavations a hundred years ago, only two Weeden Island mound centers have been investigated—Kolomoki, on the lower Chattahoochee River, and McKeithen, in the north Florida interior near Lake City. Both these mound centers were part of large settlements; no vacant mound centers have been identified.

McKeithen Mound Center   The McKeithen site was excavated by Jerald Milanich and his students in the early 1980s.[62] It included a horseshoe-shaped ring midden with a clean interior plaza. Three mounds were built on the ring midden, one on each end and one at the center of the horseshoe. Excavations revealed that the mounds covered platforms that had been used to elevate a mortuary, a charnel house, and a residence. Structures on each platform had been burned and covered with a dome-shaped layer of earth. The mortuary processing mound was screened from the village. There were several pits in which bodies presumably were buried, allowed to decompose, exhumed, and cleaned for storage in the charnel house until later reburial. Several large posts, some almost 4 ft in diameter, had been raised on this platform. The residential mound supported a rectangular building that was apparently the residence of the person buried there. A charnel house was on the third mound and it apparently was emptied before being burned. The remains of at least 36 people were buried at about 5-ft intervals around the edge of the platform. A cache of at least 18 pottery vessels was found beside the southeast edge of

---

[61] Examples of Moore's excavation reports are Moore, 1901, 1903, and 1907.

[62] See Milanich *et al.*, 1984, for details about the McKeithen site excavation.

the mound. Rocks were placed on the southwest edge of the platform before it was capped with sand.

Jerald Milanich theorizes that the McKeithen residential mound was the home of a Big Man (the skeleton was identified as male), who used special pottery containers and was given special food. Members of his kin group who died were prepared for reburial on the mortuary mound by the resident specialist, who also used special pottery containers and plates reserved for the elite. When the Big Man died he was buried in the floor of his residence, the charnel house was emptied, and all the structures were ritually burned and buried. The stored bone bundles were then spread around the charnel house, and the mounds were covered with additional layers of earth. Use of this mound ceased about A.D. 475. The settlement remained occupied, but its size and importance declined. Milanich suggests that the interval of mound use was related to the emergence of a local leader who could command special treatment, mound building, and special mortuary rituals for his kin group. During the Big Man's heyday, the settlement was the center of sociopolitical events.

Kolomoki Mound Center   Kolomoki is located near Blakely, Georgia, about 200 mi northwest of the McKeithen site. It is by far the largest Weeden Island period civic-ceremonial center.[63] It too had a horseshoe-shaped village that enclosed four mounds, and there were four additional mounds outside the village area. The main village occupation and mound construction period was between A.D. 300–500, the period of McKeithen florescence. The largest mound at Kolomoki is a platform mound 56 ft tall with a rectangular 325 × 200-ft base. The uppermost layers of this mound are a red clay cap covering a layer of white clay. Little else is known about it.

Two dome-shaped burial mounds of white or yellow clay with red clay caps covered low platforms. These mounds contained the remains of 86 people, all of whom were apparently buried at an event associated with the burial of the highest-status individual. Mound D contained four burial tombs with logs and stone slabs beneath a building that was buried under four layers of earth. The other burial mound had a primary mound covered with rocks. The mounds also contained 42 single skull burials, cremations, and bundle burials. Several of the remains are believed to be those of adults killed for the mass burial event. The only grave goods were personal ornaments, such as shell beads and copper-covered earspools. However, elaborate mortuary pottery vessels were cached on the eastern side of both primary mounds. Human skulls were placed in one vessel cache. There mortuary vessels, especially those from Mound D, have become well known in the Southeast, not only because of their quantity and quality, but because many were stolen from the museum that was built over part of Mound D. A few have since been recovered.

[63] See Sears, 1956, for details on Kolomoki excavations.

Kolomoki appears to have been the sociopolitical center of a Big Man or Big Woman and his or her kin group during the first half of the Weeden Island period. It appears that when the leader died, the charnel houses were burned, and the cremated and bundled remains of kinsmen who had died previously were placed on the platforms and mounds were built over them. Some adults seem to have been killed and buried in tombs under the mounds.

After about A.D. 750, the construction of Weeden Island mound centers and elaborate burials ceased, although Weeden Island culture continued for several centuries. Small amounts of ornamental mortuary pottery was placed in burial mounds throughout the period. Burial mound construction continued and may even have increased in frequency due to the dispersal of the population. These late burial mounds appear to have been used primarily as cemeteries for surrounding small settlements.

Summary   The Weeden Island culture was a late Woodland period Gulf Coastal Plain culture with groups living on the coastal strip and in the interior river valleys. Traditional hunting, gathering, and fishing continued to support the population. Weeden Island culture is best known for the elaborate mortuary ceramics placed in burial mounds built in the first half of the period. Such ceramics were often made into animal effigies, especially birds, and represent the height of prehistoric ceramic art in eastern North America. Weeden Island mortuary customs suggest that society was made up of equally ranked kin groups. Periodically, a leader emerged who commanded authority to have mound centers constructed. These were temporary, as power was not inherited, and such communities were either abandoned or simply declined upon the demise of the person in power. During the last half of this period, population growth and resulting pressure on food resources led to a dispersal of small groups into the interior and up tributary valleys.

Baytown–Coles Creek Culture and the Lower Mississippi Valley

Since the 1940s, long-term research projects have been conducted in the Mississippi Valley by the federal government, the Peabody Museum of Harvard University, the Arkansas Archaeological Survey, Tulane University, and a number of other organizations. As a result, a trememdous amount of archaeological information has been generated from this great river valley, and the dynamics of the late Woodland period are reasonably well understood.[64]

The Woodland chronological chart shows that the late Woodland period in the lower Mississippi Valley has been divided at A.D. 700 into two periods: Baytown and Coles Creek. This culture area encompasses the area from the mouth of the Arkansas River to the coast, and many local phases not shown on the culture area map have been identified for each period. These are

---

[64] For further reading on Baytown–Coles Creek see Kidder, 1992, Morse and Morse, 1983, Nassaney and Cobb, 1991, and Phillips, 1970.

distinguished primarily by pottery types and varieties.[65] Pottery of the Baytown and Coles Creek periods was tempered with small pieces of crushed pottery called grog, with occasional additions of sand, grit, bone, and shell. Surface textures range from soft and chalky to smooth and hard. Vessel forms included beakers, bowls, and globular jars, some of which are shown in Figure 6.23. Rims were commonly thickened by folding and bases were either round or flat. Some pottery continued to be made with Gulf tradition themes, and included incised and punctated designs. Cord marking was also popular in the Baytown period. However, most vessel surfaces were not decorated, but were smoothed, or sometimes polished. A stemmed, small point was used by the Coles Creek societies, shown in Figure 6.23A, rather than the triangle-shaped point used in other parts of the Southeast.

Baytown and Coles Creek sites were very abundant in the Mississippi Valley. In fact, there are more Baytown–Coles Creek sites in this area than from any other prehistoric period, with the possible exception of the Mississippian in some regions. The site density represents both population growth and mobility. In the coastal portion of the valley, marine resources continued to be of primary importance. Shell middens, such as the Morton shell mound, continued to expand.

In the rest of the valley, wetlands provided most of the food supply, and settlements were located along the mainstreams or on large tributaries.[66] A typical small streamside settlement is the Powell Canal site, a Baytown settlement near Eudora, Arkansas. Recent excavations have revealed an organized community plan and activity areas.[67] Food preparation, evidenced by a cluster of flat-based storage pits filled with kitchen refuse, was conducted at one end of the site. The residential area was just to the east of the food preparation area. A small cemetery with four burials (and no grave goods) was located on the other side of the residential area. Pottery vessels in this household cluster included a wide variety of cooking, storage, and serving containers. Faunal studies from this and other similar settlements indicate that these were fishing camps. They were likely used when spring floods brought fish into the surrounding oxbow lakes where they were trapped as the water receded. A wide variety of other flood plain food resources were utilized. Plant food studies indicate that wild plants were gathered, but there was no indication that maize was an important part of the diet.

During the Coles Creek period, the relatively simple, egalitarian society was transformed into a complex, incipiently stratified society with mulitcommunity political units governed by a small group of elites.[68] The evolution of Coles Creek society was not accompanied by such tangible evidence as

---

[65] For ceramic chronology details see Phillips, 1970, and Williams and Brain, 1983.

[66] For details of Coles Creek subsistence, see Kidder, 1992, and Fritz and Kidder, 1993.

[67] For details on the Powell Canal site see House, 1990.

[68] See Kidder, 1992, for details of Coles Creek sociopolitical evolution.

differential mortuary treatment, distinctive status goods, or significant plant cultivation. The main indications of this sociopolitical transformation are the construction of multistage platform mounds that supported residences of the elite, the development of civic-ceremonial centers, and particular patterns of community planning and architecture. The centers indicate that social and political power were centralized into a small group of elite who controlled trade and who could command communal labor to construct large multiple-mound centers.

During the early Coles Creek period, platform burial mounds were constructed at several locations, including Mt. Nebo, Greenhouse, and Lake George in northeastern Louisiana. These burial platforms were relatively low, with burial pits containing several extended primary burials or secondary bundle burials in the summit. Several platform burial mounds supported charnel houses. In one such mound at Greenhouse, 84 skeletons were scattered on the summit in poorly defined shallow depressions and covered with a layer of midden. Vincas Steponaitis suggests that these platform burial mounds were used by several generations of the same ruling family.

The general civic-ceremonial center plan consisted of a vacant area called a "plaza" in which political, religious, and social activities were conducted. Most plazas were rectangular and platform mounds were located along the sides. Approach ramps usually led to the mound summits. Most platform mounds were rectangular or square, but a few were circular, as is the Morgan mound center in southwest Louisiana. The number of mounds varied. Centers generally began with a few mounds around a plaza, and new mounds and occasionally new plazas were added over time. The location of mounds was often well planned. At many centers, mounds were aligned with solstices through the use of tall poles set on top of or near mounds. Many mounds were spaced at intervals in multiples of 155 ft. Clay Sherrod and Martha Rollingson studied mound configurations at 33 centers in the Mississippi Valley and discovered that 75% had at least one solar alignment.[69] A common multiple alignment involved a three-mound triangle with a base mound forming alignments with the other two mounds, one to the winter and one to the summer solstice. Typical Coles Creek mound centers consist of three platform mounds less that 15 ft tall arranged round a rectangular plaza. The alignment of mounds to solar events could have been a method of time keeping based on the predictable change in the location of the sunrise on the horizon. Some of the better known late Woodland civic-ceremonial centers in the Mississippi Valley with solar alignments are Greenhouse, Insley, and Toltec.

The beginning of a site hierarchy with two or three tiers appears to have emerged by about A.D. 1000. At the top of this hierarchy was the multimound civic-ceremonial center. Next were settlements with one or two mounds, followed by settlements without mounds. These societies with ranked settle-

[69] See Sherrod and Rollingson, 1987, for details of mound alignments.

ments are thought to be incipient or "petty" chiefdoms. The transformation from egalitarian to ranked society has been well documented at two Coles Creek sites—Lake George and Osceola.[70] These settlements slowly changed from moderate to large villages, and then to multiple-mound civic-ceremonial centers. During this time, mounds were also built at other settlements within 10–20 mi of these larger centers, but their role and function is not well understood.

In summary, the late Woodland Baytown and Coles Creek societies in the Mississippi Valley underwent sociopolitical transformation from unranked, egalitarian lineages to ranked lineages, centralization of power in a small elite group, and ranking of communities. From changes in mound center organization and use, it appears there was a consolidation of power from the kin group to a small number of people. The material culture was rather drab, but showed a strong continuity with previous periods. Subsistence activities included hunting, gathering, and fishing, especially in wetlands. There was very little, if any, cultivation of plants. The population significantly increased as did mound building. Most people lived in small, single- and multiple-household settlements scattered throughout the landscape.

Central Mississippi Valley

Plum Bayou Culture   On the nothern fringe of the Coles Creek culture area was the Plum Bayou culture, which has been the subject of intense research led by Martha Rollingson and the Arkansas Archaeological Survey in central Arkansas.[71] Within Plum Bayou society, there was a four-tiered settlement hierarchy: scattered households, multiple households, larger settlements with one mound, and multiple-mound centers. The bulk of the population was dispersed throughout the landscape in scattered single or multiple-household settlements. These have rich surface middens of domestic materials, clusters of pits, and postholes from structures. Larger settlements had an adjacent conical or dome-shaped mound, which was usually less than 10 ft tall, and one settlement had four mounds. The largest mound center was Toltec, located on an oxbow of the Arkansas River near Little Rock. Toltec was surrounded by a mile-long moat and earth embankment that enclosed 15 platform mounds and three conical mounds, shown in Figure 6.26. Toltec was the largest late Woodland civic-ceremonial center in the Southeast. The platform mounds were oval, linear, square, and rectangular, and arranged around two plazas. Mounds were aligned with the solstices and spaced at 155-ft intervals. Some of the mounds were quite tall, which facilitated their survival during the period of intensive mechanized agriculture at the site prior

---

[70] See Williams and Brain, 1983, for the Lake George site and Kidder and Fritz, 1990, for the Osceola Site.

[71] For details about the Plum Bayou culture see Rollingson, 1982 and 1990.

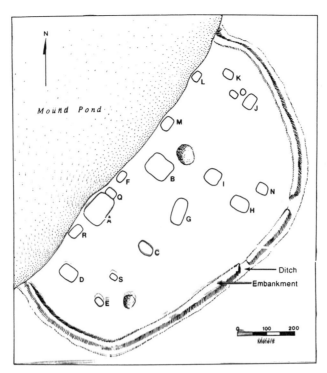

FIGURE 6.26 Toltec, a late Woodland civic-ceremonial center near Little Rock, Arkansas. (From Rollingson, 1990.)

to its purchase by the state of Arkansas. The tallest mound, Mound A, is an oval platform mound almost 50 ft high, and another is 35 ft high.

Six of the mounds at Toltec have been tested by Rollingson and the Arkansas Archaeological Survey. The upper 25 ft of platform mound B contained summits covered with thick midden deposits separated by layers of earth. The rich, organically enriched middens are thought by Rollingson to have been formed from residences on the mound summits. Mound D was also a residential platform mound, with four stages of construction that increased its length and width rather than its height. The faunal remains in the Mound D middens indicate that the occupants ate choice cuts of meat, especially deer, turkey, and raccoon. Mound A, E, and S are also thought to have been residential platform mounds. The high dome-shaped Mound C is a burial mound that appears to have been built in a single episode. Two pit burials without grave goods have been recovered from the mound and other burials have been found nearby. Radiocarbon dates from Toltec indicate that most mound building took place between A.D. 800 and 900.

Over 90% of the pottery made and used at Toltec was not decorated. There were more stone artifacts, stone raw materials, and minerals found at this mound center than at any of the surrounding settlements. The abundance and diversity of materials such as quartz crystals, copper, galena, and marine shells indicate that the occupants of Toltec controlled the local exchange network. There are no thick midden deposits except on the mounds at Toltec, indicating that there was not a large permanent population. Toltec is thought to have been a "vacant" center with a small permanent resident population of elites and periodic influxes of large numbers of people for social, religious, and political events.

The subsistence of the Plum Bayou culture was the traditional Woodland one of hunting, gathering, and fishing. There is no evidence of maize cultivation or reliance on any other cultivated plants. The wild food resources in the Arkansas drainage were sufficient to support the construction of a large mound center and support a sociopolitical hierarchy.

Northern Arkansas and the American Bottom   Farther up the Mississippi Valley important changes were taking place that would soon affect most of the Southeast. Here archaeologists have most thoroughly defined the Emergent Mississippian stage of development, with its maize agriculture, shell-tempered pottery, and and the chiefdom level of sociopolitical organization.[72] The late Woodland way of life ended in this area by a.d. 800, probably spurred by the cultivation of maize.

Chipped stone hoes and shell-tempered pottery were added to the artifact assemblage of the Big Lake, Patrick and Dohak cultures in this area. The hoes, shown in Figure 6.23F, were distinctive and most were made from Mill Creek chert, a stone that outcrops in southwest Illinois. The appearance of these hoes correlates with the increased use of maize, and archaeologists suggest such hoes were the primary agricultural tool used to break up the clayey soils of the flood plain.

The Zebree site in northeastern Arkansas, and a number of sites in the American Bottom, such as the Range site, have provided critical information about the transformation from the Woodland to the Mississippian stage of cultural development. One of the key developments was the steady increase in the use of cultivated starchy plants, especially maize. This is documented in the number of maize cobs and kernels in archaeological sites and by the simultaneous appearance of chipped stone hoes and maize-related, shell and limestone-tempered cooking and storage containers. There was also a rapid increase in the size and number of deep pits that were used to store maize. Dan Morse and Phyllis Morse state that the average storage pit at Zebree could have held 52 bushels of maize. Community food storage pits also appeared for

---

[72] For details on the Emergent Mississippian see Kelly *et al.*, 1984, Morse and Morse, 1983 and 1990, and B. D. Smith, 1990.

the first time, and there was a reduction in the number of earth ovens. This reflects an increase in open hearth cooking, which maize requires, using large, shell-tempered pots that could withstand long periods of direct heat. Other community-level changes that took place reflect a shift in social organization. Settlements developed separate residential areas surrounding a central open plaza and house shapes changed from circular to rectangular.

In the American Bottom, maize made up 40% of the diet of the late Patrick and Dohak phases by A.D. 700–800. The communities appear to have been agrarian settlements that were abandoned when nearby soils were depleted. Settlements were reoccupied when the soil fertility increased after lying fallow for some time. Population density increased in the American Bottom between A.D. 800–1000, with a trend toward smaller but more densely occupied communities and scattered farms. Mound centers were being built by at least A.D. 900, and they were consistently spaced 10 to 14 mi apart near the mouths of major streams. Although most of the people lived in scattered household settlements, some communities became larger, with populations that may have numbered in the hundreds by A.D. 950–1000.

By the end of this period, cleared-field maize agriculture was practiced in northern Arkansas and the American Bottoms, and maize was a very important part of the diet. There was still a strong reliance on the cultivation of native plants, gathering of wild plants, and hunting. Wild game, especially deer, turkey, and fish, was critically important throughout this and later periods. There is no evidence that domestic dogs were eaten in the Southeast, and there were no other domestic animals, so hunting and fishing were the only sources of meat.

Summary of the Late Woodland Period

The Southeast was occupied by relatively diverse cultures separated by geographical boundaries during the late Woodland period. The integration fostered by the Hopewellian ceremonial complex during the previous period was gone.

Subsistence of southeastern cultures continued to be based on hunting, gathering, fishing, and varying amount of horticulture. Cultigens, including maize, were only minor food sources in most areas. In the northern central Mississippi Valley maize horticulture, shell-tempered pottery, and the chipped stone hoe developed after about A.D. 700.

During the latter centuries of this period, population growth put pressure on food resources in several areas of the Southeast. The settlement pattern expanded to include small settlements in new areas.

Mound building continued in most of the Gulf Coastal Plain and the Mississippi Valley. The function of the mound centers in the Mississippi Valley changed from a primarily mortuary focus to a sociopolitical one.

SUMMARY OF THE WOODLAND STAGE

The Woodland stage began about 1000 B.C. and ended about A.D. 1000. It is conventionally divided into three periods, early, middle, and late, with general dividing lines placed about A.D. 0 and A.D. 500.

The beginning of the Woodland stage is marked by the spread of pottery manufacture throughout the Southeast. During this period, pottery technology rapidly advanced. Clay was tempered with materials other than fiber and the coiling method and the paddle and anvil technique of welding coils together were developed. These innovations allowed pottery containers to be made in a variety of shapes and sizes that could be used for direct heat cooking, storing, and serving food. By the Middle Woodland, ornamental pottery vessels were made and ceramic art had reached a high level of development. There were four major pottery traditions in the Southeast: Northern, Middle Eastern, Gulf, and South Appalachian. Each of these pottery traditions had a relatively distinctive decorative style and was made in a limited geographic area.

Mound building was also a hallmark of the Woodland stage. It first flourished during the middle period in association with the spread of the Hopewellian ceremonial complex. Some mounds were for human burials, often the local elite, while others were platforms for special activities. Some spectacularly large mound centers were built during this stage, but most mounds were singular and the majority of settlements did not have mounds. Placement of personal prestige grave goods with the dead was practiced in all periods. During the Late Woodland period in the Mississippi Valley, mound centers became the sociopolitical centers of local societies. Platform mounds became the dominant type of mound in the Mississippi Valley and many were resided upon by the elite and used for special activities. Platform mound centers in this region became the hub of social, political, and religious events, while the general population was dispersed in the countryside in relatively small settlements.

The sociopolitical organization of the middle and late Woodland periods in most of the Southeast was characterized by relatively equal, unranked kin groups that could rise to power through the ambitions of self-made leaders called Big Men and Big Women. This triggered sociopolitical advancement from the band level of complexity to the segmented lineage or tribe. The achieved rank of kin groups was temporary, and power could shift when the leader died. In the Mississippi Valley during the late Woodland, it appears that the leaders of the ruling kin group had begun to centralize power, and hereditary ranking of lineages and communities emerged. This rise of social inequality set the stage for the development of powerful chiefdoms in the Mississippian stage.

7

MISSISSIPPIAN STAGE:

A.D. 1000–1500

KEY MISSISSIPPIAN FEATURES
Chiefdoms
Southeastern Ceremonial Complex
Platform Mound Centers

IMPORTANT DEVELOPMENTS
Large Civic-Ceremonial Centers
Ranked Societies

INTRODUCTION AND OVERVIEW

The Mississippian is the last and most complex stage of prehistoric Indian culture in the Southeast. The key features of the Mississippian stage are the development of chiefdoms and the Southeastern Ceremonial Complex, and Platform Mound Centers.

The primary features of the Mississippian stage were first identified in the Mississippi Valley, and early researchers named the archaeological culture after that valley. When sites with similar features are encountered elsewhere in the southeast and Midwest they are called "Mississippian" to reflect the similarity with those first seen in the Mississippi Valley.

Despite severe impacts from European and American contact and colonialism, some southeastern Indian groups survived and several continue to practice elements of traditional Mississippian culture and speak the traditional Muskogean, Siouan, and Caddoan languages. This chapter will deal only with prehistoric Mississippian culture (i.e., up to European contact). Chapter 8 will deal with the postcontact era.

Not everyone in the Southeast adopted the Mississippian way of life. Groups in the mid-Atlantic Coastal Plain and much of the Carolina Piedmont became part of the mid-Atlantic cultural tradition. This tradition is culturally and linguistically distinct from the Mississippian way of life. The core of the mid-Atlantic cultural tradition was in Virginia, Maryland, Delaware, and New Jersey.

CHRONOLOGY

The prehistoric Mississippian stage existed between about A.D. 1000 and 1500. There are three internal periods within these five centuries, which reflect changes in material culture and sociopolitical developments. The events that identify Mississippian periods were not synchronous throughout the region. Most archaeologists agree with the dates for the internal periods and phases that are shown in the Mississippian chronological chart (Figure 7.1).

Subsistence

It was once thought that all Mississippian societies practiced maize agriculture. We know now that while maize agriculture was present in some form in most of the Southeast, it was not a requirement for the advancement to the Mississippian level of cultural development. However, archaeologists believe that a still undefined minimum threshold of food surplus was needed to support the extra demands of the chiefdom level of government. In some areas, this extra surplus was produced by adding maize farming and targeting particular wild food sources. In other areas, it was possible to support the

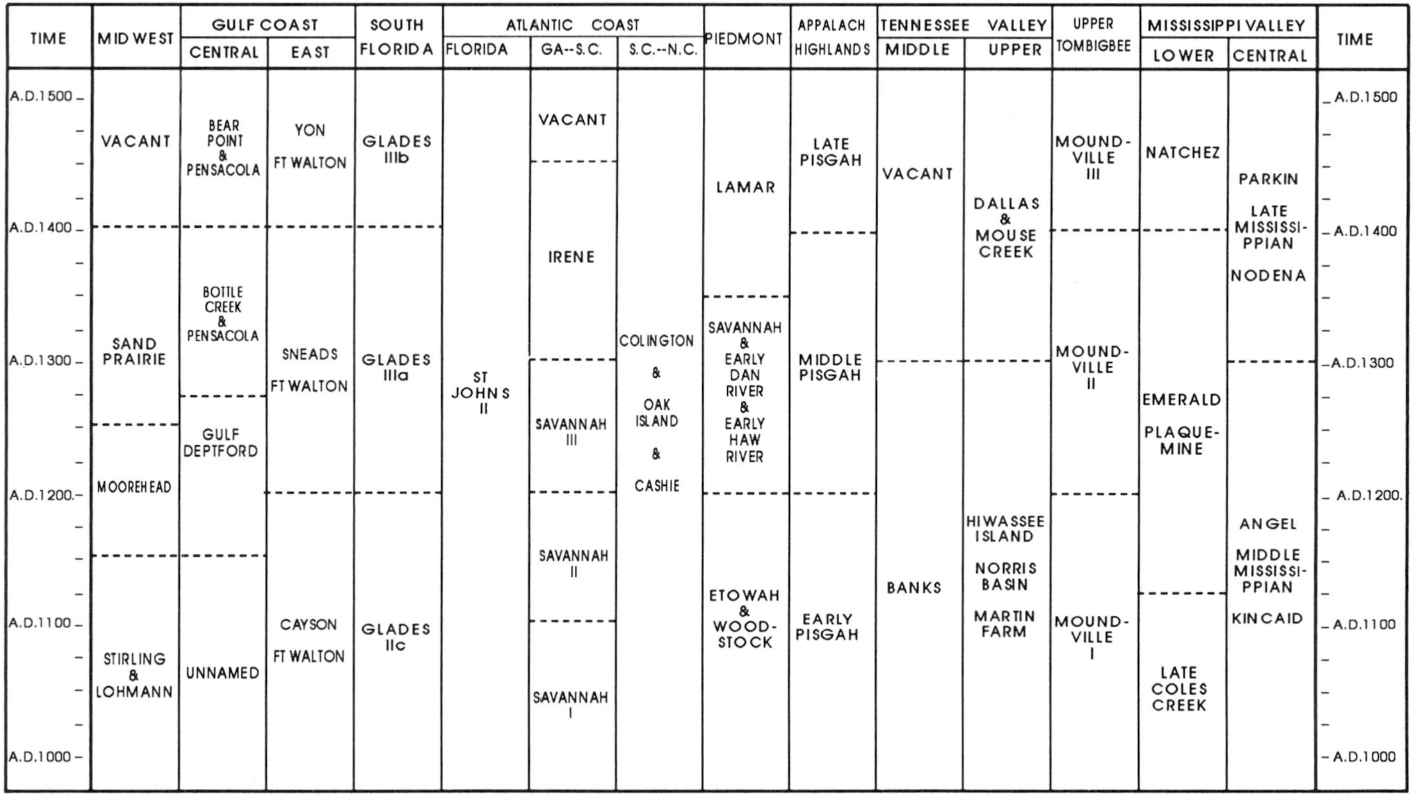

TIME	MID WEST	GULF COAST CENTRAL	GULF COAST EAST	SOUTH FLORIDA	FLORIDA	ATLANTIC COAST GA–S.C.	ATLANTIC COAST S.C.–N.C.	PIEDMONT	APPALACH HIGHLANDS	TENNESSEE VALLEY MIDDLE	TENNESSEE VALLEY UPPER	UPPER TOMBIGBEE	MISSISSIPPI VALLEY LOWER	MISSISSIPPI VALLEY CENTRAL	TIME
A.D. 1500	VACANT	BEAR POINT & PENSACOLA	YON (FT WALTON)	GLADES IIIb		VACANT		LAMAR	LATE PISGAH	VACANT	DALLAS & MOUSE CREEK	MOUNDVILLE III	NATCHEZ	PARKIN / LATE MISSISSIPPIAN	A.D. 1500
A.D. 1400	SAND PRAIRIE	BOTTLE CREEK & PENSACOLA	SNEADS (FT WALTON)	GLADES IIIa	ST JOHNS II	IRENE	COLINGTON & OAK ISLAND & CASHIE	SAVANNAH & EARLY DAN RIVER & EARLY HAW RIVER	MIDDLE PISGAH			MOUNDVILLE II	EMERALD	NODENA	A.D. 1400
A.D. 1300	MOOREHEAD	GULF DEPTFORD				SAVANNAH III				BANKS	HIWASSEE ISLAND		PLAQUEMINE	A.D. 1300
A.D. 1200	STIRLING & LOHMANN	UNNAMED	CAYSON (FT WALTON)	GLADES IIc		SAVANNAH II		ETOWAH & WOODSTOCK	EARLY PISGAH		NORRIS BASIN / MARTIN FARM	MOUNDVILLE I	LATE COLES CREEK	ANGEL / MIDDLE MISSISSIPPIAN	A.D. 1200
A.D. 1100						SAVANNAH I								KINCAID	A.D. 1100
A.D. 1000															A.D. 1000

FIGURE 7.1 Chronology of the Mississippian stage.

requirements of Mississippian chiefdoms by intensifying existing hunting, fishing, gardening, and gathering.

There were two basic Mississippian subsistence patterns: riverine and coastal. The main difference lies in the ratio of cultivated to wild food in the diet. Soils along the coast are generally quite poor, and cultivated crops can play only a limited role in the diet. In the rich soils of the flood plains, cultivated crops can play a significant role.

Riverine Mississippian Subsistence Pattern

Archaeologists have conducted a great deal of research on Mississippian riverine subsistence since 1980. These studies have revealed that Mississippian societies living in river valleys practiced relatively similar subsistence patterns throughout the Southeast.[1] River valley societies used both domesticated plants and wild food resources in river flood plains. Flood plains are characterized by a patchwork of seasonally flooded oxbow lakes, swamps, swales, and levees. Indians generally planted fields on levees, if possible. There, the soil is enriched during springtime floods by organic material and mineral-rich silt. In addition to cultivated crops on the flood plain, people harvested fish in the oxbow lakes, captured migratory water fowl (especially along the major flyways), hunted animals (especially deer, raccoon, and turkey), and gathered nuts, fruits, berries, and seeds. Indians targeted specific foods because they were dependable, they occurred in high densities at predictable locations, they withstood heavy harvesting, and they were accessible to people tied to farms in the flood plain.

Primary Mississippian crops were maize, squash, sunflower, marsh elder, and gourd. Beans became important in some areas after A.D. 1200. These crops, especially maize, provided an important supplement to wild foods, which were always a significant part of the food supply. While the ratio of cultivated to wild foods varied in the Southeast, Indians continued to rely upon both sources, despite the agricultural potential of the soil.

Figure 7.2 is a diagram of the riverine Mississippian annual subsistence cycle. Fall was the busiest season because more food was available, especially maize, deer, and nuts. Food sources were least available during the winter, and people primarily depended on stored food. The spring fish runs and bird migrations provided the first plentiful supply of fresh meat of the year. In the late spring and early summer, fields were cleared and planted. Edible plants such as fruits, berries, greens, and green maize were gathered throughout the summer; fishing was also important. Of course, there were variations in this riverine subsistence pattern due to local differences in weather, plants, animals, and flood plains.

The riverine Mississippian subsistence pattern was centered on maize. There is little direct archaeological evidence of agricultural methods; however,

---

[1] See Smith, 1985c, for a detailed summary of Mississippian riverine subsistence system.

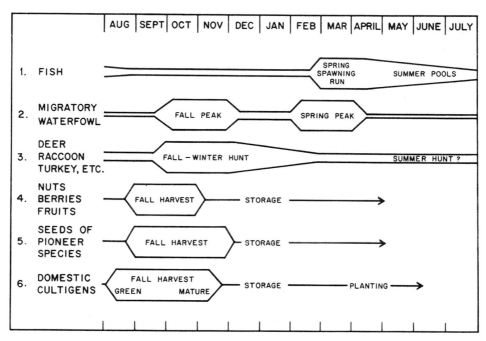

FIGURE 7.2   Riverine Mississippian annual subsistence cycle. (Reprinted with permission from Bruce D. Smith, 1985a, *Alabama and the Borderlands,* R. Reid Badger and Lawrence A. Clayton (eds.), University of Alabama Press, copyright © 1985, all rights reserved.)

archaeologists have found portions of fields preserved under some large mounds, such as the Ocmulgee mound center near Macon, Georgia, shown in Figure 7.3 and located in Figure 7.4. Observation of prehistoric fields, and the writings of some early European explorers in the Southeast, reveal that Indian fields usually had long rows about 1 ft high separated by footpaths. Another method of planting was to put corn, beans, and squash together in small hills. The beans used the cornstalk for support, and the squash thrived in the hill at the base. Archaeologists presume that prehistoric fields were cleared by cutting and burning, which was documented in the historic period. This type of cultivation is known as swidden or slash-and-burn agriculture. It has been estimated that at least 22 to 26 bushels of maize were produced per acre of flood plain soil by this agricultural method.[2]

While beans were introduced into the eastern Woodlands about A.D. 1000, they did not become an important crop in some areas until about 200 yr later. Beans are rich in protein and an excellent complement to a maize-

---

[2] For more information on production capacity of slash-and-burn maize agriculture see Muller, 1987.

FIGURE 7.3 Ridges of a prehistoric maize field buried under a platform mound at Ocmulgee near Macon, Georgia.

based diet, since maize is high in carbohydrates and low in protein. Beans also enhance maize growth because they enrich the soil with nitrogen. By A.D. 1200, maize and beans were often grown together.

Coastal Mississippian Subsistence Pattern

Along the outer Coastal Plain of the Southeast, soils are generally poorer than in the river valleys, and, consequently, they have a lower production capacity. The annual coastal Mississippian subsistence cycle, shown in Figure 7.5, depended heavily on wild food sources and only limited swidden agriculture was practiced.[3] In the coastal area, the few soils capable of growing crops are scattered in small patches and are not annually fertilized by flooding. This situation limits crop production and life of the fields and requires frequent moves to new fields. In contrast, fields on river flood plains were larger, richer, and could be used for long periods of time.

[3] For details on the coastal subsistence cycle see Crook, 1986.

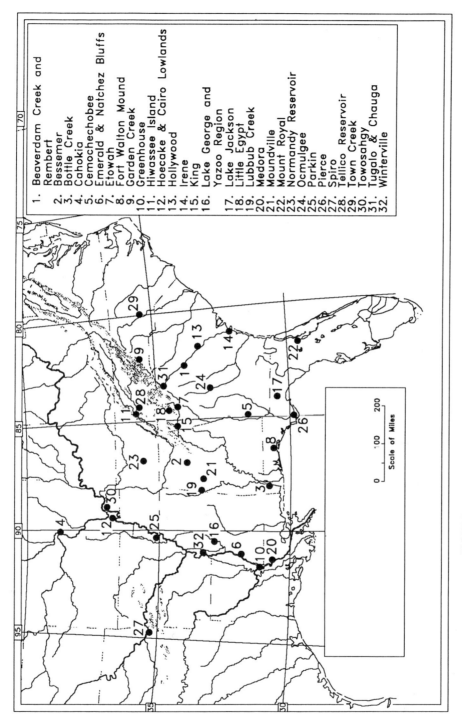

1. Beaverdam Creek and Rembert
2. Bessemer
3. Bottle Creek
4. Cahokia
5. Cemochechobee
6. Emerald & Natchez Bluffs
7. Etowah
8. Fort Walton Mound
9. Garden Creek
10. Greenhouse
11. Hiwassee Island
12. Hoecake & Cairo Lowlands
13. Hollywood
14. Irene
15. King
16. Lake George and Yazoo Region
17. Lake Jackson
18. Little Egypt
19. Lubbub Creek
20. Medora
21. Moundville
22. Mount Royal
23. Normandy Reservoir
24. Ocmulgee
25. Parkin
26. Pierce
27. Spiro
28. Tellico Reservoir
29. Town Creek
30. Towosahgy
31. Tugalo & Chauga
32. Winterville

Scale of Miles

0   100   200

FIGURE 7.4   Some Mississippian sites and areas in the Southeast.

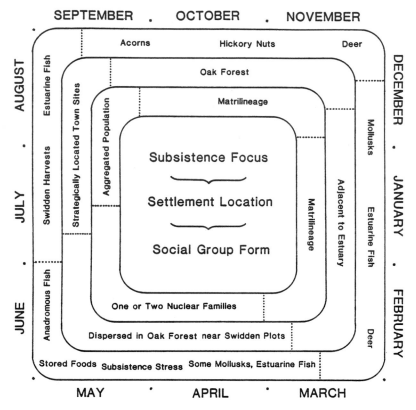

FIGURE 7.5   Coastal Mississippian annual subsistence cycle. (From Crook, 1986.)

Coastal populations were scattered in small groups for most of the year. They tended small, scattered fields, hunted, fished, and gathered the same wild food sources as they had during the Woodland stage. Archaeological evidence of maize, beans, and squash has been found in only a few coastal Mississippian sites; however, early explorers observed and documented agriculture in many areas along and near the coast. The Florida Timucuan farming scene near Jacksonville, Florida, shown in Figure 7.6, was drawn in the mid-1500s.

Summary

There were two types of Mississippian subsistence patterns: riverine and coastal. The riverine subsistence pattern was characterized by relatively permanent fields on river flood plains, in which maize, beans, squash, sunflower, marsh elder, and gourd were grown. Wild plants and animals, especially nuts, deer, and birds, were also important food sources. These people were relatively sedentary and procured wild foods on the flood plain near their fields.

FIGURE 7.6 Historic sketch of coastal Timucuan Indians farming near Jacksonville, Florida, by LeMoyne in 1564. (Reprinted with permission of the Rare Books and Manuscripts Division, The New York Public Library, Astor, Lenox and Tilden Foundations.)

In the coastal Mississippian subsistence pattern, farming played a much smaller role. Primarily, people hunted, gathered, and fished; cultivation was limited to small plots that were quickly exhausted. Coastal agriculturalists had to continually shift fields, and people spent much of the year in small groups tending scattered plots and collecting seasonal marine and terrestrial wild foods.

Chiefdoms

During the Mississippian stage, most southeastern societies evolved to the chiefdom level of sociopolitical organization.[4] A chiefdom is defined by cultural anthropologists as an organization made up of several communities that are controlled by one kin group, usually a lineage group, which has centralized power.

The most distinct characteristic of chiefdoms is the pervasive inequality of people. Chiefdoms usually have two general social classes or ranks: elite and commoner. Within the elite class are several internal ranks. The most powerful positions are held by a group called the ruling elite. They usually

[4] See Earle, 1987, and Service, 1971, for classic anthropological studies of chiefdoms; see Anderson, 1990a,b, and Knight, 1990, for details on the organization of southeastern chiefdoms.

reside at the sociopolitical center of the chiefdom, which is usually the largest settlement with the largest civic-ceremonial area. At the top of the ruling elite are the chiefly elite, who occupy the three most powerful positions—chief, head of the military, and religious leader. Only individuals from a particular family can be members of the chiefly elite, and genealogical distance from the current chief determines an individual family member's status and chance of obtaining a higher position. People were born into the chiefly elite; such status was not conferred through service or merit. One of the primary differences between tribal and chiefdom levels of sociopolitical organization is the inheritance of power and position in chiefdoms. At the tribal level of organization, individuals in kin groups have essentially an equal opportunity to gain power; it is not inherited. In chiefdoms, one kin group dominates the others and power and prestige are passed down to succeeding generations.

Political and religious power are often inseparable in chiefdoms, and both reinforce the status and legitimacy of the chiefly elite. Within the chiefly elite family there may be several individuals eligible for each power position. Personal accomplishments and political ability are important in the selection of specific individuals. Consequently, there is much competition within the ruling family for the limited number of high positions. Schemes and internal plots against the chiefly elite by the kin groups not in power are common in chiefdoms.

Crucial to the chiefdom is centralization of control over several communities. One measure of power is the number of communities the ruling elite controls. Normally, each subservient community is required to pay tribute to the chief and ruling elite in the form of food, crafts, or labor. Often, the ruling elite reward local elites for their allegiance with gifts of imported prestige items, which the ruling elite control. These gifts help maintain the status of the local leaders at home and cement their political alliance to the chief.

Cultural anthropologists and archaeologists are very interested in chiefdoms because they are a recurrent type of social organization worldwide. Simple and complex chiefdoms have been defined with differences relating to the number of localities under centralized control and the number of levels of authority, as diagrammed in Figure 7.7.[5] Simple chiefdoms are political units composed of several communities controlled by the elite at one community. There is only one level of authority or administration above the local community leaders: the ruling elite of the chiefdom. Complex chiefdoms are composed of several simple chiefdoms. There are two levels of authority and administration above the local community. There is also a paramount chiefdom, which consists of several complex chiefdoms or a combination of simple and complex chiefdoms.

Simple chiefdoms are self-sufficient organizations. Shortages and surpluses in member communities are usually balanced through small-scale ex-

[5] See Anderson, 1990b, Peebles and Kus, 1977, and Steponaitis, 1978, for details on chiefdoms.

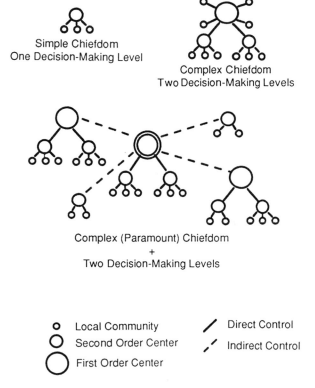

Simple Chiefdom
One Decision-Making Level

Complex Chiefdom
Two Decision-Making Levels

Complex (Paramount) Chiefdom
+
Two Decision-Making Levels

o Local Community

O Second Order Center

◯ First Order Center

╱ Direct Control

╱͗ Indirect Control

FIGURE 7.7 Diagram of the organization of simple and complex chiefdoms. (From Anderson, 1990b, reproduced with permission of the author.)

changes that take place at public events held at the chiefdom center. Food tribute is paid to the ruling elite during social occasions such as festivals and public rituals. At least part of the food given to the ruling elite is stored in public storehouses and used as a reserve. Another form of tribute is labor used in mound building, farming fields for the elite, and war. Festivals are particularly important events as they help solidify the chief's power and strengthen social ties between the different communities in the chiefdom. Public events allow chiefdom members to socialize, find spouses, and trade surplus goods. Lacking problems caused by external events, such as a threat of war or famine, there are few practical reasons for simple chiefdoms to combine into larger political units.

Complex chiefdoms are relatively unwieldy organizations in which communication and control are difficult. Often, they are established through force by an ambitious chief of a simple chiefdom. They also form in defense against threats from nearby complex chiefdoms. Complex chiefdoms are politically unstable because the poorly defined lines of succession result in rivalries between multiple candidates for power positions. There are risks of a coup d'état by the elites of subservient chiefdoms, as well as threats of their secession. The ruling elite in complex chiefdoms are always under pressure to find creative or forceful methods to keep subordinate chiefdoms together and under control. Especially critical were times when power positions were vacant, as when an important person died.

Cycles of rise, expansion, and breakup of complex and paramount chiefdoms are characteristic of the chiefdom level of political development. Centers of power shift as first one community and then another assumes prominence.

Commoners are less directly involved in chiefdom politics, because they have no legitimate claim to power. However, leaders of the elite have to have the support of the commoners to be successful. Typically, the successful leader is the one with the most followers. While commoners are generally pawns in political struggles of the elite, they vote with their feet and therefore decide who will have power.

Why did chiefdoms develop in the first place? Anthropologists have suggested several causal factors including warfare and defense, competition among elites, and resource control and redistribution.[6] While the causes differ, most anthropologists agree that the process of chiefdom development was gradual. However, once a chiefdom was present in a region, new ones formed quickly. Many southeastern archaeologists think that early chiefdoms developed in particularly rich river valleys due to the increased dependency of a growing population on maize and fish. As any farmer or fisher knows, production varies from year to year. With increasing population, it became necessary to protect areas of good soil and fishing to feed the growing number of people.[7] Rich food resources such as fishing grounds and nut groves had to be managed to prevent overutilization by member communities, and resources had to be protected from outsiders. The chiefdom provided an organizational structure necessary for planning and carrying out such management and defense activities.

Identifying past chiefdoms in the archaeological record involves documenting two features: a settlement hierarchy and the inheritance of social rank. A settlement hierarchy is identified by the presence of a large sociopolitical center with mounds (usually platform mounds) around a plaza and smaller nearby communities surrounded by small farmsteads or special procurement sites. Archaeologists recognize inherited social rank primarily through burial analyses. When young individuals are buried with high-status items in separate areas (such as mounds), archaeologists infer that these individuals inherited, rather than earned, their high status. Earning status takes time, and is usually accomplished in adulthood, not childhood.

---

[6] See Anderson, 1990a,b, Carneiro, 1981, Flannery, 1972, and Service, 1971, for more on chiefdom formation theories.

[7] For more details on this inference, see Griffin, 1985.

In summary, anthropologists define chiefdoms primarily by the existence of inherited social rank and centralized political control. Chiefdoms developed for many reasons and at different rates, but once they emerged, chiefdoms developed rapidly in a region. Complex chiefdoms form, enlarge, and fragment through time with the ambition and expertise of particular chiefs.

Southeastern Ceremonial Complex

The Southeastern Ceremonial Complex, also called the Southern Cult, was the central belief system of the people of the Mississippian stage. Three themes were emphasized: ancestor worship, war, and fertility. An important aspect of the Southeastern Ceremonial Complex was that the participants formed a network of interacting societies. Symbols of the southeastern ceremonial complex spread from the Caddo culture area in Oklahoma to the St. Johns culture area in northeast Florida, and from Wisconsin to southwestern Mississippi. The complex developed out of earlier Woodland ceremonial complexes, which share many features, such as particular bird and serpent motifs, elaborate burials for the elite, the use of mounds for elite burials, and the elevation of special structures on earth platform mounds. During the early Mississippian period, the Southeastern Ceremonial Complex was similar to late Woodland ceremonial complexes in the central Mississippi Valley and the Gulf Coastal Plain. Civic-ceremonial centers were larger, but the special objects reserved for high-status use and burial were similar to those used previously: special pottery vessels, shell beads and other shell items, and objects made from imported minerals such as copper, mica, and greenstone. The importance of the Southeastern Ceremonial Complex in the early Mississippian is revealed by the increased size of ceremonial centers and the number of platform mounds around plazas.

While ancestors were important to all kin groups, they were especially important to the chiefly elite because they were their source of power and authority. During most of the Mississippian stage, the chiefly elite conducted elaborate ancestor-related rituals at the civic-ceremonial centers of chiefdoms, where the ancestral leaders were buried. Charnel houses on mound summits were common and they became ancestor shrines during the Mississippian stage. In them were stored not only the bones of the recently dead elite, but also special ancestor-related items, such as carved images of the early ancestors and sacred animals or totems of the family. Charnel houses also held special ritual objects that symbolized chiefly power and were often used to seal political agreements. These symbolic items included special costumes, copper hair ornaments, headdresses, engraved shell cups, strings of shell beads, and symbolic weapons (especially stone axes) that had been passed down through the generations, some of which are shown in Figure 7.8.

The Southeastern Ceremonial Complex reached its peak between ca. A.D. 1200–1400, when complex and paramount chiefdoms developed and the prin-

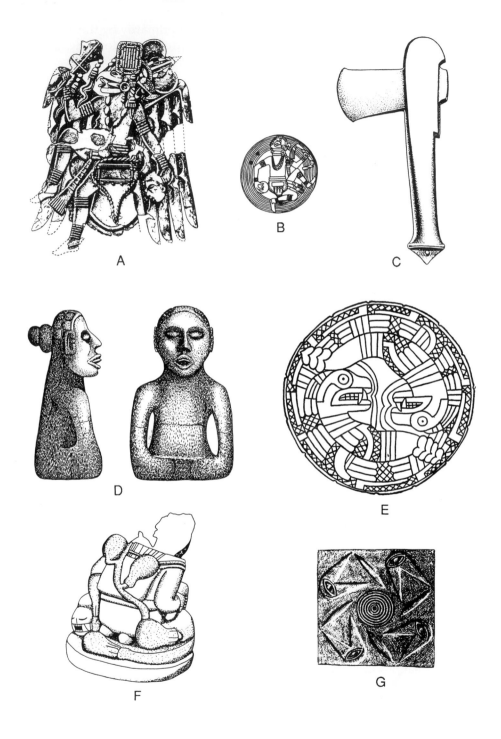

cipal elites expressed much of their authority through elaborate rituals and ceremonies. The elites emphasized the rituals of the Southeastern Ceremonial Complex as never before. The power of the ruling elite was symbolized by special ritual items and the number and size of mounds, public buildings, and plazas at political centers. Ancestor worship by the chiefly elite was powerful. Warfare became an important part of Mississippian political control, and the raptor (probably the peregrine falcon), which was the symbol of war, played a large part in the Southeastern Ceremonial Complex iconography. War-related items such as the forked-eye, falcon costumes and symbolic weapons became the most powerful ritual items and status symbols of the Southeastern Ceremonial Complex. Falcon-related symbols were put on the most elaborate ornaments, such as embossed copper plates, designed to be worn on the front of headdresses, and pins set upright in the hair. Many other ritual objects of copper and shell had embossed, painted, or engraved war themes. A common power symbol is the image of a person dressed in the falcon costume of feathers, holding several heads and weapons such as long knives, monolithic axes, and celts, as shown in Figure 7.8A. Archaeologists call this image a falcon impersonator or falcon dancer. Graves and tombs of the ruling elite regularly contain war-theme ritual items, especially during the middle Mississippian period.

After ca. A.D. 1300–1400 (earlier in the American Bottom), the emphasis on mound building and elaborate rituals of the Southeastern Ceremonial Complex declined considerably in many areas. Major mound centers were abandoned as the first series of complex chiefdoms collapsed. It appears that warfare was replacing ideology as the primary means of political control. Early European observers and archaeologists have documented that southeastern Indians continued ancestor worship, the use of temples and charnel houses as centers of power, and even mound building in some areas. However, rituals associated with these practices were no longer the primary means of political control. The Southeastern Ceremonial Complex became more of a religion and philosophy than a primary political tool. Many rituals associated

---

FIGURE 7.8 Examples of Southeastern Ceremonial Complex artifacts: (A) embossed copper cutout of falcon impersonator (16 in.); (B) shell gorget with chunkey player (2.5 in.); (C) monolithic ground stone ax (11 in.); (D) stone ancestor statues (17.5 in.); (E) slate palette with hand and eye and rattlesnake (12.5 in.); (F) the Birger stone figurine of woman, serpent, and squash (7 in. tall); (G) embossed copper plate (10.5 in.) (A, B, and G from Phillips and Brown (1975). Copyright © 1975 by the President and Fellows of Harvard College; C from Lewis and Knebery, 1946; D from Warren King Moorehead, Exploration of the Etowah Site in Georgia. In *Etowah Papers*, Yale University Press, copyright © 1932, all rights reserved; E from Hodge, 1912; F from Prentice, 1986. Reproduced by permission of the Society for American Archaeology from *American Antiquity*, vol. 51(2).)

with the Southeastern Ceremonial Complex are still practiced in traditional Southeastern Indian culture.

Fertility was important in the Southeastern Ceremonial Complex throughout the Mississippian Stage. The reproduction of plants, animals, and humans was emphasized. Images of serpents, cats, nonraptorial birds, and women appear to symbolize fertility, and were likely totems for kin groups. Fertility images are found in stone statuary, such as the Birger figurine from the St. Louis area, shown in Figure 7.8F, and in wood statuary, pipes, and pottery. The serpent, panther, woodpecker, and other birds were the most popular animals. These motifs are found in many contexts, including graves, refuse pits, and midden deposits of all size settlements.

To summarize, the Southeastern Ceremonial Complex was the belief system of Mississippian culture. Its main themes were ancestor worship, war, and fertility, and these themes were expressed in a myriad of symbols and artifacts. The religion flourished between ca. A.D. 1200 and 1400, when rituals and mound building traditions were the primary means of political control. The roots of this belief system can be traced back to the Archaic and Woodland stages of southeastern Indian cultural development, and elements survive in contemporary southeastern Indian culture.

Periods of the Mississippian Stage

As mentioned above, three periods, early, middle, and late, are recognized in the Mississippian stage. The general characteristics of the Mississippian previously described were expressed quite differently during these stages at different locales within the Southeast. The early Mississippian period, A.D. 1000–1200, was marked in many areas of the Southeast by the spread of maize agriculture and shell-tempered pottery, and by the development of simple chiefdoms, primarily in river valley societies. However, sociopolitical development did not proceed at the same pace everywhere; Cahokia, a paramount chiefdom across the river from present-day St. Louis, was at its height during the early Mississippian period. Interior populations concentrated on flood plain farms and grew rapidly. Civic-ceremonial areas were expanded at chiefdom capitals where the elite lived and were buried. Probably due to environmental factors (poor soil and abundant wild foods) there was relatively little change in the lives of Indians in coastal areas during the early Mississippian period.

The primary distinction of the middle Mississippian period, A.D. 1200–1400, was the development of complex chiefdoms in the areas of the Southeast that had rich agricultural soils. Civic-ceremonial areas at political centers were enlarged for the performance of the elaborate rituals of the southeastern ceremonial complex. At first, political power and authority in complex chiefdoms were maintained primarily through the religion known as the Southeastern Ceremonial Complex. Mound building, displays of symbolic artifacts, and elaborate rituals reached their peak during this period. Along the coasts during this period, the first simple chiefdoms developed and scattered plot agriculture was added to the subsistence pattern in some areas. Complex coastal chiefdoms formed late in this period, but only in those areas where maize could be grown in large quantities, especially near the mouths of large rivers, or where fish were particularly abundant. Increased hostilities and the need for protection were apparent in several parts of the Southeast as settlements were protected with elaborate stockade walls, and the warfare theme was emphasized in the Southeastern Ceremonial Complex.

In the late Mississippian period, A.D. 1400–1500, emphasis on public ritual and mound building declined in many places. Warfare became the primary means of political control, and, in many areas, the use of rituals and symbols of the Southeastern Ceremonial Complex declined. This resulted in a decrease or cessation in mound building, fewer and less-ornate symbolic items, and less-elaborate burials. Complex chiefdoms throughout the region went through cycles of factionalism, instability, violence, and reorganization. Political turmoil and warfare, coupled with a period of drought, led to massive population relocations in at least two areas. The emigrations left hundreds of miles of river valleys virtually vacant until the historic period. In other areas, people abandoned scattered farms and concentrated into new walled settlements from which they farmed the surrounding area. Most Mississippian societies in coastal areas continued the pattern of shifting field agriculture and hunting, fishing, and gathering wild foods; however, agricultural foods have been documented in very few coastal areas.

EARLY MISSISSIPPIAN PERIOD: A.D.1000–1200

During these first two centuries, the Mississippian way of life spread into many areas of the Southeast. The features of this period are maize agriculture, shell-tempered pottery, and the development of simple chiefdoms in most southeastern river valleys. Mississippian culture did not spread during this period to the lower Mississippi Valley, the Gulf coast, or south Florida. There, the late Woodland way of life persisted. During this period societies across the East and Midwest were connected by trade. Prestige goods such as copper and shell ornaments were traded between Illinois, Wisconsin, Ohio, Indiana, Arkansas, Mississippi, Oklahoma, Alabama, Florida, and Georgia.

Material Culture

The early Mississippian artifact assemblage included a variety of well-made pottery containers, as shown in Figure 7.9. Shell-tempered pottery spread from the central Mississippi Valley into western and northern parts of the South, especially the Ohio, Cumberland, Tennessee, upper Tombigbee,

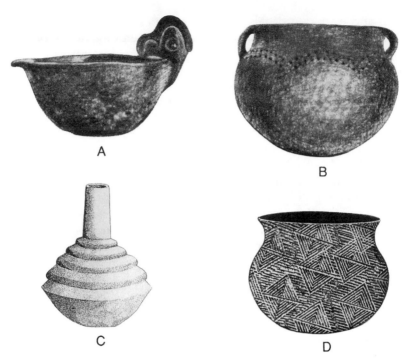

FIGURE 7.9   Early Mississippian pottery: (A) shell-tempered plain bird effigy bowl (6 in.); (B) shell-tempered punctated jar with strap or loop handles (6 in.); (C) sand-tempered bottle (13 in.), and (D) sand-tempered complicated stamped jar (10 in.). (A and B from Griffin, 1952, with permission of the University of Chicago Press, copyright © 1952 by The University of Chicago. All rights reserved; C from Schnell *et al.*, 1981; D from Caldwell, 1958, reproduced by permission of the American Anthropological Association from MEMOIR NO. 88 of the American Anthropological Association.)

and Black Warrior valleys. In the rest of the Southeast, sand or grog tempering continued to be used. The suite of pottery containers was expanded, especially in the areas practicing maize agriculture, to include many large jars, bowls, and pans. These containers could be used for long periods of direct-heat cooking (useful for producing salt and lime) and for storage. Shell-tempered pottery tended to be decorated with Gulf tradition-related incised and punctated designs. Consequently, in those areas where shell tempering was diffused, the previous ceramic tradition generally declined. In areas that did not adopt shell tempering, traditional surface decorations continued: complicated stamping in the Appalachian Highlands and Piedmont, cord marking in the Coastal Plain of Georgia and the Carolinas, and incising and punctating in the Gulf Coastal Plain, the lower Mississippi Valley, and Florida.

The stone tool assemblage of the early Mississippian period was composed largely of expedient tools, such as knives and perforators, made from chert flakes. Formal tools were limited mainly to chipped stone points. Small triangular points with straight edges and bases remained popular throughout most of the region, but small stemmed and side-notched types persisted in the western portion of the region. Chipped stone hoes, such as the Mill Creek hoe, were made in some areas of the central Mississippi Valley. Shells were also attached to long handles and used for hoes, but only a few examples have been found. We know from historical observations that wooden hoes and digging sticks were also used, as illustrated in Figure 7.6. While archaeologists have not found hoes made of the easily decayed materials, some kind of hoe or digging stick was necessary for planting and weeding.

Subsistence

The hallmark of early Mississippian period subsistence was the spread of maize agriculture into many river valleys. In some areas, maize agriculture was adopted fairly rapidly, as in the central Tombigbee and Apalachicola valleys. In other areas, like the Tennessee Valley, it was adopted more gradually. On most of the outer coastal plain there are no indications that maize was a factor in subsistence during the early Mississippian period.

An example of a gradual shift to maize agriculture was the Tennessee Valley, where gardening had been part of subsistence since the Archaic stage. The earliest dates of maize presence in the Southeast are from this valley. It was not until almost A.D. 1200, though, that full-scale maize agriculture was underway.[8] The pollen record indicates that large sections of the flood plain forest were cleared for planting at this time. An additional sign of the importance of maize agriculture is the relocation of settlements from the flood plain to higher terraces. This move is interpreted as reflecting the need to farm as much flood plain land as possible and to protect the large, permanent villages from flooding.

The most rapid shifts to maize agriculture seem to have occurred in societies with previous subsistence stress, little evidence of gardening, and the presence of good agricultural soil. While we really cannot define what "rapid" means, estimates are that it probably took less than 100 yr for the people to become fully dependent upon maize. For example, at the Lubbub Creek site in the central Tombigbee Valley, the residents were fully dependent on maize very early in the Mississippian period.[9] Studies of the preceding late Woodland Miller III diet revealed no maize, and there are good indications of depopulation of meat animals by over hunting. The shift to intense maize use in the central Tombigbee was accompanied by a distinct settlement pattern shift from the seasonal base camp–satellite camp pattern to one of scattered farmsteads.

Signs of subsistence stress in the late Woodland Weeden Island culture

[8] See Schroedl *et al.*, 1990, for details.

[9] For details on the Lubbub Creek site see Peebles, 1983a,b,c and 1987, and Welch, 1990.

were also seen in the Apalachicola Valley where most of the population had dispersed into the uplands. There are also indications that maize was experimented with by some late Weeden Island groups.[10] Maize is consistently recovered from early Mississippian Cayson phase settlements, and it appears that the switch to the riverine Mississippian subsistence pattern was quick. Pollen studies in the Apalachicola Valley have also shown that clearing of the flood plain was taking place. It is assumed that this clearing was for maize fields as 14% of the pollen from the soil of contemporary settlements is from maize.

In the central Mississippi Valley, the Mississippian riverine subsistence pattern was continued from the Emergent Mississippian and late Woodland periods. In northeast Arkansas, it appears that there was a significant increase in maize agriculture, along with rapid population growth. Maize agriculture also rapidly spread west into the Caddoan culture area in the Red and Arkansas river valleys and the Ozark highlands.[11] However, the population in these regions remained lower and more widely dispersed than in the Mississippi Valley, probably because of the poorer soil and smaller quantity of food resources.

Settlement Patterns and Mounds

Adoption of the riverine Mississippian subsistence pattern was accompanied by a significant change in settlement pattern. The new settlement pattern was characterized by a plethora of small farms, called farmsteads, scattered on the rich soils of the flood plains. Most of the population lived on these farmsteads. At the top of the settlement hierarchy was the large civic-ceremonial area, usually with several mounds around a plaza, which was located either within the largest settlement of the chiefdom or at a special ceremonial center where only the ruling and chiefly elite resided. Between the farmsteads and the chiefdom center were moderate-sized settlements with one or more associated mounds. Local elite resided at the midsized settlements. This hierarchical settlement pattern is typical of complex chiefdoms.

A good example of the settlement pattern change associated with the adoption of the Mississippian riverine subsistence system is in eastern Tennessee, where a series of chiefdoms emerged along the flood plain of the Tennessee River.[12] The site hierarchy consisted of a large settlement with a ceremonial center surrounded by smaller settlements and scattered farmsteads. The largest of the chiefdom centers was on Hiwassee Island (see Figure 7.10). The ceremonial precinct had a double pyramid mound with multiple ascending

[10] For details see Scarry, 1981 and 1990.

[11] For more about the Caddoan culture see Rogers, 1983 and 1989.

[12] For details about eastern Tennessee see Schroedl et al., 1990.

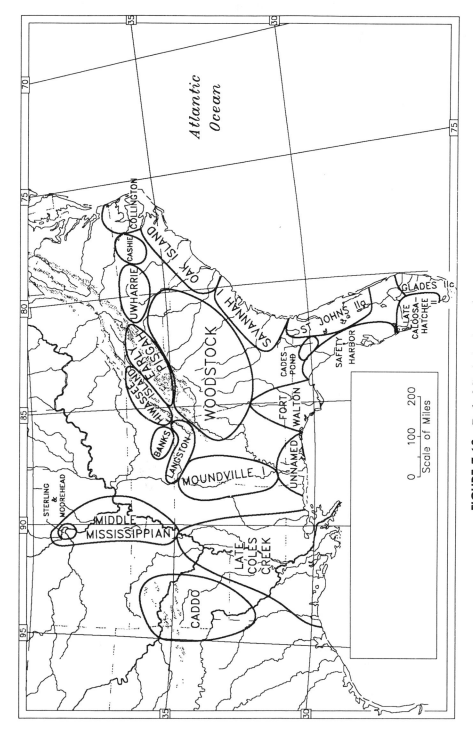

FIGURE 7.10 Early Mississippian culture areas.

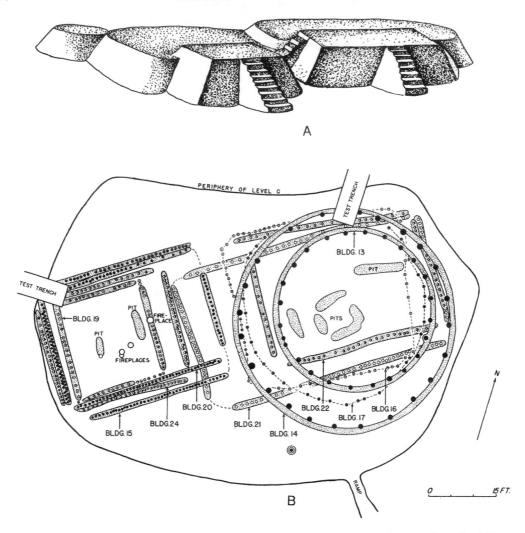

FIGURE 7.11 (A) Artist's reconstruction of the three connected mounds at the Hiwassee Island site; (B) overlay of the foundations of structures on the summits. (From Lewis and Kneberg, 1946.)

stairways and an attached flat topped conical mound. The early Mississippian mounds were not as large as the ones shown in Figure 7.11, which depicts a situation during the middle Mississippian. Early Mississippian mounds were composed of a series of buried summits, each of which had supported a large public building with raised rectangular clay platforms, raised clay seats, and raised clay hearths.

The residences of commoners at the Hiwassee Island and other chiefdom centers were rectangular and made of slender saplings placed in foundation trenches and pulled together at the top. The walls were covered with a clay plaster (called daub) or panels of bark, and the buildings had hard, smooth clay floors with central hearths in raised circular and square clay platforms.

Another good example of the early Mississippian settlement pattern changes associated with the rapid adoption of maize agriculture is in the Apalachicola Valley of the Fort Walton culture area.[13] Previous Weeden Island settlements had been widely dispersed small campsites in tributary valleys and uplands. Early in the Cayson period, there was a shift to scattered farmsteads surrounding mound centers. Interestingly, the Fort Walton civic-ceremonial mound centers were arranged in pairs on both sides of rivers at intervals of about 30 mi. The Cemochechobee site, the ceremonial precinct of one Fort Walton culture chiefdom, contained two platform mortuary mounds separated by a plaza from an elite residential area.[14] Charnel houses had been constructed, emptied, razed, and buried under a series of summits. Members of the chiefly elite were buried in the mounds. Accompanying their remains were elaborate grave goods, including special mortuary pottery and Southeastern Ceremonial Complex ritual items. Such items were also cached in the mounds during construction of a new summit.

While few details are known about settlement patterns of the early Mississippian culture in the St. Johns River valley in east Florida, unusual large Mississippian mound centers were constructed during this period. Both platform and conical mounds were present and often stood at the ends of long, symmetrical ponds ("water avenues") or shell-lined causeways up to a half-mile long. Examples are the Mount Royal and the Shields mound centers, as shown in Figure 7.12. Typical early Mississippian Southeastern Ceremonial Complex items (copper plates, shell beads, greenstone celts, and special mortuary pottery vessels) were found with elite burials in the mounds at these centers, such as those shown in Figure 7.8.

In the lower Mississippi Valley, the chiefdom hierarchy of settlements developed with no signs of significant agriculture in the late Coles Creek culture.[15] At the top of the settlement hierarchy were multiple-mound centers that were often surrounded by moderate-sized settlements with single platform mounds. Most of the population lived in seasonal settlements. In the civic-ceremonial centers, platform mounds were organized along rectangular plazas, and platform burial mounds were consistently present. Mound building increased during this period. Numerous mound centers with one to three mounds were constructed, and other mound centers were enlarged. The Lake George site, for example, went from a small mound center to a large ceremonial center during this period, and it was the dominant site in the lower Yazoo Valley. Similarly, the Osceola civic-ceremonial mound center in the Tensas

---

[13] For more about the Fort Walton culture see Brose, 1984, and Scarry, 1990.

[14] See Schnell *et al.*, 1981 for details of this excavation.

[15] See Fritz and Kidder, 1993, and Kidder, 1992 and 1993, for details about late Coles Creek.

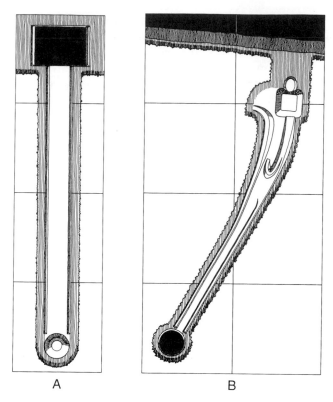

FIGURE 7.12   St. Johns Mississippian civic-ceremonial centers. (A) Mount Royal near Palatka, Florida, and (B) shields near Jacksonville, Florida (squares are 660 ft on each side). (From W. N. Morgan, 1980, *Prehistoric Architecture in the Eastern United States.* Reprinted with permission of MIT Press, copyright © 1980, all rights reserved.)

Basin was expanded, and it was surrounded by no fewer than eight lesser mound centers within a 12-mi radius. A small amount of maize has been found and only at the Osceola site. It is a presumed that maize agriculture was not a significant part of the late Coles Creek subsistence.

Warfare

Signs of increased warfare and the need for defensive fortifications have been documented in several early Mississippian culture areas: the Cherry Valley Phase in the central Mississippi Valley, the Moundville I Summerville Phase in the central Tombigbee Valley, and the Langston culture area in the central Tennessee Valley. The central settlement of the Summerville chiefdom,

Lubbub Creek, was surrounded with a stockade wall with regularly spaced bastions. Inside this fortified settlement, the civic-ceremonial precinct was enclosed by an additional stockade. Warfare in the Summerville society is also suggested by burials of men who had died from arrow wounds, and there was a separate area in the cemetery reserved for men buried with war symbols, such as copper plates embossed with the falcon impersonator. In the Langston culture in the central Tennessee Valley, chiefdom centers were located in particularly secure defensive locations and were strongly fortified with walls and bastions.

Mortuary Patterns

Burial practices of the early Mississippian chiefdoms reflect the development of ranked social stratification in the consistently different mortuary treatment, segregation, and distinctive grave goods of elites and commoners. Elite members of all ages were buried in separate areas with elaborate grave goods, and sometimes with what appear to be retainer burials (sacrifices). In many areas, the elite were buried exclusively in or near mounds at the civic-ceremonial centers; in others, they were buried in separate cemeteries or in special areas within cemeteries. The elite were usually buried with high-status items of the Southeastern Ceremonial Complex, such as copper plates embossed with the falcon or the sun, copper-covered ear-spools, shell beads, or special mortuary pottery. Use of log-lined tombs for the elite continued in the Mississippi Valley and other parts of the Southeast.

Commoners were usually buried in or near their houses or in cemeteries, with utilitarian items, large pieces of pottery, or nothing at all. They were usually buried in the flesh in the extended position facing east. Bundled and flexed burials are infrequent. The most frequent grave goods placed with commoners were pottery containers, but they were not necessarily elaborately decorated or particularly well made.

In the Appalachian Mountain and Piedmont areas, a new type of ceremonial structure—the earth lodge—was constructed in the Pisgah culture area. This was an above-ground building that had either an earth-covered roof or a high earthen embankment around the outside walls. Inside some earth lodges were raised clay benches along the inside walls, raised clay hearths and animal effigies in the center, and tunnel-like passageways to the outside.[16] The use of the earth lodge as a ceremonial building in the Appalachian Highlands and Piedmont coincides with the beginning of the early Mississippian period, about A.D. 1000–1100. Earth lodges were elevated on platform mounds and like other elevated structures were periodically destroyed, buried under a layer of earth, and rebuilt on a new and higher summit.

[16] For details on earth lodges see Rudolph, 1984.

Summary

The early Mississippian period was characterized by the spread of well-made pottery, maize agriculture, and the chiefdom level of sociopolitical organization in many areas of the Southeast. By A.D. 1200, most cultures had adopted some version of the Mississippian culture, as evidenced by the settlement hierarchy, the Southeastern Ceremonial Complex, and ranked social status. The riverine subsistence pattern, characterized by maize agriculture, was practiced in most river valleys of the Southeast by the end of this period. In much of the outer Coastal Plain and the lower Mississippi Valley, chiefdoms developed that were supported only by hunting, gathering, and fishing. Transformation to the chiefdom level of sociopolitical organization did not require maize agriculture.

Examples of Early Mississippian Cultures

The Woodstock and coastal Savannah cultures will be discussed as typical examples of early Mississippian period cultures in the Southeast. I have also included the Cahokia culture in the American Bottom in this section. While the Cahokia culture is not typical, it was very important to the development of Mississippian culture in the rest of the Southeast. This society also constructed the largest and most complex Mississippian mound center ever built, Cahokia.

Woodstock Culture

The Mississippian way of life appeared earliest in the Macon-Atlanta-Rome portion of the Woodstock culture area.[17] This area of Georgia holds important clues to how Mississippian culture spread in the Southeast, though the subject is still not yet well understood. Within this culture area, the Macon Plateau society warrants special attention.

Macon Plateau Mississippian

In the Macon Plateau, the Mississippian way of life appeared full-blown just before A.D. 1000. The riverine maize-based subsistence pattern, the Southeastern Ceremonial Complex, the chiefdom level of sociopolitical organization, and shell-tempered pottery were all present. Although radiocarbon dates are few, they suggest the earliest Mississippian settlements on the Atlantic Slope were in the Macon Plateau area, and no transition from late Swift Creek to Macon Plateau Mississippian has been found.

Only two Macon Plateau Mississippian settlements have been documented: Ocmulgee and Brown's Mount. Both were large fortified settlements with large and complex civic-ceremonial precincts. Ocmulgee had an immense plaza, four platform mounds, two earth lodge mounds, and a stockade and

---

[17] For detailed summaries of Woodstock see Anderson and Joseph, 1988, and Hally and Langford, 1988.

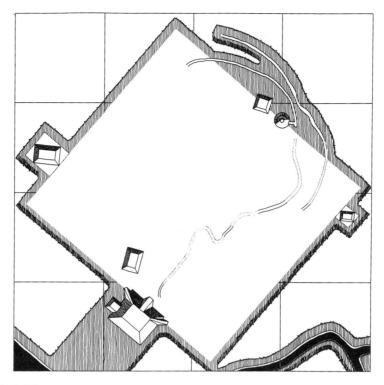

FIGURE 7.13 Ocmulgee, an early Mississippian mound center near Macon, Georgia (squares are 660 ft on each side). (From W. N. Morgan, 1980, *Prehistoric Architecture in the Eastern United States*. Reprinted with permission of MIT Press, copyright © 1990, all rights reserved.)

moat encircling the entire complex, as shown in Figure 7.13.[18] The largest platform mound was 50 ft high with three ascending ramps and an attached smaller platform mound. Opposite the plaza was a circular mound with an earth lodge 42 ft in diameter. The earth lodge had a roof of heavy logs covered with earth and sod and a long covered entryway. Inside was a clay bench along the wall 6 in high, with 47 individually molded seats and a raised central clay hearth. Beside the central hearth were three elevated seats and a large bird effigy with a forked eye made of fired clay. The platform mound on the northwest side of the plaza had a series of charnel houses on its summits, and elaborate high-status burials were placed in tombs in the mantles covering the mortuaries.

Questions about the origin of the Macon Plateau society have been raised by archaeologists ever since it was first excavated in the 1930s. Because of the

[18] See Fairbanks, 1946 and 1956, for a detailed description of the excavations at Ocmulgee.

early dates, the lack of local precedents, and the fact that it was a full-blown Mississippian culture, the Macon Plateau society is viewed by most archaeologists as belonging to a group of immigrants or colonists. James B. Griffin and others have long held that pottery similarities suggest that the Macon Plateau immigrants came from the early Mississippian culture in east Tennessee.[19] Research has supported this theory, and it appears that an invasion of the Macon Plateau region took place about A.D. 1000. Mississippian colonizers established a chiefdom in the area previously occupied by late Woodland societies. The success of the invasion is thought to have triggered a wave of defensive chiefdom formations in societies of the region that were previously organized at the tribal level. The need for defense is evidenced by the presence of fortifications at all early Mississippian settlements in northwest Georgia, some of which were over 100 mi from the Macon Plateau. The rise of the Etowah chiefdom near Atlanta, Georgia, beginning about A.D. 1100–1200, also appears to have been directly effected by the Macon Plateau colonizers, as shell-tempered pottery first introduced by the Macon Plateau colonizers has been found below the earliest platform mounds at Etowah.[20] Archaeologists suggest that the earliest Etowah chiefdoms may well have threatened their neighbors to the north and east, thus instigating the defensive formation of more chiefdoms. The threat represented by the Macon Plateau Mississippian colony may have started a domino effect of imitation and defense. Current thinking is that the Mississippian way of life spread throughout the Atlantic Slope over about 200 yr in this manner.

The simple chiefdoms that developed in the Woodstock culture area were linearly arranged in river valleys and had the typical chiefdom settlement hierarchy. At the top was the largest settlement with the largest and most mounds located in a well-defined civic-ceremonial center. Next were a few moderate-sized settlements without mounds, and at the base were scattered farmsteads on the flood plain. Most large chiefdom centers were clustered at the Fall Line in the river valleys of the inner Coastal Plain. Farther out on the Coastal Plain, chiefdom centers were more regularly spaced in the river valleys. In northwest Georgia, most settlements, even small ones, were fortified with stockades and ditches, but these defensive measures have not been documented in the Savannah River Valley.

Early Mississippian elite were buried only in civic-ceremonial mound centers, and they alone were interred with high-status grave goods. Their skeletons showed physical evidence of a better diet than that of commoners, and they had generally better health.[21] The earth lodge was a consistent Mississippian ceremonial structure in this area, and several have been excavated, including ones at Tugalo and Chauga in the Upper Savannah Valley.

---

[19] For details see Anderson, 1990a,b, Griffin, 1946, and Phillips *et al.*, 1951.

[20] James B. Griffin, personal communication, 1993.

[21] For details see Anderson *et al.*, 1986.

At both chiefdom centers, earth lodges were found on the summits of platform mounds. At Tugalo, the earth lodges were square to rectangular in shape with walls about 25 ft long with a thick, high earth embankment along the outside walls. Walls were made of individually set posts with a large post at each corner. A central hearth was present as was an entryway through the earth embankment near the northeast corner. High-status burials were placed in the earth mantles of the platform mounds covering dismantled earth lodges.

In summary, early Mississippian culture in the Piedmont and Atlantic Coastal Plain in Georgia and South Carolina appears to have been initiated by the immigration of a group of people from the eastern Tennessee early Mississippian culture area, just before A.D. 1000. Afterward, the Mississippian way of life began to spread in a west-to-north-and-east pattern. The expansion of Mississippian culture after the Macon Plateau invasion appears to have been a defensive and imitation process. Local societies politically reorganized into chiefdoms, the elite adopted the new version of the Southeastern Ceremonial Complex, and shell-tempered pottery and the maize subsistence system were universal.

Coastal Savannah I Culture

The Savannah I culture on the outer Atlantic Coastal Plain of Georgia and South Carolina is the only well-documented example of coastal early Mississippian culture in the Southeast.[22] Research conducted over the past six decades documents the transition from the Woodland to the early Mississippian period at about A.D. 1150–1200. The initiation of the Mississippian way of life is indirectly related to the Macon Plateau intrusion, and its ripple effect initiated the development of Mississippian culture on the Atlantic Slope. The main archaeological indicator of the transition to the Mississippian on the Georgia coast is the emergence of the classic chiefdom settlement hierarchy. The largest Savannah I settlements have platform and burial mounds and are surrounded by smaller seasonal settlements. Some pottery changes coincided with this sociopolitical transition, but there was no switch to shell-tempered pottery with incised and punctated decorations. Grit tempering replaced grog, a finer type of cord marking was used, and some typical Mississippian containers such as the large open bowl were present.

From the distribution of settlement types, it appears that there were two Savannah simple chiefdoms. Each was loosely associated with the lower valley of a major river system, these being the Savannah and Altamaha.[23] The chiefdoms included the lower portions of the river valleys, adjacent uplands, the estuaries, the coast near the river mouth, and the barrier islands. The chiefdom shared basic features, such as burial mounds and the settlement hierarchy. However, each chiefdom had distinctive pottery types. Only two Savannah

[22] See Crook, 1986, and Thomas and Larsen, 1979, for good summaries.
[23] For details about these chiefdoms see Crook, 1986, and Pearson, 1977 and 1978.

I platform mounds were built, both of which were in the Irene chiefdom at the mouth of the Savannah River. One platform mound was built at the Irene site at the mouth of the Savannah River, and the other at the Indian Hill site on St. Helena Island.

Savannah I societies practiced the coastal Mississippian subsistence pattern, and maize has not been recovered from any site. The model of the coastal Mississippian subsistence cycle and settlement pattern shown in Figure 7.5 was based primarily on early discriptions of the historic Guale, who are the descendants of the Savannah I culture. They practiced small-plot maize agriculture.[24] It is theorized that early Mississippian Savannah I societies practiced the traditional coastal hunting-gathering-fishing seasonal round. Marine foods, especially finfish, along with deer and nuts, were the primary food sources, although they were supplemented with many other plant and animals.

To summarize, the Savannah I culture area appears to have adopted the Mississippian way of life late in this period, about A.D. 1150–1200. The initiation of the Mississippian culture was probably part of the imitation-and-defense process of chiefdom formation that spread from the interior riverine chiefdoms to the west. Chiefdoms were centered around the lower portions of each of the major rivers in this portion of the outer Atlantic Coastal Plain. The evidence of chiefdom formation is seen in the archaeologic record primarily in the hierarchy of settlements, especially in the Irene chiefdom, where two platform mounds were constructed. Neither shell-tempered pottery nor maize agriculture was adopted by this coastal society.

American Bottom and Cahokia

As you will recall from the last chapter, Indian societies in the American Bottom and northeast Arkansas of the central Mississippi Valley had developed into the Emergent Mississippian culture during A.D. 800–1000. The shift to maize agriculture, limestone-tempered pottery, and the development of the chiefdom level of settlement hierarchy all occurred before A.D. 1000. In the American Bottom during the Stirling Phase, A.D. 1050–1150, the Mississippian riverine subsistence pattern prevailed, the population grew rapidly, and the first complex chiefdoms developed.

What was unusual about the American Bottom is the density and size of the civic-ceremonial mound centers that were constructed, especially at centrally located Cahokia.[25] This settlement, opposite present-day St. Louis, is one of the most famous archaeological sites in North America. It reached the height of its power in the Stirling and Moorehead phases between A.D. 1050 and 1250, when it grew to cover over 5 square mi and had over 100

---

[24] See Crook, 1986, for details on coastal Mississippian subsistence.

[25] See Milner, 1990, Milner *et al.*, 1984, and Fowler, 1978, for summaries of Cahokia and the Mississippian stage in the American Bottom.

mounds, as shown in Figure 7.14. The central civic-ceremonial area included the multiterraced Monks Mound and the other large platform mounds laid out in parallel rows on either side of the large central plaza. This central ceremonial area was protected by a stockade with a series of bastions. Monks Mound was 1000 × 700 ft at the base and was 100 ft high. It is the largest prehistoric earth mound ever built in the United States. There were many different types of mounds at Cahokia including platform, conical, oval, and linear. Most mounds cluster along the central ridge of the site and are grouped around open plazas. Most are platform mounds that supported elite residences or public buildings. Four circles between 240 and 480 ft in diameter and comprised of large posts are thought to have been solar observatories called woodhenges. They may have been used for determining celestial events such as solstices and equinoxes. New residential areas were built with a clear organization of residences, platform and burial mounds, and plazas. As time went by, older residential sectors were razed to make way for new mounds. The settlement was occupied for about 500 yr. Archaeologists do not agree about how many people lived at Cahokia at any point in time. The large mounds and overall size of the settlement do not necessarily mean large numbers of people lived there. Archaeologist George Milner estimates that the peak population at Cahokia numbered in the thousands, not tens of thousands. The bulk of the American Bottom population was dispersed on flood plain farms and practiced the riverine Mississippian subsistence pattern. This dispersed population likely was periodically required to contribute labor to build the mounds at Cahokia. Remember, mounds were built in stages, not all at once.

By A.D. 1000–1050, a ranked society with a ruling elite stratum was present at the Cahokia mound center and throughout the American Bottom. The ruling elite are identifiable by special and elaborate mortuary treatment. At Cahokia, the graves of elite included not only finely crafted and often imported grave goods, but also many sacrifices or retainer burials. One well-known instance is the mass grave in Mound 72. In this mound, Melvin Fowler found a male burial laid out on a platform covered with 20,000 shell beads. The burial was accompanied by three men and women whom Fowler suspects were close relatives killed for this burial. Grave goods included about 800 arrow points in a quiver made in one point style from only one flint type, sheets of copper and mica, and 15 chunkey game stones. Nearby were the skeletons of four decapitated men with their hands also cut off. More than 50 women between 18 and 23 yr old were buried in a pit nearby. Fowler suspects they were strangled. This burial ritual clearly indicates the power and authority of the ruling elite at Cahokia.

At smaller mound centers, the elite were buried in a less elaborate manner. Their remains were often prepared elsewhere and bundled, then placed in a mound in a mass burial. Such burials often were accompanied by limited amounts of grave goods such as shell beads and whelk shells. Commoners

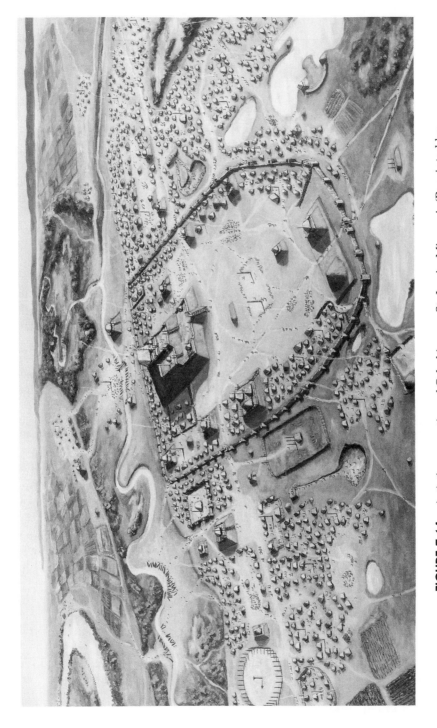

FIGURE 7.14 Artist's conception of Cahokia near St. Louis, Missouri. (Reprinted by permission of the artist, William R. Iseminger.)

were primarily buried in cemeteries of outlying settlements, along bluff tops, and at mound centers. Grave goods were limited and utilitarian, but there were occasional individuals accompanied by large numbers of ornamental items such as shell beads or copper objects; these individuals are thought to have been local leaders.

The settlement hierarchy in the American Bottom had four levels. At the top was the Cahokia mound center. The next level consisted of large settlements (over 120 acres) with several mounds. Next were smaller settlements with a single platform mound. At the base of the settlement hierarchy were small moundless settlements and farmsteads scattered on the flood plain. Why was Cahokia so large, what was its role in the hierarchy, and how did their system work? These questions have intrigued archaeologists ever since Cahokia was discovered. First, Cahokia had an excellent loaction. It lies just below the confluence of the Illinois and Missouri rivers with the Mississippi River, and it is not far from the Ohio-Tennessee-Cumberland entry into the Mississippi. It lies in the center of a mammoth flood plain with great expanses of marshes and hundreds of oxbow lakes and large deposits of flint nearby.

The political organization of the early Mississippian chiefdoms in the American Bottom is the subject of debate. Melvin Fowler and his colleagues theorize that there was a single paramount chiefdom in the American Bottom that was controlled socially and economically by the elite residing at Cahokia.[26] They also suggest that the success of this chiefdom was due to their monopoly of both long-distance trade and the manufacture of ceremonial and ritual items. They theorize that the subordinate chiefdom centers in the American Bottom were trading hubs strategically located along major waterways to provide the best access for canoe-based trade. According to Fowler's theory, trading success was the key to the material wealth and elaborate mound construction seen at Cahokia.

Another explanation of the organization of the American Bottoms chiefdoms is put forth by George Milner. He regards the chiefdoms on this rich flood plain as too large and complex to have been managed under one paramount chief at Cahokia.[27] He argues that it was unlikely, given the weaknesses inherent in chiefdom politics, that any one chiefdom could completely control the mosaic of strong, wealthy chiefdoms in this area. Milner suggests that while Cahokia was surely the dominant chiefdom in the American Bottom, the other chiefdoms were semi-independent and not under the thumb of the Cahokia elite. These chiefdoms were centered at large mound centers located at intervals along the rivers. Here, local elite resided and directly controlled the surrounding population on the flood plain. He suggests that these simple chiefdoms likely took advantage of rare or locally distributed resources, such as galena, to interact with the elite at Cahokia. He agrees, though, that Cahokia

[26] For more about this theory see Fowler, 1978, and Peregrine, 1991.

[27] See Milner, 1990, for details of his theory.

was a complex chiefdom, and that the elite at Cahokia maintained connections of some kind with the local chiefdoms. Close relations would have provided the Cahokians with the labor needed to build their monumental mounds, and in return, they supplied the outlying chiefdom elite with quantities of ritual and high-status items. In summary, Milner thinks that the American Bottom Mississippian chiefdoms were socially and politically segmented into complex chiefdoms controlling more-or-less discrete territories and interacting symbiotically with Cahokia.

Archaeologists agree that the Cahokia system was the most organizationally complex of all Mississippian societies. They also agree that the huge Cahokia mound center dominated the American Bottom. What they do not agree upon is how the sociopolitical system worked. The relative strength of Cahokia and the outlining mound centers and their respective roles are not clear. Only further research can solve this puzzle.

Summary of the Early Mississippian Period

The early Mississippian period was characterized by the spread of the Mississippian way of life throughout much of the Southeast. The most common shared trait was the chiefdom level of sociopolitical organization, which was expressed archaeologically in a settlement hierarchy and ranked social status which was ascribed, not achieved.

There were two basic Mississippian subsistence patterns: riverine and coastal. Riverine subsistence was centered on small farms in flood plains on which several crops were grown, of which maize was the most important. Wild foods were also important, and hunting and gathering continued. The coastal subsistence pattern lacked any significant maize agriculture; hunting, gathering, and fishing accompanied seasonal population movements. Both subsistence patterns supported the development of chiefdoms.

The mechanics of the spread of Mississippian culture are not well understood; however, the imitation-and-defense reaction seen in the well-documented Macon Plateau invasion was undoubtedly important. The adoption of maize agriculture was also important in the areas of good soils.

MIDDLE MISSISSIPPIAN PERIOD: A.D. 1200–1400

The principal features of the middle Mississippian period were the formation of complex chiefdoms and the florescence of the Southeastern Ceremonial Complex in many areas of the Southeast. The Mississippian chronological chart, Figure 7.1, and the culture area map, Figure 7.15, show that new culture periods have been defined in most areas. These new periods are usually distinguished by changes in pottery styles and attributes that serve as temporal markers.

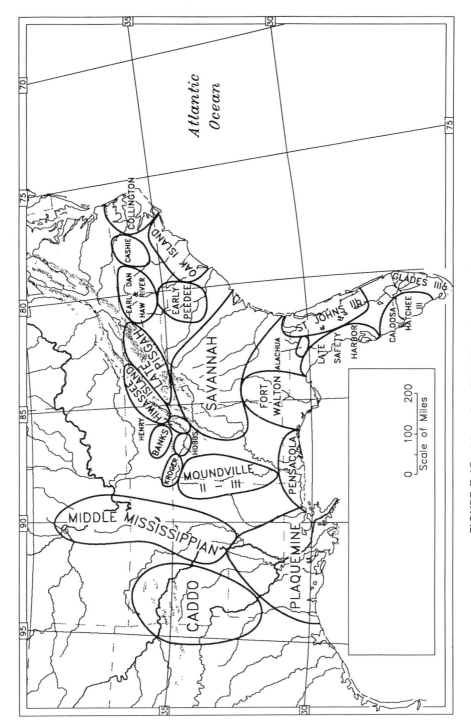

FIGURE 7.15 Map of middle Mississippian culture areas.

Material Culture

The artifact assemblage of the middle Mississippian period remained relatively unchanged from the early period. The adoption of shell tempering continued to spread eastward and southward, and it is used as a marker for many middle Mississippian artifact assemblages. Shell tempering was not adopted by many of the Mississippian cultures in the eastern part of the Coastal Plain. Pottery containers, regardless of tempering agent, included a wide range of bowls, bottles, jars, beakers, and pans.

Sociopolitical Developments

The middle Mississippian period is marked by the decline of Cahokia and the rise of complex chiefdoms in the Southeast. In the American Bottom of the Mississippi Valley, Cahokia chiefdoms began to decline at the very beginning of this period, and by A.D. 1400 only a series of simple independent chiefdoms remained. The number of farms and settlements decreased, and many of the mound centers were abandoned or minimally occupied. The site of Cahokia was still used, but it was not an important chiefdom center. During these two centuries, commoners' residences were built in many areas that formerly had been reserved for ceremonial purposes and commoners were buried on the surfaces of many mounds.

As Cahokia was declining, the first complex chiefdoms in the Southeast were forming, and the sociopolitical landscape was changing. Cultural anthropologists and archaeologists theorize that in environments that can produce an adequate surplus, simple chiefdoms grow relatively quickly in population and territory. The size of simple chiefdoms is limited by the distance that can be traveled for public events, payment of tribute, and enforcement of policies. To increase the amount of territory and number of people under their control, the chiefly elite formed complex chiefdoms. It is suspected that the process started with the union of a few simple chiefdoms, either by force or mutual agreement, and the centralization of power by the establishment of a new tier of ruling elite. The new tier of ruling elite was an expanded, restructured, and reorganized version of one of the participant simple chiefdoms. Complex chiefdoms have two tiers of authority, which meant that the elite of subservient chiefdoms not only collected tribute from their own communities, but had to pay tribute to the ruling elite of the complex chiefdom. The additional layer of tribute-demanding elite necessitated the production of more surplus than was necessary in simple chiefdoms. The additional "cost" of complex chiefdom formation limited their development to only the most productive natural environments of the Southeast and many areas continued to be characterized by simple chiefdoms.

Studies of living and extinct complex chiefdoms have shown that the ruling elite of new complex chiefdoms must quickly establish their authority because they are not necessarily related to the local elite of subservient chiefdoms. One of the most common means of establishing power and authority is to convince people that the new ruling elite have a divine right to govern. This legitimizes their hold on the power and is often accomplished through flamboyant demonstrations of that power. There is usually an initial period of great emphasis on ritual and ceremonialism shortly after the formation of complex chiefdoms. These rituals are much more elaborate than those held in simple chiefdoms. Following this elaborate ceremonial phase, complex chiefdoms generally undergo a decline in ritual and symbolic displays of power and an increase in secular ways of maintaining authority and privileges, especially through military and poltical pressure.

Archaeologists have documented the scenario just described in many areas of the Southeast during the middle Mississippian period. Complex chiefdoms formed quickly and there was an explosion in ceremonialism and elaborate rituals at their civic-ceremonial centers. There were also dramatic increases in mound building activity and iconography of the Southeastern Ceremonial Complex. The archaeological record shows that ties to ancestral territories and the physical remains of the ancestral chiefly elite became very important.[28] Charnel houses, ceremonial buildings, and mound complexes were enlarged during the middle Mississippian period as never before. Archaeologists interpret the acceleration in mound building as directly related to the establishment of a divine right to rule by the chiefly elite of new complex chiefdoms. Mounds became an expression of power, and mound building episodes are consistently connected with the death and elaborate burial of the chief of a complex chiefdom. Therefore, growth in mound size was physical evidence of the continuity of ruling families; the larger the mound, the longer the ruling family had been in power. Each construction stage was a symbol of the transfer of power from the last generation to the new chief. The ceremonial destruction and burial of the old mortuary and ceremonial buildings and construction of new mortuaries, ceremonial buildings, and residences clearly established that a new generation was in charge.

The elaborate iconography of the Southeast Ceremonial Complex that developed during the middle Mississippian period was also linked to the emergence of sacred authority of the new set of ruling elite. Elaborate costumes and emblems of office such as the columella pendant and heart-shaped apron must have been regularly worn in public rituals. They are consistently found buried with the chiefly elite. The use of the falcon motif, costume, and symbolic weapons reached a peak during the middle Mississippian.

---

[28] See Brown, 1985, Knight, 1986, and Galloway, 1989, for analyses of the Southeastern Ceremonial Complex.

Civic-Ceremonial Mound Centers

Many sites in the Southeast clearly reflect the efforts of the ruling elite to develop a sacred basis for their power. Most new civic-ceremonial mound centers had been the sociopolitical center of a former simple chiefdom. The better-known middle Mississippian complex chiefdom mound centers include Moundville, Etowah, Spiro, Lake Jackson, Lake George, Towosahgy, Irene, and Bottle Creek, which all had previously been centers of simple chiefdoms. Each had a large civic-ceremonial compound that was either part of a larger permanent community or was occupied only by the ruling elite. The expansion of these centers began with an acceleration of mound building, an elaboration of Southeastern Ceremonial Complex iconography, and the initiation of elaborate mortuary rituals. The initial flurry of activity leveled off for a time and was followed by either a general decline in mound building, rituals, and iconography, a renewal of mound building and elaborate rituals, or an abrupt end to ceremonial activity. When a sociopolitical center declined, another formed and expanded and the cycle repeated. Toward the end of the middle Mississippian period, a region-wide decline in mound building and elaborate ceremonialism occurred. Many large mound centers were abandoned after A.D. 1400; those that continued were only slightly enlarged. Burial of the elite in mounds continued in many areas, but often old mounds were used and new ones were not constructed. The elite continued to be buried with high-status goods and symbols of their power, but the use of elaborate tombs, large caches of ornate items, elaborate costumes, and iconography decreased.

Middle Mississippian civic-ceremonial centers across the Southeast were generally similar, but each was distinctive in the number and organization of mounds, favored iconography, or specific mortuary practices. While mound centers were built in all parts of the Southeast, the majority are in the Mississippi Valley. There are fewest mound centers on the coast; the largest clearly were constructed by people living in rich natural environments that could produce sizable food surpluses.

Moundville

Moundville, near Tuscaloosa, Alabama, is one of the best known and researched of the middle Mississippian civic-ceremonial centers. Excavations have been conducted there since 1905. While the bulk of the fieldwork took place between 1905 and 1941, over 30 yr passed before much of the material was intensively studied. Christopher Peebles, then with the University of Michigan, along with his students and colleagues undertook the task.[29] Moundville is the largest Mississippian civic-ceremonial center in the Southest. It is within the extraordinarily rich soil zone called the "black belt" of central Alabama. Located on a high bluff along the Black Warrior River, the mound

---

[29] See Peebles, 1971, 1974, and 1987 for summaries of the Moundville center.

complex covers more than 100 acres, and there are 20 mounds, as shown in Figure 7.16. During the early Mississippian period, Moundville had been just one of the four single-mound centers in the lower Black Warrior Valley. They probably were the political centers of simple chiefdoms. By about A.D. 1250, the beginning of the Moundville II period, Moundville had become the largest chiefdom center in the valley, with four platform mounds instead of one, and the site had grown in size from 5 to 125 acres. The majority of the population continued to live on dispersed farmsteads organized around single-mound centers. During the following two centuries, mound construction was accelerated at Moundville, and by about A.D. 1400, it had 20 mounds and a 100-acre plaza and covered 200 acres. Six of the settlements near Moundville grew in size and added single-platform mounds. It is thought these settlements were centers of simple chiefdoms under Moundville's control. It is estimated that at its peak, about 3000 people lived at Moundville.

In the civic-ceremonial precinct of Moundville, platform mounds were arranged along the margins of the plaza. The mounds alternated in form and function between those with large platforms and no burials and those with small platforms and elaborate burials. Large public buildings were located at ground level in the northeast and northwest corners of the plaza. In one of these, there were caches of skulls buried along the north wall, which was a pattern in ceremonial buildings at Moundville. Residential areas were outside the plaza to the west and east. The elite residential area was located on the bank of the small creek east of the plaza. Although most refuse was thrown in deep ravines in the area, there was enough material left on the site for Peebles to determine where specific craft manufacturing took place. For example, debris from shell bead manufacturing was concentrated outside the northeast part of the plaza; paint pigments and debris from copper-working were concentrated inside the northeast corner of the plaza; and pottery manufacturing debris was concentrated on the west side of the plaza.

A total of 3051 burials have been excavated at Moundville. While burials were located almost everywhere other than in the plaza, most were in the northeast and southern sectors of the settlement. In a study of over 2000 burial locations and associated grave goods, Christopher Peebles reconstructed the Moundville social-ranking system. Elites and commoners were present, and there appear to have been two internal ranks within the elite stratum. Each social rank had specific burial locations and grave goods. Higher-status individuals were buried in mounds, and as the status of the buried individuals decreased, the distance from the northernmost mounds increased. The elite buried in or near platform mounds were accompanied by stone palettes, monolithic axes (shown in Figure 7.8), copper axes, infants, and single skulls. Seven adult males in this group were accompanied by a particular subset of grave goods: ceremonial axes, and ground stone palettes. These men apparently were chiefs who inherited their positions. The status of the remainder of the ruling elite apparently was at least partially earned, because the amount

A

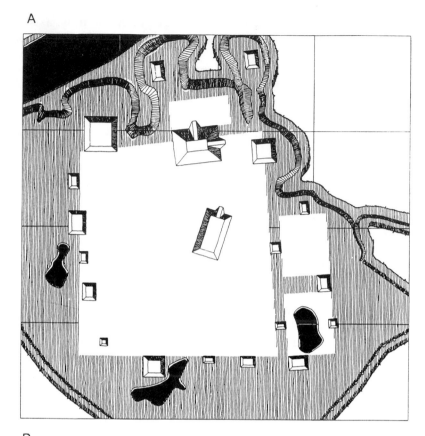

B

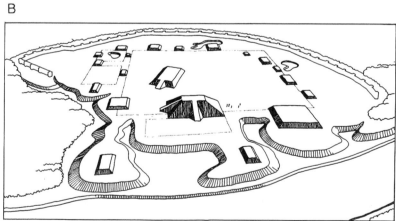

FIGURE 7.16 (A) Drawing of Moundville near Tuscaloosa, Alabama (squares are 660 ft on each side); (B) bird's eye view. (From W. N. Morgan, 1980, *Prehistoric Architecture in the Eastern United States.* Reprinted with permission of MIT Press, copyright © 1980, all rights reserved.

and type of grave goods correlated with age, sex, and, presumably, achievements. Peebles theorizes that the ascription of high rank on the basis of birth alone defined only one small, though very powerful, segment of the elite. Burials of commoners, who made up 95% of the population at Moundville, either had no grave goods at all, or had items appropriate to their particular age and sex.

Studies of the Moundville complex chiefdom have resulted in the theory that the single-mound centers closest to Moundville served primarily to funnel tribute. Paul Welch suggests that they were moving the greatest volume of tribute goods and that their locations were selected to reduce transportation costs.[30] The Moundville economic system is diagrammed in Figure 7.17. Subsistence goods, such as choice cuts of meat and corn, were contributed to Moundville, and in return, the chiefly elite awarded special Southeastern Ceremonial Complex items such as copper plates, stones palettes, and shell beads to the local elite, which increased their status and preserved their allegiance.

Spiro

Spiro, in the Caddoan culture area, was the sociopolitical center of a complex chiefdom in the Arkansas Valley, was a different type of middle Mississippian mound center.[31] This mortuary center had primarily conical mounds rather than platform mounds, shown in Figure 7.18. Spiro is well known to southeastern archaeologists for two reasons: the extraordinarily rich litter burials of the elite and the shameless looting of the burial mounds during the Depression.[32]

Because the looting of Spiro was so severe, the circumstances are well known. It all began in 1935 when the new owner of several of the mortuary mounds on the eastern edge of the site leased digging rights to two partners for two years for $100. They formed the "Pocola Mining Company" and hired coal miners to dig huge craters and tunnels and even to dynamite the mounds. The relics were sold. The diggers soon reached what later was determined to be a mortuary building containing remains of the chiefly elite and an abundance of symbolic Southeastern Ceremonial Complex items. These ritual and status items, such as monolithic stone axes and engraved shell cups and carved shell gorgets, brought high prices from private collectors and museum agents who began to converge on the site. More coal miners were hired and a maze of tunnels was dug into the mound to get more saleable relics. A commerical camp sprang up at the mounds, and items were sold on the spot to the highest bidder. News coverage of the finds brought crowds of buyers

---

[30] See Peebles, 1978, Steponaitis, 1978, and Welch, 1991, for details on Moundville chiefdom organization.

[31] For details on Spiro and Caddoan archaeology see J. Brown, 1966 and 1971, and Rogers, 1983, 1989.

[32] See Phillips and Brown, 1978, for a summary of the looting and artifacts from Spiro.

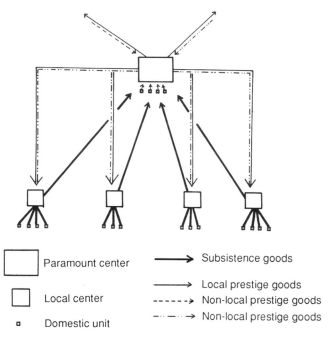

FIGURE 7.17 Diagram of the Moundville tribute system. (From Paul D. Welch, 1991, *Moundville's Economy*, University of Alabama Press, copyright © 1991, all rights reserved.)

and prices skyrocketed. The relic diggers pulled grave goods out and rushed to the end of their tunnels to sell them. An unsuccessful attempt was made to blast away the mound with dynamite. Some of the items looted from the mounds were skulls with strands of hair and headbands, fabric robes, costume ornaments, and hundreds of delicately carved shell gorgets. It is only from newspaper accounts and later interviews with some of the diggers that anything is known about the incredible finds that had been scattered all over the world. This looting episode is one of the most tragic events in southeastern archaeology. However, the outcry from archaeologists and the public prompted the passage of one of the first state antiquities laws in the United States. Since this disastrous mining episode, only professional archaeologists have directed the work at Spiro. In additon, many of the artifacts looted during the Depression have been recovered and documented.

There have been several episodes of professional excavation and study at Spiro, and researchers have determined that the 12 mounds at this center were arranged into two groups. There was an upland ring of six mounds—two platform and four dome-shaped—surrounding the edge of a 13-acre plaza that probably had a large central post. The second mound group consisted of six conical mounds lining the edge of the first terrace over 1000 ft from the

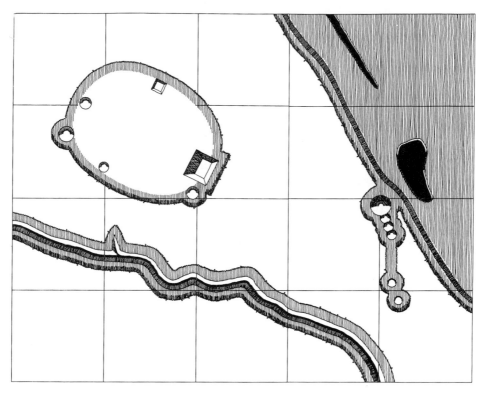

FIGURE 7.18   Drawing of Spiro in eastern Oklahoma (squares are 660 ft on each side). (From W. N. Morgan, 1980, *Prehistoric Architecture in the Eastern United States.* Reprinted with permission of MIT Press, copyright © 1980, all rights reserved.)

mound-plaza complex. It is suspected that the area between the mound and plaza and the conical mounds was residential. It is thought that during the middle Mississippian period, only a small group of elite resided permanently at Spiro. The site had a much larger residential population during the early Mississippian, when it had been one of several simple chiefdom centers in the valley.

The largest conical mound along the river terrace edge, the Craig Mound, has been the subject of intensive study. The initial looting of this mound indicated that there might have been a structure buried under it, and the most spectacular grave goods had been taken from there. Professional research has revealed that the core of the Craig Mound did have a buried structure, and it is one of the most spectacular mortuary structures ever encountered in North America. It was a 2,000-square-ft building, often called the "Great Mortuary," the floor of which was covered with split cane mats and heaps of ornate Southeastern Ceremonial Complex symbolic items, especially carved shell. On top and between these heaps of ritual items were the skeletal remains of the chiefly elite. At least 12 cedar pole litters were present, such as the one shown in Figure 7.19. These had been stacked with Southeastern Ceremonial Complex items, such as engraved shell cups and gorgets, beads of shell and pearls, carved stone pipes, and fabric robes. Scattered between the litter burials were partially disarticulated skeletons. These appear to have been the second tier of ruling elite and were surrounded by a few elaborate items, including three copper plates embossed with the falcon warrior. The remains of individuals from a third tier of elite were also found. Their bones had been defleshed and placed in basket chests along with embossed copper plates. The mortuary building had been buried under a mound of earth with additional caches of Southeastern Ceremonial Complex items at the base. The engraved shell artifacts recovered from Spiro are unparalleled in North America. Archaeologists studying these items theorize that most of the shell and copper ornaments were imported to Spiro in finished form.

The local elite at subservient Spiro chiefdoms were buried with different and less elaborate Southeastern Ceremonial Complex items than those at the

FIGURE 7.19   Drawing of one of the burial litters in the Craig Mound at the Spiro mound center. (From Phillips and Brown, 1959. Copyright © 1975 by the President and Fellows of Harvard College.)

multiple mound center at Spiro. Their graves contained items made of pottery and stone, and they had no elaborately engraved shell cups and gorgets. Commoners were buried in separate cemeteries under or near their houses, with a restricted set of utilitarian grave goods.

Lake Jackson

Another type of middle Mississippian mound center is the Lake Jackson site, which was the sociopolitical center of the Apalachee Fort Walton complex chiefdom. Located on a large lake, seven platform mounds were arranged around two plazas, shown in Figure 7.20. Only one platform mound has been investigated at this site, but it was particularly informative. A 17-ft-high platform mound was partially and hurriedly excavated by B. Calvin Jones just prior to its destruction by the landowner.[33] It was a mortuary mound with a series of 12 summits, each of which had a structure. These had been demolished and buried under a mantle of earth. Eight of the structures had deep tombs containing elaborate burials beneath the floors. The summit buildings were rectangular with single post walls, and Jones suspects they were mortuaries for the elite. Continuity of use is indicated by the placement of new graves so as not to intrude on previous interments. The average length of time between mound building episodes was 20 yr, beginning about A.D. 1300. The number of graves in each mound summit ranged from one to three, except for the last layer that had 10 or more. The elite were interred in elaborate costumes with symbols of office and status, such as copper plates embossed with the falcon dancer, as illustrated in Figure 7.8A, copper headdresses, round plain copper breastplates, strings of pearls and shell beads, and celts of copper and stone.

Jones noted several trends in burial patterns and construction of the Lake Jackson mound over the 250 yr it was used. The first layers of earth in the mound were thick, which would have meant a rapid increase in mound height. The burials associated with these first thick layers were very elaborate. In the middle stages of mound construction, the layers decreased in thickness and burials had less ornate items. The final stages saw a resurgence in grave goods and layer thickness. These trends are interpreted by Jones as reflective of the power of the Lake Jackson chiefs. The first cycle of elaborate grave goods and rapid increase in mound height presumably reflects the initial efforts of the chiefly elite of the new complex chiefdom to establish the divine right to rule. The leveling off and decrease of these activities in the middle layers is interpreted as reflecting the successful attainment of that right to power and maintenance of this position. The later revival of the elaborate mortuary rituals and significant mound construction is thought to represent an attempt to revive the power and authority of the chiefly elite.

Bioarchaeologist Rebecca Storey has studied the skeletons of the elite

---

[33] For details of the Lake Jackson excavation see Jones, 1982 and 1991.

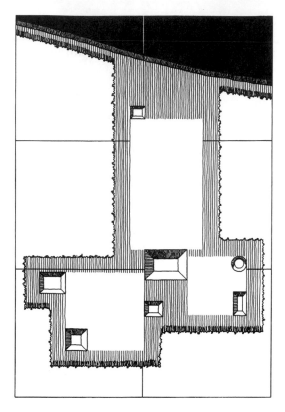

FIGURE 7.20   Lake Jackson mound center near Tallahassee, Florida (squares are 660 ft on each side). (From W. N. Morgan, *Prehistoric Architecture in the Eastern United States*. Reprinted with permission of MIT Press, all rights reserved.)

buried in the tombs of the platform mortuary mound at Lake Jackson. She found that all individuals showed signs of childhood stress. She also found that 12 of the individuals had a peculiar inherited trait of their teeth, which is a good indicator that they were all part of the same family.[34] There were two females among the ruling elite buried in elaborate tombs with copper plates embossed with a falcon dancer. Although this is unusual, female chiefly elite have been found at four other Mississippian mound centers in the Southeast. From her studies of patterns of inheritance of the elite in the middle Mississippian period, Storey concludes that although adult males were preferred for the chiefly elite power positions, a female or a boy could be appointed in the absence of an adult male. Southeastern Indians had a strong tradition of inheritance through the female line (matrilineal), although males usually held political positions.

[34] For details of the bioarchaeology see Storey, 1991.

Summary of Middle Mississippian Civic-Ceremonial Mound Centers

From these examples, it is apparent that middle Mississippian civic-ceremonial mound centers shared a basic organization with Southeastern Ceremonial Complex items. Distinct local variations reflected separate culture histories and differences in wealth, resources, and political situations. Research at each of these centers has contributed information about different aspects of middle Mississippian society. From Moundville, we have a detailed picture of the organization of mounds, craft activites, internal social ranking, and the economic and tribute system in a complex chiefdom. From Spiro we have an idea of how an elaborate ancestor shrine and vacant center operated. From the Lake Jackson center we can detect subtle political and economic changes during the 250-yr reign of paramount chiefs from a single family line.

Warfare

There are indications that warfare became more important in the Southeast during the middle Mississippian period. Archaeologists find evidence of warfare in the presence of defensive fortifications at settlements. Three basic fortification plans existed: a stockade around the entire settlement, a stockade around only the civic-ceremonial area, or stockades around both. Stockades were made of large poles set vertically either in long trenches or in individual pits. Additional defensive structures were often added to the stockades. Bastions (enclosed projections) were placed at close intervals to prevent the walls from being scaled and wide ditches were dug outside the stockade. Often, settlements along major waterways were not stockaded on the water side, such as Etowah, shown in Figure 7.21. Cahokia is an example of a stockaded civic-ceremonial center within a community (shown in Figure 7.16). Archaeological evidence of repair, maintenance, and other alterations to stockade walls is common. In the Savannah River valley, sometime after A.D. 1300, even small outlying settlements were fortified. Such defenses are interpreted as signs of population pressure, competition for tillable soil, and political instability.

Examples of Middle Mississippian Cultures

The interior riverine Savannah culture is typical of cultures in the interior river valleys during the middle Mississippian. The Pensacola culture is representative of the coastal Mississippian way of life. It, along with the Safety Harbor and Calusa cultures, demonstrate several interesting variations in Gulf coast Mississippian cultures.

Savannah Culture

The Savannah culture area was one of the largest in the Southeast during the middle Mississippian period, located in Figure 7.15. It encompassed all

A

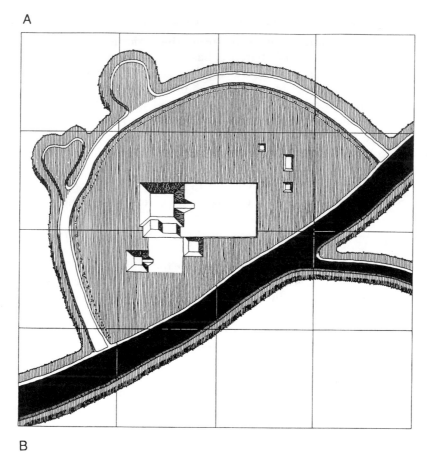

B

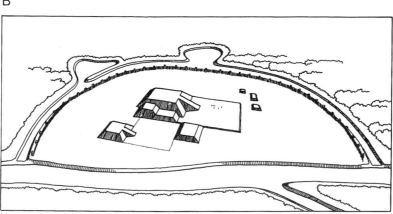

FIGURE 7.21   (A) Drawing of Etowah mound center near Atlanta, Georgia (squares are 660 ft on each side); (B) bird's eye view. (From W. N. Morgan, 1980, *Prehistoric Architecture in the Eastern United States.* Reprinted with permission of MIT Press, copyright © 1980, all rights reserved.)

of Georgia, most of South Carolina, and northeast Alabama. While many sections of this culture area have received significant research, the Ridge and Valley portion of northwest Georgia and the Savannah River valley are discussed here.[35]

In these areas, the middle Mississippian pottery change consisted of a relative decrease in shell and limestone tempering and an increase in the use of grit. The quality of stamp designs and the execution of stamping were poorer than in the early Mississippian period. The typical Mississippian containers continued to be made, including bowls (some with loop handles), jars, and bottles. The surfaces of most pottery containers continued to be decorated with curvilinear complicated stamps, but many were plain.

In the Ridge and Valley area of northwest Georgia, near Rome, David Hally and his colleagues have documented a complex chiefdom site hierarchy consisting of a large multiple-mound center, several single-mound settlements, smaller moundless settlements, and scattered farmsteads. The settlements in the chiefdom were organized into clusters up to 9 mi long. The clusters of settlements were separated from other chiefdom clusters by buffer zones at least 18 mi long.

Extensive research has been done at the sociopolitical center of the Etowah complex chiefdom, the Etowah site, which is just north of Atlanta, Georgia. Etowah had six mounds. It was surrounded by six settlements with single platform mounds, five of which were located directly on the flood plain. In the Etowah chiefdom there were at least seven smaller settlements without mounds and many small farmsteads. The Etowah site was located on the upstream edge of the chiefdom, not in the center. While this location may have caused logistics problems, Etowah was located on the richest agricultural soil in the chiefdom.

Several areas of the Etowah mound center have been excavated.[36] The settlement was about 50 acres in size and was heavily protected by a 30 × 10-ft moat and a stockade complete with bastions, as shown in Figure 7.21. The ceremonial center had three platform mounds and two plazas. The largest mound faced a 3-ft-high, square, raised clay plaza 330 ft in size. The southernmost mound was for mortuary purposes. It has been most intensively investigated by Lewis Larson. The mound was 25 ft high and had a series of five summits characterized by mortuaries that had been demolished and covered with layers of fill. It contained over 350 burials. Stockades had been placed around the base of the mound each time it was raised, and chiefly burials had been placed on the toe of the mound, just inside the stockade wall. The chiefly elite had been buried in log tombs in elaborate costumes with symbolic ornaments and weapons of the Southeastern Ceremonial Complex, some of

---

[35] For the Ridge and Valley area see Hally and Langford, 1988; for the Oconee Valley see Shapiro, 1990, and Williams and Shapiro, 1990; for the Savannah Valley see Anderson et al., 1986, and Anderson and Joseph, 1988.

[36] For details of Etowah excavations see Larson, 1971, and Moorehead, 1932.

which are shown in Figure 7.22. The costumes in which the chiefs were buried were very similar. Perhaps the best-known burial recovered from this mound is the very last one interred. As usual, a large log tomb had been placed at the base of the approach ramp just inside the surrounding stockade wall. This tomb contained the dismembered bodies of four people, two large, stone human statues, one of which was broken, and a variety of personal ornaments and Southeastern Ceremonial Complex items. Based on the positions of the body parts, the broken stone statues, and the general disarray of the materials, Lewis Larson suggested that this burial event must have taken place under unusual circumstances. He thinks the ruling elite had been overthrown and that the surviving members had hurriedly buried the contents of their mortuary, along with their special stone ancestor images and relics, just before departing. Two other stone statues have been found buried at Etowah, but both had been carefully placed. One was in its own stone-lined grave, and the other had been placed in the grave of a female chief.

Similar chiefdom political events were taking place at about the same time in the Savannah River valley.[37] By A.D. 1200, a series of simple chiefdoms had formed. They seem to have been organized into three or four clusters about 30 mi apart in the valley. At least seven and possibly ten mound centers were in use in these simple chiefdoms. About A.D. 1300, two complex chiefdoms had organized out of these simple chiefdoms. The Rembert and Mason's Plantation sites were the multimound chiefdom centers. Within a century, the political landscape changed again, and Mason's Plantation was abandoned while Rembert and Tugalo, a single-mound center, remained in use. At the mouth of the Savannah, the Irene Center was revitalized late in this period, and it again became the dominant center for the lower Savannah Valley and coastal area. At Irene, the platform mound that had previously supported a structure was converted to a burial mound and doubled in size. A rotunda (council house) was constructed on ground level and a mortuary was built. Both the latter structures were modified and rebuilt several times. The presence of the rotunda has led David Anderson to suggest that the society had developed a less authoritarian decision-making process. Council houses were observed in many southeastern groups during the early historic period. They were used for many public events, including public forums and discussions where decisions were made. An authoritarian decision-making process would not have necessitated construction of a council house.

In review, the Savannah culture included most of Georgia and some of South Carolina. During the middle Mississippian period, several complex chiefdoms rose and fell. These political dynamics are inferred through the

---

[37] See Anderson, 1990a,b, for a detailed summary of the Mississippian stage in the Savannah Valley.

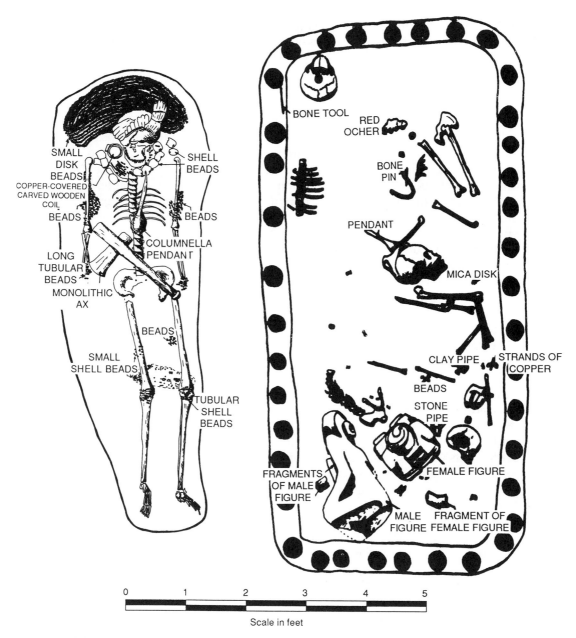

FIGURE 7.22 Drawing of graves of ruling elite in Mound C Etowah: (A) typical well-prepared and organized burial; (B) final burial which is disorganized and contains two stone statues. (From Larson, 1971. Reproduced by permission of the Society for American Archaeology from *American Antiquity*, vol. 36(3).)

construction, abandonment, enlargement, and revitalization of various mound centers seen in the archaeological record; such changes in mound centers reflect power shifts within and between chiefdoms.

The Eastern Gulf Coast

There were three middle Mississippian cultures along the eastern half of the Gulf of Mexico: Pensacola, Safety Harbor, and Calusa. These cultures were different than the interior, agriculturally based middle Mississippian cultures, and not all southeastern archaeologists believe they are properly classified as Mississippian. However, most agree that they were at the chiefdom level of sociopolitical organization, had platform mound centers, and participated in the Southeastern Ceremonial Complex. For these reasons, they are considered Mississippian despite their lack of an agricultural base.

Pensacola Culture   The Pensacola culture was located between the Pearl River in Louisiana and Choctawhatchee Bay in northwest Florida, as shown in Figure 7.15. Within this 200-mi-long area, the artifact assemblage, especially pottery, was exceptionally consistent. At the beginning of this period, shell tempering was added to the traditional sand and grit, and typical Mississippian containers were added, although bottles were rare. Pottery surfaces continued to be decorated by incising and punctating in Gulf tradition designs as shown in Figure 7.23. Pottery of the Pensacola culture was very similar to that of the Plaquemine culture in the lower Mississippi Valley. Most archaeologists believe these similarities reflect considerable interaction along the coast during the middle Mississippian period.

During this period a series of simple chiefdoms developed that were centered around the bay systems of the coast.[38] One or more single-mound settlements were usually present around each bay system with outlying settlements clustered in the vicinity. While very few of the platform mounds have been investigated, they appear to have served to elevate public buildings. Mound burials are scarce. In this culture area, cemeteries were more often used for burial of both elite and commoners.

Only one complex chiefdom has been documented in the Pensacola culture area: Bottle Creek.[39] The simple chiefdoms that participated in the Bottle Creek

---

[38] For details see Bense, 1989, and Phillips, 1989.

[39] See Brown and Fuller, 1994, Knight, 1984a,b, and Stowe, 1985, for details.

FIGURE 7.23   Examples of middle and late Mississippian pottery: (A) Fort Walton incised bowl; (B) Safety Harbor incised jar; (C) Walls engraved bottle; (D) Plaquemine brushed jar; (E) Nodena red-on-white painted bottle; (F) Nodena human effigy bottle; (G) Lamar complicated stamped bowl with incised shoulders. (A and B from Willey, 1949; C and F from Morse and Morse, 1983; D and E from Phillips, 1970. Copyright © 1970 by the President and Fellows of Harvard College; G from Snow, 1977.)

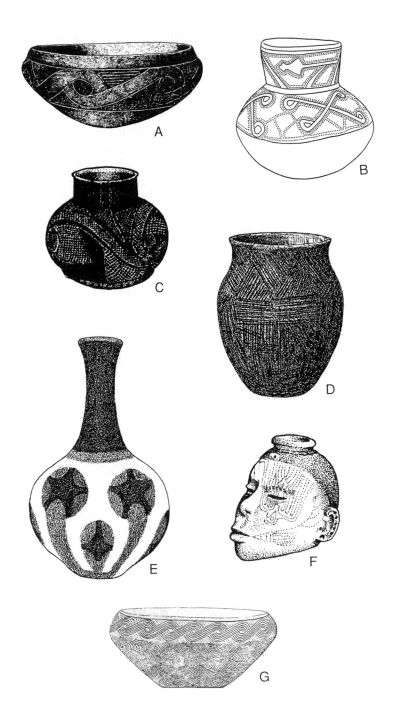

complex chiefdom were scattered along both sides of the delta of the Mobile and Tensas rivers and along Mobile Bay. The Bottle Creek multiple-mound center was located deep in the delta on a low island. This mound center had at least 13 mounds, the highest of which is still over 40-ft tall. It also had a canal, a stockade, and a possible burial mound, shown in Figure 7.24. Although Bottle Creek has been known for over 150 yr, very little archaeological work has been conducted, due to its remote location. Only very recently has the site even been mapped, and long-term research has just begun.

The complex chiefdom of Bottle Creek is unique in the Pensacola culture area. Archaeologists explain its existance by the unique environment. Large expanses of tillable soil occur on the flood plain and delta, which are annually flooded. Most of the delta is ringed with high bluffs on which permanent settlements were located. The richness of the natural environment in this river delta area is unique along the Gulf coast. This seems to have allowed development of a maize-based riverine Mississippian subsistence pattern supplemented by locally rich wild food resources. These unique environmental features provided the surpluses necessary to support the demands of a second tier of ruling elite. Other middle Mississippian coastal culture areas in the Southeast were also organized into simple chiefdoms except at the mouths of large rivers. As at Bottle Creek, complex chiefdoms developed at the mouths of the Apalachicola, Altamaha, and Savannah rivers.

Outside the unique Bottle Creek region in the Pensacola culture area, the coastal environment was relatively poor and could support only simple chiefdoms. These were contained within individual bay systems and very few mounds were constructed. Cemeteries were extensively used for burial of elite and commoners. More extensive surveys have been performed in the Choctawhatchee Bay system than the others. Pensacola chiefdoms in this area consisted of several settlements clustered around either a cemetery or a single mound that was the sociopolitical center of the chiefdom.[40] The coastal subsistence pattern of the Woodland stage continued. In the 1980s, maize was recovered from a Pensacola site in the Choctawhatchee Bay system. Maize may have at least supplemented hunting, gathering, and fishing along this coast. In the Pensacola Bay system, several large and small cemeteries containing both commoners and elite have been documented. Examples are the small chiefly elite cemetery of Hickory Ridge and the mixed elite and commoner Gulf Breeze cemetery. Only one possible mound has thus far been identified in the Pensacola Bay system.[41]

The Pensacola culture area typifies middle Mississippian coastal cultures not only in the prevalence of simple chiefdoms in the bay systems strung along the coast but also in strong material similarities over long distances. Coastal archaeologists agree these similarities were the result of frequent

---

[40] See Thomas and Campbell, 1992, for details in the Choctawhatchee Bay area.

[41] See Bense, 1989, for an overview and Phillips, 1989, for details of Pensacola cemeteries.

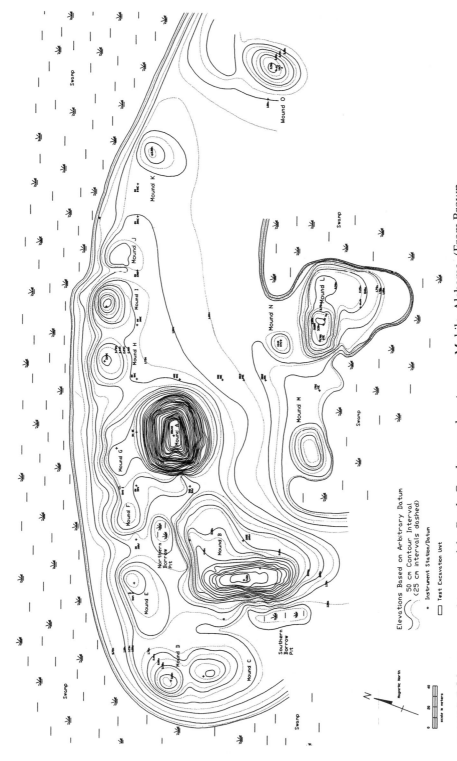

FIGURE 7.24 Topographic map of the Bottle Creek mound center near Mobile, Alabama. (From Brown and Fuller, 1992.)

interaction, interaction that was feasible due to the ease of traveling along the coast in watercraft. Canoes dating to the Woodland and Mississippian stages are frequently found along the Gulf coast.

Safety Harbor Culture   The Safety Harbor culture extended farther down the Gulf coast, from the Fort Walton culture area to present-day Sarasota, located in Figure 7.15. Population was most dense in the Tampa Bay area.[42] At least 13 simple chiefdoms developed along this coast in the Mississippian period, each of which had a large sociopolitical center with a platform mound and a ceremonial percinct. These centers were located on bay or lagoon shores and many smaller special purpose settlements were nearby. There were 15–20 pyramid mounds in the Tampa Bay area, many of which were situated where streams enter the bay. There also appears to have been an inland Safety Harbor chiefdom 50 mi east of Sarasota. Each large settlement having a platform mound is thought to represent the sociopolitical center of a simple chiefdom.

Safety Harbor chiefdom centers were large linear settlements along inland bodies of water. Today they are shell middens. Ceremonial precincts were located on the landward side of the settlements and consisted of at least one platform mound and plaza. Platform mounds used for burials had charnel houses on their summits, but, in this culture, they were not located in or near the ceremonial precinct. They were located well away from the village and mound area. A suite of special ceraminc vessels, such as those shown in Figure 7.23, were common grave goods in elite burials, and they also were cached in mounds. Southeastern Ceremonial Complex items such as copper-covered earspools were imported by the Safety Harbor elite and also buried with them. Safey Harbor ceramics are similar to Pensacola and Apalachee Fort Walton types, again indicating communication along the Gulf coast. While the internal chronology of the Safety Harbor culture is not well refined, most researchers agree the culture developed about A.D. 1200. No evidence for maize cultivation in the Safety Harbor culture has been recovered, and it seems that the subsistence base was hunting, gathering, and fishing with perhaps some gardening.

Calusa Culture   Still farther south along the Gulf coast was the Caloosahatchee (or Calusa) culture area.[43] Spanish records show that in the sixteenth century the Calusa had a complex chiefdom with a nonagricultural (fishing) subsistence base. The position of chief was inherited and the chief controlled a large portion of southwest Florida. How and when Calusa chiefdoms developed is not well known; neither is the extent to which they exhibited Mississippian characteristics. Calusa ceramics were primarily plain, including those

---

[42] For details on the Safety Harbor culture see Leur and Almy, 1981, and Milanich and Fairbanks, 1980.

[43] For details of the Calusa see Marquardt, 1992, and Widmer, 1988.

used as grave goods. No Southeastern Ceremonial Complex items have been recovered from Calusa sites. The most Mississippian feature of the Calusa was the construction of mound centers. Such centers had several platform mounds that were often connected by shell causeways, canoe canals, plazas, and sunken plazas called "water courts." Sand burial mounds continued to be built and used, and pottery was placed with at least some of the burials. As in the Safety Harbor culture area just to the north, burial mounds were removed from settlements and mound centers. Some burial mounds, such as the Englewood mound near Sarasota, contained submound burial pits covered with ocher. Other mounds, such as the Laurel Mound near Sarasota, were built over several burials placed in a circular pattern. The skulls were in the center, with the bodies arranged like wheel spokes and covered with red ocher. Additional burials were placed in the mound fill layers.

The Calusa (and Glades) cultures subsisted only on fishing and gathering, not agriculture. The waters around the mangrove islands and swamps along this portion of the Gulf coast are among the richest fishing grounds in the world. Some archaeologists have theorized that these productive fishing grounds were managed like agricultural fields to produce large surpluses capable of supporting complex chiefdoms.

Summary of the Middle Mississippian Period

The key features of this period were the formation of complex chiefdoms and the florescence of the Southeastern Ceremonial Complex. Complex chiefdoms developed only in areas capable of producing the surpluses necessary to support an additional layer of administration and elite. Development of complex chiefdoms was thus restricted to those areas with exceptionally rich soil or other natural resources.

The ceremonial precincts of new complex chiefdoms underwent rapid expansion as platform mound building and the Southeastern Ceremonial Complex reached their peaks in southeastern prehistory. Mound centers of the Southeast were similar in many ways, but there were also local differences in mound, favored iconography, and specific mortuary practices.

During this period, secular forms of political control, particularly warfare, began to replace ceremonialism in many culture areas. An increase in violence is detected in an escalation of settlement fortification and a decrease in mound building and elaborate mortuary rituals.

LATE MISSISSIPPIAN PERIOD: A.D. 1400–1500

The final century of the prehistoric Mississippian stage is noted for increases in political turmoil and population relocations. It is suspected that the cycle of formation and fragmentation inherent in complex chiefdoms resulted in large population movements in the Southeast. This left hundreds of miles of river valleys either virtually abandoned or sparsely populated by A.D. 1450. Some complex chiefdoms west of the Mississippi Valley permanently collapsed during this period. The Mississippian way of life ceased and people returned to Woodland lifeways.

Material Culture

Late Mississippian pottery continued to be tempered with shell in the central Mississippi, Tennessee, and Tombigbee drainages, as well as most of the Pensacola culture area on the northern Gulf coast. Clay tempering predominated in the Natchez culture area in the Lower Mississippi Valley and Louisiana coast, with only occasional shell tempering. Grit and sand tempering continued in the eastern half of the Southeast. Stylistic changes in pottery included new surface treatments, and vessel shapes, such as those as shown in Figure 7.23. Surface decoration techniques that became popular included brushing before firing and engraving designs after firing. Also, complicated stamped designs were often poorly applied or obliterated, and incised and punctated designs were often carelessly done. Small, projecting lug handles applied to vessel rims and loop or strap handles were popular in some places. Rims were often thickened and decorated with pinches, notches, nodes, and cane punctations along the bottom. In northeast Arkansas, elaborate shell tempered red and white painted ceramics were popular as grave goods, and often were made in the shape of ornamental bottles and human heads, much like death masks, such as the one illustrated in Figure 7.23.

Sociopolitical Events and Warfare

During the late Mississippian, several complex chiefdoms went through significant changes due to economic and political problems. Four examples of these political changes are given below: the collapse of the Spiro chiefdom, the fragmentation of the Moundville chiefdom, the relocation of Natchez political centers, and the reorganization of the Apalachee Fort Walton chiefdom.

Fall of Spiro

The complex chiefdoms of the Arkansas basin (in the western portion of the Mississippi drainage) collapsed during the late Mississippian period and the Mississippian way of life ended in much of the Caddoan culture area.[44] In the Spiro chiefdom, virtually all mound use and mound building stopped, and the Spiro mound center was abandoned. Inherited social status disappeared and participation in the Southeastern Ceremonial Complex ceased. While the population remained in place, there were significant changes in

[44] See Kay *et al.*, 1989, and Wycoff, 1980, for more details.

their subsistence and settlement patterns. Settlements were smaller and farther apart, and the use of large storage pits to conceal stored foods substantially increased. This suggests that settlements were abandoned for long periods of time and above-ground storage cribs could no longer be used. Plant and animal remains from these settlements indicate a dramatic increase in seasonal hunting and gathering in the uplands. Researchers point to two related causes that probably led to these changes: a reduction in rainfall and the disruption in the long-distance trade network. The weather had been getting dryer in this area since about A.D. 1200, and by A.D. 1400 rainfall had been cut in half.[45] This area is on the fringe of the arid Plains, and even slight changes in rainfall patterns seriously affect agricultural production (as was the case during the dust bowl of the 1930s). Archaeologists theorize that the Spiro elite experienced chronic political problems with lowering maize production. This is reflected in a steady decline in the number of imported shell cups and gorgets, which were symbols of authority and power. The combination of a decline in food production and related problems in securing status symbols is thought to have broken the ability of the elite to govern. The continuing drought forced the Caddoans to change their economic focus from maize agriculture to hunting, gathering, and fishing. Farms were abandoned and the population became once more dependent upon wild foods, leading to seasonal movements between base camps and satellite camps.

Breakup of Moundville

At the beginning of this period, the sociopolitical center of Moundville was heavily fortified by a surrounding stockade with bastions, shown in Figure 7.17.[46] Archaeologists have detected a steady decline in the amount of imported and manufactured Southeastern Ceremonial Complex items at Moundville in the early decades of the fifteenth century. Even simple chiefdoms on the perimeter of Moundville's influence refortified their mound centers about A.D. 1500. The Lubbub Creek settlement, the center of the Summerville chiefdom on the central Tombigbee, was consolidated to fit inside the stockade walls. This reflects concern about the growing unrest in Moundville and the escalation of warfare in the general area. All these factors signal to Moundville archaeologists that the chiefly and ruling elite had become defensive, likely because subservient chiefdoms had gained power and had become a physical threat. Sometime ca. A.D. 1500, the chiefly and ruling elite at the Moundville Center lost the battle for power, and the mound center was all but abandoned. Researchers speculate that the underlying reasons for Moundville's breakdown were a combination of an overdependence on maize, a rapid rise in the population, and an overextension of tribute demands by the ruling elite (especially for food and mound building). The political change

[45] See Bareis and Bryson, 1965, for more on climatic changes during this period.
[46] For a summary of the breakup of Moundville see Peebles, 1987, and Welch, 1991.

at Moundville was not accompanied by the rise of one of the formerly subservient chiefdoms. Rather, the complex chiefdom organization splintered into a series of simple chiefdoms.

Relocation of Natchez Political Centers

In the Yazoo and Natchez Bluffs region of the Natchez culture area in the lower Mississippi Valley, sociopolitical centers were relocated to more defensible positions during the late Mississippian.[47] Mound centers located along main channels of rivers, such as Winterville and Lake George, were abandoned for locations that were more difficult to approach and that could be more easily defended. There was a reduced emphasis on mound construction at these new locations, and the settlements were smaller. One of the largest mound centers established during this period is the Emerald site, situated on a 40-ft-high bluff 6 mi from the main river channel. The civic-ceremonial center had eight platform mounds (one 35 ft tall) arranged symmetrically around a plaza. Most Natchez mound centers were smaller with fewer platform mounds.

Reorganization of Apalachee Fort Walton

During the late Mississippian period the Lake Jackson mound center was abandoned. The Anhaica (Martin) site became the new governmental center and was heavily fortified.[48] No mounds were constructed at this new center and all former mound centers were abandoned. Mound building throughout the chiefdom ceased. The use of imported Southeastern Ceremonial Complex items also greatly declined. These changes during the late Mississippian are interpreted by researcher John Scarry as an indication that the ruling and chiefly elite residing at the Lake Jackson mound center had been overthrown by a rival faction. When this occurred, the center of the defeated elite was abandoned and a new center established at the victor's ancestral home. The cessation of mound building and the use of Southeastern Ceremonial Complex items indicates that the importance of mounds and ceremonialism as symbols of chiefly authority had waned and were replaced by the rise of warfare. The Apalachee complex chiefdom remained strong. It was visited by Hernando de Soto, who occupied the capital at Anhaica during the winter of A.D. 1539–40. De Soto considered the Apalachee among the richest and most powerful chiefdoms he encountered in the Southeast.

Ceremonialism

While mound building and elaborate Southeastern Ceremonial Complex rituals declined in many areas, they were continued in many others, including the Lamar, Dallas, and Pensacola culture areas, the Mississippi Valley, and all

---

[47] See Brain, 1978, and Williams and Brain, 1983, for details.
[48] See Scarry, 1990, for details.

the Florida peninsula. A good example of the continuance of the Southeastern Ceremonial Complex is the central Mississippi Valley chiefdom of Nodena in Arkansas. There, the elite were buried with unprecedented elaborate mortuary pottery made into the shape of human heads, full human bodies and animals, and compound and stirrup vessels, as shown in Figure 7.23F. These elite mortuary ceramics were often painted a striking red and white. The burials also included such traditional Southeastern Ceremonial Complex objects as copper sheets embossed with images of birds, humans, and snakes, copper disks, and chunkey stones.

Population Movements and Settlement Pattern Changes

One of the consequences of the increase in warfare in the Southeast during the late Mississippian period was population reorganization. Two types of population relocation took place: emigration to new areas and concentration of the populace into well-fortified, walled settlements.

Population Movements

Major emigrations occurred in the central Mississippi-Ohio-Tennessee-Cumberland valleys and most of the Savannah River valley. The most extreme emigration affected the 600 plus mi of river valleys in the central Mississippi drainage. This area has been labeled the "Vacant or Empty Quarter" (located in Figure 7.25) by Stephen Williams, who first suspected that the central Mississippi Valley was vacant by A.D. 1500, prior to the arrival of the first Spanish explorers.[49] Most southeastern archaeologists agree at least that the population in this area was greatly reduced. No one has unraveled the details of the abandonment. Swift population movements are not necessarily assumed, although there are places where abandonment and purposeful burning of settlements has been documented (the Powers Phase in southeast Missouri, for example). It is also possible that portions of the Vacant Quarter were slowly emptied. The destination of the immigrants has not been identified, but several researchers think that many went down river, where there was an increase in the number of late Mississippian sites. The movement of the population was probably related to the increased competition within and between complex chiefdoms during this period, aggravated by drought.

More is known about the details and timing of the abandonment of the Savannah River valley by societies of the Lamar culture.[50] As mentioned above, this river valley was densely occupied during the early and middle Mississippian periods. There had been a steady increase in the number of settlements, and by A.D. 1400, complex chiefdoms had developed in the upper, middle, and lower portions of the valley, (see Figure 7.26). However, no settlements after A.D. 1450 have been documented in the valley except at the

[49] See Williams, 1982 and 1990, for details on the Vacant Quarter.
[50] See Anderson, 1990a,b, and Anderson and Joseph, 1988 for details.

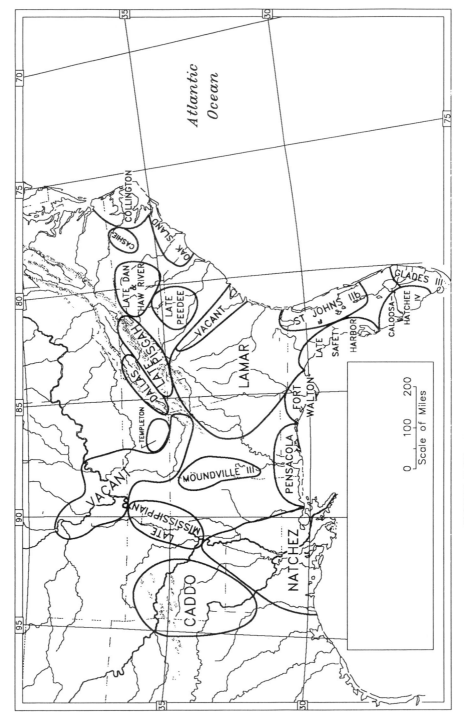

FIGURE 7.25 Late Mississippian culture areas.

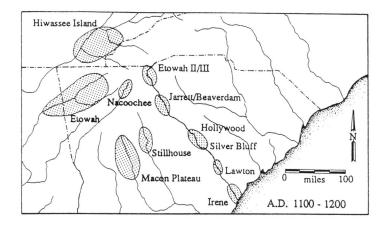

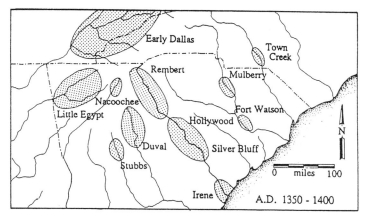

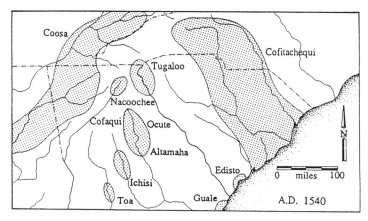

FIGURE 7.26 Mississippian chiefdoms in the Atlantic Slope. (From Anderson and Joseph, 1988.)

headwaters. About the same time, a number of mound centers in western South Carolina were also abandoned.[51] When Soto explored the middle Savannah valley in A.D. 1540, it was uninhabited, and it served as a large buffer zone between the rival chiefdoms of Ocute to the north and Cofitachequi to the south.

David Anderson has analyzed the archaeological record of the late Mississippian Lamar societies in the Savannah River valley and nearby areas for clues to the abandonment process. He has deduced that drought and political turmoil were the leading causes of the emigration from this valley. He suggests that the rise of the rival neighboring chiefdoms of Ocute and Cofitachequi either directly attacked or at least seriously threatened the chiefdoms in the Savannah Valley. This is evidenced by the fortification of settlements throughout the valley before A.D. 1450. Anderson concludes that the inability of the ruling elite to protect their subservient settlements plus the pressure of drought and harvest shortfalls eroded their support. Without sufficient protection or support from the ruling elite of the Savannah Valley chiefdoms, Anderson theorizes that the populace simply moved into the neighboring chiefdoms where they would be unharmed or perhaps even supported in return for their allegiance and tribute. Given that over 200 mi of rich farmland was abandoned in the Savannah Valley, it is clear that the need for agricultural land was not the cause of the migration. Some of the populace moved upstream to the Tugalo chiefdom at the headwaters, but many moved out of the valley into other chiefdoms, such as the Oconee chiefdom of Ocute. At that time there was a sharp rise in the late Mississippian sites with pottery similar to that of the Savannah River valley.

Population Reorganization

The second type of population relocation, a concentration into protected sites, has been well documented in the central Mississippi Valley of Arkansas just south of the Vacant Quarter.[52] During A.D. 1350–1400 almost all of the Mississippian settlements scattered throughout the Cairo Lowlands were abandoned. The populace moved to the meander belt of the Mississippi, St. Francis, and White rivers. In the Powers Phase portion of the Cairo lowlands, settlements were burned upon abandonment. In the meander belt near the mainstream, there was a flurry of new settlement. Six chiefdoms formed in the area. Instead of the previous settlement pattern of scattered farmsteads surrounding a single mound center, the population was concentrated into compact, fortified settlements. These were, without exception, located on exceptionally large expanses of fertile land on large streams. Apparently, it was too dangerous for people to live on isolated farmsteads. The location of

---

[51] For details on South Carolina see DePratter, 1983.

[52] For more details see Morse and Morse, 1983, and Price, 1978.

the new defensive settlements on only the very richest soils ensured a steady food supply for the residents.

A specific example of these new defensively organized chiefdoms is the Parkin chiefdom. The multimound settlement of Parkin was the sociopolitical center of the chiefdom and was heavily fortified by a moat and a stockade, illustrated in Figure 7.27. Residences were located only inside the walls and up to 400 houses had been built, burned, buried, and rebuilt. This concentration of activity raised the area inside the walls more than 3 ft above the surrounding area. This settlement had a large ceremonial precinct including a sunken plaza and six platform mounds supporting homes of the elite. Other settlements in the Parkin chiefdom were smaller, but were similarly fortified and were located at regular intervals along the river. As no Parkin farmsteads have been found between the fortified settlements, the spacing of the walled settlements is thought to reflect the amount of land needed for their support. The one exception was Parkin itself, which archaeologists estimate did not have enough land surrounding it to support its dense population, and food tribute is thought to have made up the difference.

Summary

It should be clear that this century was characterized by an increase in political turmoil in the Southeast. In some areas there was a decline or even total cessation of mound building and ceremonialism. Complex chiefdoms

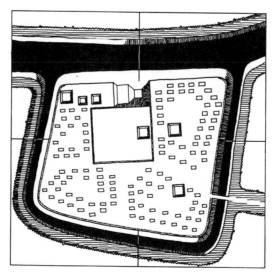

FIGURE 7.27 Drawing of the Parkin site in Arkansas near Memphis, Tennessee (squares are 660 ft on each side). (From W. N. Morgan, 1970.) (Reprinted with permission of MIT Press, copyright © 1970, all rights reserved.)

went through cycles of factionalism, violence, and reorganization throughout the region. In at least two areas, the scale of political turmoil and warfare coupled with drought led to massive population emigrations that left hundreds of miles of river valleys virtually vacant. In other areas, the constant threat of attacks forced the abandonment of isolated farmsteads on the flood plains and the concentration of the population into walled settlements.

Examples of Regional Culture: Dallas Culture

The late Mississippian Dallas culture in the Tennessee Valley has long been familiar to southeastern archaeologists. A well-circulated and illustrated 1946 publication featured the excavation by Madeline Kneberg and Thomas Lewis of the large Mississippian mound center on Hiwassee Island.[53] Since then, much new information about the Dallas culture has been discovered, especially through investigations in the Tellico Reservoir on the Little Tennessee River by Richard Polhemus, Gerald Schroedl, and others at the University of Tennessee.

One of the major differences between the Dallas period, which began about A.D. 1300, and the preceding Hiwassee Island period was the change to a defensive settlement pattern. The populace concentrated into a series of compact walled settlements (called towns) with at least one mound each, and scattered farmsteads disappeared. The fortified towns of individual chiefdoms were clustered together and separated by wide buffer zones from the next town cluster. Evidence of centralized power is seen in the size and extent of public works, such as mounds, large public buildings, and large defensive works at the towns. Communities with the largest of these features are thought to have been the chiefdom centers. Archaeologists describe Dallas complex chiefdom organization as characterized by temporary and expedient political alliances between independent chiefdoms according to military ability, cleverness of chiefs, and pressures from other chiefdoms.

Dallas towns were well planned and laid out as shown in Figure 7.28. Each town had a public civic-ceremonial area, a surrounding residential area, and a defensive stockade. The towns of Toqua and Hiwassee Island were laid out with the central axis oriented to the winter solstice (northwest-southeast). Public buildings and elite residences were usually elevated on platform mounds. One such building was a high-status residence with an attached pavilion for public activities. Both structures were enclosed by a clay embankment. Inside the elite residence was a central open area and clay benches along the wall. The walls and ceiling of both the public buildings and elite residences on the mounds were covered with a clay plaster (daub), probably to prevent fires, and painted.

[53] See Lewis and Kneberg, 1946, Polhemus, 1987, and Schroedl, 1986, for details about the Dallas culture.

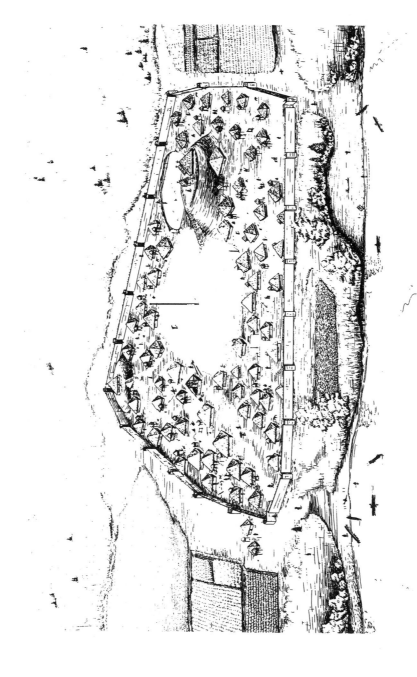

FIGURE 7.28 Artist's conception of Toqua, near Knoxville, Tennessee. (From Polhemus, 1987.)

The size of residences within the towns correlated with proximity to the civic-ceremonial precinct. Larger residences were located nearest the plaza and size decreased with distance. Residences were organized into clusters of about six structures that faced a shared courtyard. It is suspected that the clusters were residential units of an extended family. Houses averaged about 400 square ft and were sqaure to rectangular in shape. They had a central open area with a central clay hearth and a series of benches between the main roof supports and the outside walls. Interior walls were covered with daub, and some had been painted red with white designs. There was a food-processing area and storage shed adjacent to every house.

Defense was a priority in Dallas towns and much effort was put into the design, construction, and maintenance of stockade walls. At Toqua, there were three phases of stockade building; each new wall was covered with a layer of daub. The first stockade had been destroyed by fire, suggesting that the town had been overrun and burned. The second stockade had been improved by placing bastions with internal platforms raised on posts about every 60 ft along the wall. The third stockade enclosed a much smaller area. This wall is thought to have been a last effort to maintain a defensive perimeter during the historic period. Over 3,000 posts were used in the stockades at Toqua.

The burials at Toqua revealed two social ranks, and there was evidence of both ascribed and achieved status. The elite were buried in mortuary mounds and residential platform mounds accompanied by rich grave goods and retainers. An interesting difference has been observed in the kind of objects buried with individuals in residential and mortuary mounds. In the residential platform mound, many individuals were buried with weapons, such as arrows and celts. In the mortuary platform mound, no one was buried with weapons; instead, they had shell cups and pottery. Archaeologists suspect that this reflects the division of society into two basic groups, red (war) and white (peace). Such a division was well documented among the Cherokee in the historic period. Shell items included bead necklaces, cups, dippers, gorgets, and columella. Pottery items were decorated bottles and bowls. By comparing grave goods with the age, sex, and location of the burials, it has been documented that status was both inherited and achieved. Commoners were buried under the floors of their houses, either along the inside edge of the wall or under the benches near the center.

Studies of 439 Dallas skeletons from Toqua by Kenneth Parham revealed that the status of individuals correlated with two biological features. First, the skulls of many commoners (56%) were flattened in the front and back of the head (frontal-occipital flattening) as infants. Eleven percent of the elites buried in the mound had this trait. They were all adults, and Parham inferred that these individuals had been born as commoners but had achieved elite status during their life. Second, there were clear correlations between status and health. The elite were generally healthier than commoners and from this it is inferred that they ate better food. The skeletons of commoners revealed that they were generally in poor health and suffered from nutritional deficiencies and infectious diseases. Studies of the plant and animal remains at Toqua confirmed the correlation of diet and status. Bones from better grades of meat and better-quality maize were found in elite residential areas and the elite residential mound.

The skeletal studies of the Toqua population revealed that 60% of the population survived the stresses of early childhood. While individuals had a reasonably good chance for survival into adulthood, few people lived past 40–45 yr.

In summary, the late Mississippian Dallas culture was characterized by simple chiefdoms composed of clusters of walled towns on the flood plain separated by buffer areas. These chiefdoms were organized into complex alliances, and warfare had increased to the point that the entire populace lived in compact, fortified towns. Platform mounds were constructed to elevate elite residences, public buildings, and mortuaries. The ruling elite were buried in these mounds with substantial ornate grave goods, and commoners were buried in the floors of their houses with utilitarian items. The elite showed evidence of a better diet and health.

Summary of the Late Mississippian Period

The late Mississippian period was characterized by an increase in political turmoil, warfare, and population relocation. Some complex chiefdoms broke apart and some reorganized after being overthrown.

Two types of population relocation occurred: emigration and reorganization. By A.D. 1450, large stretches of river flood plain appear to have been virtually abandoned in the central Mississippi and Savannah River valleys. Reorganization of the population into defensive walled towns also occurred in the Mississippi and Tennessee valleys.

While mound building and elaborate Southeastern Ceremonial Complex rituals declined in many areas, they continued unabated in many others, including the Lamar, Dallas, and Pensacola culture areas, the Mississippi Valley, and all the Florida peninsula.

SUMMARY OF THE PREHISTORIC MISSISSIPPIAN STAGE

The Mississippian was the last prehistoric Indian stage of cultural development, and existed between A.D. 1000 and 1500. The hallmarks of the Mississippian stage are the development of chiefdoms, the florescence of the Southeastern Ceremonial Complex, and the expansion in platform mound centers.

There were two patterns of Mississippian subsistence: riverine and coastal. Riverine subsistence was characterized by the use of crop rotation on fields in which maize, beans, squash, sunflower, marsh elder, and gourd were grown. River valley Mississippians were relatively sedentary and procured wild foods in the woods near their fields. In the coastal subsistence pattern farming played a much smaller role, if any, and hunting, gathering, and fishing of marine and terrestrial food sources was emphasized. Cultivation was limited to small-plot, shifting-field agriculture. Much of the year was spent in seasonal settlements, where people tended scattered farm plots and procured wild seasonal marine and terrestrial foods.

Two types of chiefdoms developed in the Mississippian stage: simple and complex. Simple chiefdoms were composed of several communities under the control of the ruling elite residing at one of the participant communities. Complex chiefdoms were composed of several simple chiefdoms controlled by the ruling elite of one of the chiefdoms. A more complicated form of complex chiefdom also existed, the paramount chiefdom, which consisted of either several affiliated complex chiefdoms or an affiliation of both simple and complex chiefdoms.

The Southeastern Ceremonial Complex was the belief system of people of the Mississippian stage. The main themes were ancestor worship, war, and fertility, and these themes were expressed in a myriad of symbols and objects. This complex flourished in the middle Mississippian, between about A.D. 1200 and 1400, when rituals and mound building were a primary means of political control. The roots of this belief system can be traced back to the Archaic and Woodland stages of southeastern Indian cultural development, and elements still survive today.

The early Mississippian, A.D. 1000–1200, was characterized by the spread of the Mississippian way of life throughout much of the Southeast. The most common shared trait was the chiefdom level of sociopolitical organization, which is detected in a hierarchy of settlements and inherited social status. The mechanics of the spread of Mississippian culture are not well understood, and both general diffusion and migration are thought to have been important processes. The documentation of the Macon Plateau Mississippian intrusion from eastern Tennessee, which triggered defense-and-imitation chiefdom formation in the Atlantic Slope, is one example of how the Mississippian way of life spread in the Southeast.

During the middle Mississippian, A.D. 1200–1400, complex chiefdoms formed in many areas and the Southeastern Ceremonial Complex reached its peak. Complex chiefdoms were organized primarily in areas with exceptionally rich soil and exceptional fishing grounds. Sociopolitical centers of the complex chiefdoms usually underwent a rapid expansion, and platform mound building reached its highest level in southeastern prehistory, as did the use of the rituals and paraphernalia of the Southeastern Ceremonial Complex to establish power and authority. There were many similarities between the mound centers of complex chiefdoms across the Southeast, but there were also local differences in mounds, preferred iconography, and specific mortuary practices. Warfare began to replace ceremonialism as the primary means of political control in many areas during this period.

The late Mississippian period, A.D. 1400–1500, was characterized by political turmoil and population relocations. Environmental and political problems in different areas led to cycles of instability, violence, and reorganization of complex chiefdoms. Two types of population relocation occurred: emigration and consolidation into walled towns. Although mound building and elaborate southeastern ceremonial complex rituals declined in most areas, they continued in many places.

8

EUROPEAN STAGE:
A.D. 1500–1821

KEY FEATURES

First European and African Materials and Settlements

Incorporation of European Items into Indian
Material Culture

Reorganization of Indian Settlement Pattern

IMPORTANT DEVELOPMENTS

European Encroachment

Indian Population Reduction and Chiefdom Collapse

Deerskin Trade

INTRODUCTION AND OVERVIEW

The European stage began with the arrival in the early 1500s of Europeans and ended with the termination of European ownership in the Southeast by the annexation of Florida into the United States in 1821. The archaeological features of this stage consist of the (1) First European and African Materials and Settlements, (2) Incorporation of European Items into Indian Material Culture, and (3) Reorganization of Indian Settlement Pattern. During this period, Europeans and their African slaves increasingly infiltrated the Southeast and had a significant impact on the Indians living there. One major effect of European colonization on the Indians was a population reduction due to epidemics of diseases brought by the Europeans. This led to their sociopolitical reorganization. As Europeans, Africans, and Indians adapted to the new natural and social environment, the shape of modern southeastern culture began to change.

Historical Archaeology

Beginning with this period, the archaeological record is supplemented with a new source of information about the past—written documents. While Europeans did not write down everything they did or saw, they nevertheless produced a wealth of documents. Their documents include reports and letters to sponsors, business records such as account books and shipping bills, court records, tax records, wills, and probate records, descriptions written by journalists, naturalists, adventurers, and survivors of expeditions, and drawings. Historical records and archaeological remains are used together in historical archaeology and produce a more realistic picture and explanation of the past than can be reconstructed by either discipline alone. While historical archaeology has developed in only the last 25 yr, it is one of the fastest growing fields in American archaeology. This growth is due primarily to public interest in the development of United States American culture and the realization that historical archaeology can reveal significant information about our past.

In the European stage, historical documents dealt almost exclusively with European activities and events. Little was written by Indians or Africans, and the documents that contain information about them were written from the European perspective. Historical archaeological studies of Indian and African culture are filling the void about the development of modern Indian and African-American ways of life.

Indians and Disease

In addition to the visible material items that Europeans brought with them to the New World, they also brought invisible, microscopic germs and viruses.

While it is difficult to comprehend in our age of high-speed travel, until the arrival of Europeans, American Indians in the New World had been almost completely isolated from the rest of the world for at least 10,000 yr. As a result, they had not been exposed to and had no immunity to the viruses, germs, and parasites introduced by Europeans and Africans. Archaeologists and historians agree that disease was the great killer of southeastern Indians. Epidemics followed on the heels of the first encounters with European and Africans and often the effects were intensified by multiple or tandem outbreaks of diseases such as mumps, measles, flu, smallpox, and pneumonia. Diseases spread like wildfire, and many Indian populations were reduced by 90% by the 1600s.

European Politics in the Southeast

During the three centuries of this stage, Spain, France, and England claimed and occupied portions of the Southeast. These countries had long histories of shifting political alliances and war, and each country had its own priorities and policies toward the Indians living in the New World. The recovery of gold, silver, and other valuable natural resources found in the New World changed the balance of power in Europe and resulted in new alliances and conflicts throughout this period.

Despite piracy and periodic attempts at settlement by the English and French, Spain had the Southeast to itself until 1670. Spain's principal interests in the New World were in Mexico, the Caribbean, and Central and South America, where great quantities of gold and silver were obtained. Initial explorations of the Southeast and Southwest in the early 1500s had revealed no valuable minerals, and Spain chose to use these areas as a buffer zone to protect the gold and silver-producing areas in the tropics. Because of this, historians have labeled the Southeast and Southwest the "Spanish Borderland." Spain tried to build forts along the Atlantic coast to protect the gold fleets sailing from the Gulf to Spain. Catholic Indian missions were established to convert Indians to Catholicism and to provide labor and supplies to the fort populations.

In the late 1600s, the French and English made inroads into Spain's claim on the Southeast. In the eastern half of the region, the English established the Carolina colony with plantations along the Atlantic coast and a lucrative Indian deerskin trade. The French moved into the western part of the region, between the Mississippi Valley and central Alabama. They established the colony of Louisiana, and set up a series of trading posts in the lower Mississippi and Alabama-Tombigbee valleys. The American Revolution caused European claims to the Southeast to rapidly dwindle, and by 1821, the last of Spain's holdings, the Floridas, was acquired by the United States.

Summary

The European stage of Southeastern archaeology will be divided into two parts. The Contact period, 1500–1670, was characterized by exploration and settlement by the Spaniards, rapid reduction of many Indian populations, and the establishment of Catholic Indian missions. The Colonial period, 1670–1821, was distinguished by the encroachment of the French and British into the Southeast, the spread of plantation agriculture, the importation of African slaves, and the reorganization and relocation of Indians. Trade with the Indians for deerskins became a big business, and the American Revolution created the first independent European-derived country in the New World—the United States of America.

CONTACT PERIOD: A.D. 1500–1670

Three major European-related events occurred during the Contact period: the first explorations and settlements, the first Indian epidemics, and the establishment of Catholic missions. A brief historical sketch of each is presented, followed by a summary of the archaeology.

First Explorations and Settlements

Historical Sketch

The very first Spaniards contacted by southeastern Indians were probably shipwrecked sailors and Spanish slave raiders from the Caribbean. The first official expedition was by Juan Ponce de León, who landed in 1513 on the east and southwest coasts of the Florida peninsula, as shown in Figure 8.1, and returned to Puerto Rico.[1] Throughout his voyage, Ponce de León had hostile encounters with Florida coastal Indians, including the Calusa near Charolotte Harbor. The Spaniards stayed there nine days and found a Calusa Indian who spoke Spanish, indicating previous contact with Spaniards, probably through Spanish Indian enslavers or shipwrecked sailors. He named the newland *"Pascua de la Florida"* because he made the discovery during Easter week, the passover of flowers.

A series of Spanish voyages to La Florida followed Ponce de León. Pedro de Salazar was the first Spaniard to land north of the Florida peninsula, when in 1514–15 he disembarked on the barrier islands off the Carolina coast and captured 500 Indians. Francisco Hernández de Córdoba visited southwest Florida in 1517, landing there on his return voyage to Cuba from the Yucatán Peninsula. The first settlement attempt was by Ponce de León, who returned to southwest Florida in 1521 with 200 colonists. The Calusas successfully

---

[1] See Coker and Shofner, 1991, for a summary of the early explorations in the Southeast.

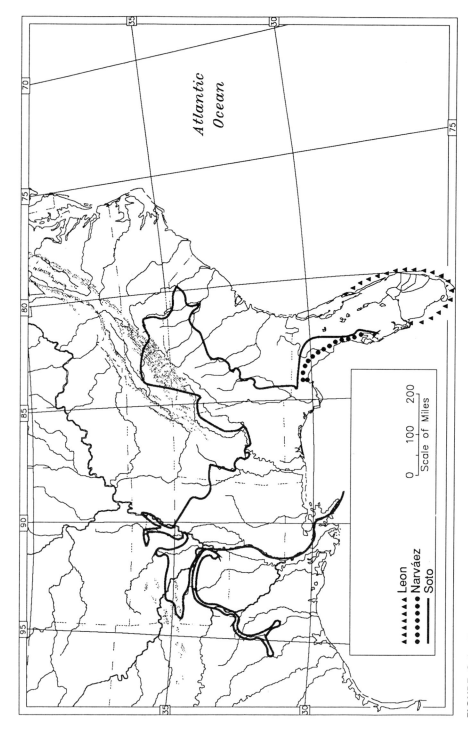

FIGURE 8.1 Routes of Ponce de León in 1513, Panfile de Narváez in 1528, and Hernando Soto, 1539–1541, in the Southeast.

attacked and fatally wounded Ponce de León, and the undertaking was abandoned. In 1521, Lucas Vásquez de Ayllón and Francisco Gordillo landed at the mouth of the Santee River in South Carolina and abducted 60 Indians. Impressed with the agricultural potential of the area, Vásquez de Ayllón returned in 1526 with 600 people and started a settlement at Sapelo Sound on the Georgia coast, which he named San Miguel de Gualdape. Ayllón died only two months afterward, along with 350 others. Four months later, the survivors abandoned the colony.

Narváez   The next colonization effort was led by Panfilo de Narváez in 1528. His force of 400 soldiers and 40 horses landed on the Florida peninsula, probably near Tampa Bay, where the Indians had some gold items. When they were told that the gold came from the land of the Apalachee to the north, Narváez made plans to go there. He sent his supply ships to Apalachee Bay, and he and his group marched up the western side of the Florida peninsula. Their interactions with Indian groups were consistently hostile, and one of their key tactics was to take a chief hostage for ransom and intimidation. They found the Apalachee, camped with them for a short while, and took a chief hostage. But they found no gold, and Apalachee hostility soon forced them to flee south to the coast near a village called Aute or Ochete, near present-day St. Marks, Florida. Starving, Narváez's men killed their horses for food. At least 40 of them had died of sickness on the trip, and others had been killed by the Apalachee. They decided to abandon the expedition and escaped by water by making rafts and drifting west along the coast. Narváez's rafts were soon scattered by a storm and most men, including Narváez, were lost. A few Spaniards landed on the Texas coast, perhaps on Galveston Island, and lived among the Indians. Eight years later, four survivors reached Mexico. One of the survivors, Álvar Núñez Cabeça de Vaca, originally the expedition's constable and treasurer, wrote a much-read account of this ill-fated expedition. He strongly suggested the possibility of finding riches in the interior. This account is the first observation of the Indians on the Texas coast, and it is a very important historical document.

Soto   The next Spanish expedition was led by Hernando de Soto, along a route shown in Figure 8.2. In 1539, he also landed in Florida, probably in Tampa Bay, with an army of over 600 men, 200 horses, and large attack dogs. He also carried food supplies for 18 mo, including a herd of pigs. Soto's Indian policy was aggressive and he used intimidation rather than negotiation. Like Narváez, he often kidnapped important Indian leaders for ransom, intimidation, and forced labor. Women were also regularly kidnapped for sexual exploitation. Knowing the Spanish Indian policy from their experience with Narváez, the Florida Indians fled from Soto, burned their villages and food supplies, and harassed the Spaniards with guerrilla warfare. However, Soto surprised the Apalachee at their capital town of Anhaica, which the Indians

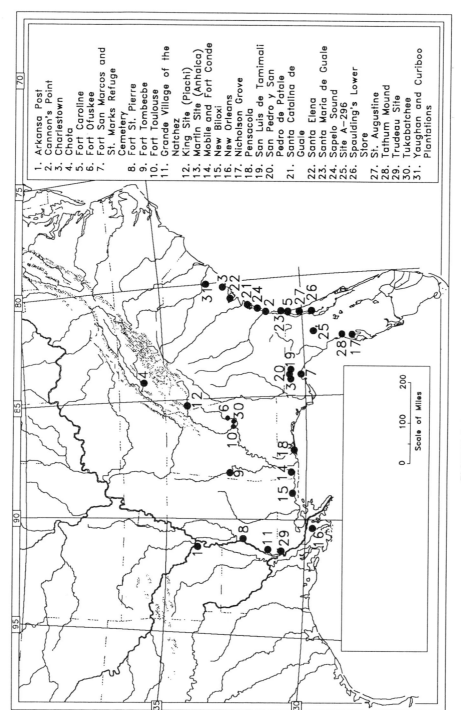

1. Arkansa Post
2. Cannon's Point
3. Charlestown
4. Chota
5. Fort Caroline
6. Fort Ofuskee
7. Fort San Marcos and
   St. Marks Refuge
   Cemetery
8. Fort St. Pierre
9. Fort Tombecbe
10. Fort Toulouse
11. Grande Village of the
    Natchez
12. King Site (Piachi)
13. Martin Site (Anhaica)
14. Mobile and Fort Conde
15. New Biloxi
16. New Orleans
17. Nicholson Grove
18. Pensacola
19. San Luis de Tamimali
20. San Pedro y San
    Pedro de Patale
21. Santa Catalina de
    Guale
22. Santa Elena
23. Santa Maria de Guale
24. Sapelo Sound
25. Site A–296
26. Spaulding's Lower
    Store
27. St. Augustine
28. Tathum Mound
29. Trudeau Site
30. Tukabatchee
31. Yaughan and Curiboo
    Plantations

FIGURE 8.2 Some European stage sites.

had abandoned but not burned, and the expedition spent the winter of 1539–40 there, harassed by guerrilla attacks. Soto met his supply ships at the Bay of Horses (Apalachee Bay), probably near where the Narváez men built their rafts. He told his supply convoy captain to meet him at Ochuse, Pensacola, the next year, and he took a Pensacola chief hostage to act as a guide.

In the spring season, Soto marched into part of Georgia and the Carolinas, crossed the Appalachians into east Tennessee, and followed the Coosa River into central Alabama, where he fought a damaging battle against the Coosa at Mabila, probably near Selma and Montgomery. Despite the traditional bitter rivalry between the Coosa and himself, the chief named Tascaluza apparently led the Coosas in the fight against Soto at Mabila. Almost every Spaniard was wounded and more than half their supplies were lost. Soto then turned northwest and spent the winter among the Chickasaw in Mississippi. He did not meet his supply ships in Pensacola Bay, although his pilot, Captain Francisco Maldonado, made several trips to Pensacola Bay and cruised the Gulf and Atlantic coasts looking for him. The next spring, Soto marched west, crossed the Mississippi River, and spent the year searching Arkansas for valuables. He returned to the Mississippi, where he spent the winter, and died there of a fever. The next year, the group tried to walk west to Mexico, but gave up and retraced its steps to the Mississippi. There they built boats and floated to the Gulf and then to Pánuco (Tampico), Mexico, where 311 survivors arrived in 1543.

Three accounts of the Soto expedition, and part of a fourth, were written by participants, and a secondhand account was written later. These accounts are among the most valuable historical documents about the southeastern United States that exist today. They contain detailed descriptions of sixteenth century Indian settlements, materials, ceremonies, political organization, warfare, and a myriad of other details. These descriptive accounts provide the first, and sometimes the only, glimpse of many late Mississippian Indian societies in the Southeast, and researchers throughout the Southeast continually use these documents.

Luna   Pressured by the plight of shipwrecked sailors and the need to hold on to the buffer zone of La Florida, Spain organized yet another settlement attempt in 1559. Led by Tristán de Luna y Arellano, the mission was to establish two permanent settlements, one at Pensacola on the Gulf, and one at Santa Elena on the Atlantic. Luna's group was formed in Mexico, and it consisted of 500 soldiers (several from the Soto expedition), 900 civilian men, women, and children, 100 Aztec warriors, and six priests. When the group arrived at Pensacola, they found very few Indians, and, consequently, no supply of food or labor. Five weeks after their arrival a hurricane sank all but three ships, killed many people, and destroyed most of their supplies. Luna abandoned plans to build a settlement at Pensacola and moved the group into the interior in search of Indians with food. Luna went to the central Alabama River, and others went as far as Coosa in northwest Georgia, but the Coosa chiefdom settlements visited by Soto twenty years earlier had deteriorated in the interim, and the Spaniards found little food. The food supply problem plus dissension in the ranks caused Luna to abandon plans to go on to establish a settlement at Santa Elena, and he returned to Pensacola. Frustrated by Luna's problems and the need for a settlement at Santa Elena, the Spanish government replaced Luna with Angel de Villafañe in 1561, who took the remaining expedition members by sea to reach Santa Elena. At sea a storm destroyed two of his ships and killed 25 more people, and the endeavor was canceled.

Ribault and Laudonnière   The very next year, 1562, the French tried to establish a foothold where the Spaniards had failed. Jean Ribault led an expedition of 150 people and built a small fort, called Charles Fort, on the South Carolina coast. All but one of the men at Charles Fort rebelled and sailed back to France. A second expedition under René de Laudonnière arrived in 1564 with three ships and 300 people. He relocated the settlement to the mouth of the St. Johns River and built a new fort, which he called Fort Caroline.

Menéndez   Spain sent Pedro Menéndez de Avilés with six ships and 600 men to expel the French in 1565. He quickly established St. Augustine near Fort Caroline, and surprised the French and killed most of them, including Ribault. In 1566, Menéndez built a fort at Santa Elena near the earlier French fort, on present-day Parris Island, South Carolina. The next year he sent Captain Juan Pardo to build another fort at Santa Elena and to explore the interior for a route to Mexico. Pardo made two long interior treks, reaching the Appalachians and eastern Tennessee, and he built several settlements and small garrisons. Within 2 yr they all were destroyed by Indians. Menéndez made Santa Elena the capital of La Florida in 1571, but troubles with the Indians, massacres of priests, problems with supplies, lack of settlers, and the death of Menéndez in 1574 prevented its success. In 1576, the capital was moved to St. Augustine, which was attacked and burned in 1586 by the English buccaneer Sir Francis Drake. This attack caused the Spaniards to evacuate Santa Elena and consolidate their forces at St. Augustine. The town and fort were rebuilt there, and Spain's hold on the Southeast remained unchallenged for almost a century. The English concentrated their efforts in the Caribbean and New England, and the French expanded in Canada and the upper Mississippi drainage.

Historical Archaeology

Thus far, the earliest historical archaeological sites in the Southeast are associated with the Soto and possibly the Narváez explorations.[2] These are the earliest historic archaeology sites in the United States.

Narváez Refuge Cemetery Site   Only one site has been located that possibly is associated with the Narváez expedition, the Refuge Cemetery, near St. Marks, shown in Figure 8.2.[3] There, on Apalachee Bay, European-made grave goods consisting of small hawk-bells (called Clarksdale bells), *Neuva Cádiz* glass beads, over 800 small silver disk beads, and perforated disks of brass, gold, and silver have been found in an Indian cemetery. Archaeologists presume that the metal was salvaged from Spanish shipwrecks and reworked into traditional Mississippian clothing decorations and ornaments. However, the account of the Narváez expedition specifically mentions a gift of bells to a Florida chief. While archaeologists cannot be certain whether the European items in the Refuge Cemetery were from the Narváez or the Soto expedition, they suggest that the cemetery was probably from the Narváez expedition because of the site's location on Apalachee Bay, where the Narváez team lived for a while and built their rafts. Archaeologists are cautious, though, in the association of the cemetery site with Narváez because Soto also resupplied in this vicinity 12 yr later, in the spring of 1540.

Soto Archaeology   Archaeologists, historians, ethnohistorians, the general public, and politicians have been fascinated with the Soto expedition through the Southeast. On several anniversaries of the expedition, commissions have been established to trace and mark the route, research the documents, and find the archaeological sites of Indian settlements where Soto visited. As a consequence, there have been many historical archaeological studies of the Soto expedition. A few examples of the archaeological research from this large field of research are described.

Tathum Mound   Just north of Tampa, early sixteenth century European artifacts and metal ornaments have been found as grave goods in three nearby burial mounds: Weeki Wachee, Ruth Smith, and Tathum.[4] The Tathum mound, discovered in 1984, has been excavated by Jeffery Mitchem and Jerald Milanich of the Florida Museum of Natural History. The mound contained the remains of several hundred people buried with hundreds of sixteenth century glass beads, many objects of reworked metal, especially iron made

---

[2] See Thomas, 1990, and Milanich and Milbrath, 1989, for a series of papers on early historic archaeology in the Southeast. Also see Hudson, 1987, for details of the Pardo expedition and Hudson *et al.*, 1990, for a description of the De Luna expedition.

[3] See Marrinan *et al.*, 1990, and Mitchem, 1989, for details on Narváez archaeology.

[4] See Mitchem, 1989, 1990, for details on the Tathum mound excavations and Narváez archaeology.

into tools such as chisels, as well as traditional Safety Harbor Mississippian pottery vessels. Mitchem suggests that the iron probably came from a cache of iron implements and other supplies buried by Soto at the Indian settlement of Cale, believed to be nearby. The Indians might well have found the cache and traded the items to neighboring groups. Direct contact between Europeans and the Indians buried in the Tathum Mound was documented by means of sword wounds on two skeletons. Indirect evidence of contact with Europeans is interpreted from a mass grave of at least 77 people. Archaeologists suggest that these people probably died from a local epidemic of European diseases. The association of the European-related wounds and artifacts in the three burial mounds with the Soto expedition rather than the Narváez expedition, which also passed this way, is based on the amount of iron implements used for grave goods and proximity of the Soto iron tool cache at nearby Cale.

Martin Farm   Farther north in Florida, near Tallahassee, the Martin Farm site has been confirmed as the location of Soto's winter encampment of 1539–40 among the Apalachee at Anhaica.[5] While only a small part of this village of 250 houses has been excavated, key European time markers and military artifacts have been found, some of which are shown in Figure 8.3. Spanish artifacts include chain mail links, a crossbow tip, two copper Spanish coins (*maravedís* minted between 1515 and 1517), three Portuguese copper coins, nails, ceramic storage jars called "olive jars," and tableware ceramics. While these artifacts can place the occupation of this site sometime in the early sixteenth century, they cannot by themselves be used to determine whether the occupation was by the 1528 Narváez or the 1539–40 Soto expedition. However, the recovery of a shattered jaw of a pig eliminated the Narváez theory. Soto had read the Cabeça de Vaca account of the Narváez expedition, and knew that he would be unable to live entirely off the land (and the Indians), so he brought along a herd of pigs for food. Pigs are not native to the New World and Narváez had not brought any on his expedition. Soto was the first to introduce pigs into the Southeast, and the recovery of the pig jaw at the Martin Farm site provided conclusive evidence that this was Soto's winter encampment.

Coosa Chiefdom   Historical archaeologists in Georgia, Tennessee, and South Carolina also have studied the Soto expedition to test our ability to identify Indian prehistoric chiefdoms from the archaeological record. Researchers Charles Hudson, Marvin Smith, David Hally, and Chester DePratter have concentrated on reconstructing the Coosa complex chiefdom using the Soto accounts and archaeological excavations.[6] Soto visited several provinces of the Coosa complex chiefdom, and expedition narratives often describe their

[5] See Ewen, 1989, 1990, for details on the Martin site excavation.

[6] For details of the Soto route and Coosa chiefdom historical archaeology see Hudson *et al.*, 1985 and 1990, Hally *et al.*, 1990, and Smith 1987.

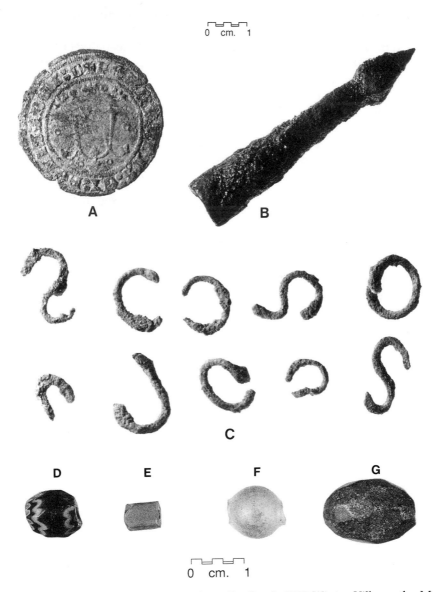

FIGURE 8.3 Early Spanish artifacts from De Soto's 1539 Winter Village, the Martin site (Anhaica) near Tallahassee, Florida: (A) Spanish coin, (B) crossbow tip, (C) chain mail links, (D) faceted chevron glass bead, (E) *Nueva Cadíz* glass bead, (F) blown-glass bead, (G) faceted glass bead. (From Ewen, 1990.)

settlements in detail, and the political organization and relationships between the affiliated chiefdoms. Hudson and his colleagues have been able to identify the chiefdoms of this complex chiefdom, which are shown in Figure 8.4. Combining historical documents and archaeological data, they have identified some archaeological correlates of chiefdoms. For example, the settlements of simple chiefdoms had clusters of sites about 12 mi long, which were separated from other similar clusters by at least 18 mi. Within the simple chiefdom site clusters, the typical simple chiefdom site hierarchy was present, consisting of one large settlement with the most mounds, several smaller settlements

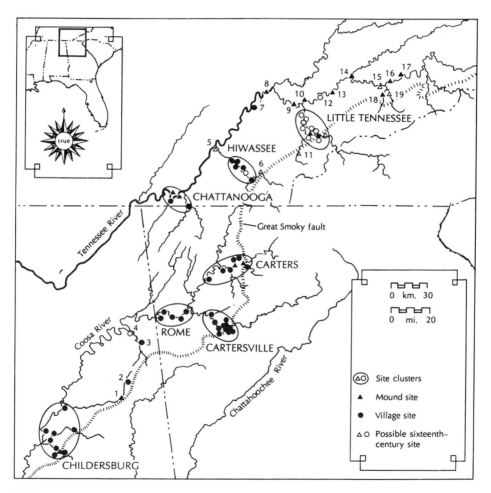

FIGURE 8.4 Location of site clusters thought to be simple chiefdoms politically aligned in the Coosa complex chiefdom visited by Soto in 1540. (From Hally *et al.*, 1990.)

with a few mounds, and scattered farmsteads. There also is a strong similarity of material culture within the chiefdom settlement clusters, especially pottery temper and surface decorations. The researchers could not easily detect archaeologically that the individual chiefdoms had been politically affiliated into the complex chiefdom as described in the Soto documents. As shown in Figure 8.4, the Coosa chiefdoms were located in two different river valleys (the Coosa and Tennessee), and the general artifact assemblages are quite different. Archaeologists and ethnohistorians suggest that comparisons of the grave goods of the ruling elite of the different chiefdoms may best reveal distinctive categories of status markers shared by the political allies.[7] One such shared status marker, the Citigo type of carved shell gorget associated with the Southeastern Ceremonial Complex, has been tentatively identified in the Coosa complex chiefdom. The Citigo gorget has only been found within the boundaries of the Coosa complex chiefdom in both the Coosa and Tennessee valleys and therefore may be an archaeological marker of this political unit.

While several Coosa settlements visited by Soto have been identified and excavated, the King site in the Rome, Georgia, chiefdom has revealed significant evidence of armed conflict between the Indians and Spaniards.[8] This site is thought to be the community called Piachi where Soto spent one or two days in 1540. There, archaeologists have found that 20% of the burials had wounds from metal weapons. The wounded individuals were either women in their 20s or men and women in their 40s and 50s. Forensic studies of the skeletons revealed animal gnawing marks on the bones of some individuals, which indicates that they had lay in the open for weeks before burial. While researchers agree that the sword wounds were from Soto's men, there are two conflicting theories about where the wounds occurred. One theory proposes that the wounded individuals were from a group of people captured by Soto for slaves when he visited Piachi, who were taken to Mabila, where they were wounded and killed in the big battle that occurred there. The wounded escaped and made their way home where they died and were buried, and the dead were retrieved from the battleground several weeks later for burial at home. The second theory proposes that the injuries were inflicted at Piachi by Soto's men as part of their standard intimidation of Indians who resisted capture in the settlements they visited. This theory explains the exposed bodies as those of people who had been wounded and managed to flee into the surrounding area where they died. Their bodies were retrieved a few weeks later and buried at Piachi.

Early Spanish Settlements   Long-term historical archaeological studies are ongoing at both the former Spanish Florida capitals of Santa Elena and St. Augustine. Santa Elena is located on current-day Parris Island, near Beaufort, South Carolina, and St. Augustine is in northeast Florida. The historical ar-

[7] See Anderson, 1990b, for details of chiefdom signatures.
[8] For details of the King site archaeology see Blakely, 1988.

chaeology at these early Spanish communities in the Southeast United States continues to shed new light on how Spaniards dealt with the Southeast and Indians that lived there.

Santa Elena   The first capital of La Florida, Santa Elena, has been intensively studied by a team of researchers headed by Stanley South from the South Carolina Institute of Archeology and Anthropology.[9] This team has identified portions of two forts that have been partially eroded and the residential community positioned between them, as shown in Figure 8.5. Although South initially identified the two forts as those built by Menéndez, Fort San Felipe II and Fort San Marcos, he is beginning to suspect the eastern fort may be Charles Fort, built by the Frenchman, Jean Ribault, in 1562, four years before Menéndez arrived.[10] Excavations inside the eastern fort have located the moat, stockade, bastions, and a strong house (*casa fuerte*) of 50 × 70 feet.

Recently, Stanley South and his colleagues have been testing the area north of the two forts, looking for the elusive third fort. While the third fort has not been found, they have made the surprising discovery of the oldest Spanish pottery kiln in North America.[11] The 4 × 4-feet square subterranean kiln has brick walls 2 ft below the ground and a firing chamber. South suggests that this kiln was originally about 3 ft deep. Inside the kiln were several complete ceramic vessels with bulbous bodies, thin necks, and handles similar to those made in Spain at the time and which reflect the Moorish influence on Spanish material culture.

Excavations in the residential area of Santa Elena have revealed five residences. Four were built in the traditional rectangular Spanish design, but one is circular. As shown in Figure 8.6, all residences were placed around a central courtyard. The Spanish style houses were small, 18 × 20 feet maximum, and the walls were made of upright posts to which cornstalks and canes were fastened and then covered with a plaster made of clay mixed with moss or grass. The plaster was made in nearby pits that were later filled with refuse.

A large barrel well, with the lower barrel intact, has been found outside Structure 2. Barrels were often used to make well shafts in colonial settlements. Construction consisted of digging a pit to the water table, where an openended barrel was forced down into the wet sand at the water table and the sand removed. A series of open-ended barrels were then stacked to the surface, and the construction pit was filled in around them. Water was confined in the shaft formed by the stacked barrels and was drawn up with a bucket. Barrel wells usually lasted only 10–15 yr and when no longer useable, the upper barrels were often removed and the shaft was filled. Three barrel wells also have been found in the eastern fort, and one is shown in Figure 8.7.

The artifacts from Santa Elena and their distribution patterns have revealed much about this early Spanish and Indian community (Figure 8.8). As an

---

[9] For a summary of Santa Elena archaeology see South, 1987.

[10] Stanley South, personal communication, 1993.

[11] Stanley South, personal communication, 1993.

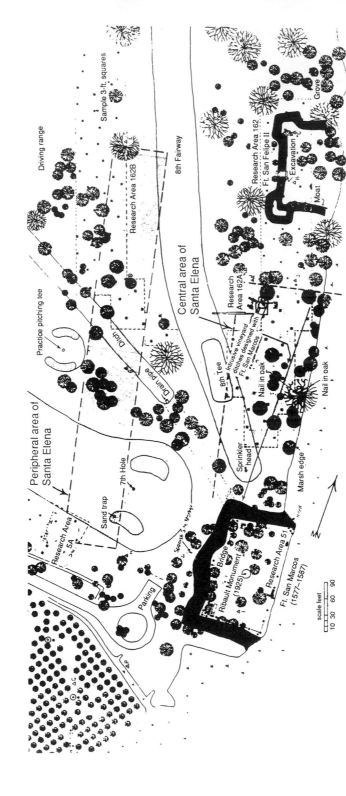

FIGURE 8.5 Map of the site of Santa Elena, on Parris Island, South Carolina. (From South, 1980.)

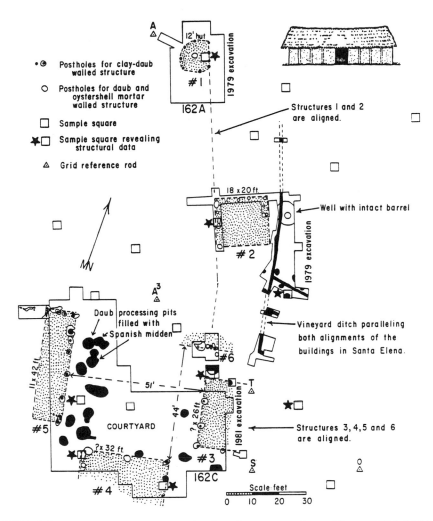

FIGURE 8.6 Spanish structures and other features at Santa Elena (1566–1587) on Parris Island, South Carolina. (From Stanley *et al.*, 1988.)

example, there were many more Spanish-made items in the fort than in the Spanish-style residences, and they were rare in the circular residence. All Spanish items had to be imported and were in demand. South has inferred from the distribution of the valuable items that access appeared to be related to a person's rank and social position. The highest-ranking Spaniards were in the military and lived in the fort, where there were more Spanish items than elsewhere. Spanish civilians were second in rank and social position and they lived in the Spanish-style rectangular houses outside the fort where many Spanish items were found, but in lower quantities than in the fort. The

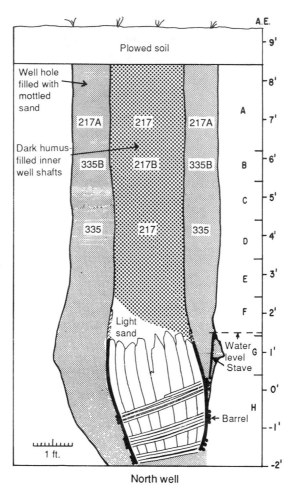

FIGURE 8.7   Profile drawing of a barrel well at Santa Elena in the eastern fort showing the relationship of the water level, lowest barrel, and outer and inner shafts. Note the well shaft has been filled in leaving only the lowest barrel in place. (From South, 1985.)

lowest social rank was that of Spanish laborer, and these people lived in the Indian-style hut where Spanish items were rare. On the other hand, expensive items, such as Ming porcelain, were recovered only from the Spanish residences. South interprets the distribution of expensive items outside the fort as an indicator that the civilians at Santa Elena were relatively wealthy and were the only people who could afford to buy expensive materials.

The differential distribution of Indian pottery at Santa Elena revealed the different roles of different Indians in this community. The general importance

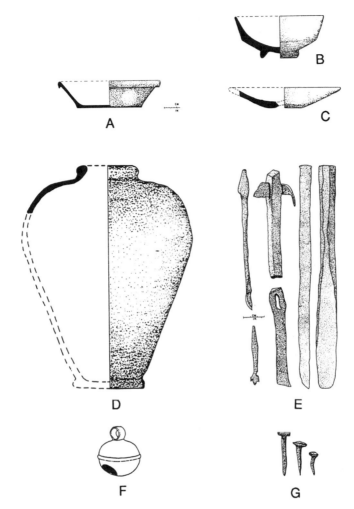

FIGURE 8.8   Early Spanish artifacts. (A) lead-glazed *Lebrillo* dish (4.5 in.); (B) Isabella polychrome majolica *escudilla* (bowl) (5 in.); (C) Isabella polychrome majolica *plato* (plate) (8 in.); (D) flat-based olive jar (16 in.); (E) wrought-iron auger bits, broken auger shafts, and gouge (13–14 in.); (F) Clarksdale brass bell (1 in.); (G) wrought-iron nails (1.5 in.). (From South *et al.*, 1988.)

of Indians is reflected in the fact that Indian pottery made up 42% of all artifacts recovered from the excavations. Within the Indian pottery, there were two distinct groups. One group was made by the local Indians from around Santa Elena and was found mainly in the fort. The pottery made by the Indians from St. Augustine was found primarily in the residential area outside the fort. South has made several interpretations from this differential distribution of Indian pottery. First, the presence of Timucuan Indian pottery indicates that Menéndez must have brought Indians with him from St. Augustine. From the fact that their pottery was abundant only in the residential area, South suggests that they were probably Timucuan women who were house servants, concubines, and wives of the Spanish civilians. The Timucuan Indian women either brought their pots with them from Florida or made them in Santa Elena. South interprets the abundance of local Indian pottery inside the fort as related to gifts of food brought in their pottery containers by local Indians. The pottery containers were then used and broken inside the fort. Much additional information has been found from the historical archaeology research at Santa Elena, but these examples of the findings demonstrate the productive combination of history and archaeology.

St. Augustine   In St. Augustine, one of the main research interests of Kathleen Deagan and her students has been the cultural adaptations made by the Spaniards to life in Florida.[12] They found that this early Spanish community was organized according to the pattern established in Spain, with a strategically placed fort, residences centered around an open plaza, and a church. Deagan targeted for excavation specific house lots that had good historical records about the early Spanish occupants, such as race, occupation, family size, and status. From excavating these lots, Deagan has discovered that all types of residential dwellings had foundation trenches lined with oyster shells on the bottom, barrel wells positioned at the same place along the streets, trash pits along backyard fences, and sheet midden in backyards. The pattern of archaeological deposits was the same on all Spanish house lots in St. Augustine.

There was a differential distribution of Spanish-made artifacts at St. Augustine, which correlated with the social status of house lot residents, similar to that found at Santa Elena. There were consistently more Spanish artifacts found on house lots belonging to higher-status residents than on those belonging to lower-status residents. Further analysis revealed that the most popular Spanish artifacts were items with high visibility such as dining and serving wares and drinking glasses. Items with less social visibility were often Indian-made, especially things used in the kitchen, such as cooking pots and storage jars.

Another revealing source of information about how the Spaniards adapted to life in the New World in St. Augustine is their food remains.[13] Deagan and her students and her associates, Elizabeth Reitz, Stephen Cumbaa, and Margret Scarry, compared the relationship of social status and diet in sixteenth century Spain to contemporary St. Augustine society. Their research revealed that the diet of almost all socioeconomic classes in the Spanish homeland

---

[12] For details of St. Augustine see Deagan, 1983; for a summary see Deagan, 1990.

[13] For paleobotany details see Reitz and Cumbaa, 1983, and Reitz and Scarry, 1985.

consisted of domesticated plants and animals. The reason was that long-term overpopulation in Spain had depleted the countryside of habitats for edible animals and plants. Wild food, especially game, was extremely scarce. Fish were available in many areas in Spain, but fish were regularly eaten only by the poor and were considered a lower-class food. Only the upper class ate wild game because they owned private forests and hired private hunters. Wild birds were especially favored by the elite, but all wild game was considered an upper-class food. Most Spanish colonists came from urban areas and had always purchased their food at markets. Therefore, the skills of farming and hunting were not well known by most of the Spaniards who arrived in St. Augustine. Archaeology in early Spanish St. Augustine has substantiated that house lots of higher-status residents contained the highest amounts of imported domesticated grains, such as wheat and barley, and more wild game, such as deer and birds. This correlates with historical documents that state that higher-status people hired Indian or African hunters to get their wild game. Archaeology at house lots of lower-status households has produced lower amounts of imported grain and, as in Spain, they ate wild animals that are easily captured, especially fish. The archaeological record of Spanish St. Augustine has revealed a strong correlation between status and diet, similar to the pattern in contemporary Spain.

Summary

The examples of archaeological research of the first Spanish exploration sites and settlements demonstrate how historical archaeology is providing information about how Spaniards adapted to the Southeast and dealt with the people and environment that they encountered. By combining the descriptive accounts of the early explorations with the archaeology of the sites that were visited, researchers are able to detect the direct and indirect effects of the Indians and Spaniards on each other. By using the narratives to confirm the boundaries of specific chiefdoms and isolating their specific archaeological assemblages, archaeologists are also gaining a better understanding of how the archaeological record does and does not correlate with Indian sociopolitical organizations. From the work being done in Santa Elena and St. Augustine, we also are getting a better understanding of the very beginnings of the development of the Spanish-American community. From historical archaeology we are beginning to track how traditional Spanish cultural values were applied and modified in the Southeast, and how Indians were integrated into Spanish society.

Indian Epidemics and Population Decline

Another area of archaeological research of the Contact period in the Southeast is the biological and cultural aftereffects of European explorations and first settlements: epidemics and the collapse of many of populations.[14] The direct effects of the explorations on Indians are readily recognizable by the presence of European artifacts in graves and sword wounds in human remains. The indirect effect of European diseases is more subtle and difficult to detect.

The early occurrence of epidemics of European diseases in Indian populations is known because the early explorers witnessed many epidemics and saw the results of others. For instance, at the town of Talomeco in 1540, on the South Carolina Fall Line, Soto saw hundreds of bodies stacked up in front of buildings, and when asked about this, the Indians said that epidemics had depopulated several towns in the area. These epidemics are thought to have stemmed from the Spanish Allyón settlement in 1526 on the Georgia coast. Soto's men discovered European items in their mortuary temple that are believed to have come from that colony. Indian epidemics were also documented by expeditions that followed routes of previous parties. Accounts of previous expeditions were often used to plan the routes of new ones, and previously visited large Indian settlements were targeted for revisitation to obtain labor and food supplies. Often members of previous parties were used as guides. However, when the second exploratory group reached the location of former large agricultural settlements, they usually had been decimated by sickness following the previous visit, and food was in short supply. This was the case when Luna followed the Soto route to Coosa, and when he arrived at the once rich chiefdom, he found only seven small villages with very little food. This situation caused Luna to abandon his expedition to Santa Elena and return to Pensacola. Luna also found few Indians in the Pensacola area, and it is likely that they had been infected with European diseases from Soto's resupply team, which anchored in Pensacola Bay in 1541 and visited the Indian settlements in the area. The planners of the Luna expedition had counted on Indians and their food both in Coosa and Pensacola, but it appears that epidemics started by Soto had caused their demise.

Several researchers have studied the dynamics of the Indian epidemics in the Southeast.[15] Isolation from the rest of the world for at least 10,000 yr had prevented the spread of European and African diseases to the American Indians. Magnifying this situation was the powerful disease history of both Europeans and Africans. In Europe, the disease and death rate in the dirty and crowded Middle Age cities had been so high that constant immigration from the countryside was required to maintain their population. Waves of epidemics had also swept Europe during this time, the worst of which was the epidemic of bubonic plague known as the "Black Death" during the fourteenth century, which killed an estimated 25 million people in Europe,

---

[14] See Verano and Ubelaker, 1992, and Thomas, 1990, for recent studies on disease and demographic changes. See Dobyns, 1983 and 1991, Milner, 1980, and Stannard, 1991, for examples of detailed research.

[15] Examples are Stannard, 1991, Dobyns, 1991, and Ramenofsky, 1990.

25–33% of the total European population. Female survivors of the epidemics and diseases passed their antibodies to their children, which greatly reduced the effects on later generations of such illnesses as whooping cough, smallpox, influenza, and measles. While Europeans still contracted these diseases, they usually suffered light cases in childhood, and afterwards were immune. Tropical Africa also has a disease-ridden history, and the survivors of their diseases, some of whom were brought to the New World, had a wide range of antibodies and disease-fighting biological properties, such as the sickle cell trait, which wards off the malaria parasite.

When Indians were first exposed to a European and African disease, almost everyone in a settlement contracted a severe case, because they had no inherited antibodies to reduce the effects of the disease. Indians usually died from mumps, measles, colds, and influenza, which were relatively minor threats to Europeans. Another reason disease had such an explosive impact on Indians was that diseases came in waves. As communities recovered from one epidemic, another disease would be introduced. The weakened state of survivors made them very susceptible to the new disease. The high death rate was also intensified because usually everyone in a community was sick at the same time. Therefore, important activities such as drawing water, gathering firewood, getting food, and caring for the sick were not possible, and many potential disease survivors died from malnutrition, dehydration, and lack of care.

In an historical study of the epidemics and population decline of the Timucuan Indians in northeast Florida, Henry Dobyns catalogued the series of sicknesses suffered by this population. The first recorded epidemic was smallpox in 1519, which apparently was started by a Spaniard with this disease. Dobyns estimates that 50% of the Timucuans died in this smallpox epidemic. A series of Timucuan epidemics followed: a gastrointestinal infection outbreak in 1528, bubonic plague in 1545–48, typhus in 1549, mumps in 1550, influenza in 1559, and bubonic plague again in 1613–1617. Sickness among the Timucuans was also documented by the early explorations as Spaniards once saw the effect of the newly introduced diseases and witnessed half the people in a village dying. Some of the French drawings of the Timucuans near Fort Caroline during 1562–1565, such as the one shown in Figure 8.9, actually depict sick Indians who probably were in the midst of an epidemic.

Marvin Smith investigated the possibility of Indian epidemics and subsequent depopulation and reorganization in the Coosa complex chiefdom in the interior of the Southeast.[16] While the Coosa have a sparse historical record, there is extensive archaeological information from the excavation of many sixteenth and seventeenth century sites. In his study, Smith reasoned that if the Coosa suffered epidemics spread by the explorations of Soto, Luna, and Pardo, their population would have been reduced in the sixteenth and seven-

[16] See M. Smith, 1987 and 1989, for details of the Coosa study.

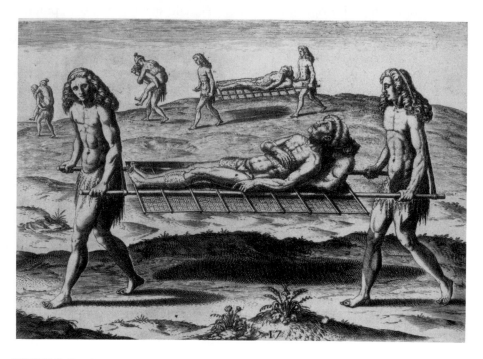

FIGURE 8.9   1564 LeMoyne drawing of sick Timucuans likely suffering from an epidemic of a European disease. (Reprinted with permission of the Rare Books and Manuscripts Division, New York Public Library, Astor, Lenox and Tilden Foundations.)

teenth centuries. He identified five archaeological indicators of the proposed Coosa population collapse and reorganization.

1. Cessation of public works such as mound and stockade building
2. Settlement abandonment, reduction in size, and relocation of survivors
3. End of the chiefdom settlement hierarchy
4. Cessation of inherited rank as reflected in grave goods
5. Decline in craft specialists as reflected in personal and status items

Smith established a refined chronology using European artifacts of four 30–40 yr periods between 1525 and 1670. His study documented that all of the archaeological indicators of population collapse listed above were evident within 30–60 yr of the Soto visit. He theorizes that there were simply not enough Coosa people to support the elite, perform public works, make special crafts, and engage in chiefly warfare. By 1700, the once-powerful Coosa complex chiefdom had been reduced to little more than a few small loosely organized settlements composed of a mixture of survivors who had banded together for mutual support and defense.

Some scholars such as Ann Ramenofsky have also tried to determine how diseases spread within different Indian populations. She has pointed out that the rate at which epidemics spread between communities should vary with their settlement and mobility patterns. In dense, sedentary populations with large settlements and much interaction, epidemics spread quickly between settlement chiefdoms. In societies with a lower and more mobile population, scattered small settlements, and only intermittent interaction, diseases spread more slowly. Regardless of the different rate of the spread of disease, most of Florida, Georgia, and at least eastern Alabama were largely depopulated by the mid-1600s.

In the end, all Indian populations in the Southeast suffered extreme population reduction, and the way of life of the reorganized survivors was different than in the prehistoric Mississippian period. The early population collapse and reorganization of many of the southeastern Indian groups has caused a serious discontinuity between the first detailed historical descriptions of southeastern Indians in the eighteenth and nineteenth centuries, and the archaeological record at the time of contact.[17] Therefore, the primary source of information about southeastern Indians in the sixteenth and seventeenth centuries is through archaeology, not documents.

Catholic Mission System

Historical Sketch

The many failed Spanish settlement attempts in La Florida had cost both private citizens and the crown a lot of money. After almost a century of effort and great expense, all that Spain had to show in La Florida was a small government-subsidized military garrison at St. Augustine. The main problems in establishing a foothold in the Southeast were the lack of a good incentive (such as gold and silver deposits) to Spaniards and the lack of a large sedentary Indian population, like in Mexico or Peru, that could be profitably exploited.

In fact, one of the biggest problems was the stiff resistance by the Indian population who attacked the Spaniards. The Spanish needed the cooperation of local Indians to supply them with food and labor because there were not enough Spaniards to do all the labor, and they did not know how to hunt, gather, and grow food in the Southeast.

Encomiendia **System**　　The first Indian policy Spain tried was the *encomienda* system. Under this policy, Indians within the domain of *encomienderos*, Spanish men in charge of expeditions or settlements could force Indian leaders to supply labor and food in return for "protection." Food and large groups of men were sent to Spanish settlements to farm, hunt, construct buildings,

---

[17] Swanton, 1946, is a classic example of these historical descriptions of southeastern Indian groups.

clear forests, and transport supplies. However, the *encomienda* system did not work well in the Southeast because of Indian hostility and population reduction from epidemics. Spain experimented with using African slaves as early as 1581 in St. Augustine to replace the dwindling number of Indian slaves and laborers, and, though limited, it was successful.[18]

Throughout the early Contact period, priests had accompanied expeditions and built churches in settlements. The Church was unhappy with the abuse of the Indians in the *encomienda* system, and although this system was outlawed in 1542, it was not well enforced. About this time, the Catholic Church began to emphasize converting Indians to Catholicism by sending out missionaries. The converted Indians became obedient Christian Spanish subjects who would follow the priests' orders to work for the Spanish. Seeing the advantage in this missionizing policy, the Crown agreed to provide transportation and pay the friars' salary, if the missions would supply the settlements with food and labor from their Indian converts. The first religious order assigned this missionization task was the Jesuits, but they made little headway. In 1573, after a series of failures and massacres on the Georgia coast and in Chesapeake Bay, they gave up on missionizing in the Southeast.

Franciscan and Apalachee Missions   Franciscans were then assigned the responsibility of the missions, but they too had problems with the Indians, who had become anti-Spanish because of food and tribute demands and harassment by the military. A Guale rebellion against the Franciscans in 1597 on the Georgia coast destroyed the newly established Franciscan mission system. In retaliation, the Spaniards launched a series of reprisals out of St. Augustine in 1598. At this point, Spain seriously considered abandoning La Florida altogether, but the Church convinced them to continue. Missions were reestablished on the Georgia coast, and the Guale, who by then had been seriously depleted by epidemics and Spanish retaliations, realized that they simply could not stop the Spaniards. Rather than perish, the Guale began to seek protection through religious conversion. New missions were established on the Georgia and Florida Atlantic coast, but they were only marginally successful due to the Indian population decline and the demands for food and labor by St. Augustine.

By 1633, in an effort to find a new source of Indian converts to supply St. Augustine, the Franciscans expanded their missions to the western Timucuan and Apalachee groups. The rapid dwindling of the Guale and Timucuans increased demands on the Apalachee, who revolted in 1647. A reprisal by the Spaniards defeated the Apalachees, and they also realized that they could not stop the Spaniards. So, like the Guale before them, they began to seek protection from the Spaniards by accepting the Franciscan priests, helping

---

[18] See Landers, 1990, for details of this experiment.

them build missions, and converting to Catholicism. By 1674, there were 36 Franciscan missions in La Florida, as shown in Figure 8.10.

The Franciscans modified their missionary and worked within the Apalachee political and social structure. The friars also kept the Spanish military from brutalizing their Indian converts. Franciscan friars realized that Apalachee chiefs had real power over their subjects, and so they targeted the chiefs as their first converts. After a chief's conversion, the rest of the population was willing to follow. The Franciscans also located their missions in the chief's settlement, which was the sociopolitical center of the chiefdoms. They placed their church on the plaza in the civic-ceremonial area across from the Indian council house. This revised strategy of the Franciscans was very successful with the Apalachee. The friars protected the Indians from the brutality of the military, and through the required obedience of the Indian converts, the friars were able to provide food and labor to St. Augustine as well as to produce surplus for sale.

The Catholic missions were on the frontier of Spanish–Indian contact, and they became the first Indian trading centers.[19] With a strong demand for leather and agricultural products, Indians were encouraged to bring these items into the mission settlement to exchange for trade goods. The Apalachee raised cattle and farmed, and other Indian groups brought in large numbers of deerskins. By 1639 the Gulf port of San Marcos was established at the mouth of the St. Marks River near Tallahassee, and there was a lively, if illicit, traffic with Havana. While the main commodity for trade was hides, large amounts of tallow, maize, beans, and wild turkeys were also shipped. Many traders preferred the port of San Marcos because they could evade the royal taxes and transportation costs associated with St. Augustine. Of course, the Apalachee population was rapidly decreasing, but during the last half of the 1600s, this Franciscan mission system was Spain's greatest economic success in Florida.

Mission Archaeology

There has been an impressive amount of mission archaeology since the 1970s in the Southeast, including several long-term research projects in Florida and coastal Georgia and South Carolina.[20] In this research, six missions have been extensively excavated and many have been investigated. From this historical archaeology, we are beginning to accumulate a great deal of information about life in and around the missions, some of which is summarized below.

Archaeologists have documented that the layout of Spanish Catholic mis-

---

[19] For more about seventeenth century trade see Waselkov, 1989b.

[20] For more on Spanish mission archaeology see Thomas, 1990, and McEwan, 1991c. Examples of specific mission archaeology studies are David Thomas, 1987 and 1988, Saunders, 1988, and Weisman, 1988.

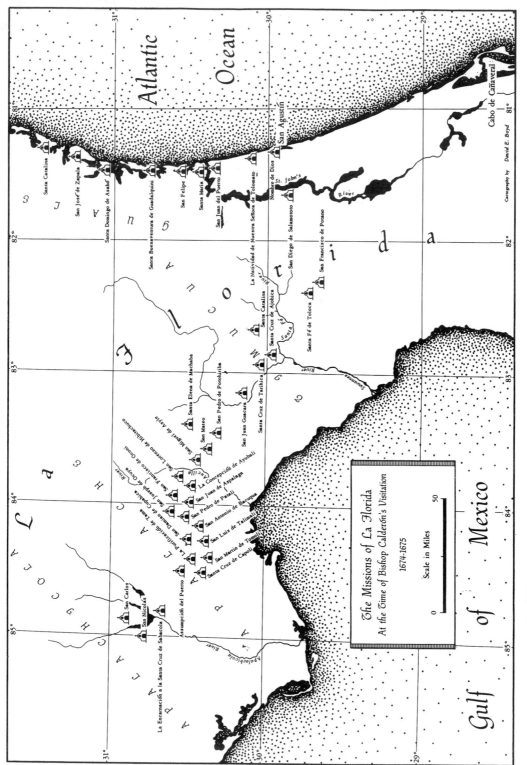

FIGURE 8.10 Catholic Missions of La Florida in 1674–1675. (From Gannon, 1965.)

sions varied with time, available supplies, and Indian labor.[21] Most buildings were made of wooden posts with wattle and daub walls, and thatch roofs. A typical mission had four parts: church, cemetery, *convento* (friary residence), and kitchen. Early missions among the Guale and Timucua were separated from Indian settlements, although they were often nearby. Later, among the Apalachee, missions were well integrated into the chief's settlement. The church was usually placed on the plaza across from the Indian council house. The residential areas for the priests and lay Spaniards, however, were separated from the Indian residential areas in the settlement.

Mission churches were rectangular with an earth floor, sometimes made of special soil such as clay. At the Santa Catalina de Gaule mission on St. Catherine's Island, the complete floor of the church, built in 1604 and used until 1680, has been excavated by David Hurst Thomas and the American Museum of Natural History.[22] The church was 65 × 36 ft in size, the walls were made of posts covered with wattle and daub, and it had a gabled thatch roof. Thomas determined that the altar was raised, and he even found wheat grains in the sacristy (a small room off the altar), which perhaps were from the grain used to make bread for communion. The church faced a 50 × 50-ft plaza covered with shells and enclosed by a low wall. Portions of several other mission churches have been found, and some had sufficient enough research to be reconstructed by an artist, as shown in Figure 8.11 of the San Juan de Aspalaga mission near Tallahassee, Florida. It was a common practice to bury Indian converts in church floors. Hundreds of Indian burials have been found under the floors of churches such as Santa Catalina de Guale on Amelia Island and San Pedro y San Pablo de Patale near Tallahassee. Burials were regularly oriented with the congregation buried in the nave of the church facing the altar, and the priest buried in the altar area facing the congregation. Cemeteries were also located outside in the churchyards of some missions.

Conventos were more variable in shape and location, due to the differing numbers of friars and available construction materials and labor. In Apalachee missions, *conventos* were usually close to or attached to the church, whereas at the earlier Santa Catalina de Guale mission, the *convento* was located directly across the shell plaza from the church. At the Franciscan mission headquarters in St. Augustine, the *convento* was rebuilt three times between 1588 and 1750, with increasingly sturdy materials. The last building was made of tabby and cut blocks of coquina limestone. The only mission kitchen that has been completely exposed is at Santa Catalina on St. Catherine's Island, and it was an open structure.

Apalachee council houses in mission settlements have been investigated at San Luis de Talimali and San Pedro y San Pablo de Patale near Tallahassee,

---

[21] For details on mission layout see Jones and Shapiro, 1990, Marrinan, 1991, and Saunders, 1990.
[22] For details of Santa Catalina excavation see David Thomas, 1987 and 1988.

FIGURE 8.11   Artist's reconstruction of the probable church at the Franciscan mission San Juan de Aspalaga near Tallahassee, Florida. (From Morrell and Jones, 1970.)

Florida.[23] Historical records state that council houses were used for Indian dances, ceremonies, civic meetings, and as a lodge for guests. The excavated council houses were large circular structures 50–120 ft in diameter, with stadiumlike benches lining the walls and central hearths, as shown in Figure 8.12. Council houses were pole and beam buildings covered with a thatch roof. The council house at San Luis de Talimali was twice the size of the one at San Pedro y San Pablo de Patale. This size difference is probably related to the fact that San Luis was the religious, administrative, and military center of the Spanish mission chain during 1656–1704. Artifacts recovered from excavations in and around council houses are overwhelmingly Indian, which directly reflects their use for traditional Indian activities.

A Spanish residential area was located and investigated at San Luis de Talimali, and two of the houses have been excavated.[24] As shown in Figure 8.13, the houses were rectangular two-room structures with thatch roofs. The walls of one structure were made from vertical boards, and the other had walls of whitewashed wattle and daub. Near the latter structure, in the vicinity of animal corrals, was a daub-mixing pit filled with refuse. The pit contained many high-status, Spanish-made items such as a brass weight, broken Spanish pottery containers, ring settings, silver sequins, large quantities of beads, and faceted jet rings. The most frequent artifact in this refuse pit, though, was Indian pottery made in the shape of European containers such as ring base bowls, pitchers, and plates. This pottery is called Colono-ware by historical archaeologists, and its high frequency is interpreted by Bonnie McEwan as reflecting the presence of Indian women house servants and cooks. The pattern of Spanish items with high social visibility (jewelry and dinnerware) and Indian items with low social visibility (kitchen pottery containers) is the same

[23] For details about the council house at San Luis see Shapiro and McEwan, 1991.

[24] See McEwan, 1991a,b, and Vernon and McEwan, 1990, for details.

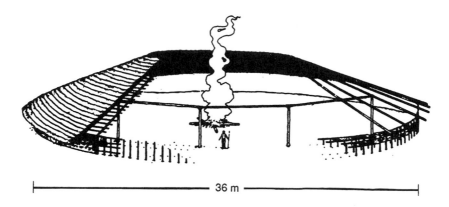

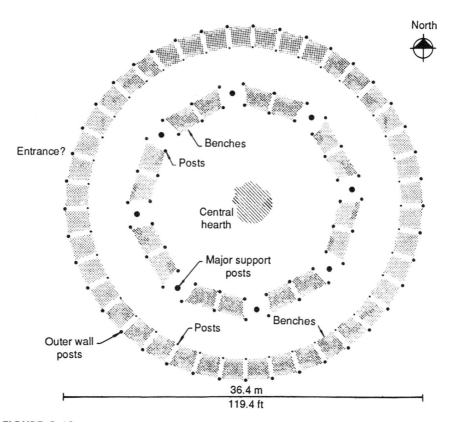

North

Entrance?

Benches

Posts

Central
hearth

Major support
posts

Benches

Posts

Outer wall
posts

36.4 m

119.4 ft

FIGURE 8.12 Artist's reconstruction of the council house at San Luis de Talimali. (From The Archaeology of Women in the Spanish New World by Bonnie McEwan, *Historical Archaeology*, 25(4):33–41, reprinted by permission of the Society for Historical Archaeology.)

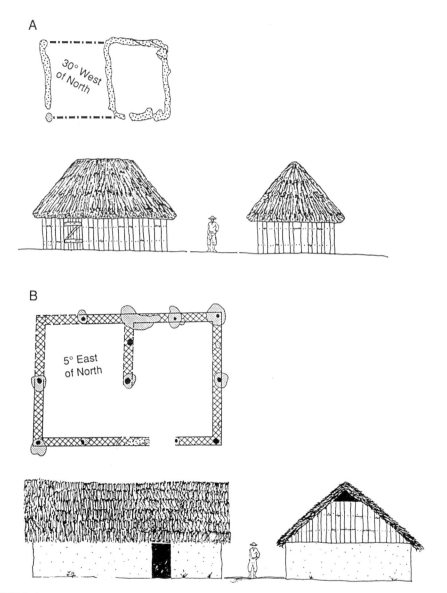

FIGURE 8.13 Artist's reconstruction of Spanish residences at San Luis de Talimali from the archaeologically documented foundations. A, vertical board with thatched roof; B, wattle and daub with thatched roof. (From Vernon and McEwan, 1990.)

as that documented in Santa Elena and St. Augustine. Studies of the faunal remains from this refuse pit revealed this household consumed primarily meat from domesticated animals. In fact, this pit had the highest proportion of domesticated meat documented of any refuse pit at any Catholic mission in La Florida. The high number of Spanish-made items and the typical Spanish diet of domesticated meat indicate that the occupants of this household were able to maintain a relatively Spanish lifestyle in this remote mission outpost.

Summary of Missions

Catholic missions were very important to the Spanish, especially in the 1600s. Apalachee missions were the most successful establishments in the Southeast, and they were the primary mechanism of Spain's hold on La Florida. Missions supplied St. Augustine with food, labor, agricultural products for trade, and effectively controlled the Indians. Mission archaeology is beginning to document how the missions were constructed and organized, the lifeways of the Indians and Spaniards living there, and how they interacted. From this historical archaeology we have also learned that Spaniards at some of the missions, such as San Luis de Talimali, could maintain a high standard of living similar to that in St. Augustine. Missions were on the frontier of Indian–Spanish contact in the Southeast during this period, and historical archaeology is providing a rich source of information about this brief but very powerful system.

Summary of the Contact Period

The first contacts between Europeans and Indians were from shipwrecked sailors, slave raids, Spanish explorations, and settlement attempts by the Spanish and French. The only successful European settlement in the Southeast during the Contact period was the military garrison at St. Augustine, established in 1565. Historical archaeology in Santa Elena and St. Augustine has indicated that the Spaniards tried to maintain a Spanish way of life and that Indians were an important part of Spanish communities and households, providing labor, food, and female companionship.

Epidemics of European diseases killed most of the Indian population in modern-day Florida, Georgia, and the river valley populations of Alabama by the mid-1600s. This early population collapse caused a historical discontinuity between pre-Contact late Mississippian Indian culture and the historical descriptions from the next century.

Catholic missions became an important part of Spain's hold on La Florida in the 1600s. Franciscan Apalachee missions were successful, and mission archaeology has shown that a high standard of living could be maintained similar to that in St. Augustine.

COLONIAL PERIOD: A.D. 1670–1821

The Colonial period began with the establishment of the first permanent English settlement in the Southeast, Charles Town (Charleston, South Carolina) and the Carolina colony in 1670, which signaled the beginning of the end of Spanish dominance in the region. During this period, England, France, and Spain all claimed and occupied parts of the Southeast. Indian epidemic survivors reorganized, relocated, and traded heavily with Europeans. The Colonial period ended in 1821 with the annexation of La Florida into the United States. Each of the three European countries occupying the Southeast during this period had different goals, strategies, and materials, which are reflected in the archaeological record. The historical and archaeological summary of this period is organized around the English, French, and Spanish activities in the Southeast.

The English

Historical Sketch

The Carolina colony was founded at Charles Town by a group of investors given large land grants from the English Crown. Although Spain claimed this area, it could not keep the English out, and eventually, England took much of the Southeast from Spain. Land grants had been made to owners of successful sugar and tobacco plantations in the Caribbean and Virginia to encourage development of the South Carolina and Georgia coasts. By 1700, two types of profitable private businesses had been developed: Indian deerskin trade and plantation agriculture. These businesses became the economic mainstays of the English colonies in the Southeast, and their success triggered the influx of thousands of immigrants from the British Isles.

Plantations   Plantations were agricultural businesses where large groups of workers of a subordinate social class produced a cash crop for members of the upper social class who marketed and sold it, usually in an international market.[25] The first plantations in the southeastern United States were located on pockets of fertile soil along the Atlantic coast and on the sea islands to facilitate water transportation of crops to market. Plantation owners shipped their crops to merchants or brokers in the port towns of Charles Town or Savannah, who then sold it to manufacturers in Europe or the New World. Population in the plantation region was generally low because plantations were self-sufficient, requiring only large amounts of land, labor, and a few trading ports. Although plantations were very large, activities were concentrated in a small and well-organized area.[26] The central activity area of a

---

[25] See Singleton, 1985, for a series of papers on plantation archaeology.

[26] See Lewis, 1985, for details on plantation layout and function.

plantation had the planter's house centrally located within a symmetrical arrangement of farm and service buildings, such as the wash house, barns, smokehouse, spinning house, slave quarters, loading dock, and vegetable and ornamental gardens. This centralized arrangement allowed easy supervision by the owners and managers of production activities, supplies, and slaves.

Need for plantation slaves affected southeastern Indians because the English were willing to trade arms and ammunition as well as trade goods for Indian captives. For the first time southeastern Indians could readily acquire guns and ammunition, as Spaniards refused to trade arms to Indians. Trade in captives for guns and ammunition led to an outbreak of internal Indian warfare, and eventually, most Indian groups became armed during the Colonial period. The English also conducted slave raids assisted by Indian rivals of the targeted group.

Indian slave trade led to the quick demise of many Atlantic coastal Indian groups, which in turn pushed the slave trade westward into the interior, where Creeks raided Choctaws and Cherokees, their traditional enemies, for captives. During the late seventeenth century, Indian-led slave trains crossed the Southeast heading for Charles Town, removing thousands of Indians from the interior. But by 1700, there were just not enough Indians left to meet the needs of the Atlantic coastal plantations, and African slaves were imported as replacements. Africans were better plantation slaves than Indians because they did not know the area, they were more resistant to disease, and they could be "seasoned" to slavery on plantations in the Caribbean. Slave trading became a big business during this period on the South Carolina and Georgia coast, and it is known as North America's "Slave Coast."

Deerskin Trade   Along with Indian slave trade, trade in deerskins grew rapidly due to the great demand for leather goods in Europe, especially for military uniforms. Deerskin trade began informally between individual planters and neighboring Indians. However, with the decline of the local Indians, the deerskin trade pushed westward where it developed into a huge industry, and the English paid high prices for hides. One of the key elements in the success of the Indian trade business was the English credit system.[27] Credit started with groups of investors or bankers in London who loaned money to manufacturers of trade goods. Manufacturers sold trade goods on credit to merchants in southeastern port towns. Trade merchants employed 20 to 30 licensed trade agents called factors, who received trade goods on credit to exchange to Indians for deerskins. The most popular trade goods were clothing, metal and glass beads, jewelry, metal axes, guns, powder and shot, and knives. Factors were usually *mestizos* (mixed Indian and European) and lived in Indian settlements. Factors usually advanced Indian hunters guns and

---

[27] See Wright, 1986, for more details on the operation of the English deerskin trade.

ammunition, and when they returned with deerskins, they settled their debt, and received the balance in trade goods. Once a year, factors took mule trains of deerskins to their trade merchant in a port town where they settled their debts, stocked up on new trade goods, and took the balance in profit. Trade merchants shipped the deerskins to England where their debts were paid, new trade goods were advanced, and the cycle was repeated.

The English deerskin trade developed into a thriving industry despite a declining Indian population and uprisings in which many traders and settlers were killed, such as the Yamassee War in 1714–15.[28] Trade merchants in port towns grew wealthy, and some formed large companies with branch stores along the coasts and interior rivers. Trading companies adjusted with the political changes in the Southeast, often moving their headquarters from one port to another, but continuing to do business in the interior as usual. Panton, Leslie, and Company, studied by William S. Coker, is a good example of large Indian trading companies in the Colonial period.[29] Panton and Leslie had been independent English trade merchants in Georgia and Carolina, but after the American Revolution they left the former colonies and formed a joint trading company headquartered in St. Augustine, then the capital of the fifteenth English colony of East Florida. When the Spanish regained the Floridas from the English in 1783, Panton and Leslie were offered incentives by the Spanish to continue doing business and to move their headquarters to Pensacola, which they did soon afterward. Spaniards needed the alliance of the Indians, and they had no trading company to replace the English deerskin trade. During the three moves of their headquarters, the Panton and Leslie trading company continued business with their network of factors and branch stores without interruption. By 1790, this company had acquired from the Spanish a virtual monopoly on Indian trade due to their connections with the Indians, who demanded the trade be continued.

Historical Archaeology

English Colonial period archaeology has focused on both English and Indian settlements. The types of English settlements that have been investigated include plantations, small rural communities, trading posts, forts, and port towns. The types of Indian settlements that have been investigated are primarily large communities and towns, but some battlefields and Indian forts also have been investigated.

Plantations   Plantation archaeology has concentrated on the social structure of the plantation and African slave culture.[30] Studies of plantation social

---

[28] For details on Indian slave and deerskin trade history see Zierden and Calhoun, 1984, and Wright, 1986.

[29] For details on Panton, Leslie, and Company see Coker and Watson, 1986, and Wright, 1986.

[30] For detailed studies on plantation archaeology see Singleton, 1985, and Otto, 1977, 1980, and 1984; for summaries see Orser, 1984, 1988, and 1990, and Singleton, 1988 and 1990.

structure have documented that the status differences of planters, overseers, and slaves can be detected in the archaeological remains of their residential areas. A good example is John Otto's work at Cannon's Point Plantation in coastal Georgia, where he determined that status differences between these three socioeconomic groups were reflected in the archaeological remains of their housing, ceramics, glass, and the ratio of domesticated to wild food remains. Other archaeological studies have also revealed the internal social structure within slave society, which was primarily determined by their assigned job (field versus domestic slaves).

As pointed out by Theresa Singleton, African slaves provided more than labor to plantations. They brought their own cultures, and in the case of the early rice plantations on the Atlantic coast, the enslaved Africans actually taught their white owners how to grow and process rice as they had done in West Africa. Historical archaeology of slave culture has also identified several features of African culture that were continued on the early British plantations and later in emancipated African-American society. For example, Thomas Wheaton and Patrick Garrow's excavations at two early English colonial plantations in South Carolina, Yaughan and Curiboo, have demonstrated that some of the slave housing and other buildings were occasionally built in the West African architectural style.[31] These houses, one of which is shown in Figure 8.14, were narrow, single- or double-room buildings with clay walls, steep thatch roofs, and no chimneys. Paintings of some early plantation slave houses also reveal rows of West African-style slave houses with high pyramidal roofs. Historical archaeology has also shown that the "shotgun" house, a long narrow structure with three rooms and no hallway still prevalent in many modern African-American neighborhoods, is also African in origin.[32] Another African trait that persisted in some parts of the Carolina colonies was handmade pottery. Leland Ferguson's studies of handmade African Colono-ware pottery concentrated in slave-occupied areas on colonial English plantations.[33] Thus far, this is the only documentation of African-made Colono-ware in the Southeast, as Indians traditionally made this pottery. Ferguson has also documented that the African tradition of using bowls as the primary eating container was continued in many slave residences, rather than adopting the European tradition of using flat plates.

Historical archaeological studies of African slave residences have also begun to reveal a different picture of slave life than is normally perceived.[34] The consistent recovery of food remains, gun parts, lead shot, and graphite in slave quarters contradicts the perception that all slaves were prohibited

[31] For details of the Yaughan and Curiboo plantation excavations see Wheaton and Garrow, 1985.

[32] For more information on the shotgun house type see Singleton, 1988.

[33] For more about African-made Colono-ware and African continuities in slave culture see Ferguson, 1980 and 1992.

[34] For details on slave diets see Gibbs *et al.*, 1980, and Reitz *et al.*, 1985; for a summary see Singleton, 1988.

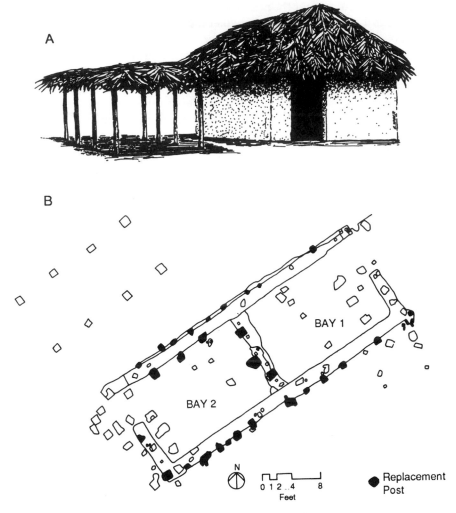

FIGURE 8.14 African-style slave house at the Curiboo Plantation in South Carolina. A, artist's reconstruction of dwelling. B, archaeological features from the slave dwelling, including foundation trenches and postmolds. (From Wheaton *et al.*, 1983.)

from cooking for themselves, having guns, or learning to read and write. Studies of food remains from hearths of slave residences reveal that in many cases, African slaves supplemented their diet with wild plants and animals. This leads to the realization that some slaves had guns, prepared their own food, and, had the time to do these tasks. This archaeological information has led to the suggestion that some traditional African cuisines continued during slavery.

Archaeologists have found that the retention of African cultural practices of slaves is associated with the "task" type of work system used on English coastal plantations. Under this system, slaves were assigned a task each day, and when it was completed, they could select their activities. Often, assigned tasks would be done by midafternoon, and slaves would garden, hunt, fish, raise livestock or chickens, and even make crafts for sale. The task labor system consequently facilitated the retention of some African traditions and the development of a relatively independent slave culture. Colonial historical documents virtually ignored slave culture. Historical archaeology is beginning to piece slave culture together, and through this research, the development of African-American culture in the United States is being understood for the first time.

Colonial Communities   Several rural English colonial towns have been investigated in the Carolinas, such as Camden and Brunswick Town.[35] From excavations at Brunswick Town, North Carolina, Stanley South developed and refined some basic principles of historical archaeology. The first principle is the association of distinctive patterns of archaeological deposits at settlements of different nationalities. He found that British residences consistently had refuse deposited next to the house, especially around windows and doorways. He called this the "Brunswick Pattern of Refuse Disposal," and he found that it was present at all types of British and early American sites, including military forts and trading posts, regardless of their location. This British colonial pattern of refuse disposal is so consistent that structure locations and orientations can be determined simply from the refuse pattern. Other depositional patterns have since been affiliated with other nationalities, but South was the first to discover the principle.

A new principle in historic archaeology identified by South from British Colonial period sites is artifact patterns. He discovered that when all artifacts from British Colonial period sites in the Carolinas were organized into functional groups and the percentages for each group determined, the proportions, shown in Table 8.1, were consistent at all British Colonial period sites, regardless of size, location, or function. He named this the "Carolina Artifact Pattern," and it reflects the typical British Colonial period artifact assemblage.[36]

South also used his British Colonial period archaeological research in the Carolinas to refine the procedure of ceramic dating. Ceramic dating is based on the historically documented manufacturing dates of specific types and patterns of pottery, and it has long been used in historical archaeology. The main use of manufacturing dates of ceramics is to determine the earliest possible date of archaeological deposits, called the *terminus post quem* (TPQ). However, many ceramic types were manufactured for long periods of time,

---

[35] For Brunswick Town archaeology see South, 1977; for Camden see Lewis, 1976, for details.

[36] See South, 1977, for details on artifact and depositional patterns and mean ceramic dating.

TABLE 8.1 Carolina Artifact Pattern[a]

Carolina artifact pattern		
Artifact group	Mean (%)	Range(%)
Kitchen	63.0	52–70.0
Architecture	25.0	20–32.0
Tobacco	6.0	2–14.0
Clothing	3.0	0.6–5.0
Activities	2.0	0.9–3.0
Arms	0.5	0.1–1.2
Furniture	0.2	0.1–0.6
Personal	0.2	0.1–0.5

[a] From South, 1977.

sometimes more than a century, and, consequently, TPQ dating often was not very specific. South developed a more precise method of ceramic dating, called the mean ceramic date. This method uses the median date of manufacture of a ceramic type, rather than the entire range, and it takes into consideration the number of pot sherds recovered from a site or specific contexts. His reasoning was based on the principle that most items are most popular midway through their manufacturing span, (i.e., the median date). He developed a formula, shown below, to derive the mean ceramic date, which multiplies the median manufacture date of each pottery type by the number of sherds of that type, adds the products together, and divides the sum by the total number of sherds of all types.

$$\text{Mean ceramic date} = \frac{\text{Sum of the median date} \times \text{Sherd count}}{\text{Sum of total sherd count}}$$

The accuracy of mean ceramic dating has been tested on historic sites with known occupation dates. Tests resulted in strong agreements between the occupation dates derived by the mean ceramic date formula and the occupation dates derived from documents. Since South's refinement of ceramic dating using eighteenth century British sites in the Southeast, it has been used extensively, and today it is a standard dating method in historical archaeology.

Larger British colonial communities, such as Charles Town, studied by Martha Zierden and her colleagues, have also been investigated.[37] The success of the deerskin trade and plantations made this community the fourth largest British colonial town, and it had a large merchant class. Zierden has focused research on how this colonial town developed through excavations of house

[37] See Zierden and Calhoun, 1984, for details and 1986 and 1989 for summaries.

lots of people of different status and locations, both within the community in the rural countryside. By comparing and contrasting the archaeological materials and deposits, many interesting details about the earliest urban residents in the Southeast have been revealed. For example, they found that English urban dwellers relied much more on domestic food than did their rural counterparts. They also identified a new type of residential unit in the colonial town, which appears to have been the urban equivalent of the plantation: the urban compound. During the Colonial period, English planters increasingly resided in cities and left the daily operation of their plantations to managers and overseers. They bought a large lot in town on which many plantation structures and activity areas were built, but they were all squeezed into an urban lot. Zierden calls these "urban compounds," and they had large main houses, outbuildings, livestock barns, slave quarters, a detached kitchen, privies, and wells. Thick midden deposits and abundant features accumulated on these lots. Research has also been conducted in the commercial core of Charleston along the waterfront, where stores, warehouses, and merchant's residences were located. Comparisons of the materials and features between urban compounds and commercial core lots have begun to reveal details of how different residential neighborhoods grew away from the commercial centers in American cities.

Forts Several British forts have been investigated in the Southeast, such as Fort Loudoun and the Tellico Blockhouse in eastern Tennessee, Ninety Six in South Carolina, and the Fort of Pensacola in Florida.[38] These investigations have revealed details about construction, structures both inside and outside the forts, the community surrounding the fortifications, and differences between the ways of life of different ethnic groups. For example, at the Tellico Blockhouse in east Tennessee, Richard Polhemus found the same type of African-made Colono-ware as found on coastal British plantations. A check of the historical records indicated that African slaves from coastal plantations were rented as laborers to construct the Tellico Blockhouse. Polhemus could then explain the African-made Colono-ware at the Tellico Blockhouse as being brought in by the rented African slaves.

At Pensacola, my colleagues and I at the University of West Florida have documented through historical archaeology the development of the British Fort of Pensacola from the initial takeover in 1763 from the Spanish to 1781 when Spain regained it by the military campaign of General Galvez.[39] Historians and archaeologist have documented many stages of expansion of this fort in those 18 yr, as shown in Figure 8.15. Excavations have provided detailed

[38] For more information on the Fort of Pensacola, Florida, see Joy, 1989; for Ninety Six, South Carolina, see South, 1971; for the Tellico Blockhouse, North Carolina, see Polhemus, 1985.

[39] For a summary of the British Fort of Pensacola archaeology see Bense, 1989; for details see Joy, 1989.

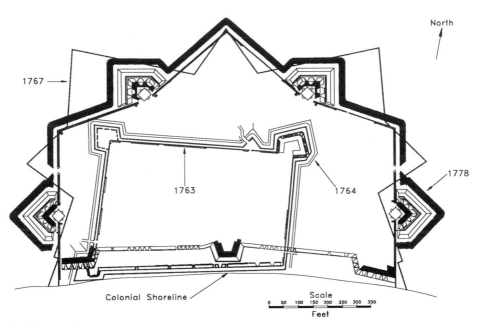

FIGURE 8.15 Overlay of the expansions of the British Fort of Pensacola between 1763–1778 in Pensacola, Florida.

information about construction techniques of military buildings, fortifications inside and outside the fort, and modifications to the fortifications that were not recorded in historical documents. We also have been able to compare and contrast the materials and food remains from areas inside the fort used by different ranks of soldiers, including the enlisted men's kitchen and barracks area and the commanding officer's compound. The material recovered from these two areas is quite different. For example, from the midden in the commanding officer's yard, we recovered pieces of expensive Chinese porcelain that were hand painted with gold gilt on the edges, as well as other fine tablewares and ornate glass such as goblets. The food remains from the commanding officer's compound was dominated by domesticated animals, especially beef that had been butchered into large roasts. The refuse pits close to the enlisted men's barracks and their kitchen contained lower-quality pottery, such as creamwares, no ornate ceramics or glass items, and their food consisted primarily of fish and oysters and some beef. Historical archaeological investigations in the Fort of Pensacola have also consistently produced only minor amounts of Indian pottery. This is consistent with the British policy of keeping relationships with Indians on a business and political level, and generally not integrating them into their households or communities. Historical records indicate that Indians generally camped in the woods outside of town and went into the British community only for trade or political meetings.

Historic Indian Towns   There have been several archaeological studies of the Indian population in the portion of the Southeast dominated by the English during the Colonial period.[40] Good examples of such investigations are Gerald Schroedel's study of the Overhill Cherokee in eastern Tennessee and Vernon Knight's research on the Creek in central Alabama. These and other researchers have focused on the effects of the deerskin trade and epidemics, and the reorganization that followed contact with Europeans.

An example of colonial Indian archaeology is Vernon Knight's investigations at the Creek town of Tukabatchee, near present-day Montgomery, Alabama. This work focused on the transition of the Creek from the late prehistoric Mississippian stage to their forced removal to Oklahoma in 1832. During the prehistoric late Mississippian period, Tukabatchee was a chiefdom center with two platform mounds. After 1600, the population grew rapidly, which Knight attributes to an influx of survivors of the epidemics started by the Spanish explorations. The refugee Creek reorganized into the Creek Confederacy at Tukabatchee, and it became the political capital. Knight excavated many houses, refuse pits, and middens from the four centuries of occupation of Tukabatchee. With good archaeological context, he was able to study, among other subjects, the role of European trade goods in Creek culture. Historians had proposed that European technological superiority was the reason behind the Indian's strong desire for trade goods.[41] The trade goods most desired by the Creek, and other Indian groups, were glass beads, brightly colored cloth, small brass bells, silver pendants and headdress bands and beads, small metal hatchets, metal medallions, guns, and ammunition. Knight offered an alternative to the historians theory for the preference for these trade goods by relating them to the Mississippian sociopolitical and belief system, in which personal ornaments were used to signify status and power. At the time of European contact, highest-status items were made of metal, such as embossed plates and axes of copper, and carved shell gorgets and beads were high-status markers. These metal and shell items were absolutely controlled by and restricted to the elite in Mississippian societies. Knight reasoned that the influx of items similar to Indian high-status goods, but made by Europeans, into the exclusionary Mississippian prestige goods system caused a clamor for them by the nonelite, who could get them only through trade with the English. Therefore, the Creek and other Indian groups traded deerskins to Europeans—for which the English paid the highest prices—to raise their social status.

While Tukabatchee houses were made by traditional construction methods, and they contained traditional Indian pottery and food, their floors and graves were littered with European trade goods. This differential use of European trade goods was a strong indication to Knight that they were acquired

---

[40] Good examples of these studies are Knight, 1985, Schroedel, 1986, and Polhemus, 1987.

[41] For details on this perspective see Crane, 1928, Cotterill, 1954, and Mason, 1963.

and displayed to raise personal status. Therefore, it was not the technological superiority of European goods, but the desire to rise in social status that was behind the Creek demand for specific trade goods. If you look closely at the Creek Indian portraits in Figure 8.16, you can see that the European-made metal pendants and medallions, nose rings and earrings, and bright clothing replaced traditional Mississippian Southeastern Ceremonial Complex items such as embossed copper plates, copper-covered earspools, robes, and shell gorgets and beads found in graves of prehistoric Mississippian elite. After the initial arming of the southeastern Indians, Knight suggests that the demand for guns and ammunition was directly related to the desire to obtain status items because it enabled them to get more deerskins to trade than the bow and arrow. Historical archaeological studies, such as Knight's at Tukabatchee, are

FIGURE 8.16 Portraits of southeastern Indians. Left: Stimafutchki, a Creek, 1790, Right: Austenaco, a Cherokee, ca. 1762. (Smithsonian Institution Photos No. 1063-q and 1169-L-3.)

expanding our understanding of the Indian's interaction with Europeans and Euro-Americans in the Southeast as well as modern Indian culture.

The French

Historical Sketch

During the same time that the English were moving into the eastern part of the South, the French were moving into the western portion. From their colonies in Canada and the upper Mississippi region, the French moved downstream into the central and lower Mississippi Valley and on to the Gulf coast.

Louisiana The French established the Louisiana colony, centered on the lower Mississippi Valley with capitals first at Biloxi, then Mobile, and finally New Orleans. The purposes of French expansion into the Southeast were to halt English and Spanish expansion and to increase French holdings and income in North America. Their colonization strategy was to build a network of government-operated fortified Indian trading posts along the rivers and Gulf coast. The French government also made land grants to encourage the development of rice, indigo, and sugar plantations. The government also tried to supply plantation labor by gathering up large groups of prisoners and poor people in France and sending them to the New World to work as indentured servants for certain periods of time, after which they would be free. Groups of private investors, such as the Company of the Indies, also funded plantation developments. In general, French plantations were not very successful early in the Colonial period due to problems with the labor supply, a high sickness and death rate (50%), and problems controlling Indian and African slaves. Plantations became much more successful, though, later in 1763 when the English acquired Louisiana east of the Mississippi and instituted their successful plantation management system.

Trading Posts In an effort to compete with the expanding English deerskin trade, the French made exclusive trade agreements with Indian leaders. These agreements set prices for deerskins, and they gave large "signing bonuses" of gifts that were annually renewed. This practice of making large payments of gifts to Indian groups was popular with the French, and it amounted to a kind of payment to Indians to occupy their land and monopolize their trade. There were several problems, though, with the government-operated French–Indian trading system. French trade goods were generally inferior to English goods, prices were much higher than the English, and the supply was especially unpredictable. Because of these problems, the French could not rely on trading alone for colonial expansion. Consequently, they promoted warfare between their Indian allies and groups that traded with the English. A good example is the high amount of gifts the French paid to the Choctaw, loyal French trade partners, for waging war on the Chickasaw, who were loyal to the English. This constant harassment distracted the Chickasaw, hurt the English Indian trade, and kept the French from having to make expensive agreements with the Chickasaw. The French deerskin trade network was in place by about 1720, with a series of fortified trading posts from Natchitoches on the Red River in Arkansas, to the Arkansas Post on the Mississippi, downstream to New Orleans, around the Gulf coast to Mobile, and up the Coosa River into central Alabama to Fort Toulouse. The French sent a few Jesuit missionaries to the Indians, but their missionizing effort was very limited and not nearly on the scale of the Spanish in Florida.

A good example of French Colonial period strategy is the series of events that took place in Alabama with the Creek and Chickasaw.[42] Over 10,000 Creek refugees had concentrated at the confluence of the Coosa and Tallapoosa rivers in central Alabama during the 1600s, and several towns such as at Tukabatchee developed. Immediately following the Yamassee-led Indian revolt against the English in 1714–15, the French took advantage of Indian hostility toward the English and, in 1716, started trading with Creek groups at the confluence of the Coosa and Tallapoosa rivers, once a strong trading area for the British. They enticed Creek leaders into trade agreements with large payments of gifts, and in 1717 they built a fortified trading post there, Fort Toulouse. The English quickly retaliated by building their own fort nearby, Fort Okfuskee, but the French Fort Toulouse was successful. From this base, French traders infiltrated the English trading areas of the Creek and Cherokee in the Carolinas and Tennessee. The Indians also used the hostility between the French and English to drive up prices for deerskins. A second French fortified trading post was also built in Alabama in 1736, Fort Tombecbe, at the junction of the Tombigbee and Black Warrior rivers. From this fort, the French made further inroads on the English deerskin trade by harassing and trading with the Chickasaw. Fort Tombecbe was successful, and it became the sixth largest supplier of deerskins in Louisiana.

The French were active in the Southeast only for about sixty years. In 1763, in the treaties that ended the Seven Years' War, England acquired all of Louisiana east of the Mississippi and north of Lake Ponchartrain. Spain acquired the land west of the Mississippi and south of Lake Ponchartrain.

Historical Archaeology

Archaeological investigations of French colonial and Indian settlements in the Southeast have included several forts, a few colonial settlements, and several Indian settlements.

---

[42] For historical summaries on the French in Alabama see Thomas, 1989, Waselkov, 1989b, and Waselkov *et al.*, 1982.

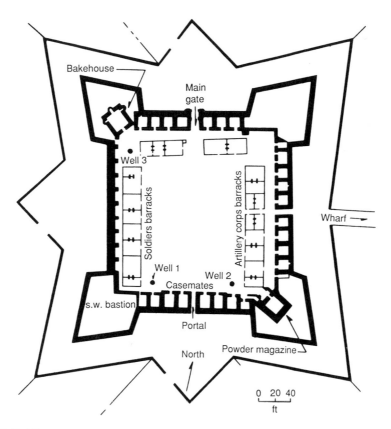

FIGURE 8.17 Floor plan of Fort Conde in Mobile, Alabama, constructed between 1717 and about 1720. (From Harris and Nielsen, 1972.)

Forts   French forts that have been investigated include the Arkansas Post and Forts St. Pierre, Conde, Tombecbe, and Toulouse. Fort Conde was the largest and most substantial French fort in the Southeast. Located in modern-day Mobile, this was a "star fort" with brick walls 20 ft high, shown in Figure 8.17, and it was the only French Colonial period brick fort on the Gulf coast.[43] Archaeologists led by Jerry Neilsen found portions of the brick walls, the moat, a bastion, and three stone-lined wells, one of which was excavated and a cross section of this well is shown in Figure 8.18. In the wet sediments at the base of the well, archaeologists recovered three complete olive jars and organic items such as leather shoes, wooden buckets, and fruit pits.

Good examples of wooden French forts that have been investigated are

[43] For details of the Fort Conde excavation see Harris and Nielsen, 1972.

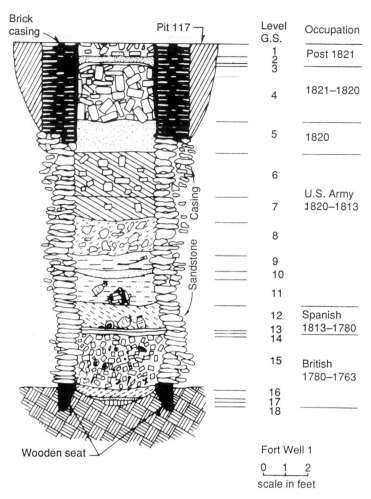

FIGURE 8.18   Cross section of excavation of Well Number 1 in the southwest corner of the French Fort Conde, in Mobile, Alabama. (From Nielsen and Harris, 1972.)

Forts Tombecbe and Toulouse, both of which were smaller than Fort Conde.[44] The walls of Fort Toulouse were made of split logs, and five structures have been excavated inside as well as a bastion powder magazine and the barracks. Excavations have documented that the walls of internal buildings were covered with a plaster called "bousillage" made of clay mixed with grass or moss and spread on wooden slats nailed to wall posts. The smooth hard surface was

---

[44] For more on Fort Toulouse archaeology see Waselkov *et al.*, 1982, and Waselkov, 1989a; for Fort Tombecbe excavations see Parker, 1982.

usually painted. Studies of the diet of the military officers from Forts Conde and Toulouse indicate that their meat consisted of two-thirds domesticated cattle and one-third deer. The shortage of French trade goods referred to in the historical records was detected archaeologically at Fort Toulouse in the low number of trade items, as well as the recovery of many English trade goods that the French apparently had purchased and traded to the Indians. Archaeological evidence of large Indian settlements made up of diverse refugee groups has been recovered near all the French forts.

Colonial Settlements Recent excavations by Gregory Waselkov at the first, though short-lived, settlement of Mobile are beginning to provide the first detailed view of a French settlement in the Southeast.[45] This site, known as "Old Mobile," was a planned 120-acre community started in 1702 and occupied until 1711, when it was moved downstream after a bad flood to modern-day Mobile. Old Mobile was the capital of French Louisiana at the time, and it had between 80 and 100 structures and about 300 inhabitants. Houses were laid out on a formal street grid with a fort at the center overlooking the river. This settlement served as the colony's military headquarters, and the fort contained the residences of colonial officials, royal warehouses, and a church. In this well-preserved site, archaeologists have found 26 structures, and two have been excavated: a residence and the blacksmith's shop. The walls of the French buildings were constructed on wooden sills that supported posts between which would have been placed small pieces of wood, over which the builders applied a thick layer of bousillage. The archaeological remains of the dwelling are shown in Figure 8.19, and from this burned home, Waselkov was able to determine details of construction. The floor was raised 3 to 6 in. inside the sills and in the largest room, floor planking was placed on joists laid directly on the clay. A fireplace was shared between the largest and adjacent room. The building looked similar to the largest building shown in the drawing of New Biloxi on Biloxi Bay in 1720, shown in Figure 8.20. Researchers at Old Mobile suggest that the architectural style was derived from the Caribbean. A surprising discovery at Old Mobile was the abundance of Spanish material and the scarcity of French artifacts, especially Spanish pottery and coins. Historical records indicate that there was some trade between Spanish Pensacola and French Mobile, but the archaeological artifacts reveal that it must have been substantial and very important to Mobilians. French colonial artifacts, especially ceramics, are also consistently found in Pensacola. Despite the fact that France and Spain were political adversaries, the exchange of goods and probably food during hard times apparently was a common practice between nearby colonial towns, which were far away from Europe and often poorly supplied.

[45] For details of Old Mobile excavations see Waselkov, 1991.

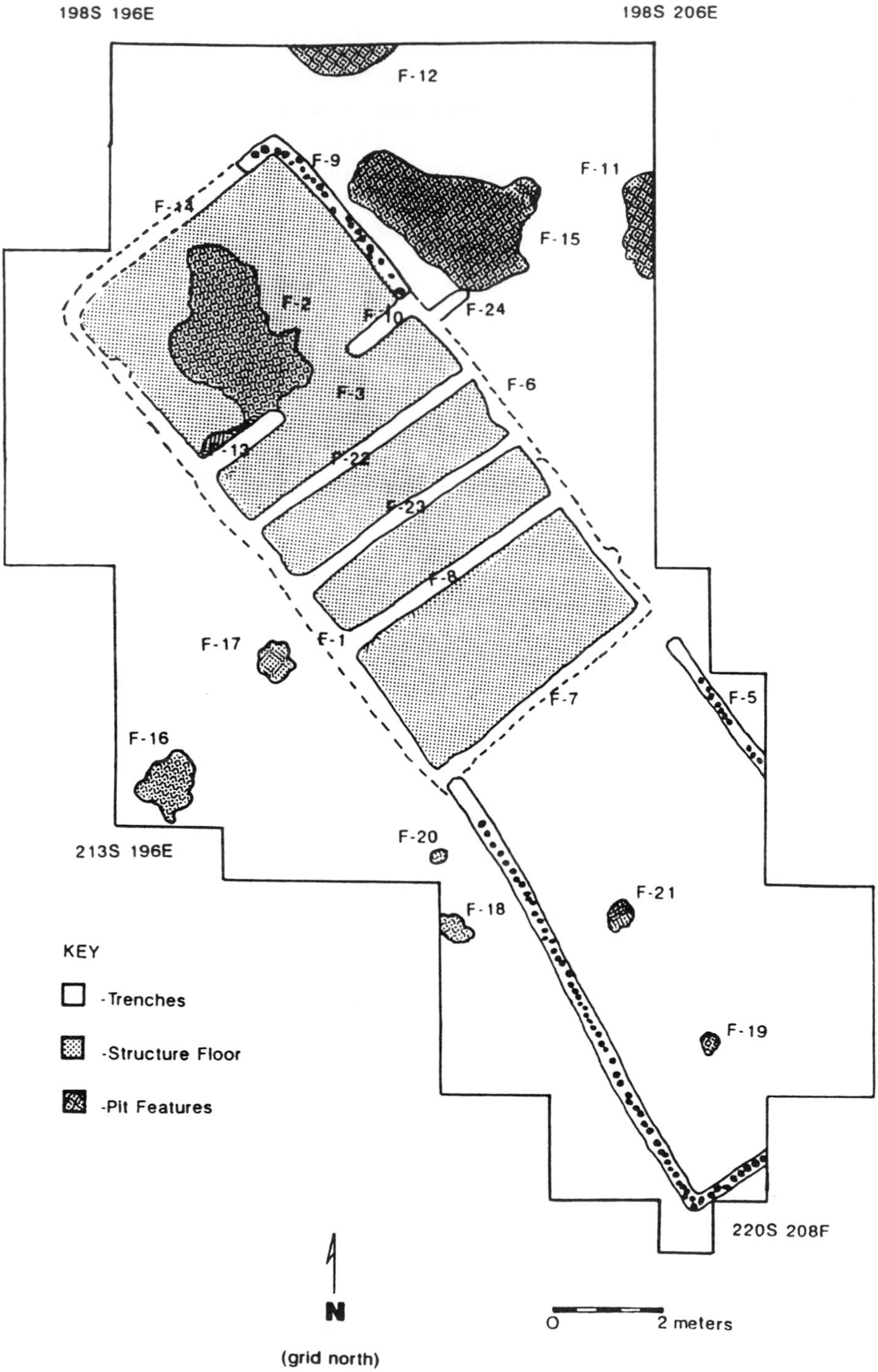

FIGURE 8.19 Archaeological remains of a dwelling at Old Mobile built about 1702. (From Waselkov, 1991.)

304

FIGURE 8.20 Drawing of the French settlement at New Biloxi in 1720. (Courtesy of The Edward E. Ayer Collection, The Newberry Library.)

Historic Indian Communities   Several Indian settlements of the Chickasaw, Choctaw, and Natchez have been archaeologically investigated, revealing contact with the French.[46] Probably the best-known of these historic Indian sites is the Fatherland site near Natchez, Mississippi. This large village, known as the Grande Village of the Natchez, had three mounds and was the capital of a Natchez chiefdom. It was visited regularly by a Jesuit missionary, Antoine Simone du Pratz, who lived there for 8 yr in the early 1700s. He wrote detailed descriptions and drew many pictures of Natchez ceremonial and daily life. While there, du Pratz witnessed the death of a chief and his burial in a platform mound, which he described and illustrated. Stuart Neitzel excavated two of the mounds and part of the residential area at the Grande Village. Neitzel documented the transition from prehistoric late Mississippian to the historic period in house style, burial practices, and incorporation of trade goods. He documented that one of the European traits that was quickly adopted was the custom of coffin burials.

Another important French–Indian Colonial period site is the Trudeau site near Tunica, Louisiana. Although burials from this eighteenth century site were excavated by an amateur archaeologist, the artifacts were studied by Harvard archaeologists Jeffery Brain and Ian Brown.[47] The Tunica group of the Choctaw were well known for their trading ability, and they were the primary suppliers of salt and horses to the French. Consequently, many Tunica became wealthy, and they acquired substantial amounts of trade goods from the French. The trade goods recovered from the 113 Tunica graves at the Trudeau site included almost 200,000 glass beads, 98 brass kettles, metal skillets, spoons, scissors, buckles, 21 glass bottles, scores of French tableware items, and stoneware mugs and pitchers. The collection also included many personal ornaments such as crucifixes, metal finger rings, bracelets, pendants, and many brass bells. There were also many guns, gunflints, and lead shot. The most common Indian-made grave good was pottery. The bulk of Indian pottery was traditional shell-tempered Mississippian vessels decorated with standard incised and punctated designs, similar to prehistoric pottery. The only Colono-ware at Trudeau was one handmade shell-tempered copy of a pitcher. These findings were paralleled in excavations at the Arkansas Post site, which uncovered hundreds of Indian graves containing a similar range of French trade goods and traditional Indian ceramics.[48]

Archaeologists have also been studying the historic Chickasaw and Choctaw in Mississippi.[49] Following Soto's passage, Chickasaw epidemic survi-

---

[46] For more information on the Natchez see Brown, 1985 and 1990, and Neitzel, 1965 and 1983; for the Choctaw see Blitz, 1985.

[47] For details of "Tunica Treasure" see Brain, 1979.

[48] For a summary of the Arkansas Post see Morse and Morse, 1983; for details see Walthall, 1991.

[49] For more on Choctaw and Chickasaw archaeology see Atkinson, 1987, Johnson and Sparks, 1986, and Blitz, 1985.

vors relocated and reorganized in northeast Mississippi, near Tupelo, during the Colonial period. Archaeological excavations in this area have documented the dual trade of the Chickasaw with the French and English as these two European powers vied for control of Indian trade. Archaeological research has also documented that while mound use ceased in this area in the 1600s, there was strong continuity in Indian-made pottery from the prehistoric to historic periods. Chickasaw Colono-ware copied European vessel shapes, and they also copied other European items, such as shell and bone buttons. John Blitz's study of the Choctaw in eastern Mississippi has documented a sharp population reduction between Soto's winter encampment in 1540 and arrival of the French in the early 1700s. The main indicator of Choctaw population reduction that Blitz found is the distinct drop in sites from the late Mississippian period to the French Colonial period.

In the Mississippi Valley, archaeologists have documented population reduction, as well as a continual influx of Indian refugees from east of the Mississippi, especially during the last half of this period.[50] Most refugee groups were small; and they were either absorbed into local Natchez societies or they joined with other refugees into independent groups of multiple ethnicities. Archaeologists in the lower Mississippi Valley have been able to document the assimilation of several immigrant Indian groups by identifying the initial appearance of different styles of Indian manufactured items, especially pottery, and tracking either the transition to resident craft styles or the continuance of the styles with which they arrived.

The Spanish

Historical Sketch

It should be clear at this point that Spain lost much of its claim to the Southeast during the Colonial period.[51] Despite boundary lines drawn on maps, the most territory that Spain controlled was what is now the state of Florida, with the northern border located between Pensacola and St. Augustine. The establishment of a small garrison at Pensacola in 1698 successfully kept the French from claiming this port when, only two months after its construction, the French had to bypass Pensacola and establish the Louisiana colony farther west.

In 1763, Spain lost all of La Florida to England after the Seven Years' War in Europe. Spaniards literally were evacuated from St. Augustine and Pensacola in 1763, ending Spanish dominance in Florida. Spain forcibly took Florida back in 1781, but many English remained, and the population in the colony became a mixture of people of many European nationalities, runaway African slaves, free Africans, and Indians.

---

[50] For details on historic Indian refugees in the lower Mississippi Valley see Brown, 1985.

[51] For details of the second Spanish period see Coker and Watson, 1986, and Weisman, 1989.

Creeks and Seminoles   By 1700 Florida was essentially empty of Indians due to the population collapse of the original groups from epidemics and missionization. This situation brought hardship on the Spanish who depended on Indians for their food supply. To relieve their food shortage, Spaniards encouraged Creeks living in Alabama and Georgia to relocate into Florida where they would give them a good market for trade.[52] As a result, bands of Creek moved into north Florida in the early decades of the 1700s, and expanded down the peninsula in the mid-1700s. These Creek bands became known as the "Seminole," which is a derivative of the Spanish word for runaways. The Creek first concentrated in the Tallahassee and Alachua areas where they shifted their economy from the deerskin trade to cattle raising. Deerskins had been their economic mainstay, but the deer population had seriously declined from overhunting, and most Spanish cattle ranches in Florida had failed. The Seminole met the demand for hides and beef by raising wild cattle. This economic shift, as well as continual encroachments of white settlers, resulted in a change in the traditional sedentary Creek-Seminole settlement pattern to a more mobile one. This settlement pattern shift also had ripple effects throughout their society. For example, the large permanent Creek towns like Tukabatchee with central civic-ceremonial plazas and council houses were no longer used and settlements became much smaller, dispersed, and more temporary.

Scores of small settlements were established by the Seminole in Florida in a general north-to-south pattern throughout this period. With the British takeover of Florida in 1763, the Seminole became more distant and hostile. Runaway African slaves from English plantations joined Seminole communities in increasing numbers. Despite their hostility towards Europeans and Euro-Americans, many Seminole had prosperous farms, large agricultural plantations, and large cattle herds during the late Colonial period. Some Seminole owned slaves and were quite affluent. Their agricultural products literally supported the settlements of St. Augustine and Pensacola, and they were in demand by both the English and Spaniards. Despite their general success, though, many Creek-Seminoles became indebted to the trading stores through the credit system. Often this debt got out of control and the local Creek-Seminole leaders ceded parcels of land to the traders to satisfy debts of their followers. Near the end of the Colonial period, there was an influx of Creek Red Sticks from their defeats in the Creek War of 1813–1814 and the First Seminole War of 1816–1818.

Historical Archaeology

Archaeological research in the late Colonial period of Spanish Florida has focused on two topics: Indian and European-American communities.

---

[52] See Weisman, 1989, for a detailed summary of Seminole history.

Seminole Archaeology   Seminole archaeology was pioneered by Hale Smith and Charles Fairbanks.[53] Archaeological investigations of trading posts of the Panton, Leslie, and Company branch store on the St. Marks River in northwest Florida by Pheriba Stacy, the Spaulding Lower Store, and a post on the St. Johns River near Gainesville in north Florida by Kenneth Lewis have given us our best picture of Seminole material culture during this period. Also, a residential Seminole settlement of this period, the A-296 site near Gainesville, has been excavated, which documented the conservative ceramic styles and the association of unique rim styles with female potters' clan memberships. From this evidence, archaeologist Brent Weisman has suggested that it was in this period that the strong matrilineal clans of the Seminole were organized. Pottery continued to be made in the traditional Mississippian manner, and it was decorated primarily by brushing with a corncob.

Despite their separation from the larger Creek society, historical archaeology has documented that the Seminole continued many of their traditional Mississippian customs. An example is the continuance of the practice of placing status items in graves, such as the Zetrouer site near Gainesville. Archaeologists uncovered the burial of a Seminole man buried with many grave goods, including a trade ax, mirror, knife, pouches of shot and flints, a leather buckled belt, a brass kettle, brass buckles, coils of copper wire, a file, rasp, gun parts and two pocket knives. These items were all available at the nearby Panton, Leslie, and Company Spaulding branch trading store. The amount and variety of the trade items buried with the Zetrouer Seminole as well as similar amounts found in Seminole graves in Nicholson Grove, just northeast of Tampa, reveal the general wealth of some Seminole people during this period. However, after the American Revolution, there was a flood of settlers into Florida who raided Seminole settlements, causing the collapse of their profitable agriculture. Consequently, the Seminole and their African compatriots retreated south to the Everglades, where they settled on land poorly suited to agriculture or cattle ranching, but which afforded some security.

St. Augustine   Colonial period historic archaeology in St. Augustine has shown that after the Spanish were forced to evacuate St. Augustine along with their Indian converts, the British community was quite different.[54] The English did not try rigidly to transplant English culture in the New World and they had more structured relationships with Indians and Africans. As a result, the community was more segregated along ethnic lines than during the Spanish occupation. Another difference between Spanish and British St. Augustine that Kathleen Deagan and her colleagues have discovered through historic archaeology was the change in refuse disposal pattern. The British in

---

[53] See Weisman, 1989, for details of Seminole archaeology; see Milanich and Fairbanks, 1980, for summary.

[54] See Deagan, 1983, for details on St. Augustine Spanish Colonial period archaeology.

St. Augustine followed the Brunswick pattern defined by Stanley South in the Carolina colony and threw their trash out their doorways, in the streets, and in low areas nearby. This contrasted with the Spanish disposal pattern, which consisted of placing refuse in a series of small pits at the rear of the backyard. These and other studies of colonial St. Augustine are providing information about how two different European cultures adapted to the New World.

Pensacola   Archaeological research in colonial Pensacola, the other settlement in Spanish Florida, has thus far focused primarily on the Spanish and British military installations built and used during this period.[55] All the major colonial military installations have been identified, including three Spanish and one British fort, outlying defensive works, and the associated civilian and military communities. Archaeologists are just beginning to compare the information from Pensacola to that from St. Augustine, and we are finding many similarities between the two settlements. From the work at Pensacola and St. Augustine, archaeologists are beginning to get a more complete picture of life in Colonial period Florida.

Summary of the Colonial Period

The Colonial period was signaled by the encroachment of England and France into the territory claimed by Spain in the Southeast. Spain was able to defend and occupy only the area from St. Augustine and Pensacola to peninsular Florida. The period concluded with the end of European ownership in the Southeast and the incorporation of all land into the United States.

The English established Charles Town in 1670 as an expansion of their Virginian and Caribbean plantation systems. Their first and largest success was the deerskin trade, which was followed by the establishment of successful rice and cotton plantations on the Atlantic coast. Plantation archaeology has revealed that many elements of African culture were incorporated into plantation culture, especially handmade ceramics (Colono-ware), architecture, and rice production. Archaeology has also revealed the similarities and differences in social status and occupation on plantations.

The French settled the western portion of the Southeast, especially the Mississippi and Tombigbee drainages. They competed with the English in the deerskin trade and established several settlements and fortified trading posts. Archaeology has revealed that the French had supply problems and

---

[55] For details on Pensacola Spanish historic archaeology see H. Smith, 1965, Joy, 1989, and Bense, 1989.

used considerable amounts of both English and Spanish materials, but they had a distinctive architectural style.

Spanish Florida became a refuge for Creek and runaway Africans in the colonial period as they filled the vacuum left by the extinction of Florida's Indians. The Seminoles emerged from these immigrants, and they were successful in keeping a distance from Europeans and Euro-Americans, yet prospering in trade in foodstuffs and deerskins.

SUMMARY OF THE EUROPEAN STAGE

The European stage of culture in the Southeast began with the arrival in the Southeast of Europeans and ended with the incorporation of the region into the United States in 1821. The first contacts between Europeans and Indians were with shipwrecked sailors and slave raiders, but soon afterwards the Spanish and French sponsored explorations and settlement attempts. The only successful settlement in the Contact period was by the Spanish at St. Augustine, which was founded in 1565. Archaeology of Spanish exploration sites and the early settlements has indicated that the Spaniards tried to establish the Spanish way of life in the Southeast, and that Indians were an important part of their households and community labor. During the sixteenth and seventeenth centuries, epidemics of European diseases greatly reduced the Indian population in modern-day Florida, Georgia, and east Alabama. The rapid population reduction caused sociopolitical reorganization of the survivors, which has been documented in several areas by historical archaeology. The early population reduction caused a serious historical discontinuity between late prehistoric Indian culture and the first historical detailed descriptions in the late 1700s and 1800s. Missions became an important part of Spain's hold on La Florida in the 1600s. After a series of failures, Indian groups along the Atlantic coast and in north central Florida began to accept missionaries into their communities. Franciscan missions to the Apalachee were particularly successful, and mission archaeology has shown that, at least on some Apalachee missions, a high standard of living was maintained similar to that in St. Augustine.

The Colonial period was initiated by the encroachment of England and France into the Southeast, beginning with the establishment of Charles Town on the Atlantic coast in 1670. Spain was able to defend and occupy Florida only between St. Augustine and Pensacola and to the south. The English economy in the Southeast was based on the deerskin trade and plantations. Indians participated in the deerskin trade to acquire European ornaments for use in the traditional Mississippian manner for social advancement. Plantation archaeology has revealed that African culture was incorporated into African slave culture, including handmade ceramics, architecture, and rice production.

In the western portion of the Southeast the French established the colony of Louisiana and tried to stop the advancement of the British. They entered the deerskin trade business and established several settlements and fortified trading posts. Spanish Florida became a refuge for the Creek and runaway Africans as they filled the vacuum left by the loss of the original Florida Indians. The Seminole emerged from these immigrants, and they were successful in keeping a distance from Europeans and Euro-Americans, but they also prospered in trade with them.

9

AMERICAN STAGE:
A.D. 1821–1917

KEY FEATURES

Mass Production of European and American Materials
Severe Reduction in Indian Material after Removal
Increase in Urban Deposits

IMPORTANT DEVELOPMENTS

Indian Removal
Florescence and Fall of Plantations
Civil War
African-American Cultural Coalescence
Small Farm Expansion
Increase in Towns and Cities

INTRODUCTION AND OVERVIEW

The American stage in the Southeast began with the acquisition of Florida into the United States in 1821, and it ended with United States entry into World War I in 1917. Technically, this period extends to World War II, but archaeologists are just beginning to conduct research of the period between World War I and II, and there is not enough information to compose a regional summary. The key archaeological features of this period are (1) Mass Production of European and American Material, (2) Severe Reduction in Indian Material after Removal, and an (3) Increase in Urban Deposits. Most of the Indian population in the Southeast was forcibly removed from the Southeast between 1828 and 1835 and relocated on reservations west of the Mississippi River. Immediately following Indian removal, European-Americans spread rapidly into the interior of the Southeast, establishing an agricultural of plantations and small farms. The Civil War resulted in serious social and economic changes with the destruction of most infrastructure in the region and the abolition of slavery. Most plantations were converted to tenancy or broken into small farms. African-American culture developed as societies became more consolidated with emancipation.

The American stage is divided into two periods: Antebellum and Victorian. Historians define the Antebellum period as the period of time between the American Revolution and Civil War and the Victorian period as the span of Queen Victoria's life (1819–1901) or her reign (1837–1901). In this book, the Antebellum period marks the period between the acquisition of Florida and the end of the Civil War (1821 and 1865), and the Victorian period begins with the end of the Civil War to the beginning of World War I (1865–1917). The spans of the Antebellum and Victorian periods for the purposes of this book are based on their cultural distinctiveness in the Southeast.

In the first two decades of the Antebellum period, over 100,000 Indians were forcibly removed from the Southeast. The removal was spearheaded by Andrew Jackson, the "Indian Fighter," who, along with the U.S. Congress, advocated and funded the removal of Indians from the Southeast. As soon as the United States began acquiring tracts of Indian land after specific groups were removed, government lotteries and land sales were held for European-Americans, and there was an immediate wave of settlers, some bringing their African slaves. Plantations, independent farms, and small towns were quickly established on former Indian lands, which transplanted the British and African-based American cultures into most of the South, where it remains dominant to the present. Agriculture dominated the economy of the Southeast throughout the Antebellum period. The invention of the cotton gin in 1793 made it economically feasible to grow short-fiber cotton as a cash crop, and it could be grown almost anywhere in the region.

After the Civil War, most plantations were operated on the tenant or sharecropping systems. Expansion of independent and tenant farming in the Southeast led to the establishment of thousands of small European-American towns to meet the merchandise and service needs of the small farmers. Port towns such as Charleston, Savannah, and New Orleans grew into large urban centers, and new cities were established at major railroad hubs, such as Atlanta. After the Civil War, new industries such as lumber, iron, the railroad, and factories developed in the South. The one-party political system and the practice of segregation isolated free African-Americans from mainstream European-American society.

Historical archaeology is beginning to unravel the cultural realities of the Antebellum period of southeastern culture. The most frequent entity studied has been the plantation. Studies of African-American culture before the Civil War have focused on plantations, although a few studies of African-American urban communities, both free and slave, have been conducted. There has been growing archaeological interest in Indian culture during the Antebellum period, especially the Seminole, Creek, and Cherokee, and this research is beginning to document how these groups coped with the increasing European-American pressure of this period.

Archaeologists studying the Victorian period in the Southeast have focused on the development of rural European-American or "southern" culture. Studies of small farms are revealing how farming families adapted to the effects of the Civil War and the Industrial Revolution. A few archaeological studies of small towns and cities also have been conducted. Industrial archaeologists have studied how towns and cities grew around railroad yards, steam-driven factories, and wharfs. There also have been some archeological studies of African-American urban neighborhoods and segregated towns during the Victorian period, which reflect not only their social and economic conditions, but the coalescence of African and European influences into modern African-American culture. There is a significant gap in the documentary record of this culture, and historical archaeology is making an important contribution to filling the void.

The sheer volume of the archaeological record takes a great leap during the Victorian period, especially in towns and cities. The Industrial Revolution facilitated mass production of consumer goods, and there was a dramatic increase in the amount of materials in all but the poorest households. People purchased and used thousands of items of glass, pottery, and metal.

The Antebellum and Victorian periods were perhaps the most dynamic of all periods of human occupation in the Southeast. There were massive population movements, a pan-regional war, and the Industrial Revolution. The effects of these events on Indian, European, American, and African societies in the Southeast is well reflected in their archaeological remains, which are summarized below.

ANTEBELLUM PERIOD: 1821—1865

The major events of the Antebellum period were the forced removal of Indians out of the region and an immigration surge of Europeans, Americans, and Africans into the recently vacated lands. The immigrants established a socially ranked agricultural society of plantations and independent or yeoman farms that produced cotton as the main cash crop. Plantations were cleared and worked by African slave labor, and small farms were usually operated by European-American families. Indians, Europeans-Americans, and African-Americans had relatively distinct histories and cultures during this period, and this historical and archaeological summary will be organized accordingly.

Indian Culture and Removal

Historical Sketch

There was an increased demand for Indian land in the U.S. Congress from planters, politicians, and land speculators, due primarily to the invention of the cotton gin in 1793. The gin substantially increased the profitability of existing coastal long-fiber cotton farming, and it enabled short cotton, which could be grown on a wider variety of soils, to be successfully farmed. Thomas Jefferson first proposed the relocation of all the southeastern Indians to reservations west of the Mississippi as a solution to the demand for more land. Justifications for Indian removal and the seizure of their lands included claims that European-Americans could use the land "more productively" than Indians, reservations would protect Indians from abusive frontiersmen, there would be an increase in tax revenue from European-Americans settlers, and the idea that it was the United States' "Manifest Destiny" to own North America. There were few defenders of Indian land rights during this period other than a few missionaries. The Cherokee Indians were the most acculturated to European-American ways. They became successful farmers in great numbers. Cherokee built water-powered grist and saw mills, and Sequoyah, a Cherokee scholar and leader, wrote a syllabary for the Cherokee language and soon established a press and newspaper. The Cherokee also set up a centralized democratic government modeled after the United States, including a constitution with three branches of government.

In 1827, John C. Calhoun was designated to organize Indian removal, and when Andrew Jackson was elected President in 1828, he sponsored the Indian Removal Act, passed in 1830, which gave the federal government authority to "help" Indians leave. This law authorized the president to grant Indian groups new land in the unsettled western prairie, and an annual payment (annuity) in exchange for their lands. From the beginning, there were many problems with Indian removal. The first impasse was Indian refusal to trade their homeland for unfamiliar prairie land. What started out as a peaceful process involving a treaty agreement giving Indians an option to remain evolved into a military campaign forcing Indians from their homes, concentrating them in camps, and taking them to Oklahoma under armed guard. Resisters had their legal rights stripped away, and they could no longer own property or be protected by law enforcement. Therefore, Indians were left without recourse when the United States Army arrived at their doorstep to take them away. Bounties were placed on runaway Indians, and they were vulnerable to capture everywhere.

Some groups of Indians managed to remain in the Southeast. The best known resisters are the Seminole, against whom the United States Army waged three wars. Only about 300 Seminoles actually escaped into the Everglades, where their descendants live today. A group of approximately 1,000 Cherokee escaped into the Appalachians, and some Choctaw in Louisiana banded together to form the Houma and escaped removal by hiding in the marshy bayous where they intermixed with the French Acadians. Some Cherokee and Creek also escaped into southwestern Louisiana and formed the group known as the "Red Bones." Other small groups of resisters were scattered in remote areas, including the Chitimacha in Louisiana, the Catawba in South Carolina, the Choctaw in Mississippi, and scattered Creek communities throughout the region. From 1830 until 1925, when American Indians were awared United States citizenship, Indians in the Southeast had to remain hidden to avoid capture and forced removal to a reservation in the West.

Historical Archaeology

Archaeological research of Southeastern Indians during this period has included Indian sites occupied prior to removal, especially Cherokee and Creek, and sites of resisters after removal, principally the Seminole. Historical archaeology has documented that most southeastern Indians underwent significant changes during this period. Some groups adopted European-American practices and materials while others rejected them and continued traditional customs.

Cherokee Archaeology   Several old Cherokee towns have been archaeologically investigated, such as Chota, Citico, and Starnes in the Little Tennessee Valley of Tennessee, and New Echota in Georgia (see Figure 9.1).[1] However, archaeological studies have confirmed that it was during this period that the Cherokee changed their traditional settlement and subsistence patterns and adopted European-American practices. Large traditional Cherokee towns were generally abandoned, and people moved to small farms, lived in log cabins, and used European-American materials, especially tablewares, clothing, farm tools, construction tools, and hardware. One such farm has

[1] See Chapman, 1985, and Schroedl, 1986, for details on Tennessee sites; for Georgia see M. T. Smith, 1992.

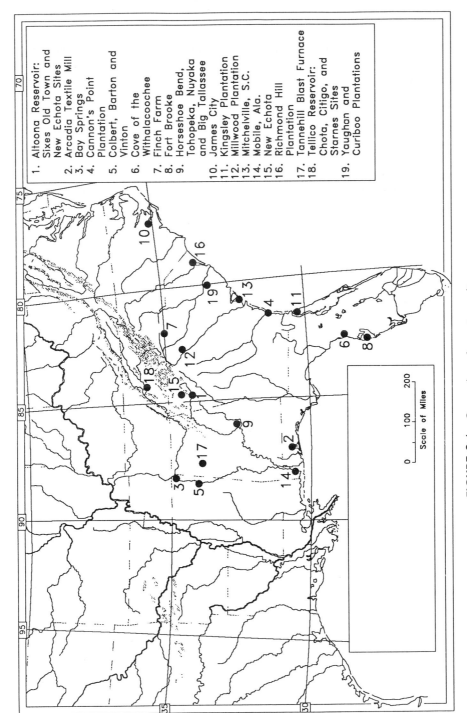

FIGURE 9.1 Some American stage sites.

1. Altoona Reservoir: Sixes Old Town and New Echota Sites
2. Arcadia Textile Mill
3. Bay Springs
4. Cannon's Point Plantation
5. Colbert, Barton and Vinton
6. Cove of the Withalacoochee
7. Finch Farm
8. Fort Brooke
9. Horseshoe Bend, Tohopeka, Nuyaka and Big Tallassee
10. James City
11. Kingsley Plantation
12. Millwood Plantation
13. Mitchelville, S.C.
14. Mobile, Ala.
15. New Echota
16. Richmond Hill Plantation
17. Tannehill Blast Furnace
18. Tellico Reservoir: Chota, Citigo, and Starnes Sites
19. Yaughan and Curiboo Plantations

Scale of Miles

0   100   200

been studied, the Bell Rattle farm, in the Little Tennessee Valley. At the Bell Rattle farmstead, 75% of the ceramics were European-American. A Cherokee farming community in northwest Georgia has also been studied by historical archaeologists. The farms in the community, known as Sixes, had fruit tree groves, cornfields, horses, cattle, pigs, and log buildings.[2] Two of the 26 Cherokee farming families were relatively wealthy. A new Cherokee capital town of New Echota in Georgia was established and occupied between 1826 and 1838. This new town was laid out like contemporary European-American towns, with platted streets, houses, and a tavern. All buildings were constructed in the European-American frontier log building style.[3] Excavations at several residences in New Echota have revealed that some of the Cherokee residents were wealthy, highly acculturated, and used European-American materials. In one cellar, hundreds of pieces of lead type with characters of the Cherokee language were recovered, and it is interpreted that this building was used for publishing a newspaper for the town. Only one building was built in traditional Indian style, which was a council house or rotunda. The council house was built in the traditional circular shape and it was constructed of posts, but some posts had been squared in the European-American manner. Archaeological information from these and other Cherokee settlements during the early Antebellum period have documented that many Cherokee had become quite wealthy, had large homes, sometimes made of brick, and were successful farmers.

Seminole Archaeology   Historical archaeology has documented that the Seminole adopted the opposite strategy of the Cherokee to the encroachment of European-Americans. Most Seminole tried to maintain their Creek-derived traditions and resisted European-American materials and customs. A good example of Seminole archaeology is the research done by Jerald Milanich and Brent Weisman in the cove of the Withlacoochee wetlands, about 60 mi north of Tampa, which was the stronghold for Seminole resisters led by Osceola during the Second Seminole War. United States Army Lt. Henry Prince pursued the Seminoles through this area, and using his diary as a guide, historical archaeologists found Osceola's village.[4]

Prince's diary described Osceola's town as having a ceremonial area called a "square ground" in the center surrounded by matrilineal clan camps. The distribution of artifacts from Weisman's excavation and analysis from the archaeological site thought to be Osceola's settlement revealed that the archaeological materials were clustered around a large area without artifacts in the center of the site. The differential distribution was interpreted by Weisman as follows. The large clean area in the center of the site probably was the

---

[2] See Ledbetter *et al.*, 1987, for details on historical archaeology at Sixes Old Town.

[3] For details and a good summary of New Echota archaeology see M. T. Smith, 1992.

[4] See Weisman, 1989, for details of the search for and archaeology of Osceola's town.

ceremonial square ground and the surrounding clusters of artifacts are from the matrilineal clan camps of related women and their husbands and families, which were described as living around the borders of the square ground. Within each artifact cluster were distinctively decorated traditional brushed Creek Lamar pottery. This finding reinforced the theory that the clusters were female-headed clan camps, because pottery was traditionally made by Creek and Seminole women and passed down to daughters that would have lived together for their lifetime with their husbands and families. Another revealing archaeological finding in Osceola's town was the recovery of only a few European-American artifacts, none of which were European or American pottery or decorative personal items. This low amount of European and American items is consistent at most contemporary Seminole sites, and it is interpreted as a reflection of their isolation from and rejection of European-American culture.

Over a dozen American military forts were built in Florida for the Second Seminole War, and a few have been studied by historical archaeologists, such as Fort Brooke in Tampa. This particular fort was built to monitor activities on temporary Seminole reservations that had been set up as concentration camps between Ocala and Tampa. Fort Brooke was also a major depot for shipping emigrating or captured Seminoles to the West. The location of the fort is now in downtown Tampa, and when the city was constructing a parking garage, the fort cemetery was discovered and partially excavated by Harry and Jacqueline Piper.[5] As shown in Figure 9.2, the 38 Seminole burials were organized into clusters, which is interpreted by the Pipers as a reflection of the matrilineal clans. Eyewitness historical accounts document that the United States Army usually allowed Seminole clan members to be buried together. Most of the Seminoles in the Fort Brooke cemetery were buried wearing traditional ornamental trade goods.

Creek Archaeology   There have also been several archaeological investigations of contemporaneous Creek settlements in the Montgomery area of Alabama.[6] The amount of European and American items and trade goods recovered from the sites has varied considerably. Tukabatchee, the capital, had by far the most trade goods, and Vernon Knight has remarked that after 1790, every home in this Creek town possessed considerable European-American ceramic tableware, including plates, cups, saucers, platters, serving bowls, and even teacups. He also documented that despite the purchased European-American tableware, the Creek diet remained traditional. However, at sites related to the Creek War, such as Horseshoe Bend, Tohopeka, or

---

[5] For details on the Fort Brooke excavations, see Piper and Piper, 1982 and 1993, and Piper *et al.*, 1982.

[6] For examples of excavations of Creek sites in central Alabama see Knight and Smith, 1980, and Knight, 1985.

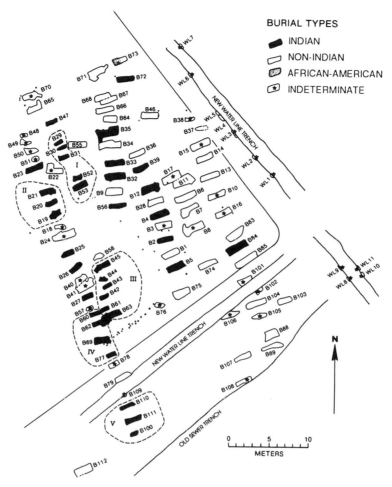

FIGURE 9.2 Probable Seminole matri-clan grave organization of burials at Fort Brooke Cemetery, Tampa, Florida. (From Piper and Piper, 1982.)

Nuyaka, there were very few European or American items, and virtually no European-American made personal ornaments.[7] Archaeologists attribute this to the interruption of trade by the Creek War and the rejection of European-American culture, much like Osceola's settlement in Florida. The Creek were part of the Indian nativistic movement, which spread in eastern North America during this time. Indian prophets emerged in several places who were thought to be invincible to European-Americans and preached a fundamentalist doctrine of driving out European-Americans and returning to their precontact,

[7] For more information on Indian battle-related sites in central Alabama see Dickens, 1979.

"native" ways. At these settlements such as Nuyaka, there are few to none European-American materials.

Summary   While there have been many other archaeological studies of Indian settlements in the Antebellum period in the Southeast, the Cherokee, Creek, and Seminole studies previously summarized are good examples. Southeastern Indian groups tried both to assimilate into and reject European-American culture, and these strategies are well reflected in their archaeological remains.

European-American and African-American Culture

Historical Sketch

After Indian removal, there was a rapid expansion of European-American and African-American culture in the Southeast. The standard practice of land acquisition was that the wealthier planters purchased large tracts of rich flood plain soil, and poorer independent farmers purchased small parcels of inferior soils in the remaining hilly uplands. The continual opening of large areas through Indian removal during this period fostered the attitude that there would always be more new land available. This transient or frontier attitude was especially strong in independent farmers, and as a consequence, they quickly exhausted soil and timber on their small upland parcels and moved on. This frontier attitude fostered little or no conservation of soil or other natural resources, and severe erosion occurred in the uplands of the Southeast. Plantation owners in the valleys, however, considered their agricultural businesses as permanent entities, and as a consequence, they practiced considerable conservation of natural resources.

The small towns that emerged in the Southeast during the Victorian period functioned primarily as service and exchange centers for independent small farmers. Farmers sold their surplus and cash crop, usually cotton, to merchants in the small towns to buy necessities that were difficult to make at home, such as hardware, bottles, cloth, and window panes, as well as some luxuries that made frontier life more pleasant. Plantation owners did not usually trade at nearby small towns as they continued the practice of shipping cotton directly to brokers in large port cities, where they also purchased materials and supplies.

Three kinds of European-American communities developed during the Antebellum period: rural hamlets for servicing farmers, county seats for general government-related administration, and small towns for transportation-related services. Cities continued to be located only at deep water coastal ports at the mouths of major rivers, and, during this period, cities grew in size and complexity due to general population increase, the accumulation of wealthy merchants, and absentee plantation owners.

African-Americans continued to be confined primarily to plantations in the Southeast during the Antebellum period. While most new slaves during this period were born in the United States, some were still imported, legally and illegally, from Africa. The continued importation of African slaves kept infusing African traditions into plantation slave culture. A few slave and free African-American communities did emerge in cities during this period. Some African-American slaves were rented by their resident owners to work on construction projects in the growing urban areas. Urban slaves often lived in separate slave quarters within the cities or near the construction sites on which they worked. Some free African-Americans also lived in urban areas and worked for wages. African-American communities in cities were segregated, and usually located in undesirable, low, and wet areas in the city or on the outskirts.

Historical Archaeology

The summary of the historical archaeology of European-American and African-American cultures during the Antebellum period will be organized by the main cultural divisions that existed in the Southeast during this time: plantations, independent farms, rural industries, and towns and cities.

Plantation Archaeology   There were two types of plantations in the Southeast during the Antebellum period, coastal and interior. There has been much more archaeological research on coastal plantations than interior planta-tions, and at least 20 have been studied.[8] The layout of Antebellum plantations followed two basic patterns: nuclear and conglomerate. The nucleated pattern continued from the European period on coastal plantations, where the owner's house, service and industrial buildings, and African slave quarters were clus-tered in a central activity area, as shown in Figure 8.16. The conglomerate plantation layout was used primarily on interior plantations and consisted of several building clusters scattered around the plantation due to the need to rotate fields every 3 to 5 yr. The building clusters, which were primarily slave quarters, were placed near fields under cultivation to avoid long walks to and from the fields from the main house area.

Archaeology on both types of plantations has shown that there are clear differences in the material remains from owner, manager, and slave residential areas. One of the clearest differences is in architecture. Owners' buildings were always the largest on the plantation and made of the best materials, although specifics varied with the wealth and spending practices of individual planters. For example, excavations at the owner's house on the large and prosperous coastal cotton plantation of Cannon's Point Plantation on St. Si-mon's Island revealed it had carefully poured tabby wall foundations support-ing a large two-story wooden frame house with large fireplaces and chimneys.[9] Tabby is a concretelike substance made from crushed shells, sand, shell-lime, and fresh water. The detached kitchen and baking oven were near the main

[8] See Singleton, 1985 and 1990, and Orser, 1990, for summaries of plantation archaeology.
[9] For details on the Cannon's Point Plantation archaeology see Otto, 1984.

house. At the smaller and less successful Richmond Hill rice plantation in South Carolina, the owner's house was much more modest.[10] The foundations, shown in Figure 9.3, were individual brick piers or pilings that elevated a wooden structure off the ground. The house was simple with a two-story front, a single-story back, and no detached kitchen. Although the Richmond Hill plantation was near the coast, this type of owner's house was similar to those generally built on interior cotton plantations. However, there were some quite elaborate main houses on interior plantations and in small towns. An example is the Waverly plantation on the Tombigbee River near Aberdeen, Mississippi.[11] There, the large luxurious planter's house even had built-in lights that operated on turpentine gas piped in from a brick-lined chamber (called a retort) of slow-burning pine knots. Regardless of location or wealth, though, historical archaeology has documented that, in general, plantation owner's residences were the best and biggest residences on the plantation when in comparison to other dwellings.

During the Antebellum period there was a trend toward standardization of slave housing, which is interpreted by archaeologist Theresa Singleton as a reflection of a reform movement to improve the health of slaves and acculturate them more to European ways.[12] By the 1830s, southern agricultural magazines recommended that a standard slave dwelling should be wooden, 16×18 ft in size, raised on piers, have a plank floor and fireplace, and be located at least 75 ft from other dwellings. The archaeological evidence for slave housing on coastal plantations during the Antebellum period confirms the preference for this type of slave dwelling. Of course, a few plantations had other types of slave structures, such as at the wealthy Kingsley Plantation near Jacksonville. Charles Fairbanks found that the Kingsley slave cabins were exceptionally nice with tabby floors and walls and halls and parlors.[13] Other plantations, such as Cannon's Point, had duplex cabins. A few slave quarters also continued to use African-style construction with thatch roofs and a linear arrangements of rooms with dirt floors.

In addition to architectural differences between the dwellings of plantation owners and slaves, historical archaeology has revealed differences in the artifacts they left behind. For instance, slave artifact assemblages usually have no more than 30% kitchen artifacts, whereas owner assemblages average 60%. Within kitchen artifacts, cheaper banded annular wares are much more

[10] See Michie, 1990, for details on the Richmond Hill Plantation archaeology.

[11] See Brose, 1991, for a summary and Adams, 1980, for details on Waverly Plantation archaeology.

[12] Singleton, 1988, has details on slave facility standardization.

[13] Kingsley Plantation excavations are reported in Fairbanks, 1974.

FIGURE 9.3 Architectural reconstruction of the owner's house at the Richmond Hill plantation (A) based on the foundations revealed through archaeology (B). (From Michie, 1990.)

A

B

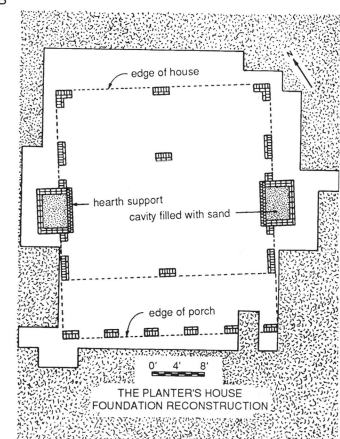

edge of house

N

hearth support

cavity filled with sand

edge of porch

0'　　4'　　8'

THE PLANTER'S HOUSE
FOUNDATION RECONSTRUCTION

numerous in slave contexts, while expensive transfer wares were more numerous in owner contexts, as shown in Figure 9.4. Slave areas also have more bowls and less flatware (plates and saucers), while the reverse is true for planter areas. During this period, there also was a decrease in African-style Colono-ware.

Interesting similarities and differences have also been revealed by archaeology in the food remains of owners and slaves.[14] For example, both planters and slaves on coastal and interior plantations consumed a wide variety of wild plants and animals, but the owners' families ate more meat from domesticated animals than slaves. Another indication of the difference in status and activities of slaves and owners is reflected in food preparation methods. For example, on Cannon's Point plantation, food bones from slave households were usually cracked open to release more nourishment by boiling in one-pot stews, the typical slave meal, which were simmered during the workday. John Otto has suggested the preference of slaves for stews and soups may not be just a function the work schedule, but it could be a continuation of the cuisine of several contemporary African cultures from which many of the slaves originated. From the plantation owner's kitchen midden, food bones had been carefully sawn and butchered into roasts that had to be cooked just prior to serving. Dietary research studies by archaeologists such as these examples are beginning to reveal details of the day-to-day lives of plantation residents, as well as the overall effects of the size and financial condition of individual plantations.

Comparisons of slave diets on different types of plantations have shown that 70–80% of the meat eaten by slaves on coastal plantations was from wild game, but on interior plantations, wild game made up much less of the slave diet. The difference in wild animal meat consumption is interpreted by historical archaeologists as a reflection of the different labor systems used on coastal and interior plantations. The task system on coastal plantations allowed slaves more time for supplemental subsistence activities such as hunting. The gang system used on interior plantations worked slaves all day long, which allowed them less free time to hunt game.

Independent Farm Archaeology   While plantations greatly increased in the Southeast during the Antebellum period with the opening up of Indian land, small independent farms actually dominated the landscape in the Southeast during this period. For example, in 1860, 66% of Georgia was in small farms, and 60% of Georgians owned no slaves. These proportions are fairly representative for most southern states during the Antebellum period.[15] Because most small farms were occupied only for a few years, a very sparse

---

[14] For details on slave diet studies see Reitz, 1987, and Reitz et al., 1985.

[15] For more historical information on the antebellum South see Moore and Williams, 1942, and Owlsley, 1949.

FIGURE 9.4 Pottery types: (A and B) cheaper banded annular bowls frequently found in slave sites, and (C) more expensive transfer printed plates from owner's sites. (From Otto, 1984.)

archaeological record was left behind. Often the material left on these sites has been washed away by the soil erosion caused by poor farming practices, modern forest clear-cutting, mechanized agriculture, and reforestation. Many small farms have been archaeologically investigated in the Southeast, and most of the Antebellum period material is either disturbed or buried.

Despite the problems with finding intact Antebellum small farm sites, a few studies, such as Marlesa Gray's examination of early small farm organization in the Savannah River valley, have been conducted.[16] Gray's study revealed that the buildings on small independent farms were positioned according to the sexual division of labor, which consisted of female-housekeeper and male-farmer. Female-related structures such as the smokehouse, milk house, and chicken pen were near the house, and male-related structures such as barns and forges were located farther from the house. Family cemeteries were generally located near the main house. The specific organization of buildings on small farms, however, was not well structured because structures were built and located according to need and convenience. However, the sex-role-related building position pattern was quite consistent on independent European-American farms throughout the Southeast.

Rural Industrial Archaeology   During this period, water-powered mills to grind grain and saw lumber were built on the frontier and mills often were the first building constructed in a new community. There also were some attempts to build water-powered industrial complexes in the South. The two most frequent attempts at southern industrialization were textile factories and iron furnaces. My colleague John Phillips and I have recently investigated a large water-powered Antebellum mill complex near Pensacola, Florida.[17] At the complex known as Arcadia, a large sawmill was converted into a two-story brick cotton textile factory that was operated by up to 100 female African-American slaves. The mill burned in 1845, and despite repeated salvaging of brick and metal over the past 150 yr, we found hundreds of artifacts from the carding and spinning machines, looms, mule-drawn railroad, and even the base of the crane that lifted cotton bales into the factory, as shown in Figure 9.5. By carefully plotting the location of the machinery parts, building foundations, and the crane, part of the internal layout of the factory was reconstructed.

Another rural industry that developed in the Antebellum period was iron smelting. In iron-rich Alabama, forges and blast furnaces were built to make agricultural tools, weapons, and sheet iron. During the Civil War, the Confederate government put considerable resources into building iron furnaces in west central Alabama near Tuscaloosa, and historical archaeologists have investigated several blast furnaces. Blast furnaces used iron ore mined from the nearby area, water-powered bellows, charcoal for fuel, clay to remove

[16] For details of Gray's study see Gray, 1983.

[17] For details on the excavations at the Arcadia industrial site see Phillips, 1993.

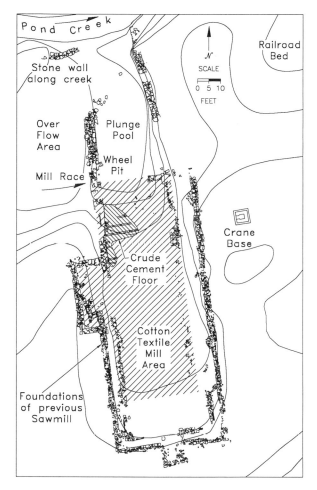

FIGURE 9.5 Foundations of Arcadia, an Antebellum water-powered cotton textile factory near Pensacola, Florida. (From Phillips, 1993.)

impurities in the molten metal, and a stone furnace, shown in Figure 9.6.[18] Large volumes of ore and wood were required for blast furnaces, and large tracts of land, called "iron plantations," were purchased to support them. Like agricultural plantations, activities and buildings were centralized in one area, which consisted of the furnaces and forges, dwellings for the ironmaster and workers, storage buildings, and often fields for raising food crops and animals. Several blast furnaces have been archaeologically investigated, as at Tannehill near Tuscaloosa, which was one of nine large furnaces and forges

[18] For details on the antebellum iron industry see Joseph and Reed, 1987, and Jones and Meyer, 1991.

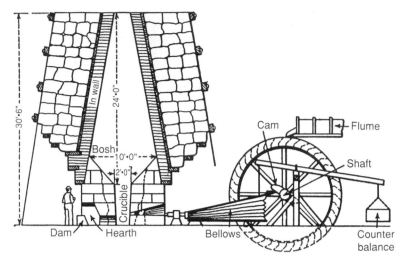

FIGURE 9.6   Cross section and operation plan of a typical water-powered iron ore blast furnace in the Southeast in the nineteenth century. (From Joseph and Reed, 1987.)

operating in this area during the Civil War.[19] The remains of the water-powered bellows house at the Tannehill Furnace, shown in Figure 9.7, provide a good example of the type of stone foundation found at blast furnace sites. The artifacts recovered from this and other blast furnace sites are very specialized and were used exclusively in the production of ore or building construction.

Town and City Archaeology   Small towns, with their merchants, professionals, craftsmen, and transportation facilities, played an important role in the agricultural cotton-based economy, because small farmers traded agricultural products for money, goods, and services. One of the few archaeological studies of Antebellum period small towns has been at a group of sites on the Tombigbee River: Colbert (1834–1847), Barton (1848–1870), and Vinton (1850–1920).[20] Excavations were conducted at several residences, a hotel, blacksmith shop, brick kiln, cotton gin, and general store. One of the surprises to the researchers was the sparsity of architectural remains on house lots, such as foundations, bricks, glass, or nails. Archaeologists explain the lack of architectural remains by the use of wood as the primary building material even for piers, shutters, and chimneys.

[19] See Jones and Meyer, 1991, for details of the Tannehill iron furnace investigation.

[20] For details on the Colbert, Barton, and Vinton excavations see Cleland and McBride, 1983, McBride, 1990, and McBride, 1991; for a summary see McBride and McBride, 1987.

FIGURE 9.7   Brick foundations of the water-powered blower house at the Tannehill Blast Furnace near Tuscaloosa, Alabama. (From Jones and Meyer, 1991.)

Despite sparse architectural remains, there were several types of residential features on the house lots in Colbert, Barton, and Vinton. Features included detached cooking areas, wells, smokehouses, outhouses, gardens, sheds, fence post lines, trash pits, trash-filled cellars, garden furrows, wagon ruts, and brick walkways. Wells had square shafts that were occasionally lined with brick or wood. Not surprisingly, the location of structures and activity areas on town lots followed the sexual-division-of-labor building pattern found on small farms. Male-related buildings such as barns, large animal pens, and storage sheds were located farthest from the house, and female-related buildings such as the smokehouse, garden, and well were closest to the house. Comparing the artifacts between house lots, Kim and Stephen McBride discovered that the materials on a merchant's house lots reflected only a modest standard of living compared to that of other professionals, such as lawyers and physicians, who had a high standard of living. Overall, the standard of living reflected in the archaeological remains from house lots of merchants and professionals in small towns is generally midway between that of wealthy town-dwelling planters and rural small farmers. In other words, historical archaeologists have detected the beginning of the emergence of the middle class in European-American southern culture in the professionals living in small towns.

Archaeological studies in Antebellum cities have revealed a very different archaeological record from that found in small towns.[21] Cities are large and complex archaeological sites, called city-sites, with different patterns of settlement, architecture, subsistence, commercialism, refuse deposition, and material items. Archaeologists have studied city taverns, house lots, urban compounds, wharfs, markets, and residential and commercial lots. They have found, for example, that in the cramped urban house lots, the backyard was the primary area for refuse disposal during this period. Large pits were dug along the perimeter of each backyard and filled with household garbage. Garbage was also thrown on the surface of the ground in the backyard, in what is called "sheet midden." Eventually, household garbage became too much for backyard deposition, and it was deposited on nearby vacant lots and unpaved streets, used as landfill in low and wet areas, and was thrown into creeks and rivers. This refuse disposal pattern, called secondary deposition, is an archaeological characteristic of city-sites and causes difficulty in determining the specific producers of the archaeological material found in refuse pits, wells, cellar holes, or sheet midden deposits. As a result, urban archaeology of Antebellum period and later cities generally focus on large areas of the city, such as a neighborhood or the commercial core, rather than on specific house lots of commercial establishment.

Expansion of shipping and commercialism in Antebellum period port cities usually resulted in modification to the shoreline. In the Colonial period, ships would generally anchor offshore and small flatboats called "lighters" would be used to load and unload cargo. With increased commerce in cotton in the Antebellum period, waterfronts of coastal cities were extended into the water by seawalls and landfill so ships could be directly loaded from a dock. Fireproof brick warehouses were built on the new landfilled wharfs to press and store cotton for shipment, and finger wharfs were extended directly to ships. Often several rows of streets and wharfs were built into the water on landfill placed behind sea walls, such as in Mobile, which is shown in Figures 9.8 and 9.9.[22] Archaeological investigations into the Mobile wharf as well as other contemporary ports have revealed early sea walls of huge timbers that were built on the lot lines of submerged or marshy lots. The sea walls were organized into huge open boxes called "cribs" and were usually initially covered with planks. Over time, the cribs were filled with a variety of materials including household garbage, sawdust, sunken boats, and even animals. This unsanitary landfill often caused problems, and city councils frequently restricted wharf landfill to "clean" materials such as sand, ballast stones, or demolition debris. The Antebellum period wharf in Mobile, Alabama, recently

---

[21] See Zierden and Calhoun, 1984, and Joseph and Reed, 1991, for examples of Antebellum urban archaeology.

[22] For more about Antebellum ports and archaeology of the Mobile, Alabama, wharf, see Joseph and Reed, 1991.

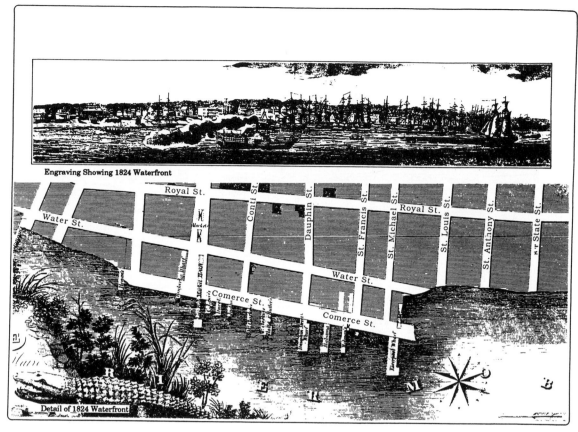

Engraving Showing 1824 Waterfront

Detail of 1824 Waterfront

FIGURE 9.8   Map of the wharf front in Mobile, Alabama in 1824. (From Joseph and Reed, 1991.)

investigated by J. W. Joseph and Mary Beth Reed revealed strata of landfill and the foundations of a series of brick warehouses built on the changing surfaces.

Archaeological research of urban African-American communities has just begun in the Southeast. However, J. W. Joseph has completed an investigation in Augusta, Georgia, of the Springfield African-American community that was occupied during and after the Civil War.[23] He found the remains of an Antebellum period house that was constructed using both European and African elements. The house had a European post and frame construction, but the walls were finished in the African style using wattle and daub. The

[23] The investigations of the Augusta Springfield African-American community are included in Joseph, 1993.

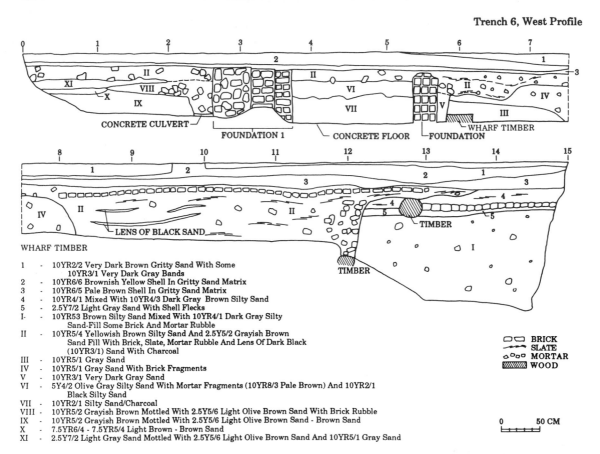

FIGURE 9.9 Profile of archaeological trench in the wharf area of Mobile, Alabama. Note the timbers from wharf construction and foundations and floors of brick warehouses. (From Joseph and Reed, 1991.)

floor plan of the house was also in the African tradition. It was a long and narrow with two small rooms and a possible in-line addition. The pottery vessels were dominated by bowls (75%), which were similar to the pottery found in slave areas on contemporary plantations. Joseph suggests that the similarity in pottery containers between the rural plantations and urban households may indicate the continuation of African dietary practices from slave to free settlements. Analysis of the food remains from the Springfield house site revealed pork jowls and feet, a wide variety of wild food, and a high percentage of bone, much of which was burned from cooking meat in an open fire. These food remains traits coincide with that found from contemporary African-American slave areas on plantations. The pattern of the food remains is considered to be distinctive of the African-American cuisine, which developed during the Antebellum period in the Southeast.

Summary of the Antebellum Period

The archaeological record of southeastern Indians during this period reveals rapid acculturation by some groups, resistance by others, and relocation of all groups.

European-Americans and African-Americans immigrated throughout the region and an agricultural economy was established consisting of cotton plantations and independent small farms. Plantation archaeology has revealed distinct differences between plantation owners and slaves in architecture, ceramics, and diet. Artifacts found in slave sites also reveal that many slaves hunted with guns and traps, learned to read and write, and cooked their own food. Studies of small farms have revealed that the placement of buildings was determined by the sex roles of female-housekeeper and male-farmer.

Small towns and cities grew as trade centers with the booming cotton industry. The archaeological remains of urban Antebellum house lots have a distinct pattern of concentrated backyard refuse disposal. Another urban archaeological pattern that developed was secondary deposition of refuse and other debris on vacant lots and landfill. Archaeology in urban African-American communities is beginning to reveal similarities to contemporaneous plantation slave communities and the continuation of many African-related traditions in architecture and diet.

VICTORIAN PERIOD: A.D. 1861–1917

The Victorian period encompasses the time between the Civil War and World War I. The Civil War destroyed most of the infrastructure and industries in the Southeast and the abolishment of slavery fundamentally changed the economic base of the region. Spurred by rebuilding, expansion of the railroads, and the Industrial Revolution, the Southeast experienced an economic boom during the Victorian period. The history and archaeology of the Victorian period will be summarized according to the main cultural divisions that characterized it: tenant plantations, small independent farms, small towns, and cities.

Tenant Plantations

Historical Sketch

Plantations were generally returned to their former owners by the United States government after the Civil War, and the price of cotton was high enough to encourage planters to reestablish production. However, without human slaves, major changes had to be made in plantation operation.[24] By law,

---

[24] For summaries about tenant plantations see Anderson and Joseph, 1988, and Weaver and Doster, 1982.

employers had to enter into some form of voluntary contract with people for their labor. There were problems with labor contracts, though, due to the plantation owners lack of cash for wages and the reluctance of African-Americans to enter into annual wage contracts with former slave owners. As a consequence, there often was a shortage of labor on plantations. In the transition from slavery, plantation owners experimented with many types of contracts. Tenant farming quickly became the most successful arrangement, and it became the new economic system as well as a social institution.[25] Two types of tenancy developed based on ownership of equipment, tools, and mules: sharecropping and cash rental. Housing was provided by the landowner. Sharecroppers were provided all equipment, tools, and mules by the landlord, which were kept near the landlord's house. A predetermined portion or "share" of the crop produced by the tenant was kept by the landowner for use of the land and equipment. Cash renters, also called tenant farmers, owned their own equipment and mules and paid a fixed rent price in cash or crops. Cash renters were relatively independent and generally rented larger parcels than sharecroppers. Plantations were generally divided into parcels of 50 to 500 acres, but over time, the parcels became smaller, averaging less than 100 acres by 1920. There also was a shift in tenant farmers from predominantly African-American immediately after the Civil War to predominantly European-American after 1900.

In the last half of this period, tenant farming became a form of "debt-peonage" in many areas. In an effort to deal with the problems of labor supply to keep tenants economically bonded to their land, many landowners refused to let tenants have gardens or raise animals, thereby forcing them to purchase supplies at the landowner's general store on credit against the next year's crop. This debt system kept many tenants bound to tenant farms that they otherwise would have left. Other sharecropper and tenant abuses included cheating during crop division at the cotton gin and encouraging tenants to spend their cash at harvest time on unnecessary luxuries, thereby increasing their debt at the landowner's store. Despite these problems, tenant farming was the dominant type of agriculture in the South during the Victorian period.

Historical Archaeology

Tenant Plantation Archaeology   In the middle Savannah River valley, near Abbeville, South Carolina, Charles Orser's archaeological study of the Millwood Tenant Plantation provides a good example of the conversion of a plantation from former slave labor to tenants.[26] In a comparison of the artifacts found at the dwellings of African-American tenants, European-American manager and owner, and the owner's personal African-American servant, Orser

---

[25] For detailed studies of tenant farming see Brooks and Crass, 1991, and Moir and Jurney, 1987.

[26] See Orser, 1988, for details and Orser and Nekola, 1985, for a summary of Millwood plantation investigation.

found that ceramics best reflected socioeconomic differences. For example, there were many more different types of pottery and vessels at the owner's site than at tenant sites. Higher-status residences also had the much more decorated and expensive ceramics, while tenants had the lowest amount.

At other tenant plantations, such as Waverly and Sharpley's Bottom on the Tombigbee River, historical archaeology has documented that one of the characteristics of tenant house sites is sparsity.[27] The plantations were converted to tenancy immediately after the Civil War, and many of the former African-American slaves and their families continued as tenants until the 1930s. From the ledgers of the landowner's store at Waverly Plantation, William Adams documented that most tenant purchases were for food and clothing. When Adams compared the purchase list of a household to the material he excavated at the house site, he found that very little of the artifacts survived. In fact, the survival rate of the documented purchased materials by a tenant household and what was actually recovered from their house site was only 9%. The same phenomenon occurred at Sharpley's Bottom Plantation, as well as other tenant farms in the Southeast.[28] Archaeologists and historians explain the lack of artifacts at tenant house sites as a consequence of poor housing supplied by landowners, poverty of the tenants, swept yards, and high mobility of tenant families. Because tenant farmers were poor, they bought few durable goods, saved and repaired most of their possessions, and took everything of use when they moved to the next farm. Although the debt-peonage system forced some tenants to remain on farms for relatively long periods of time, the average occupation span of tenants on the same farm was only 4–6 yr, which inhibited tenants from making improvements to their houses.[29] Michael Trinkley, who studies tenant plantations in South Carolina, describes the evolution of a tenant farm as one of gradual decay and removal of all functional and repairable items.

Independent European-American Small Farm Archaeology Independent farms continued in the Southeast in the Victorian period, and as before, they usually were located in the hilly uplands. There have been several archaeological studies of independent farms of the Victorian period, especially in the Carolinas and Mississippi. Historical archaeology has shown that there was a strong continuity between independent small farms of the Antebellum and Victorian periods, unlike the disruption and changes that occurred on plantations. An example of the archaeological studies of Victorian-period small farms is the work led by William H. Adams in the Bay Springs community

---

[27] See Adams, 1980, for details on the Waverly plantation and Kern et al., 1982 and 1983, for Sharpley's Bottom.

[28] Examples of tenant archaeology are Orser, 1988, Trinkley, 1983, Agee and Evans, 1969, and Anderson and Muse, 1982.

[29] For a historical perspective see Woofer et al., 1936.

in northeast Mississippi.[30] Eight European-American farms in the dispersed farming community were investigated using archaeology and oral history. Researchers found that the settlement pattern was based on extended families that lived in separate areas. Each extended family area had a central area with a small general store, cotton gin, and church. The dominant families within the extended family lived on high ground in their central area next to the main roads.

The Eaton Farm is a representative example of the Bay Springs farms. As shown in Figure 9.10, the residence, built by the owner, was placed on high ground next to the road. The house was a two-room wooden structure raised on wooden piers. If other houses were built on the farm for tenants, they were smaller, made of poorer materials, and located away from the owner's house. The placement pattern of farm structures continued to be based on the sexual division of labor. During the Victorian period, household refuse on small farms was burned in or near the backyard as well as dumped in nearby gullies. Like tenant farms, poorer independent farms generally left sparse archaeological remains. Archaeologists explain the low artifact density as a result of general poverty, the lack of durability of most items, and a high amount of salvaging and recycling. For example, fences and even sheds were often constructed of odd pieces of salvaged metal, nails, logs and scrap lumber. The practice of salvaging abandoned or burned buildings for bricks and hardware was pervasive, and salvaging often removed most durable artifacts from the archaeological record of structures.

Archaeologists have also studied larger and more successful small independent farms. A good example of such a study is the Finch Farm near Spartanburg, South Carolina, shown in Figure 9.11.[31] The owner was a college-educated teacher, and he had one tenant farmer. The Finch Farm was started in the late 1800s and it had clusters of buildings around the main house, the tenant farm, and a series of farm buildings. When J. W. Joseph and his colleagues compared the artifacts from the owner's house to those found at the tenant house, they found a surprising similarity. The ceramics, for example, were so similar that no socioeconomic differences were reflected, which was opposite the pattern found on tenant plantations. Researchers found that socioeconomic status was expressed not in cultural material, but in architecture and landscaping. There was a significant difference between the size and design of the houses of the owner and tenant. While the houses were both locally designed and built, the owner's house was a large stylized version of the "Folk Victorian" type with many rooms, a hall and much exterior decorative trim. The tenant house was small and plain with only a few large rooms and no decorative trim. The differences in size, design, and ornamentation

---

[30] See Adams *et al.*, 1981, and Smith *et al.*, 1982, for historical archaeology at Bay Springs.

[31] For details on the Finch Farm excavation see Joseph *et al.*, 1991.

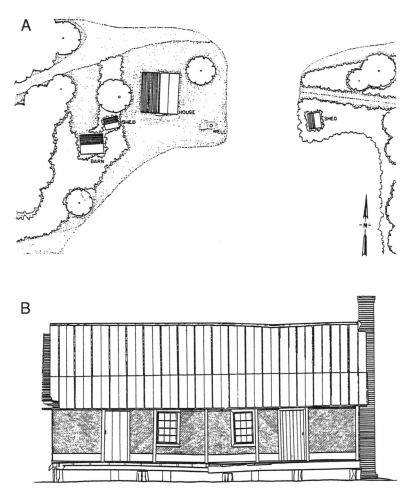

FIGURE 9.10 Diagram of a poor independent farm layout (A) and farmhouse (B) of the Victorian Period: the Eaton Family Farm in Bay Springs, Mississippi. (From Smith *et al.*, 1982.)

of the houses on the Finch Farm directly reflected the social position of the occupants to any passerby, as did the owner's landscaped yard.

The link between architecture and social standing was developed and encouraged by farming magazines and journals (such as *The Progressive Farmer*), which reflected a change in attitude of independent farmers during this period. The frontier had generally stopped expanding, and farmers were forced to consider their farms as long-term homesteads rather than short-term stopping points.[32] As a consequence of a long-term commitment, independent

---

[32] For details on the change in farmer's perspective see Joseph, 1992.

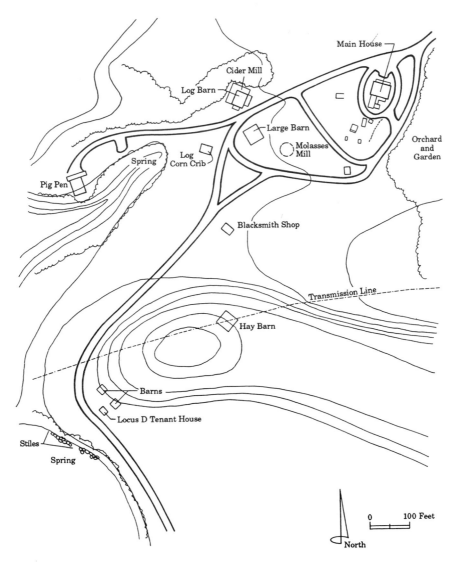

FIGURE 9.11 Diagram of the layout of a middle class farm of the Victorian period: the Finch Farm near Spartanburg, South Carolina. (From Joseph *et al.*, 1991.)

farmers built better-quality homes and grounds and practiced soil conservation.

Researchers at the Finch Farm also documented a change in the refuse disposal pattern that was representative of the successful independent farms. The initial disposal pattern was to spread household refuse in the backyard, creating a sheet midden. During the late 1800s and early 1900s, the volume of trash increased and became a problem. Trash burning in the backyard became common and the residue was dumped nearby. The off-site dumping pattern has been labeled the "Piedmont Disposal Pattern" by Leslie Drucker, and she correlates it to the increase in mass production and improved distribution of consumer goods that occurred at the turn of the twentieth century.[33] Most trash dumps have a very high percentage of bottles, which Drucker explains is due to the fact that bottles did not burn, they were dangerous to leave in the yard, and bottles had become cheap enough to throw away.

Small Towns

Historical Sketch

With the abolition of slavery, the development of tenant plantations, and an increase in independent farms during the Victorian period, small towns popped up across the Southeast to provide merchandise, services, and transportation. The presence of free African-Americans, however, caused changes in the organization of many towns. African-Americans in the South were segregated from European-Americans socially, commercially, and residentially. Emancipation and segregation also generated the establishment of entirely separate African-American communities.

Several new African-American communities were started in the South by the United States Army during and following the Civil War, on land confiscated from plantation owners. The communities generally started as refugee camps for rescued and escaped African-American slaves. Later, the camps became planned communities with blocks, lots, and streets platted out for residences, and farms were laid out nearby, which were given to African-Americans.

Few African-Americans lived in European-American small towns. Despite the fact that in many areas African-Americans made up over 60% of the population, they lived in the country on tenant farms, not in towns. African-Americans generally went to towns only to trade, usually on Saturday mornings when European-Americans customarily stayed away.

Small European-American towns rose, fell, and changed during the Victorian period as railroads replaced steamboats as the mode of transportation after the Civil War.[34] In general, most river towns died and new towns were built along railroad lines. There also was a concerted push by small town councils during this period to develop local industries to diversify the economy and provide jobs. Consequently, cotton gins and presses, brick kilns, iron blast furnaces, and grist and lumber mills were built in many railroad towns. The presence of the railroad and the concentration of light industries expanded the market radius of small towns to about 25–50 mi. Many small towns became

[33] See Drucker *et al.*, 1982, for details on farming and the Industrial Revolution in the South.
[34] For a summary of small Victorian towns see Anderson and Joseph, 1988.

centralized service centers, which led to the growth of a true merchant class in southern towns. Local store owners became pivotal in the cotton industry and economy. The new town-based light industries spurred population growth in many towns, especially among landless wage laborers and managers. Neighborhoods began to develop as town populations increased with the new job alternatives to farming. The increased town population in turn supported the growing commerical districts in small towns.

Historical Archaeology: Small Town Archaeology

African-American Towns   Two African-American towns have been studied by historical archaeologists: James City near New Bern, North Carolina, and Mitchelville, near Hilton Head, South Carolina.[35] Both these communities were at their highest population during and just after the Civil War, decreased in size by the end of the nineteenth century, and are extinct today. In James City, Thomas Wheaton and his colleagues studied half of a city block that had once held nine house lots. After carefully removing the topsoil with a bulldozer and a road grader, archaeologists identified and mapped hundreds of features, shown in Figure 9.12. Although the houses had been removed and there were very few architectural remains, individual house lots could be identified by fence post lines. House lots of recently emancipated African-Americans were characterized by trash pits lining the back fence and rear portions of the side fences and by many internal fences within yards. Only two lots had outhouses along the back fence, and only two wells were discovered, both in the center of the block. Historical records and archaeological remains (furrows) revealed that gardens were located on nearby vacant lots in James City rather than on individual house lots. Although there were sparse architectural remains at James City, that was not the case at Mitchelville. Michael Trinkley found the houses of African-American residents of Mitchelville typically had a large room with a large fireplace and a kitchen off to one side with a smaller fireplace called an "ell."

Artifacts from Mitchelville and James City showed little variation between houses or blocks. Archaeologists believe this reflects a lack of internal social stratification and the presence of a communal, relatively egalitarian, society. The centrally located wells reflect the sharing of resources as well as a high level of social interaction. A strong sense of community probably developed among freed African-Americans due to their common background as slaves, their physical and social isolation from European-American society, their roles in the tenant farm economy, and their common struggle for independence. Historical archaeology has revealed that, unlike most European-American communities, the inhabitants of James City appear to have had a community that focused on the group rather than the individual.

---

[35] For details on Mitchelville see Trinkley, 1986; for details on James City see Wheaton *et al.*, 1990.

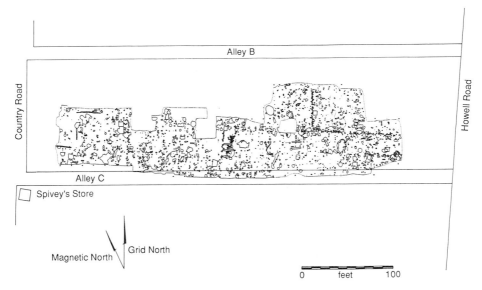

FIGURE 9.12 Drawing of the features in half of a residential block of the now extinct African-American town of James City, North Carolina. Note the outline of lots by the fence postholes. (From Wheaton *et al.*, 1990.)

By studying the choices made by the first free African-American communities, historical archaeologists have a glimpse of the effects of slavery on African cultural heritage. These studies have demonstrated that European-American material culture dominated the house styles and everyday materials. Archaeologists studying James City were surprised at the similarities between sites of poor European-Americans and free African-American sites, and they stated that, archaeologically, the two groups are indistinguishable. Because of the similarity of material culture between poor African-Americans and poor European-Americans, archaeologists are beginning to think that poverty may mask ethnicity in the archaeological record.

European-American Towns There has been little historical archaeology done on Victorian occupations of European-American southern towns. One of the few studies was done in association with the Tennessee-Tombigbee Waterway, which included part of one river town, Vinton, on the Tombigbee River near Columbus, Mississippi.[36] But Vinton was not representative of the typical small southern town. It was a very small, relatively impoverished town that served local tenant farmers with a mercantile store, cotton gin, and a ferry. The archaeology of several house lots in this town revealed a strong continuity with the previous period, and similarities with poor indepen-

---

[36] See Minnerly, 1982 and 1983, and Cleland and McBride, 1983, for details on Vinton archaeology.

dent small farms. The location of buildings on Vinton house lots followed the sexual-division-of-labor pattern found on independent small farms. The female-related house was surrounded by a detached kitchen, well, smokehouses, gardens, and sheds. Male-related animal pens, sheds, and barns associated with agricultural activities were farthest from the house. Artifacts were slightly more abundant on the town house lots than on rural tenant farms or independent farms. The pattern of trash deposition on the town house lots was similar to that of contemporaneous independent farms. Household refuse was thrown in the backyard and side yards, piled up along the fence rows, and thrown in abandoned wells. Garbage was also dumped away from the house lot in low areas, and these dumps contained a high amount of glass.

There is a big gap in archaeological studies of Victorian period European-American small towns. Hopefully, researchers will soon begin to focus their attention on them, because they were the center point of the development of southern culture as we know it today.

Cities

Historical Sketch

Just as the growth of light industry changed small towns, the growth of heavy industry changed Victorian cities into centers of industrial capitalism. Industrialization and urbanization were central to the development of cities in the Victorian period. The industrialization of the South spread from the Northeast spearheaded by textiles. Cotton mills sprang up with such speed that by 1900 more cotton cloth was made in the South than in the Northeast. With the advances in the steam engine for both railroads and sawmills, the expansive pine forests of the South could be profitably harvested, and by 1900, the South led the nation in lumber production. In addition, railroad construction generated a strong demand for iron, and as a result, the iron industry boomed as well as locomotive works, railroad yards, and switching centers.

Industrial development in cities resulted in plentiful jobs, and cities filled with workers from diverse ethnic backgrounds, especially African-Americans, rural European-Americans, and European immigrants. The expanding city population separated into neighborhoods along ethnic and economic divisions. Advances in transportation, especially the streetcar, allowed better-paid city workers to live in cleaner neighborhoods on the periphery of the city. Never before had so many people concentrated in cities, and they were the scene of sweeping cultural changes. The social effects of industrialization's population concentration in cities were striking. Cities became unsanitary, polluted, crowded, and had unsightly slums. Because of these problems, city officials began to change from a "hands off" to a "hands on" management style to improve the environment and conditions of cities.

Historical Archaeology

City Archaeology   The most striking difference in Victorian archaeological deposits from Antebellum deposits in cities is the increase in amount of materials and the thickness of deposits. This change is interpreted by urban archaeologists as a reflection of the dense population and mass production of cheap consumer goods. Buildings were built close together and land was used and reused with unprecedented intensity.

Victorian period archaeology has been done in many cities in the Southeast in residential neighborhoods, industrial areas, commercial cores, and cemeteries. One example of archaeology in an upper-class Victorian neighborhood is the research my colleagues and I have done in Pensacola, Florida.[37] This neighborhood, North Hill, was established in the 1880s after the trolley line provided transportation to and from the commercial core downtown. Middle- and upper-class European-Americans built large Victorian homes on the highest part of the hill. A new African-American residential community also sprung up around the base of the hill, composed of the families of domestic employees who walked up the hill to work for the European-Americans living on the hill. There have been several patterns identified in the archaeological deposits of North Hill house lots. First, backyards have a thick midden (about 1 ft deep) with dense artifacts and a high volume of coal residue from heating and cooking, which makes the midden very black and distinctive. Conversely, front and side yards have a very thin midden with few artifacts. As shown in Figure 9.13, features are concentrated in the backyard where scores of refuse pits were excavated and filled along the fence lines; refuse was also piled along the fence line, thrown in old privies, and used for filling in low areas in and around the yard. Large features are often buried in side yards, such as large brick cisterns for roof runoff and coal bins. Landscaping features from fences and gardens are the most common features in the front and side yard areas.

Urban African-American neighborhoods grew significantly during this period because of the availability of jobs. Most neighborhoods were established near employment areas such as commercial districts, wharfs, and railroad yards. Some archaeological investigations have been done in these urban African-American communities, such as in Pensacola and Augusta.[38] The studies have shown that while there was a general shift to European-American architectural styles, there was a continuation of the African-related preference for bowls in their ceramic assemblages. Historic archaeologists suggest the high amount of bowls, plus food remains, indicate that at least part of the African-related cuisine was continued in urban neighborhoods. There are many pit features and hearths in the yards of urban African-Americans, which

[37] For details on Victorian period archaeology in Pensacola, Florida, see Bense, 1989.
[38] For Pensacola see Bense, 1985; for Augusta see Joseph, 1993.

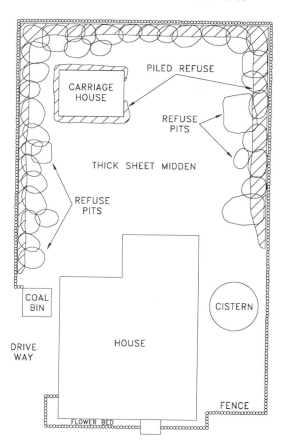

FIGURE 9.13   Typical pattern of archaeological deposits in a Victorian period upper- and middle-class residential neighborhood in Pensacola, Florida.

suggests continuity of the African-related custom of using the yard for a wide variety of activities, including cooking.

The commercial core of cities also expanded during the Victorian period. Archaeological deposits continued to build up, and they became increasingly complex with continual reuse of land. In general, there was a decrease in residential deposits in the downtown areas and an increase in industrial and commercial deposition.

Industrial Archaeology   There have been some archaeological studies of industrial areas in Victorian period cities, such as a railroad yard in Chattanooga and a commercial pottery in Knoxville, Tennessee.

The Union Railyard in Chattanooga is a good example of Victorian period urban industrial archaeology in cities. Railroad yards were present in every

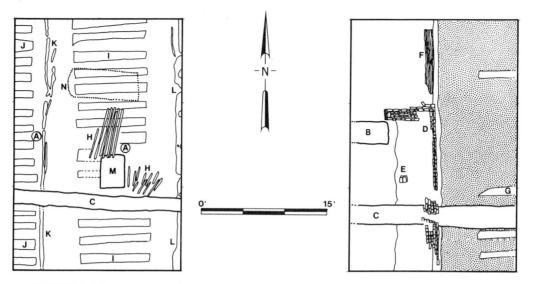

FIGURE 9.14 Drawing of the railroad crossties, railroad beds, building foundations, and plan view of excavation at the depot of the Union Railyards in Chattanooga, Tennessee. (From Council and Honercamp, 1984.)

city in the Southeast during this period.[39] The stratigraphy at the Union Railyard site clearly reflected the fuel change after the Civil War from wood to coal, as coal fragments made up most of the strata. Although the railyard had been cleared of buildings prior to excavation, archaeologists found the underground drainage system, rail beds with crossties and tracks, and the foundations of several buildings, including the depot and engine house with the turntable. As shown in Figure 9.14, the archaeological features were exceptionally clear, which is typical of other industrial sites. There was a narrow range of artifacts recovered from the railyard, and all were specifically related to the railroad and workers. Artifacts included track spikes and rail clamps and plates, mechanical, electrical and hydraulic fittings, tools such as picks, parts from the engines and cars, pieces of general yard equipment, switches, signs, and seals from freight hauled in the cars. Workers' artifacts included ceramics, glass, and personal items such as pipes, clothing fasteners and jewelry.

At the commercial Weaver Pottery in Knoxville, archaeologists found the base of the circular kiln and brick piers that supported the pottery shop-warehouse.[40] The pottery factory produced utilitarian cooking and storage jars, pipe, chimney flues, and decorative curbing tiles. The range of artifacts

[39] See Council and Honercamp, 1984, for details of the Union Railyards excavation.
[40] See Faulkner, 1982, for details of the pottery kiln excavation.

recovered from this ceramic factory site was very narrow and specifically related to pottery manufacture. The artifacts consisted primarily of broken pottery, kiln furniture, kiln debris, and fuel waste. Charles Faulkner found that the artifacts and strata at this industrial site correlated with the ceramic products manufactured there and the sequence of production frequency through time. In other words, the order of the strata and the different frequencies of pottery items matched the history of company production.

Cemetery Archaeology   Victorian period cemeteries were usually associated with specific churches or denominations. While many European-American middle- and upper-class cemeteries still remain in cities today, there is an increasing problem in cities with the discovery of "lost" cemeteries, especially from lower socioeconomic and non-European-American ethnic groups.[41] The main cause of abandonment of cemeteries is the increasing value of land and the decreasing amount of easily developed land in cities. Abandoned urban cemeteries often contain hundreds or thousands of graves, and usually there are no cemetery records. Historical archaeologists with increasing frequency are called to investigate Victorian period cemeteries discovered during urban construction, in legal disputes by descendants who find their family's graves and cemetery impacted by development, and in the removal of graves from an old to a new cemetery prior to development. As a consequence of increased investigations, cemetery archaeology is beginning to produce much new information about different urban ethnic and socioeconomic groups during the Victorian period. Much of the information is a result of forensic studies done on the skeletons to determine the sex, age, and cause of death to aid in identification of burials.

Some urban archaeologists are also investigating city dumps from the Victorian period to get a better understanding of the urban way of life. For example, Paula Davidson found that in Englewood, a middle- and lower-class residential suburb of Atlanta, the residents purchased all their meat.[42] From studying the food remains, she was able to confirm that the portion of the dump she excavated had been deposited in the winter, due to the high number of turkey bones (Thanksgiving and Christmas meals), the large number of soup bones (winter food), and the absence of fruit pits (spring and summer foods). She also documented that meat preferences were beef, pork, and chicken in that order.

Summary of the Victorian Period

Abolition of slavery changed plantation agriculture in the Southeast to the tenant system. Archaeological remains of tenant farms are typically sparse due to the general poverty of the occupants, the lack of durability of their

---

[41] For examples of "lost" urban cemeteries see Blakely and Beck, 1982, and Shogren *et al.*, 1989.
[42] For details of the dump investigation see Davidson, 1982.

materials, and the short occupation time of tenant families. Artifact assemblages from different status groups on tenant plantations reflect the socioeconomic differences, primarily in ceramic types and vessel forms.

Independent European farms continued through the Victorian period with little change, especially on poorer, smaller farms. On larger, more successful farms, the artifact assemblages are larger because of the resident's higher purchasing ability and mass production, and household refuse began to be burned in backyards and the residue dumped nearby. Larger independent farmers developed a more permanent perspective with the disappearance of the frontier. More emphasis was placed on permanent improvements that reflected differential status, especially architecture and landscaping.

Small towns underwent several changes during this period. The first free African-American communities were established and the archaeological record reveals that they were cohesive social units with much sharing of space and facilities. European-American-dominated towns concentrated along the railroads, which expanded throughout the region, and there was new concentration of public industries such as cotton gins, presses, and mills. Archaeology of residential house lots reveals a pattern similar to that of the Antebellum period.

Cities in the South became centers of capitalist industrial development and a pattern of downtown commercial cores and peripheral residential neighborhoods emerged. Archaeology at commercial and residential sites has revealed that there are strong patterns to the archaeological deposits, and artifact assemblages are specific to individual types of neighborhoods, businesses, and industries.

SUMMARY OF THE AMERICAN STAGE

The American stage in the Southeast began with the acquisition of Florida into the United States in 1821 and it ended with the United States entry into World War I in 1917. The key archaeological traits of this period are (1) an increase in European and American materials and sites, (2) a severe reduction in Indian material and sites after removal of the population, and (3) an increase in urban deposits in small towns and cities. Most Indians were forcibly removed from the Southeast by the United States Army between 1828 and 1835, and they were relocated on reservations west of the Mississippi River. Following Indian removal, European-American plantations and small farms spread rapidly across the Southeast, and an agricultural society was established. Although the Civil War essentially destroyed most of the infrastructure in the Southeast, its biggest effect was the abolition of slavery, which significantly changed the agricultural economic base of the region. Most plantations were broken into myriad of small tenant farms operated primarily by African-Americans. With their freedom, African-Americans traveled and interacted much more than ever before, and this fact added a new dimension to the culture they had brought from their previous plantation-based slave period. Spurred by the rebuilding and expansion of the infrastructure, especially the railroads and the Industrial Revolution, the Southeast experienced an economic boom during this period and cities and industry greatly expanded.

During the Antebellum period, the archaeological record of southeastern Indians reveals rapid acculturation by some groups, resistance by others, and relocation of all groups. Plantation archaeology has revealed distinct differences between planters and slaves in architecture, ceramics, and diet. Artifacts found in slave sites also reveal that many slaves hunted with guns and traps, learned to read and write, and cooked their own food. Studies of small farms have revealed that the placement of buildings was determined by the sex roles of female-housekeeper and male-farmer. Antebellum towns and cities grew and became trade centers associated with the booming cotton industry. The archaeological remains of urban Antebellum house lots have a distinct pattern of concentrated backyard refuse disposal. Another urban archaeological pattern that developed was secondary deposition of refuse and other debris on vacant lots, and its use as landfill in low areas and wharf construction. The archaeological remains of Antebellum cities reflect over-crowding and competition for urban land, which produced new patterns of refuse disposal, settlement, commercial development, and wharfs.

During the Victorian period, tenant farms and poor independent small farms left sparse archaeological records due to the general poverty of the occupants, the lack of durability of their materials, and the temporary nature of most tenant farmers. Artifact assemblages from different status groups on tenant plantations reflect socioeconomic differences, primarily in ceramic types and vessel forms. Larger independent European-American farms changed from temporary to more permanent with the closing of the frontier, and archaeology has revealed that status differences were expressed in the architecture and landscaping features.

Cities expanded with the advances in capitalist industrial development and became characterized by a commercial industrial core and peripheral residential neighborhoods. There are patterns to the archaeological features and artifact assemblages specific to neighborhoods as well as industrial sites. The archaeological assemblages of urban industrial sites have a narrow range of items that are specific to the particular industry at each site.

In sum, the South became dominated by European-American culture during this period with a ranked agricultural and industrial culture. The archaeological record of this period is rich, and historical archaeology has revealed that we can learn a great deal from it about the development of modern culture in the Southeast.

References

Adams, William H. (editor)
  1980   *Waverly Plantation: Ethnoarchaeology of a Tenant Farming Community*. Resource Analysts, Inc., Bloomington, Indiana. Submitted to Heritage Conservation and Recreation Service, Atlanta.

Adams, William H., Steven D. Smith, David F. Barton, Timothy R. Riordan, and Stephen Poysner
  1981   *Bay Springs Mill: Historical Archaeology of a Rural Mississippi Cotton Milling Community*. Resource Analysts Inc., Bloomington, Indiana. Submitted to the National Park Service, Albuquerque, New Mexico.

Agee, James, and Walker Evans
  1969   *Let Us Now Praise Famous Men: Three Tenant Families*. Houghton, Mifflin, Boston.

Anderson, David G.
  1985   Middle Woodland Societies on the Lower South Atlantic Slope: A View from Georgia and South Carolina. *Early Georgia* 12:29–66.

  1990a Stability and Change in Chiefdom-Level Societies. In *Lamar Archaeology: Mississippian Chiefdoms in the Deep South*, edited by Mark Williams and Gary Shapiro, pp. 187–213. University of Alabama Press, Tuscaloosa and London.

  1990b *Political Change in Chiefdom Societies: Cycling in the Late Prehistoric Southeastern United States*. Unpublished Ph.D. dissertation, Department of Anthropology, University of Michigan, Ann Arbor.

351

1990c The Paleoindian Colonization of Eastern North America: A View from the Southeastern United States. In *Early Paleoindian Economies of Eastern North America*, edited by Kenneth B. Tankersley and Barry L. Isaac. Research in Economic Anthropology, A Research Annual, Supplement 5. JAI Press, Greenwich, Connecticut.

Anderson, David G., David J. Hally, and James L. Rudolph
1986 The Mississippian Occupation of the Savannah River Valley. *Southeastern Archaeology* 5(1):32–51.

Anderson, David G., and Glen T. Hanson
1988 Early Archaic Settlement in the Southeastern United States: A Case Study from the Savannah River Valley. *American Antiquity* 53(2):262–286.

Anderson, David G., and J. W. Joseph
1988 *Prehistory and History Along the Savannah: Technical Synthesis of Cultural Resource Investigations, Richard B. Russel Resource Area*. Vols. I and II. Garrow & Associates, Inc. Atlanta, Georgia. Prepared for the Savannah District, U.S. Army Corps of Engineers under Contract No. CX5000-7-0012. Submitted to Interagency Archaeological Services, National Park Service, Atlanta.

Anderson, David G. and Jenalee Muse
1982 The Archaeology of Tenancy: An Example from the South Carolina Low Country. *South Carolina Antiquities* 14:71–85.

Anderson, David G., Kenneth E. Sassaman, and Christopher Judge (editors)
1992 *Paleoindian and Early Archaic Period Research in the Lower Southeast: A South Carolina Perspective*. Council of South Carolina Professional Archaeologists, South Carolina Institute of Archaeology and Anthropology, Columbia.

Asch, David G., and Nancy Asch
1985 Prehistoric Plant Cultivation in West Central Illinois. In *Prehistoric Food Production in North America*, edited by Richard I. Ford, pp. 149–204. Anthropology Papers No. 75. University of Michigan Museum of Anthropology, Ann Arbor.

Aten, Lawrence E.
1984 Woodland Cultures of the Texas Coast. In *Perspectives on the Gulf Coast*, edited by Dave D. Davis. University Presses of Florida, Florida State Museum, Gainesville.

Atkinson, James R.
1987 Historic Chickasaw Cultural Material: A More Comprehensive Identification. *Mississippi Archaeology* 22(2):32–62.

Atkinson, James R., John C. Phillips, and Richard Walling
1980 *The Kellogg Village Site Investigation, Clay County, Mississippi*. Department of Anthropology, Mississippi State University, Starkville. Submitted to Mobile-District U.S. Army Corps of Engineers. Contract No. DACW01-77-C-0015.

Bareis, Charles J., and R. A. Bryson
1965 *Historical Climatology and the Southern Plains: A Preliminary Statement*. Oklahoma Anthropological Society Bulletin 13:69–75.

Bense, Judith A. (editor)
1983a *Archaeological Investigations in the Upper Tombigbee Valley, Mississippi: Phase I, Vol. 1*. Reports of Investigations No. 3, Office of Cultural and Archaeological Research, University of West Florida, Pensacola. Submitted to the Mobile District, U.S. Army Corps of Engineers. Copies available from the University of West Florida, Pensacola.

1983b Settlement Pattern, Climate and Marine Ecosystem Evolution Correlations in the Escambia Bay Drainage System in Northwest Florida. Paper presented at the 40th Annual Meeting of the Southeastern Archaeological Conference, Columbia, South Carolina.

1985 *Hawkshaw: Prehistory and History in an Urban Neighborhood in Pensacola, Florida*. Reports of Investigations No. 7, Office of Cultural and Archaeological Research, University of

West Florida, Pensacola. Submitted to Gulf Power Company, Pensacola. Copies available from the University of West Florida, Pensacola.

1987   *The Midden Mound Project.* Reports of Investigations, No. 6, Office of Cultural and Archaeological Research, University of West Florida, Pensacola. Submitted to the Mobile District, U.S. Army Corps of Engineers. Copies available from the University of West Florida, Pensacola.

1989   *The Pensacola Archaeological Survey.* Vol. 1. Pensacola Archaeological Society Publication No. 2. Pensacola, Florida. Copies available from the University of West Florida, Pensacola.

1993   Santa Rosa-Swift Creek in Northwest Florida. Papers of the Swift Creek Conference, Macon, GA. Copies available from the Lamar Institute, University of Georgia, Athens.

Blakely, Robert L., and Lane A. Beck
1982   Bioarchaeology in the Urban Context. In *Archaeology of Urban America: The Search for Pattern and Process,* edited by Roy S. Dickens, Jr., pp. 175–208. Academic Press, New York.

Blitz, John H.
1985   *An Archaeological Study of the Mississippi Choctaw Indians.* Archaeological Report No. 16, Mississippi Department of Archives and History, Jackson.

1988   Adoption of the Bow in Prehistoric North America. *North American Archaeologist* 9(2):123–145.

Brain, Jeffery P.
1978   Late Prehistoric Patterning in the Yazoo Basin and Natchez Bluffs Regions. In *Mississippian Settlement Patterns,* edited by Bruce D. Smith, pp. 331–368. Academic Press, New York.

1979   *Tunica Treasure.* Papers of the Peabody Museum of Archaeology and Ethnology Vol. 71. Harvard University, Cambridge.

Brookes, Samuel O.
1979   *The Hester Site: An Early Archaic Occupation in Monroe County, Mississippi, A Preliminary Report.* Archaeological Report No. 3, Mississippi Department of Archives and History, Jackson.

Brooks, Richard David, and David Colin Crass
1991   *A Desperate Poor Country: History and Settlement Patterning on the Savannah River Site, Aiken and Barnwell Counties, South Carolina.* Savannah River Archaeological Research Papers No. 3, Occasional Papers of the Savannah River Archaeological Research Program, South Carolina Institute of Archaeology and Anthropology, University of South Carolina, Columbia.

Brose, David S.
1984   Mississippian Period Cultures in Northwestern Florida. In *Perspectives on Gulf Coast Prehistory,* edited by Dave D. Davis, pp. 198–215. University of Florida Press, Florida State Museum, Gainesville.

1991   *Yesterday's River: The Archaeology of 10,000 years along the Tennessee-Tombigbee Waterway.* The Cleveland Museum of Natural History, Cleveland, Ohio.

Brown, Ian W.
1985   *Natchez Indian Archaeology: Culture Change and Stability in the Lower Mississippi Valley.* Archaeological Report No. 15, Mississippi Department of Archives and History, Jackson.

1990   Historic Indians of the Lower Mississippi Valley: An Archaeologist's View. In *Towns and Temples Along the Mississippi,* edited by David H. Dye and Cheryl Anne Cox, pp. 227–238. University of Alabama Press, Tuscaloosa, London.

Brown, Ian W., and Richard S. Fuller (editors)
1992   *Bottle Creek Research, Working Papers on the Bottle Creek Site (1Ba2) Baldwin County, Alabama.* Journal of Alabama Archaeology. In press.

Brown, James A.
1966   *Spiro Studies, Volume 1. Description of the Mound Group.* University of Oklahoma Research Institute, Norman, Oklahoma.

1971   The Dimensions of Status in the Burials at Spiro. In *Approaches to the Social Dimensions of Mortuary Practices,* edited by James A. Brown. Memoirs of the Society for American Archaeology 25:92–112.

Broyles, Bettye J.
1968   *Reconstructed Designs from Swift Creek Complicated Stamped Sherds.* Proceedings of the 24th Southeastern Archaeological Conference, Bulletin No. 8:49–75.

1971   *The St. Albans Site, Kanawha County, West Virginia.* Second Preliminary Report. West Virginia Geological and Economic Survey, Morgantown, West Virginia.

Bryan, Alan L. (editor)
1986   *New Evidence for the Pleistocene Peopling of the Americas.* Center for the Study of Early Man, University of Maine, Orono.

Bullen, Ripley P.
1962   Indian Burials at Tick Island. *American Philosophical Society, Yearbook* 1961:477–480.

Butler, B. M.
1979   Hopewellian Contacts in Southern Middle Tennessee. In *Hopewell Archaeology: The Chillicothe Conference* edited by David S. Brose and N. Greber, pp. 150–156. The Kent State University Press, Kent, Ohio.

Byrd, Kathleen M.
1974   *Tchefuncte Subsistence Patterns, Morton Shell Mound, Iberia Parish, Louisiana.* Unpublished Master's thesis, Department of Anthropology and Geography, Louisiana State University, Baton Rouge.

1976   Tchefuncte Subsistence: Information Obtained from the Excavation of the Morton Shell Mound, Iberia Parish, Louisiana. *Southeastern Archaeological Conference Bulletin* 19:70–75.

Caldwell, J. R.
1958   *Trend and Tradition in the Prehistory of the Eastern United States.* American Anthropological Society Memoir No. 88, Mensasha, Wis.

Caldwell, Joseph R. and Robert Hall (editors)
1964   *Hopewellian Studies.* Scientific Papers No. 12. Illinois State Museum, Springfield.

Carbone, V. A., A. V. Segovia, J. E. Foss, M. C. Sheehan, D. R. Whitehead, and S. T. Jackson
1983   The Changing Piedmont Landscape from Late Glacial to Recent Times. Paper presented at the 48th Meeting of the Society for American Archaeology, Pittsburgh.

Carlisle, R. C. and James M. Adovasio
1982   *Meadowcroft: Collected Papers on the Archaeology of Meadowcroft Rockshelter and the Cross Creek Drainage.* University of Pittsburgh, Pittsburgh.

Carneiro, Robert A.
1981   The Chiefdom: Precursor of the State. In *Transition to Statehood in the New World,* edited by Grant D. Jones and Robert R. Kautz, pp. 37–79. Cambridge University Press, Cambridge.

Chapman, Jefferson
1973   *Icehouse Bottom Site, 40MR23.* Reports of Investigations No. 13. University of Tennessee, Department of Anthropology, Knoxville.

1985   *Tellico Archaeology: 12,000 Years of Native American History.* Reports of Investigations No. 43, Occasional Paper No. 5, University of Tennessee, Knoxville. Tennessee Valley Authority Publications in Anthropology No. 41.

1990   *The Kimberly-Clark Site and Site 40LD207.* Tennessee Anthropological Association Miscellaneous Paper No. 14, Reports of Investigations No. 51, The University of Tennessee, Department of Anthropology, and Frank H. McClung Museum Occasional Paper No. 8.

Chapman, Jefferson and James M. Adavasio
1977   Textile and Basketry Impressions from Icehouse Bottom, Tennessee. *American Antiquity* 42:620–625.

Chapman, Jefferson, and Andrea B. Shea
1981   The Archaeobotanical Record: Early Archaic Period to Contact in the Lower Little Tennessee River Valley. *Tennessee Anthropologist* 6:61–84.

Claassen, Cheryl
1986   Temporal Patterns in Marine Shellfish Species Use Along the Atlantic Coast of the Southeastern United States. *Southeastern Archaeology* 5(2):120–137.

Clausen, Carl J.
1964   *The 8-A-356 Site and the Florida Archaic.* Unpublished Master's thesis. Department of Anthropology, University of Florida, Gainesville.

Clausen, Carl J., H. K. Brooks, and Al B. Wesolowsky
1975   The Early Man Site at Warm Mineral Springs, Florida. *Journal of Field Archaeology* 2:191–213.

Clausen, Carl J., A. D. Cohen, Cesaire Emeliana, J. A. Hoffman and J. J. Stipp.
1979   Little Salt Spring, Florida: A Unique Underwater Site. *Science* 203:609–614.

Cleland, Charles E., and Kim A. McBride (editors)
1983   *Oral Historical, Documentary and Archaeological Investigations of Barton and Vinton, Mississippi: An Interim Report on Phase III of the Tombigbee Historic Townsites Project.* The Museum, Michigan State University, East Lansing. Report to the Mobile District, U.S. Army Corps of Engineers.

Coe, Joffre L.
1964   The Formative Cultures of the Carolina Piedmont. *Transactions of the American Philosophical Society.* New Series Vol. 54, Pt. 5.

Coker, William S. and Jerrell H. Shofner
1991   *Florida from the Beginning to 1992.* A Jubilee Commemorative. Pioneer Publications, Inc., Houston, Texas.

Coker, William S. and Thomas D. Watson
1986   *Indian Traders of the Southeastern Borderlands: Panton, Leslie and Company and John Forbes Company, 1873–1847.* University Presses of Florida, University of West Florida Press, Pensacola.

Cole, Gloria G.
1981   *The Murphy Hill Site (1Ms300): The Structural Study of a Copena Mound and Comparative Review of the Copena Mortuary Complex.* Research Series, No. 3. University of Alabama, Office of Archaeological Research, Tuscaloosa and Tennessee Valley Authority Publications in Anthropology No. 31.

Cotter, J. L. and J. M. Corbett
1951   *Archaeology of the Bynum Mounds, Mississippi.* Archaeological Research Series No. 1. National Park Service, U.S. Department of the Interior, Washington.

Cotterill, R. S.
1954   *The Southern Indians: The Study of the Civilized Tribes before Removal.* University of Oklahoma Press, Norman.

Council, R. Bruce and Nicholas Honercamp
1984   *The Union Railyards Site: Industrial Archaeology in Chattanooga, Tennessee.* Publications in Anthropology, No. 38, The Tennessee Valley Authority and The Jeffery L. Brown Institute of Archaeology, University of Tennessee, Chattanooga.

Crane, Verner W.
   1928   *The Southern Frontier, 1670–1732.* Duke University Press, Durham, North Carolina.

Crites, Gary D.
   1991   Investigations into Early Plant Domestication and Food Production in Middle Tennessee: A Status Report. *Tennessee Anthropologist* 16:69–87.

Crook, Morgan R., Jr.
   1986   *Mississippi Period Archaeology of the Georgia Coastal Zone.* Georgia Archaeological Research Design Papers No. 1. University of Georgia, Athens.

Daniel, I. Randolph, Jr., and Michael Weisenbaker
   1987   *Harney Flats: A Florida Paleo-Indian Site.* Baywood Publishing Co., Inc., Farmingdale, New York.

Davidson, Paula Edmiston
   1982   Patterns in Urban Food Ways: An Example from Early Twentieth-Century Atlanta. In *Archaeology of Urban America,* edited by Roy S. Dickens, Jr., pp. 381–398. Academic Press. New York, Orlando.

Deagan, Kathleen
   1983   *Spanish St. Augustine: The Archaeology of a Colonial Creole Community.* Academic Press, New York.

   1990   Accommodation and Resistance: The Process and Impact of Spanish Colonization in the Southeast. In *Columbian Consequences: Archaeological and Historical Perspectives on the Spanish Borderlands,* Vol. 2, edited by D. H. Thomas, pp. 297–328. Smithsonian Institution Press, Washington and London.

DeBoer, Warren R.
   1988   Subterranean Storage and the Organization of Surplus: The View From Eastern North America. *Southeastern Archaeology* 7(1):1–20.

DeJarnette, David L.
   1952   Alabama Archaeology: A Summary. In *Archeology of Eastern United States,* edited by James B. Griffin. University of Chicago Press, Chicago.

Delcourt, Hazel R., and Paul A. Delcourt
   1981   Vegetation Maps for Eastern North America: 40,000 B.P. to the Present. In *Geobotany II,* edited by Robert C. Romans, pp. 123–165. Plenum Publishing Corp., New York.

   1985   Quaternary Palynology and Vegetational History of the Southeastern United States. In *Pollen Records of Late Quaternary North American Sediments,* edited by Vaughn M. Bryant and Richard G. Holloway, pp. 1–37. Published by the American Association of Stratigraphic Palynologists Foundation.

DePratter, Chester B.
   1976   The Refuge Phase on the Coastal Plain of Georgia. *Early Georgia.* 4:1–15.

   1979   Ceramics. In *The Anthropology of St. Catherines Island 2. The Refuge-Deptford Mortuary Complex,* edited by David H. Thomas and Clark S. Larsen, p. 119. Anthropological Papers Vol. 56. America Museum of Natural History, New York.

   1983   *Late Prehistoric and Early Historic Chiefdoms in the Southeastern United States.* Unpublished Ph.D. dissertation, Department of Anthropology, University of Georgia, Athens, Georgia, University Microfilms, Ann Arbor.

DePratter, Chester B., and James D. Howard
   1981   Evidence of Sea Level Lowstand Between 4500 and 2500 years B.P. on the Southeast Coast of the United States. *Journal of Sedimentary Petrology* 51(4):1287–1295.

   1983   Evidence of Sea Level Lowstand Between 4500 and 2500 years B.P. on the Southeast Coast of the United States—A discussion. *Journal of Sedimentary Petrology* 53:682–685.

Dickel, David N.
1992   *Analysis of Mortuary Patterns at the Windover Site*. Unpublished MS. Bureau of Archaeological Research Division of Historical Resources, Florida Department of State, Tallahassee.

Dickel, Cynthia N., Mary A. Ashley, Philip Laipis, and William H. Hauswirth
1988   Isolation of Human DNA from Archaeological Materials. Paper presented at a symposium entitled Archaic Adaptation and Biological Diversity at the Windover Site, at the 53rd Annual Meeting of the Society for American Archaeology, Phoenix, Arizona.

Dickens, Roy S., Jr.
1979   *Archaeological Investigations at Horseshoe Bend National Military Park, Alabama*. Special Publication 3. Alabama Archaeological Society, University, Alabama.

Dickens, Roy S., and Linda R. Carnes
1983   *Preliminary Investigations at Soapstone Ridge, DeKalb County, Georgia*. Southeastern Archaeological Conference Bulletin 20:81–97.

Dillehay, T.
1988   How New is the New World? *Antiquity* 62:94–97.

Dillehay, Tom D. and David J. Meltzer
1991   *The First Americans: Search and Research*. CRC Press, Boca Raton, FL.

Dobyns, Henry F.
1983   *Their Number Become Thinned*. University of Tennessee Press, Knoxville.

1991   New Native World: Links Between Demographic and Cultural Changes. In *Columbian Consequences: The Spanish Borderlands in Pan-American Perspective*, Vol. 3, edited by D. H. Thomas, pp. 541–559. Smithsonian Institution Press, Washington and London.

Doran, Glen H.
1992   Problems and Potential of Wet Sites in North America: The Example of Windover. In *The Wetland Revolution in Prehistory*, edited by Bryony Coles, pp. 125–134. The Prehistoric Society, University of Exeter, Exeter, U.K.

Doran, Glen H., and David N. Dickel
1988   Multidisciplinary Investigations at the Windover Site. In *Wet Site Archaeology*, edited by Barbara A. Purdy, pp. 263–289. Telford Press, Caldwell, New Jersey.

Doran, Glen H., David N. Dickel, William E. Ballinger, Jr., O. Frank Agee, Philip Laipis, and William W. Hauswirth
1986   Anatomical, Cellular, and Molecular Analysis of 8,000 yr-old Human Brain Tissue from the Windover Archaeological Site. *Nature* 323(6091):803–806.

Doran, Glen H., David N. Dickel, and Lee Newsom
1990   A 7,200-year-old Bottle Gourd from the Windover Site, Florida. *American Antiquity* 55(2):354–360.

Dowd, John T.
1989   *The Anderson Site: Middle Archaic Adaptation in Tennessee's Central Basin*. Miscellaneous Paper No. 13. Tennessee Anthropological Society.

Drucker, Leslie M., Woody C. Meizner, and James B. Legg
1982   *Testing and Data Recovery at Allen Plantation (38AB102) and Thomas B. Clinkscales Farm (38AB221), Richard B. Russel Multiple Resource Area, Abbeville County, South Carolina*. Carolina Archaeological Services Resource Study Series 55. Russell Papers. Submitted to Interagency Archaeological Services, National Park Service, Atlanta.

Dunbar, James S., S. David Webb, and Dan Cring
1992   Culturally and Naturally Modified Bones from a Paleoindian Site in the Aucilla River, North Florida. In *Bone Modification*, edited by R. Bonnischen. Center for the Study of Early Man, Orono, Maine.

Dunbar, James S., Michael K. Faught, and S. David Webb

1988   Page-Ladson (8Je603): An Underwater Paleo-Indian Site in Northwestern Florida. *Florida Anthropologist* 41(4):442–452.

Dunnell, Robert C.
1986   Five Decades of American Archaeology. In *American Archaeology Past and Future*, edited by David J. Meltzer, Don D. Fowler, and Jeremy A. Sabloff, pp. 23–49. Smithsonian Institution Press, Washington.
1990   The Role of the Southeast in American Archaeology. *Southeastern Archaeology* 9(1):11–22.

Dye, David H. and Charlotte A. Wartrin
1985   *Phase I and II Archaeological Investigations at the W. C. Mann Site (22TS565) Tishomingo County, MS: Draft Report.* Department of Anthropology, Memphis State University, Memphis, TN. Report to the Nashville District, U.S. Army Corps of Engineers.

Earle, Timothy K.
1987   Chiefdoms in Archaeological and Ethnological Perspective. *Annual Review of Anthropology* 16:279–308.

Ewen, Charles R.
1989   Anhaica: Discovery of Hernando's 1539–1540 Winter Camp. In *First Encounters: Spanish Explorations in the Caribbean and the United States, 1492–1570*, edited by Jerald T. Milanich and Susan Milbrath, pp. 110–118. Ripley P. Bullen Monographs in Anthropology and History, No. 9, Florida Museum of Natural History, Gainesville, University of Florida Press, Gainesville.
1990   Soldier of Fortune: Hernando de Soto in the Territory of the Apalachee, 1539–1540. In *Columbian Consequences: Archaeological and Historical Perspectives on the Spanish Borderlands, Vol. 2*, edited by D. H. Thomas, pp. 83–91. Smithsonian Institution Press, Washington and London.

Fairbanks, Charles H.
1946   The Macon Earthlodge. *American Antiquity* 12:94–108.
1956   *Archeology of the Funeral Mound, Ocmulgee National Monument, Georgia.* Archaeological Research Series No. 3, National Park Service, U.S. Department of the Interior, Washington.
1974   *The Kingsley Slave Cabins in Duval County, Florida.* Archaeology Papers 7:62–93, Conference on Historic Sites.

Faulkner, Charles H.
1982   The Weaver Pottery: A Late Nineteenth-Century Family Industry in a Southeastern Urban Setting. In *The Archaeology of Urban America: A Search for Pattern and Process*, edited by Roy S. Dickens, Jr., pp. 209–236. Academic Press, New York.
1988   Middle Woodland Community and Settlement Patterns on the Eastern Highland Rim, Tennessee. In *Middle Woodland Settlement and Ceremonialism in the Mid-South and Lower Mississippi Valley*, edited by Robert C. Mainfort, Jr., pp. 76–98. Proceedings of the 1984 Mid-South Archaeological Conference, Pinson Mounds, Tennessee. Archaeological Report No. 22. Mississippi Department of Archives and History, Jackson.

Fenneman, Nevin M.
1938   *Physiography of the United States.* McGraw-Hill, New York.

Ferguson, Leland G.
1980   Looking for the "Afro" in Colono-Indian Pottery. In *Archaeological Perspectives on Ethnicity in America*, edited by Robert L. Schulyer, pp. 14–28. Baywood Press, Farmingdale, N.Y.
1992   *Uncommon Ground: Archaeology and Early African America: 1650–1800.* Smithsonian Institution Press, Washington.

Fisk, Harold N.
1944   *Geological Investigation of the Alluvial Valley of the Lower Mississippi River.* U.S. Army Corps of Engineers, Mississippi River Commission, Vickburg.

Flannery, Kent V.
1972   The Evolution of Civilizations. *Annual Review of Ecology and Semantics* 3:399–426.

Ford, James A.
1963   *Hopewell Culture Burial Mounds near Helena, Arkansas.* Anthropological Papers Vol. 50:(1). American Museum of Natural History, New York.

Ford, James A., and Clarence H. Webb
1956   *Poverty Point, A Late Archaic Site in Louisiana.* Anthropological Papers Vol. 46:(1). American Museum of Natural History, New York.

Ford, Richard I.
1985   *Prehistoric Food Production in North America.* Museum of Anthropology, University of Michigan, Ann Arbor.

Fowler, Melvin L.
1978   Cahokia and the American Bottom: Settlement Archaeology. In *Mississippian Settlement Patterns,* edited by Bruce D. Smith, pp. 455–478. Academic Press, Orlando.

Fritz, Gayle J. and Tristram R. Kidder
1993   Recent Investigations into Prehistoric Agriculture in the Lower Mississippi Valley. *Southeastern Archaeology* 12(1):1–14.

Futato, Eugene M.
1982   Some Notes on the Distribution of Fluted Points in Alabama. *Archaeology of Eastern North America* 10:30–33.

Gagliano, Sherwood M.
1984   Geoarchaelogy of the Northern Gulf Shore. In *Perspectives on Gulf Coast Prehistory,* edited by Dave D. Davis, p. 11. University of Florida Press, Pensacola.

Galinat, Walton C.
1985   Domestication and Diffusion of Maize. In *Prehistoric Food Production in North America,* edited by R. I. Ford, pp. 245–278. Anthropological Paper No. 75. Museum of Anthropology, University of Michigan, Ann Arbor.

Galloway, Patricia (editor)
1989   *The Southeastern Ceremonial Complex: Artifacts and Analysis.* The Cottonlandia Conference. University of Nebraska Press, Lincoln.

Gannon, Michael V.
1965   *The Cross in the Sand.* University of Florida Press, Gainesville.

Gardner, William M.
1974   *The Flint Run PaleoIndian Complex: A Preliminary Report 1971–1973 Seasons.* Occasional Paper No. 1. Catholic University of America, Archaeology Laboratory, Washington.
1977   Flint Run PaleoIndian Complex and Its Implications for Eastern North America Prehistory. *Annals of the New York Academy of Sciences* 288:251–263.

Garrison, Ervan G.
1992   Recent Archaeogeophysical Studies of Paleoshorelines of the Gulf of Mexico. In *Paleoshorelines and Prehistory: An Investigation of Method,* edited by Lucille L. Johnson, pp. 103–116. CRC Press, Boca Raton, Florida.

Garrow, Patrick H.
1975   The Woodland Period North of the Fall Line. Early Georgia 3(1):17–26.

Gibbs, Tyson, Kathleen Cargill, Leslie Sue Lieberman, and Elizabeth J. Reitz
1980   Nutrition in a Slave Population: An Anthropological Examination. *Medical Anthropology* 4:175–262.

Gibson, Jon L.
1974   Poverty Point, The First American Chiefdom. *Archaeology* 27(2):95–105.
1980   Speculations on the Origin and Development of Poverty Point Culture. In *Caddoan and*

Poverty Point Archaeology, edited by Jon L. Gibson, pp. 321–348. Bulletin of the Louisiana Archaeological Society No. 6.

Gibson, Jon L., and J. Richard Schenkel
1988 Louisiana Earthworks: Middle Woodland and Predecessors. In *Middle Woodland Settlement and Ceremonialism in the Mid-South and Lower Mississippi Valley,* edited by Robert C. Mainfort, Jr. Mississippi Department of Archives and History, Jackson, Mississippi.

Goad, Sharon I.
1979 Middle Woodland Exchange in the Prehistoric Southeast. In *Hopewell Archaeology,* edited by David S. Brose and N'omi Greber, pp. 238–436. Kent State University Press, Kent, Ohio.

Goodyear, Albert C., III
1974 *The Brand Site: A Techno-Functional Study of a Dalton Site in Northeast Arkansas.* Research Series 7, Arkansas Archaeological Survey, Fayetteville.
1982 The Chronological Position of the Dalton Horizon in the Southeastern United States. *American Antiquity* 47:382–395.

Graham, R. W., and E. L. Lundelius, Jr.
1984 Coevolutionary Disequilibrium and Pleistocene Extinctions. In *Quaternary Extinctions: A Prehistoric Revolution,* edited by P. S. Martin and R. G. Klein, pp. 223–249. University of Arizona Press, Tucson.

Gray, Marlesa A.
1983 *The Old Home Place: An Archaeological and Historical Investigation of Five Farm Sites Along the Savannah River, Georgia and South Carolina,* WAPORA, Inc. Cincinnati, Ohio. Funded by Savannah District, U.S. Army Corps of Engineers. Contract No. CX-5000-1-4062. Submitted to Division of Archaeological Services, National Park Service, Atlanta. Russell Papers 1983.

Griffin, James B.
1946 Cultural Change and Continuity in Eastern United States Archaeology. In *Man in Northeastern North America,* edited by F. Johnson, pp. 37–95. Papers of the Robert S. Peabody Foundation for Archaeology 3. Andover, Massachusetts.
1952 *Archeology of Eastern United States.* University of Chicago Press, Chicago and London.
1967 Eastern North America Archaeology: A Summary. *Science* 156(3772):175–191.
1978a Eastern United States. In *Chronologies in New World Archaeology,* edited by R. E. Taylor and Clement W. Meighan. Academic Press, New York.
1978b The Midlands and Northeastern United States. In *Ancient Native Americans,* edited by Jesse D. Jennings, pp. 221–280. W. H. Freeman, San Francisco.
1985 Changing Concepts of Mississippian Cultures. In *Alabama and the Borderlands,* edited by R. Reid Badger and Lawrence A. Clayton. University of Alabama Press, Tuscaloosa.

Griffin, John W.
1952 Prehistoric Florida: A Review. In *Archaeology of Eastern United States.* edited by J. B. Griffin, pp. 322–334. The University of Chicago Press, London.

Guidon, N., and J. Delibrias
1986 Carbon-14 Dates Point to Man in the Americas 33,000 Years Ago. *Nature* 321:769–771.

Guthrie, R. D.
1984 Mosaics, Allelochemics and Nutrients: An Ecological Theory of Late Pleistocene Megafaunal Extinctions. In *Quaternary Extinctions: A Prehistoric Revolution,* edited by P. S. Martin and R. G. Klein, pp. 259–298. University of Arizona Press, Tucson.

Haag, William G.
1985 Federal Aid to Archaeology in the Southeast, 1933–1942. *American Antiquity* 50(2):272–280.

Hally, David J. and James B. Langford, Jr.
1988 *Mississippi Period Archaeology of the Georgia Valley and Ridge Province.* Laboratory of

Archaeology Series Report No. 25 and Georgia Archaeological Research Design Paper No. 4, University of Georgia, Athens.

Hally, David J., Marvin T. Smith, and James B. Langford, Jr.
1990 The Archaeological Reality of de Soto's Coosa. In *Columbian Consequences: Archaeological and Historical Perspectives on the Spanish Borderlands, Vol. 2,* edited by D. H. Thomas, pp. 121–138. Smithsonian Institution Press, Washington and London.

Harris, Donald A. and Jerry J. Nielsen
1972 *Archaeological Salvage Investigations at the Site of the French Fort Conde, Mobile, Alabama.* Department of Anthropology, University of Alabama, University, Alabama. Submitted to the Alabama Highway Department, Montgomery.

Hodge, Federick W.
1912 *Handbook of the American Indians North of Mexico,* Vol. 20, Part 2, Bureau of American Ethnology, Smithsonian Institution, Washington, D.C., p. 86.

House, John
1990 Powell Canal: Baytown Period Adaptation on Bayou Macon, Southeast Arkansas. In *The Mississippian Emergence,* edited by B. D. Smith, pp. 9–26. The Smithsonian Institution, Washington.

Hudson, Charles, Marvin T. Smith, David J. Hally, Richard Polhemus, and Chester B. DePratter
1985 Coosa: A Chiefdom in the Sixteenth-Century Southeast. *American Antiquity* 50:723–737.

Hudson, Charles M., Marvin T. Smith, and Emilia Kelley
1990 The Tristan de Luna Expedition, 1559–1561. In *First Encounters: Spanish Explorations in the Caribbean and the United States, 1492–1570,* edited by Jerald T. Milanich and Susan Milbrath, pp. 119–134. University of Florida Press, Gainesville.

Jackson, H. E.
1981 Recent Research on Poverty Point Subsistence and Settlement Systems: Test Excavations at the J. W. Copes Site in Northeast Louisiana. *Louisiana Archaeology* 8:75–88.

Jahn, Otto L., and Ripley P. Bullen
1978 *The Tick Island Site, St. Johns River, Florida.* Florida Anthropological Society Publications, No. 10, and *Florida Anthropologist* 31(2) Pt. 2.

Jefferies, R. W.
1976 *The Tunacunnhee Site: Evidence of Hopewell Interactions in Northwest Georgia.* Anthropological Papers No. 1. The University of Georgia, Athens.
1979 *The Tunacunnhee Site: Hopewell in Northwest Georgia.* In *Hopewell Archaeology: The Chillicothe Conference,* edited by David S. Brose and N. Greber, pp. 162–170. The Kent State University Press, Kent.
1992 Current Research. *American Antiquity* 57(3):545–552.

Jenkins, Ned J.
1974 Subsistence and Settlement Patterns in the Western Tennessee Valley during the Transitional Archaic-Woodland Period. *Journal of Alabama Archaeology* 20(2).
1981 *Gainesville Lake Area Ceramic Description and Chronology of Archaeological Investigations of the Gainesville Lake Area of the Tennessee-Tombigbee Waterway, Volume 2.* Reports of Investigations No. 12. Office of Archaeological Research, The University of Alabama, Moundville.

Jenkins, Ned J., and Richard A. Krause
1986 *The Tombigbee Watershed in Southeastern Prehistory.* University of Alabama Press, University, Alabama.

Jennings, Jesse D.
1974 Prehistory of North America. McGraw-Hill. New York.

Johnson, Jay K.
1988 Woodland Settlement in Northeastern Mississippi: The Miller Tradition. In *Middle Woodland Settlement and Ceremonialism in the Mid-South and Lower Mississippi Valley.*

Proceeding of the 1984 Mid-South Archaeological Conference, Pinson Mounds, Tennessee. Archaeological Report No. 22, Mississippi Department of Archives and History. Jackson.

Johnson, Jay K. (editor)
1993   *The Development of Southeastern Archaeology.* The University of Alabama Press, Tuscaloosa.

Johnson, Jay K., and John T. Sparks
1986   Protohistoric Settlement Patterns in Northeastern Mississippi. In *The Protohistoric Period in the Mid-South: 1500–1700.* Proceedings of the 1983 Mid-South Archaeological Conference. Archaeological Report No. 18, pp. 64–82. Mississippi Department of Archives and History, Jackson.

Jones, B. Calvin
1981   The Florida Anthropologist Interview with C. Jones—Excavations of an Archaic Cemetery in Cocoa Beach, Florida. *Florida Anthropologist* 34(2):81–89.
1982   Southern Cult Manifestations at the Lake Jackson Site, Leon County, Florida: Salvage Excavations of Mound 3. *Midcontinental Journal of Archaeology* 17:1. Kent State University, Kent, Ohio.
1991   High Status Burials in Mound 3 at Florida's Lake Jackson Complex: Stability and Change in Fort Walton Culture. MS on file, Bureau of Archaeological Research, Florida Division of Historical Resources, Tallahassee.

Jones, B. Calvin, and Gary Shapiro
1990   Nine Mission Sites in Apalachee. In *Columbian Consequences: Archaeological and Historical Perspectives on the Spanish Borderlands,* Vol. 2, edited by D. H. Thomas, pp. 491–510. Smithsonian Institution Press, Washington and London.

Jones, Betsy, and Jeffery Meyer
1991   *Roupes Valley Ironworks, an Archaeological Perspective: Excavations at 1Tu604, Tannelhill Furnace Compound, Tuscaloosa County, Alabama.* Reports of Investigations No. 61, The University of Alabama, Alabama Museum of Natural History, Division of Archaeology, Moundville.

Joseph, Joseph W.
1992   Building to Grow: Agrarian Adaptations to South Carolina's Historic Landscape. *Synthesis of the Historical Archaeology of South Carolina Part I: Landscapes.* South Carolina Department of Archives and History, Columbia.

Joseph, Joseph W.
1993   *"And They Went Down Both Into the Water": Archaeological Data Recovery of the Riverfront Augusta Site, 9RI165.* New South Associates, Stone Mountain, Georgia. Submitted to the City of Augusta, Georgia.

Joseph, Joseph W. and Mary Beth Reed
1987   Ore, Water, Stone and Wood: Historical and Architectural Investigations of Donaldson's Iron Furnace, Cherokee County, Georgia. Garrow and Associates, Atlanta, Georgia. Submitted to the Mobile District, U.S. Army Corps of Engineers.
1991   *An Increase of the Town: An Archaeological and Historical Investigation of the Proposed Mobile Convention Center Site (1Mb194), Mobile, Alabama.* New South Associates, Stone Mountain, Georgia. Submitted to the Mobile District, U.S. Army Corps of Engineers.

Joseph, Joseph W., Mary Beth Reed, and Charles E. Cantley
1991   *Agrarian Life, Romantic Death: Archaeological and Historical Testing and Data Recovery for the I-85 Northern Alternative, Spartanburg County, South Carolina.* New South Associates, Stone Mountain, Georgia. Report to the South Carolina Department of Highways and Public Transportation, Columbia, South Carolina.

Joy, Deborah

1989   *The Colonial Archaeological Trail in Pensacola, Florida: Phase I.* Reports of Investigations No. 27, Institute of West Florida Archaeology, University of West Florida, Pensacola.

Kay, Marvin, George Sabo III, and Ralph Merletti
1989   Late Prehistoric Settlement Patterning: A View From Three Caddoan Civic-Ceremonial Centers in Northwest Arkansas. In *Contributions to Spiro Archaeology: Mound Excavations and Regional Perspectives,* edited by J. Daniel Rogers, Don G. Wycoff, and Dennis A. Peterson, pp. 129–158. Studies in Oklahoma's Past, No. 16. Oklahoma Archaeological Survey.

Keegan, W. F. (editor)
1987   *Emergent Horticultural Economies of the Eastern Woodlands.* Occasional Paper No. 7. Center for Archaeological Investigations, Southern Illinois University, Carbondale.

Keel, Bennie C.
1976   *Cherokee Archaeology.* University of Tennessee Press, Knoxville.
1988   *Advances in Southeastern Archaeology 1966–1986, Contributions of the Federal Archaeological Program.* Special Publication No. 6. Southeastern Archaeological Conference.

Kellar, James H., A. R. Kelley, and E. V. McMichael
1962   The Mandeville Site in Southwest Georgia. *American Antiquity* 27:336–355.

Kelly, John E., Steven J. Ozuk, Douglas K. Jackson, Dale L. McElrath, Fred A. Finney, and Duane Esarey
1984   Emergent Mississippian Period. In *American Bottom Archaeology,* edited by Charles J. Bareis and James W. Porter. University of Illinois Press, Urbana and Chicago.

Kern, John R., Ira Berlin, Steven F. Miller, and Joseph P. Reidy
1982   *Sharpley's Bottom Historic Sites: Phase II Historical Investigations, Tombigbee River Multi-Resource District, Alabama and Mississippi.* Commonwealth Associates, Inc., Jackson, Michigan. Submitted to National Park Service, Mid-Atlantic Region, Philadelphia. Contract No. C-54039(80).

Kern, John R., Judith D. Tordoff, Richard A. Knecht, C. Stephan Demeter, and Terrance J. Martin
1983   *Phase II Archaeological Investigations at Sharpley's Bottom Historic Sites, Tombigbee River Multi-Resource District, Alabama and Mississippi.* Commonwealth Associates, Inc. Jackson, Michigan. Submitted to Interagency Archaeological Services, National Park Service, Atlanta.

Kidder, Tristram R.
1992   Coles Creek Period Social Organization and Evolution in Northeast Louisiana. In *Lords of the Southeast: Social Inequality and the Native Elites of Southeastern North America,* edited by A. W. Barker and T. R. Pauketat. Archaeological Papers of the AAA No. 3. American Anthropological Association, Washington.
1993   Timing and Consequences of the Introduction of Maize Agriculture in the Lower Mississippi Valley. *North American Archaeologist* 13(1):15–42.

Kidder, Tristram R. and Gayle J. Fritz
1990   *Final Report on the 1989 Archaeological Investigations at the Osceola (16TE2) and Reno Brake (16TE93) Sites, Tensas Parish, Louisiana.* Archaeological Report No. 1, Tulane University Center for Archaeology, New Orleans.

Knight, Vernon J., Jr.
1984a   Late Prehistoric Adaptation in the Mobile Bay Region. In *Perspectives on Gulf Coast Prehistory,* edited by Dave D. Davis, pp. 198–215. University of Florida Press/Florida State Museum, Gainesville.
1984b   Protohistoric Cultural Interaction along the Northern Gulf Coast. In *Perspectives on Gulf Coast Prehistory,* edited by Dave D. Davis, pp. 216–321. University Presses of Florida, University of Florida, Gainesville, Florida.
1985   *Tukabatchee: Archaeological Investigations at an Historical Creek Town, Elmore County, Ala-*

bama. Reports of Investigations 45, Office of Archaeological Research, Alabama State Museum of Natural History, University of Alabama, Tuscaloosa.

1986 The Institutional Organization of Mississippian Religion. *American Antiquity* 51:675–687.

1990 *Excavation of the Truncated Mound at the Walling Site: Middle Woodland Culture and Copena in the Tennessee Valley.* Report of Investigations 56, University of Alabama, Alabama State Museum of Natural History, Division of Archaeology, Moundville.

Knight, Vernon J., Jr., and Marvin T. Smith

1980 Big Tallassee: A Contribution to Upper Creek Site Archaeology. *Early Georgia* 8(2):59–74.

Lafferty, Robert H., III

1981 *The Phipps Bend Archaeological Project.* Research Series No. 4, Office of Archaeological Research, The University of Alabama, Submitted to the Tennessee Valley Authority in fulfillment of contract TV-44935A. TVA Publications in Anthropology, No. 26.

Landers, Jane

1990 African Presence in Early Spanish Colonization of the Caribbean and the Southeastern Borderlands. In *Columbian Consequences: Archaeological and Historical Perspectives on the Spanish Borderlands*, Vol. 2, edited by D. H. Thomas, pp. 315–328. Smithsonian Institution Press, Washington and London.

Larson, Lewis H.

1971 Archaeological Implications of Social Stratification at the Etowah Site. *American Antiquity* 36(3), Pt. 2. Memoirs of the Society for American Archaeology No. 25.

Ledbetter, R. Jerald, W. Dean Wood, Karen Wood, and Robbie Ethridge

1987 *Cultural Resources Survey of Allatoona Lake Area, Georgia.* Southeastern Archaeological Services, Inc., Athens, GA. Submitted to Mobile District, U.S. Army Corps of Engineers.

Leur, George M., and Marion M. Almy

1981 Temple Mounds of the Tampa Bay Area. *Florida Anthropologist* 34(3):127–155.

Lewis, Kenneth

1976 *Camden: A Frontier Town in 18th Century South Carolina.* Anthropological Studies #2, Institute of Archeology and Anthropology, University of South Carolina, Columbia.

1985 Plantation Layout and Function in the South Carolina Lowcountry. In *The Archaeology of Slavery and Plantation Life*, edited by Theresa A. Singleton, pp. 35–65. Academic Press, San Diego.

Lewis, Thomas M. N., and Madeline Kneberg

1946 *Hiwassee Island.* University of Tennessee Press, Knoxville, Tennessee.

1961 *Eva: An Archaic Site.* University of Tennessee Press, Knoxville.

Lilly, Eli

1954 *Walum Olum or Red Score.* Indiana Historical Society, Indianapolis.

Lynch, T.

1990 Glacial Age Man in South America? *American Antiquity* 55(1):12–36.

Mainfort, Robert C., Jr.

1986 *Pinson Mounds.* Research Series No. 7, Tennessee Department of Conservation, Division of Archaeology, Nashville.

1988 Pinson Mounds: Internal Chronology and External Relationships. In *Middle Woodland Settlement and Ceremonialism in the Mid-South and Lower Mississippi Valley*, edited by Robert C. Mainfort, Jr., Mississippi Department of Archives and History, Jackson.

Marrinan, Rochelle A.

1975 *Ceramics, Molluscs, and Sedentism: The Late Archaic Period on the Georgia Coast.* Unpublished Ph.D. dissertation, Department of Anthropology, University of Florida, Gainesville.

1991 Archaeological Investigations at Mission Patale, 1984–1991. *Florida Anthropologist* 44(2–4):228–254.

Marrinan, Rochelle A., John F. Scarry, and Rhonda Majors

1990   Prelude to de Soto: The Expedition of Panfilo de Narváez. In *Columbian Consequences: Archaeological and Historical Perspectives on the Spanish Borderlands*, Vol. 2, edited by D. H. Thomas, pp. 71–82. Smithsonian Institution Press, Washington and London.

Marquardt, William H.
1988   Politics and Production Among the Calusa of South Florida. In *Hunters and Gatherers 1: History, Evolution and Change*, edited by Tim Ringold, David Riches and James Woodburn, pp. 161–188. St. Martin's Press, New York.
1992   *Culture and Environment in the Domain of the Calusa*. Institute of Archaeology and Paleoenvironmental Studies Monograph No. 1, University of Florida, Gainesville.

Martin, Paul S., and Richard G. Klein
1984   *Quaternary Extinctions: A Prehistoric Revolution*. University of Arizona Press, Tuscon.

Mason, Carol I.
1963   Eighteenth Century Culture Change Among the Lower Creeks. *Florida Anthropologist* 16:65–80.

McBride,, Kim A.
1990   *Tenancy and the Domestic Domain: Fertility and Household Organization Among Postbellum Mississippi Tenant Farmers*. Unpublished Ph.D. dissertation, Department of Anthropology, Michigan State University, East Lansing.

McBride, W. Stephen
1991   *Flush Times on the Upper Tombigbee: Settlement and Economic Development in Lowndes County, Mississippi*. Unpublished Ph.D. dissertation, Department of Anthropology, Michigan State University, East Lansing.

McBride, W. Stephen, and Kim A. McBride
1987   Socioeconomic Variation in a Late Antebellum Southern Town: The View from Archaeological and Documentary Sources. In *Consumer Choice in Historical Archaeology*, edited by Suzanne M. Spencer-Wood, pp. 139–162. Plenum Press, New York.

McEwan, Bonnie
1991a   Hispanic Life on the Seventeenth Century Florida Frontier. *Florida Archaeology* 44(2–4):255–267.
1991b   San Louis de Talimali: The Archaeology of Spanish-Indian Relations at a Florida Mission. *Historical Archaeology* 25(3):36–30.
1991c   The Missions of Spanish Florida (editor). *Florida Anthropologist* 44(2–4).

McMillan, R. B., and W. Klippel
1981   Post-glacial Environmental Change and Hunting-Gathering Societies of the Southern Prairie Peninsula. *Journal of Archaeological Science* 8:215–245.

Mead, Jim I., and David J. Meltzer
1984   North American Late Quaternary Extinctions and the Radiocarbon Record. In *Quaternary Extinctions: A Prehistoric Revolution*, edited by Paul S. Martin and Richard G. Klein, pp. 440–450. University of Arizona Press, Tucson.

Meltzer, David J.
1989   Why Don't We Know When the First People Came to North America? *American Antiquity* 54:471–490.

Meltzer, David J., and Bruce D. Smith
1986   Paleo-Indian and Early Archaic Subsistence Strategies in Eastern North America. In *Foraging, Collecting, and Harvesting: Archaic Period Subsistence and Settlement in the Eastern Woodlands*, edited by S. Neusius, pp. 1–30. Center for Archaeological Investigations, Southern Illinois University, Carbondale.

Meltzer, David J., and J. I. Mead
1983   The Timing of Late Pleistocene Mammalian Extinctions in North America. *Quaternary Research* 19:130–135.

Michie, James L.
    1990   *Richmond Hill Plantation 1810–1868: The Discovery of Antebellum Life on a Waccamaw Planta-tion.* The Reprint Company, Spartanburg, South Carolina.

Milanich Jerald T., J. Chapman, A. S. Cordell, S. Hale, Ann S. Cordell, Vernon J. Knight, Jr.,
Timothy A. Kohler, and Brenda Sigler-Lavelle
    1984   *McKeithen Weeden Island: The Culture of North Florida, A.D. 200–900.* Academic Press, San Diego.

Milanich, Jerald T., and Charles H. Fairbanks
    1980   *Florida Archaeology.* Academic Press, New York.

Milanich, Jerald T., and Susan Milbrath (editors)
    1989   *First Encounters: Spanish Explorations in the Caribbean and the United States, 1492–1570.* University of Florida Press, Gainesville.

Miller, James J.
    1992   Effects of Environmental Changes on Late Archaic People of Northeast Florida. *Florida Anthropologist* 45(2):100–106.

Milner, George R.
    1980   Epidemic Disease in the Postcontact Southeast: A Reappraisal. *Midcontinental Journal of Archaeology* 5:39–56.
    1990   The Late Prehistoric Cahokia Cultural System of the Mississippi River Valley: Founda-tions, Florescence, Fragmentation. *Journal of World Prehistory* 4(1):1–43.

Milner, George R., Thomas E. Emerson, Mark W. Mehrer, Joyce A. Williams, and Duane Esarey
    1984   Mississippian and Oneota Period. In *American Bottom Archaeology,* edited by Charles J. Bareis and James W. Porter, pp. 157–186. Published for the Illinois Department of Transportation by the University of Illinois Press, Urbana and Chicago.

Minnerly, W. Lee (editor)
    1982   *Oral Historical, Documentary and Archaeological Investigations of Colbert, Barton and Vinton, Mississippi: An Interim Report on Phase I of the Tombigbee Historic Townsites Project.* The Museum, Michigan State University, East Lansing. Submitted to the Mobile District, U.S. Army Corps of Engineers.
    1983   *Oral Historical, Documentary and Archaeological Investigations of Colbert, Barton and Vinton, Mississippi: An Interim Report on Phase II of the Tombigbee Historic Townsites Project.* The Museum, Michigan State University, East Lansing. Submitted to the Mobile District, U.S. Army Corps of Engineers.

Mitchem, Jeffrey M.
    1989   Artifacts of Exploration: Archaeological Evidence from La Florida. In *First Encounters: Spanish Explorations in the Caribbean and the United States, 1492–1570,* edited by Jerald T. Milanich and Susan Milbrath, pp. 99–109. Ripley P. Bullen Monographs in Anthropol-ogy and History, No. 9, Florida Museum of Natural History, Gainesville, University of Florida Press, Gainesville.
    1990   Initial Spanish-Indian Contact in West Peninsular Florida: The Archaeological Evidence. In *Columbian Consequences: Archaeological and Historical Perspectives on the Spanish Border-lands,* Vol. 2, edited by D. H. Thomas, pp. 49–60. Smithsonian Institution Press, Wash-ington and London.

Moir, Randall W., and David H. Jurney (editors)
    1987   *Historic Buildings, Material Culture, and People of the Prairie Margin: Architecture, Artifacts, and Synthesis of Historic Archaeology.* Archaeology Research Program, Institute for the Study of Earth and Man, Southern Methodist University, Dallas.

Moore, Clarence B.
    1901   Certain Aboriginal Remains of the Northwest Florida Coast (Pt. I). *Journal of the Academy of Natural Sciences of Philadelphia* 11:421–497.

1903   Aboriginal Sand Mounds of the Apalachicola River. *Journal of the Academy of Natural Sciences of Philadelphia* 12.

1905   Certain Aboriginal Remains on Mobile Bay and on Mississippi Sound. *Journal of the Academy of Natural Sciences of Philadelphia* 13:279–297.

1907   Mounds of the Lower Chattahoochee and Lower Flint Rivers. *Journal of the Academy of Natural Sciences of Philadelphia* 13:427–456.

1908   Certain Mounds of Arkansas and Mississippi. *Journal of the Academy of Natural Sciences of Philadelphia* 13:279–297.

Moore, Wilbert E. and Robin M. Williams
1942   Stratification in the Antebellum South. *American Sociological Review* 7:343–351.

Moorehead, Warren King
1932   Exploration of the Etowah Site in Georgia. In *Etowah Papers*, edited by Warren K. Moorehead, Yale University Press, New Haven.

Morrell, Ross L. and B. Calvin Jones
1970   *San Juan de Aspalaga, A Preliminary Architectural Study*. Florida Bureau of Historic Sites and Properties, Bulletin No. 1, Department of State, Tallahassee, Florida.

Morrison, J. P. E.
1942   Preliminary Report on the Mollusks Found in the Shell Mounds of the Pickwick Landing Basin in the Tennessee River Valley. In *An Archaeological Survey of Pickwick Basin*, edited by W. S. Webb and D. L. DeJarnette, pp. 337–392. Bureau of American Ethnology, Bulletin 129, Washington.

Morse, Dan F.
1975   Paleo-Indian in the Land of Opportunity: Preliminary Report on the Excavations at the Sloan Site (3Ge94). In *The Cache River Archaeological Project: An Experiment in Contract Archaeology*. Assembled by Michael Schiffer and John House. Arkansas Archaeological Survey Research Series 8:113–119.

Morse, Dan F. and Phyllis A. Morse
1983   *Archaeology of the Central Mississippi Valley*. Academic Press, Inc., San Diego.

Morse, Dan F., and Phyllis A. Morse
1990   The Zebree Site. In *The Mississippian Emergence*, edited by Bruce D. Smith, pp. 51–66. Smithsonian Institution Press, Washington and London.

Muller, Jon
1986   *Archaeology of the Lower Mississippi-Ohio River Valley*. Academic Press, San Diego.
1987   *Archaeology of the Lower Ohio River Valley*. Academic Press, San Diego.

Nassaney, M. S. and C. R. Cobb (editors)
1991   *Stability, Transformation and Variation: The Late Woodland Southeast*. Plenum Press, New York.

Neil, Wilfred T.
1958   A Stratified Early Site at Silver Springs, Florida. *Florida Anthropologist* 11(2):33–52.

Neitzel, Robert S.
1965   *Archaeology of the Fatherland Site: The Grand Village of the Natchez*. Anthropological Papers, Vol. 51, Pt. 1, American Museum of Natural History, New York.

Neitzel, Robert S.
1983   *The Grand Village of the Natchez Revisited: Excavations at the Fatherland Site, Adams County, Mississippi, 1972*. Mississippi Department of Archives and History, Archaeological Report Number 2. Jackson.

Newsom, Lee A.
1988   The Paleoethnobotany of Windover (8BR246): An Archaic Period Mortuary Site in Florida. Paper presented in a symposium entitled Archaic Adaptation and Biological

Diversity at the Florida Windover Site at the 53rd Annual Meeting of the Society for American Archaeology, Phoenix.

Newsom, Lee A., and Barbara A. Purdy
1990   Florida Canoes: A Maritime Heritage from the Past. *Florida Anthropologist* 43:164–180.

Oliver, Billy L.
1985   Tradition and Typology: Basic Elements of the Carolina Projectile Point Sequence. In *Structure and Process in Southeastern Archaeology,* edited by Roy S. Dickens and H. Trawick Ward, pp. 195–211. University of Alabama Press, Tuscaloosa.

Orser, Charles E., Jr.
1984   The Past Ten Years of Plantation Archaeology in the United States. *Southeastern Archaeology* 3:1–12.
1988   The Archaeological Analysis of Plantation Society: Replacing Status and Caste with Economics and Power. *American Antiquity* 53(4):735–751.
1990   Historical Archaeology on Southern Plantations and Farms, edited by Charles E. Orser, Jr., pp. 1–6. *Historical Archaeology* 24:4.

Orser, Charles E., Jr., and Annette M. Nekola
1985   Plantation Settlement from Slavery to Tenancy: An Example from a Piedmont Plantation in South Carolina. In *Archaeology of Slavery and Plantation Life,* edited by Theresa A. Singleton, pp. 67–96. Academic Press, New York.

O'Steen, Lisa, R. Jerald Ledbetter, Daniel T. Elliot, and William Barker
1986   Paleo-Indian Sites of the Inner Piedmont of Georgia: Observations of Settlement in the Oconee Watershed. *Early Georgia* 13:1–63.

Otto, John S.
1977   Artifacts and Status Differences: A Comparison of Ceramics from Planter, Overseer, and Slave Sites on an Antebellum Plantation. In *Research Strategies in Historical Archaeology,* edited by Stanley S. South, pp. 91–118. Academic Press, New York.
1980   Race and Class on Antebellum Plantations. In *Archaeological Perspectives on Ethnicity in America: Afro-American and Asian American Culture History,* edited by Robert Schulyer, pp. 3–13. Baywood Press, Farmingdale, New York.
1984   *Cannon's Point Plantation, 1794–1860: Living Conditions and Status Patterns in the Old South.* Academic Press, New York.

Owlsley, Frank L.
1949   *Plain Folk of the Old South.* Louisiana State University Press, Baton Rouge.

Parker, James W.
1982   Archaeological Test Investigations at 1Su7: The Fort Tombecbe Site. *Journal of Alabama Archaeology* 28:1.

Pearson, Charles E.
1977   *Analysis of Late Prehistoric Settlements on Ossabaw Island, Georgia.* Laboratory of Archaeology Series, Report No. 12. University of Georgia, Athens.
1978   Analysis of Late Mississippian Settlements on Ossabaw Island, Georgia. In *Mississippian Settlement Patterns,* edited by Bruce D. Smith, pp. 53–80. Academic Press, New York.

Peebles, Christopher S.
1971   Moundville and Surrounding Sites; Some Structural Considerations of Mortuary Practices II. In *Approaches to the Social Dimensions of Mortuary Practices,* edited by James A. Brown, pp. 68–91. Memoir 25, Society for American Archaeology.
1974   *Moundville: The Organization of a Prehistoric Community and Culture.* Unpublished Ph.D. dissertation, Department of Anthropology, University of California, Santa Barbara.
1978   Determinants of Settlement Size and Location in the Moundville Phase. In *Mississippian Settlement Patterns,* edited by Bruce D. Smith, pp. 369–416. Academic Press, New York.
1983a   *Excavations at the Lubbub Creek Archaeological Locality. Vol. 1, Prehistoric Agricultural Com-*

munities in West Central Alabama. University of Michigan, Ann Arbor. Submitted to the Mobile District, U.S. Army Corps of Engineers.

1983b *Studies of Material Remains from the Lubbub Creek Archaeological Locality, Vol. 2, Prehistoric Agricultural Communities in West Central Alabama.* University of Michigan, Ann Arbor. Submitted to the Mobile District, U.S. Army Corps of Engineers.

1983c *Basic Data and Processing at the Lubbub Creek Archaeological Locality, Vol. 3, Prehistoric Agricultural Communities in West Central Alabama.* University of Michigan, Ann Arbor. Submitted to the Mobile District, U.S. Army Corps of Engineers.

1987 The Rise and Fall of the Mississippian in Western Alabama: The Moundville and Summerville Phases, A.D. 1000–1600. *Mississippi Archaeology* 22(1):1–31.

Peebles, Christopher S. and Susan M. Kus
1977 Some Archaeological Correlates of Ranked Societies. *American Antiquity* 42:421–448.

Penton, Daniel T.
1974a The Early Swift Creek Phase In Northern Florida: Internal Expressions and External Connections. Paper presented at the Annual Meeting of the Society for American Archaeology, Washington.

1974b A Synthesis of the Santa Rosa-Swift Creek Period. MS on file. Archaeology Institute, University of West Florida, Pensacola.

Percy, George W., and David S. Brose
1974 Weeden Island ecology: subsistence and village life in Northwest Flordia. Paper presented at the 39th Annual Meeting of the Society for American Archaeology, Washington, D.C.

Peregrine, Peter
1991 A Graph-Theoretic Approach to the Evolution of Cahokia. *American Antiquity* 56(1)66–74.

Phelps, David S.
1968 Thom's Creek Ceramics in the Central Savannah River Locality. *Florida Anthropologist* 21(1):17–30.

1969 *Swift Creek and Santa Rosa in Northwest Florida.* Notebook 1, pp. 14–24. Institute of Archaeology and Anthropology, University of South Carolina, Columbia.

1983 Archaeology of the North Carolina Coast and Coastal Plain: Problems and Hypotheses. In *The Prehistory of North Carolina,* edited by Mark A. Mathis and Jeffery J. Crow. North Carolina Division of Archives and History, Department of Cultural Resources, Raleigh.

Phillips, John C.
1989 *Archaeological Testing of the Hickory Ridge Site (8Es1280): A Mississippian Stage Cemetery in Escambia County, Florida.* Reports of Investigations No. 26, Institute of West Florida Archaeology, University of West Florida, Pensacola.

1993 *Arcadia: An Early 19th Century Water Powered Industrial Complex American in Northwest Florida.* Reports of Investigations No. 44, Archaeology Institute, University of West Florida, Pensacola.

Phillips, Philip
1970 *Archaeological Survey of the Lower Yazoo Basin, Mississippi, 1949–1955.* Papers of the Peabody Museum of Archaeology and Ethnology Vol. 60, Harvard University, Cambridge.

Phillips, Phillip, James A. Ford, and James B. Griffin
1951 *Archaeological Survey in the Lower Mississippi Alluvial Valley, 1940–1947.* Papers of the Peabody Museum of Archaeology and Ethnology, Vol. 25, Harvard University, Cambridge.

Phillips, Philip, and James A. Brown
1978 *Pre-Columbian Shell Engravings from the Craig Mound at Spiro, Oklahoma.* Peabody Museum

Press, Peabody Museum of Archaeology and Ethnology, Harvard University, Cambridge.

Piper, Harry M., and Jacquelyn G. Piper
  1982   *Archaeological Excavations at the Quad Block Site, 8-Hi-998, Located at the Site of the Old Fort Brooke Municipal Parking Garage, Tampa, Florida.* Piper Archaeological Research, Inc. Report on file, Department of Public Works, City of Tampa, Florida.

Piper, Harry M., and Jacquelyn G. Piper
  1982   *Archaeological Excavations at the Quad Block Site, 8Hi998.* Piper Archaeological Research, St. Petersburg, Florida.
  1993   Locating Fort Brooke Beneath Present-Day Tampa. *Florida Anthropologist* 46(3):151–158.

Polhemus, Richard R.
  1985   *Archaeological Investigation of the Tellico Blockhouse Site: A Federal and Trade Complex.* University of Tennessee Department of Anthropology, Report of Investigations No. 26, and Tennessee Valley Authority Publications in Anthropology No. 16.
  1987   *The Toqua Site: A Late Mississippian Town.* Reports of Investigations No. 41, University of Tennessee Department of Anthropology, and Tennessee Valley Authority Publications on Anthropology No. 44.

Prentice, G.
  1986   An Analysis of the Symbolism Expressed by the Birger Figurine. *American Antiquity* 51:(2) 239–266.

Price, James E.
  1978   The Settlement Pattern of the Powers Phase. In *Mississippian Settlement Patterns,* edited by Bruce D. Smith, pp. 201–231. Academic Press, New York.

Purdy, Barbara (editor)
  1988   *Wet Side Archaeology* Telford Press. Caldwell, New Jersey.
  1991   *The Art and Archaeology of Florida's Wetlands.* CRC Press, Boca Raton, FL.
  1992   Florida's Archaeological Wet Sites. In *The Wetland Revolution in Prehistory,* edited by Bryony Coles, pp. 125–134. WARP Occasional Paper 6, Department of History and Archaeology, University of Exeter, Exeter, UK.

Purrington, Burton L.
  1983   Ancient Mountaineers: An Overview of Prehistoric Archaeology of North Carolina's Western Mountain Region. In *The Prehistory of North Carolina,* edited by Mark A. Mathis and Jeffery J. Crow. North Carolina Division of Archives and History, Department of Cultural Resources, Raleigh.

Rafferty, Janet E., B. Lea Baker, and Jack D. Elliot, Jr.
  1980   *Archaeological Investigations at the East Aberdeen Site (22Mo819), Tombigbee River Multi-Resource District, Alabama and Mississippi.* Mississippi State University, Starkville. Report submitted to Interagency Archaeological Services, National Park Service, Atlanta.

Ramenofsky, Ann F.
  1990   Loss of Innocence: Explanations of Differential Persistence in the Sixteenth-Century Southeast. In *Columbian Consequences: Archaeological and Historical Perspectives on the Spanish Borderlands,* Vol. 2, edited by D. H. Thomas, pp. 31–48. Smithsonian Institution Press, Washington and London.

Reitz, Elizabeth J.
  1987   Vertebrate Fauna and Socioeconomic Status. In *Consumer Choice in Historical Archaeology,* edited by Suzanne M. Spencer-Wood, pp. 101–119. Plenum Press, New York.

Reitz, Elizabeth J., and Stephen L. Cumbaa
  1983   Diet and Foodways of Eighteenth Century St. Augustine. In *Spanish St. Augustine: The Archaeology of a Colonial Creole Community,* edited by Kathleen Deagan, pp. 151–186. Academic Press, New York.

Reitz, Elizabeth J., Tyson Gibbs, and Ted A. Rathburn
1985   Archaeological Evidence for Subsistence on Coastal Plantations. In *The Archaeology of Slave and Plantation Life,* edited by Theresa A. Singleton, pp. 163–194. Academic Press, Orlando.

Reitz, Elizabeth J., and C. Margret Scarry
1985   *Reconstructing Historic Subsistence with an Example from Spanish Florida.* Special Publication Series, No. 3, Society for Historical Archaeology.

Rogers, J. Daniel
1983   Social Ranking and Change in the Harlan and Spiro Phases of Eastern Oklahoma. In *Southeastern Natives and Their Pasts. Papers Honoring Dr. Robert E. Bell,* edited by Don G. Wycoff and Jack L. Hoffman, pp. 17–128. Oklahoma Archaeological Survey, Studies in Oklahoma's Past, Cross Timbers Heritage Association, Contribution No. 2.
1989   Settlement Contexts for Shifting Authority in the Arkansas Basin. In *Contributions to Spiro Archaeology: Mound Excavations and Regional Perspectives,* edited by J. Daniel Rogers, Don G. Wycoff, and Dennis A. Peterson, pp. 159–176. Oklahoma Archaeological Survey, Studies in Oklahoma's Past, No. 16.

Rollingson, Martha A.
1982   *Emerging Patterns of Plum Bayou Culture.* Arkansas Archaeological Research Series No. 18, Fayetteville.
1990   The Toltec Mounds Site: A Ceremonial Center in the Arkansas River Lowland. In *The Mississippian Emergence,* edited by Bruce D. Smith, pp. 9–49. Smithsonian Institution Press, Washington and London.

Rudolph, James L.
1984   Earthlodges and Platform Mounds: Changing Public Architecture in the Southeastern U.S. *Southeastern Archaeology* 3(1):33–45.

Russo, Michael A.
1986   *The Coevolution of Environment and Human Exploitation of Faunal Resources in the Upper St. Johns River Basin.* Unpublished M. A. thesis, Department of Anthropology, University of Florida, Gainesville.
1991   *Archaic Sedentism on the Florida Coast: A Case Study from Horr's Island.* Unpublished Ph.D. dissertation, Department of Anthropology, University of Florida, Gainesville.

Russo, Michael A., Lee A. Newsom, Ray M. McGee, and Barbara A. Purdy
1993   Groves Orange Midden Site (8-VO-2601). *Southeastern Archaeology,* in press.

Sahlins, M.
1963   Poor man, rich man, big-man, chief: political types in Melanesia and Polynesia. *Comparative Studies in Society and History* 5:285–303.
1968   *Tribesmen.* Prentice Hall, New York.
1972   *Stone Age Economics.* Adline, Chicago.

Sassaman, Kenneth E.
1993   *Early Pottery in the Southeast: Tradition and Innovation in Cooking Technology.* University of Alabama Press, Tuscaloosa.

Sassaman, Kenneth E., Mark J. Brooks, Glen T. Hanson, and David G. Anderson
1990   *Native American Prehistory of the Middle Savannah River Valley.* Savannah River Archaeological Papers 1. Occasional Papers of the Savannah River Archaeological Research Program, South Carolina Institute of Archaeology and Anthropology, University of South Carolina, Columbia.

Saucier, Roger T.
1974   *Quaternary Geology of the Lower Mississippi Valley.* Research Series No. 6, Arkansas Archaeological Survey, Little Rock.

Saunders, Lorraine

1972   *Osteology of the Republic Groves Site.* Unpublished Master's thesis, Department of Anthropology, Florida Atlantic University, Boca Raton.

Saunders, Rebecca
1988   *Excavations at 8Na41: Two Mission Period Sites on Amelia Island Florida.* Miscellaneous Project Report Series, No. 35, Department of Anthropology, University of Florida, Gainesville.
1990   Idea and Innovation: Spanish Mission Architecture in the Southeast. In *The Southeastern Ceremonial Complex: Artifacts and Analysis,* edited by Patricia Galloway. University of Nebraska Press, Lincoln and London.

Scarry, John F.
1981   Fort Walton Culture: A Redefinition. Southeastern Archaeological Bulletin 24:18–21.
1990   The Mississippian Emergence in the Fort Walton Area: The Evolution of the Cayson and Lake Jackson Phases. In *The Mississippian Emergence,* edited by Bruce D. Smith, pp. 227–250. Smithsonian Institution Press, Washington and London.

Schiffer, Michael
1975   An alternative to Morse's Dalton Settlement Pattern Hypothesis. *Plains Anthropologist* 20:253–266.

Schnell, Frank T., Vernon J. Knight, Jr., and Gail S. Schnell
1981   *Cemochechobee: Archaeology of a Mississippian Ceremonial Center on the Chattahoochee.* University Presses of Florida, Gainesville.

Schoolcraft, Henry R.
1851   *Historical and Statistical Information, Respecting the History, Condition, and Prospects of the Indian Tribes of the United States.* Parts I-VI, Philadelphia. Vol 1:267–268.

Schroedl, Gerald F. (editor)
1986   *Overhill Cherokee Archaeology at Chota-Tanasee.* Report of Investigations No. 38, Department of Anthropology, University of Tennessee, Knoxville, and Tennessee Valley Authority Publications in Anthropology No. 37.

Schroedl, Gerald F., C. Clifford Boyd, Jr., and R. P. Stephen Davis, Jr.
1990   Explaining Mississippi Origins in East Tennessee. In *The Mississippian Emergence,* edited by Bruce D. Smith, pp. 175–196. Smithsonian Institution Press, Washington and London.

Sears, William H.
1956   *Excavations at Kolomoki, Final Report.* University of Georgia Series in Anthropology 5. The University of Georgia Press, Athens.
1962   Hopewellian affiliations on the Gulf coast. *American Antiquity* 28:5–18.

Service, Elman R.
1971   *Primitive Social Organization.* Random House, New York.

Shapiro, Gary
1990   Bottomlands and Rapids: A Mississippian Adaptive Niche in the Georgia Piedmont. In *Lamar Archaeology,* edited by Mark Williams and Gary Shapiro, pp. 147–162. University of Alabama Press, Tuscaloosa.

Shapiro, Gary, and Bonnie McEwan
1991   Archaeology at San Luis: The Apalachee Council House. *Florida Archaeology* 6. Florida Bureau of Archaeological Research, Tallahassee.

Shea, Andrea B.
1979   Botanical Remains. In *The Peripheries of Poverty Point,* edited by Prentice M. Thomas, Jr., Report of Investigations 12:245–260, New World Research, Fort Walton Beach, Florida.

Shenkel, J. Richard
1980   Oak Island Archaeology: Prehistoric Estuarine Adaptations in the Mississippi River Delta. MS on file. University of New Orleans.

1984   Early Woodland in Coastal Louisiana. In *Perspectives on Gulf Coast Prehistory*, edited by Dave D. Davis. University of Florida Press, Florida State Museum, Gainesville.

Sherrod, P. Clay, and Martha A. Rollingson
1987   *Surveyors of the Ancient Mississippi Valley: Models and Alignments in Prehistoric Mound Sites*. Arkansas Archaeological Survey Research Series No. 28. Arkansas Archaeological Survey, Fayetteville.

Shogren, Michael G., Kenneth R. Turner, and Jody C. Perroni
1989   *Elko Switch Cemetery: An Archaeological Perspective*. Reports of Investigations 58, The University of Alabama, Alabama State Museum of Natural History, Division of Archaeology, Tuscaloosa.

Sigler-Eisenberg, Brenda
1988   Settlement, Subsistence, and Environment: Aspects of Cultural Development Within the Wetlands of East-Central Florida. In *Wet Site Archaeology*, edited by Barbara A. Purdy, pp. 291–306. Telford Press, Caldwell, New Jersey.

Singleton, Theresa A.
1985   *The Archaeology of Slavery and Plantation Life*. Academic Press, San Diego.
1988   An Archaeological Framework for Slavery and Emancipation. In *The Recovery of Meaning: Historical Archaeology in the Eastern United States*, edited by Mark P. Leone and Parker B. Potter, Jr., pp. 345–370. Smithsonian Institution Press, Washington and London.
1990   The Archaeology of the Plantation South: A Review of Approaches and Goals. In *Historical Archaeology on Southern Farms and Plantations*, edited by Charles E. Orser, Jr., pp. 70–77, and *Historical Archaeology* 24:4.

Smith, Betty A.
1975a   The Relationship Between Deptford and Swift Creek Ceramics as Evidenced at the Mandeville Site, 9Cla1. *Southeastern Archaeological Conference Bulletin* 18:195–200.
1975b   *A Re-Analysis of the Mandeville Site, 9Cla1, Focusing on its Internal History and External Relations*. Unpublished Ph.D. dissertation, Department of Anthropology, University of Georgia, Athens.

Smith, Bruce D.
1985a   The Role of *Chenopodium* as a Domesticate in Pre-Maize Garden Systems of the Eastern United States. *Southeastern Archaeology* 4(12):51–73.
1985b   *Chenopodium berlandieri* ssp. *jonesianum*: Evidence for a Hopewellian Domesticate from Ash Cave, Ohio. *Southeastern Archaeology* 4(2):107–133.
1985c   Mississippian Patterns of Subsistence and Settlement. In *Alabama and the Borderlands*, edited by R. Reid Badger and Lawrence A. Clayton. University of Alabama Press, Tuscaloosa.
1985d   Introduction to the 1985 edition of *Report of the Mound Explorations of the Bureau of Ethnology* by Cyrus Thomas. Smithsonian Institution Press, Washington and London.
1986   The Archaeology of the Southeastern United States: From Dalton to De Soto, 10, 500-500 B.P. *Advances in World Archaeology* 5(1–92).
1990   *The Mississippian Emergence* (editor). Smithsonian Institution Press, Washington and London.

Smith, Hale
1965   *Archaeological Excavations at Santa Rosa Pensacola*. Florida State University Notes in Anthropology 10, Tallahassee, Florida.

Smith, Marvin T.
1987   *Archaeology of Aboriginal Culture Change in the Interior Southeast: Population During the Early Historic Period*. Ripley P. Bullen Monographs in Anthropology and History, No. 6. The Florida State Museum, University of Florida Press, Gainesville.
1989   Indian Responses to European Contact: The Coosa Example: In *First Encounters: Spanish Explorations in the Caribbean and the United States, 1492–1570*, edited by Jerald T. Milanich and Susan Milbrath, pp. 135–149. University of Florida Press, Gainesville.

1992   *Historic Period Indian Archaeology of Northern Georgia.* Georgia Archaeological Research Design Paper No. 7. Laboratory of Archaeology Series, Report No. 30. University of Georgia, Athens.

Smith, Stephen S., David F. Barton, and Timothy B. Riordan
1982   *Ethnoarchaeology of the Bay Springs Farmsteads: A Study of Rural American Settlement.* Resource Analysts, Inc., Bloomington, Indiana. Submitted to the Nashville District, U.S. Army Corps of Engineers. Copies available from Resource Analysts, Inc.

Snow, Frankie
1993   Swift Creek Design Investigation: The Hardford Case. Papers of the Swift Creek Conference, Macon, GA.
1977   An Archaeological survey of the Ocmulgee Big Bend Region. Occasional Papers from South Georgia College, No. 3, Douglas, Georgia, page 18.

Snow, Frankie and Keith Stephenson
1993   Swift Creek Designs: A Tool for Monitoring Interaction. Papers of the Swift Creek Conference, Macon, GA.

South, Stanley
1971   *Historical Perspective at Ninety Six with a summary of exploratory excavation at Holmes' Fort and the Town Blockhouse.* Research Manuscript Series 6, The University of South Carolina, Institute of Archaeology and Anthropology, Columbia.
1977   *Method and Theory in Historical Archaeology.* Academic Press, New York.
1980   The Discovery of Santa Elena. Manuscript Series 165. Institute of Archaeology and Anthropology, University of South Carolina.

South, Stanley
1985   *Excavation of the* Casa Fuerte *and Wells at Fort San Felipe.* Manuscript Series 196. Institute of Archeology and Anthropology, University of South Carolina.
1987   Santa Elena: Threshold of Conquest. In *The Recovery of Meaning: Historical Archaeology in the Eastern United States,* edited by Mark P. Leone and Parker B. Potter, Jr., pp. 27–72. Smithsonian Institution Press, Washington and London.

South, Stanley, Russel K. Skowronek, and Richard E. Johnson
1988   Spanish Artifacts from Santa Elena. Occasional Papers Anthropological Studies 7, The University of South Carolina, Institute of Archaeology and Anthropology, Columbia.

Stannard, Dennis E.
1991   The Consequences of Contact: Toward an Interdisciplinary Theory of Native Responses to Biological and Cultural Invasion. In *Columbian Consequences,* Vol. 2, edited by David H. Thomas. Smithsonian Institution Press, Washington and London.

Stein, Julie K.
1982   Geologic Analysis of the Green River Shell Middens. *Southeastern Archaeology* 1:22–39.

Steponaitis, Vincas P.
1978   Location Theory and Complex Chiefdoms: A Mississippian Example. In *Mississippian Settlement Patterns,* edited by Bruce D. Smith, pp. 417–453. Academic Press, New York.
1983   *Ceramics, Chronology and Community Patterns: An Archaeological Study at Moundville.* Academic Press, New York.
1986   Prehistoric Archaeology in the Southeastern United States, 1970–1985. *Annual Reviews of Anthropology* 15:363–404.

Stoltman, James B.
1966   New Radiocarbon Dates for Southeastern Fiber-Tempered Pottery. *American Antiquity* 31(6):872–874.
1974   *Groton Plantation.* Peabody Museum Monographs 1. Harvard University, Cambridge.

Storey, Rebecca
1991   Bioanthropological Studies of the Lake Jackson Site. Paper delivered at the 48th Southeastern Archaeological Conference, Jackson, Mississippi.

Stowe, Noel R.
1985   The Pensacola Variant and the Bottle Creek Phase. *Florida Anthropologist* 38(1–2):144–149.

Swanton, John R.
1922   *Early History of the Creek Indians and Their Neighbors.* Bureau of American Ethnology Bulletin 73:173. Smithsonian Institution, Washington.
1924   *Social Organization and Social Usages of the Indians of the Creek Confederacy.* Forty-second Annual Report of the Bureau of American Ethnology. 23–472. Smithsonian Institution, Washington.
1946   *The Indians of the Southeastern United States.* Bureau of American Ethnology Bulletin No. 123. Smithsonian Institution, Washington.

Tankersley, Kenneth B., and Barry L. Isaac (editors)
1990   *Early Paleoindian Economies of Eastern North America.* Research in Economic Anthropology, A Research Annual, Supplement 5. JAI Press, Greenwich, Connecticut.

Tankersley, Kenneth, B., and Cherly Ann Munson
1992   Comments on Meadowcroft Rockshelter Radiocarbon Chronology and the Recognitional of Coal Contaminants. *American Antiquity* 57(2):321–326.

Tankersley, Kenneth, B., Cherly Ann Munson, and Donald Smith
1987   Recognition of Bituminous Coal Contaminants in Radiocarbon Samples. *American Antiquity* 52(2):318–329.

Thomas, Cyrus
1894   *Report on the Mound Explorations of the Bureau of Ethnology.* Smithsonian Institution, Washington.

Thomas, Daniel H.
1989   *Fort Toulouse: The French Outpost at the Alabamas on the Coosa.* The University of Alabama Press, Tuscaloosa.

Thomas, David Hurst
1987   The Archaeology of Mission Santa Catalina de Guale I. Search and Discovery. *Anthropological Papers of the American Museum of Natural History* 63(2):47–161.
1988   Saints and Soldiers at Santa Catalina: Hispanic Designs for Colonial America. In *The Recovery of Meaning: Historical Archaeology in the Eastern United States,* edited by Mark P. Leone and Parker B. Potter, Jr., pp. 73–140. Smithsonian Institution Press, Washington and London.
1990   *Columbian Consequences: Archaeological and Historical Perspectives on the Spanish Borderlands, Vol. 2.* Smithsonian Institution Press, Washington and London.

Thomas, David Hurst and Clark Spencer Larsen
1979   The Anthropology of St. Catherines Island 2. The Refuge-Deptford Mortuary Complex. *Anthropological Papers of the American Museum of Natural History* 56:(1), New York.

Thomas, Prentice M., Jr. and L. Janice Campbell (editors)
1992   *Eglin Air Force Base Historic Preservation Plan: Technical Synthesis of Cultural Resources Investigations at Eglin Santa Rosa; Okaloosa, and Walton Counties, Florida.* New World Research, Inc. Report of Investigations No. 192. Submitted to the National Park Service, Southeast Region, Atlanta. Funds provided by the U.S. Air Force, Contract No. CX5000-2-0497.

Thornbury, William D.
1965   *Regional Geomorphology of the United States.* John Wiley and Sons, New York.

Toth, E. A.
1974   *Archaeology and Ceramics at the Marksville Site.* Museum of Archaeology Archaeological Papers No. 56, University of Michigan, Ann Arbor.

Trinkley, Michael B.
1980   *Investigation of the Woodland Period along the South Carolina Coast.* Unpublished Ph.D.

dissertation, Department of Anthropology, University of North Carolina, Chapel Hill.

1983   "Let Us Now Praise Famous Men"—If Only We Can Find Them. *Southeastern Archaeology* 2(1):30–36.

1985   The Form and Function of South Carolina's Early Woodland Shell Rings. In *Structure and Process in Southeastern Archaeology*, edited by Roy S. Dickens and H. Trawick Ward, pp. 102–118. The University of Alabama Press, Tuscaloosa.

1986   *Indian and Freedmen Occupation at the Fish Haul Site (38BU805) Beaufort County, South Carolina* (editor). Chicora Foundation Research Series 7, Columbia, South Carolina.

1989   An Archaeological Overview of the South Carolina Woodland Period: It's the Same Old Riddle. In *Studies in South Carolina Archaeology: Essays in Honor of Robert L. Stephenson*, edited by Albert C. Goodyear, III, and Glen T. Hansen. Anthropological Studies 9. Anthropological Papers of the South Carolina Institute of Archaeology and Anthropology, The University of South Carolina, Columbia.

Verano, John W. and Douglas H. Ubelaker

1992   *Disease and Demography in the Americas.* Smithsonian Institution Press, Washington, D.C.

Vernon, Richard, and Bonnie McEwan

1990   *Town Plan and Town Life at Seventeenth-Century San Luis.* Florida Archaeological Reports No. 13. Division of Historical Resources, Bureau of Archaeological Research, Tallahassee, Florida.

Walthall, J. A.

1973   *Copena: A Tennessee Valley Middle Woodland Culture.* Unpublished Ph.D. dissertation, Department of Anthropology, University of North Carolina, Chapel Hill.

1980   *Prehistoric Indians of the Southeast: Archaeology of Alabama and the Middle South.* University of Alabama Press, University, Alabama.

1991   An Analysis of Late Eighteenth Century Ceramics from Arkansas Post at Ecores Rouges. *Southeastern Archaeology* 10(2):98–113.

Walthall, John A., and Ned J. Jenkins

1976   *The Gulf Formational Stage in Southeastern Prehistory.* Southeastern Archaeological Conference Bulletin 19.

Waselkov, Gregory A.

1989a   Introduction: Recent Archaeological and Historical Research. In *Fort Toulouse: The French Outpost at the Alabamas on the Coosa* by Daniel H. Thomas. The University of Alabama Press, Tuscaloosa and London.

1989b   Seventeenth-Century Trade in the Colonial Southeast. *Southeastern Archaeology* 8(2):117–133.

1991   *Archaeology at the French Colonial Site of Old Mobile (Phase I: 1989–1991).* Anthropological Monograph I. University of South Alabama, Mobile.

Waselkov, Gregory A., Brian M. Wood, and Joseph M. Herbert

1982   *Colonization and Conquest: The 1980 Archaeological Excavations at Fort Toulouse and Fort Jackson, Alabama.* Archaeological Monograph 4, Auburn University, Montgomery.

Watts, William A.

1980   The Quaternary Vegetation History of the Southeastern United States. *Annual Reviews of Ecology and Systematics* 11:387–409.

Weaver, David C., and James F. Doster

1982   *Historical Geography of the Upper Tombigbee Valley.* The Center for the Study of Southern History and Culture, The University of Alabama, Tuscaloosa. Submitted to the Mobile District, U.S. Army Corps of Engineers. Copies available from University of Alabama.

Webb, Clarence H.

1982   The Poverty Point Culture. In *Geoscience and Man XVII*, second edition, Revised. Geoscience Publications, Department of Geography and Anthropology, Louisiana State University, Baton Rouge.

Webb, S. David, Jerald T. Milanich, Roger Alexon, and James Dunbar
1984   A *Bison antiquus* Kill Site, Wascissa River, Jefferson County, Florida. *American Antiquity* 49:384–392.

Webb, William S. and David L. DeJarnette
1942   *An Archaeological Survey of Pickwick Basin in the Adjacent Portions of the States of Alabama, Mississippi and Tennessee.* Bulletin 129, Bureau of American Ethnology, Washington.

Weinstein, R. A.
1986   Tchefuncte Occupation in the Lower Mississippi Delta and Adjacent Coastal Zone. In *The Tchula Period in the Mid-South and Lower Mississippi Valley* edited by D. H. Dye and R. C. Brister. Proceedings of the 1982 Mid-South Archaeological Conference. Archaeological Report No. 17, Mississippi Department of Archives and History, Jackson.

Weisman, Brent R.
1988   Archaeological Excavations at Fig Springs Mission (8Co1). *Florida Archaeology Reports* 11, Florida Bureau of Archaeological Research, Tallahassee.
1989   *Like Beads on a String: A Culture History of the Seminole Indians in Northern Peninsular Florida.* University of Alabama Press, Tuscaloosa.

Welch, Paul
1990   Mississippian Emergence in West-Central Alabama. In *The Mississippian Emergence,* edited by Bruce D. Smith, pp. 197–225. Smithsonian Institution Press, Washington and London.
1991   *Moundville's Economy.* University of Alabama Press, Tuscaloosa.

Wharton, Barry R., George R. Ballo, and Mitchell E. Hope
1981   The Republic Groves Site, Hardee County, Florida. *Florida Anthropologist* 34(2):59–80.

Wheaton, Thomas R., Amy Friedlander, and Patrick H. Garrow
1983   *Yaughan and Curriboo Plantations: Studies in Afr.-American Archaeology.* Submitted to Interagency Archaeological Services, National Park Service, Atlanta.

Wheaton, Thomas R., and Patrick H. Garrow
1985   Acculturation and the Archaeological Record in the Carolina Lowcountry. In *The Archaeology of Slavery and Plantation Life,* edited by Theresa A. Singleton, pp. 239–260. Academic Press, San Diego.

Wheaton, Thomas, R., Jr., Mary Beth Reed, Rita Folse Elliot, Marc S. Frank, and Leslie E. Raymer
1990   *James City, North Carolina: Archaeological and Historical Study of an African-American Urban Village,* Vol. I. New South Associates, Stone Mountain, Georgia in association with John Milner Associates, Inc., West Chester, Pennsylvania. Report to Bridge Pointe Development, Inc., New Bern, North Carolina.

White, John W.
1982   An Integration of Late Archaic Settlement Patterns for the South Carolina Piedmont. Unpublished M. A. Thesis, Department of Anthropology, University of Arkansas, Fayetteville.

Widmer, Randolph J.
1988   *The Evolution of the Calusa: A Nonagricultural Chiefdom on the Southwest Florida Coast.* University of Alabama Press, Tuscaloosa.

Willey, Gordon R.
1949   *Archaeology of the Florida Gulf Coast.* Smithsonian Miscellaneous Collections, Vol. 113.

Willey, Gordon R. and Jeremy A. Sabloff
1974   *A History of American Archaeology.* W. H. Freeman and Company, San Francisco.

Williams, Mark and Gary Shapiro

1990   Paired Towns. In *Lamar Archaeology,* edited by Mark Williams and Gary Shapiro, pp. 163–174. University of Alabama Press, Tuscaloosa.

Williams, Stephen (editor)
1977   *The Waring Papers.* Peabody Museum of Archaeology and Ethnology Papers 58.

Williams, Stephen
1982   The Vacant Quarter Hypothesis: A Discussion Symposium. Abstract in *Southeastern Archaeological Conference Bulletin* 25:iii.
1990   The Vacant Quarter and Other Late Events in the Lower Valley. In *Towns and Temples along the Mississippi,* edited by David H. Dye and Cheryl Anne Cox. University of Alabama Press, Tuscaloosa.
1992   *Fantastic Archaeology: The Wild Side of North American Prehistory.* University of Pennsylvania Press, Philadelphia.

Williams, Stephen, and Jeffery P. Brain
1983   *Excavations at the Lake George Site, Yazoo County, Mississippi, 1958–1960.* Peabody Museum of Archaeology and Ethnology Papers 74.

Wood, W. Dean, Dan T. Elliot, Teresa P. Rudolph, and Dennis B. Blanton
1986   *Prehistory in the Richard B. Russel Reservoir: The Archaic and Woodland Periods of the Upper Savannah River. The Final Report of Data Recovery at the Anderson and Elbert County Groups: 38AN8, 38AN126, 9EB17, 9EB19, and 9EB21.* Russell Papers. Interagency Archaeological Services, National Park Service, Atlanta.

Wood, W. Raymond and R. Bruce McMillan
1976   *Prehistoric Man and His Environments: A Case Study in the Ozark Highland.* Academic Press, New York.

Woofer, Thomas J., Jr., Gordon Blackwell, Harold Hoffsommer, James G. Maddox, Jean M. Massell, B. O. Williams, and Walter Wynne, Jr.
1936   *Landlord and Tenant on the Cotton Plantation.* Works Progress Administration, Division of Social Research, Monograph No. 5. U.S. Government Printing Office, Washington, D.C.

Wright, H. E., Jr.
1983   *Late-Quaternary Environments of the United States.* (editor) University of Minnesota Press, Minneapolis.

Wright, J. Leitch, Jr.
1986   *Creeks and Seminoles: The Destruction and Regeneration of the Muscogle People.* University of Nebraska Press, Lincoln and London.

Wycoff, Don G.
1980   *Caddoan Adaptive Strategies in the Arkansas Basin, Eastern Oklahoma.* Unpublished Ph.D. dissertation, Washington State University, Pullman. University Microfilms, Ann Arbor.

Wyman, Jeffries
1863   An Account of the Fresh-Water Shell-Heaps of the St. Johns River, Florida. *American Naturalist* 2(8–9):393–403, 449–463. Boston.

Wyman, Jefferies
1868   Fresh-Water Shell Mounds of the St. Johns River. *Memoirs of the Peabody Academy of Science.* 4:3–94. Salem.

Yarnell, Richard A.
1964   *Aboriginal Relationships between Culture and Plant Life in the Upper Great Lakes Region.* University of Michigan Anthropological Papers, No. 23. University of Michigan Press, Ann Arbor.

Yarnell, Richard A. and M. Jean Black
1985   Temporal Trends Indicated by a Survey of Archaic and Woodland Plant Food Remains from Southeastern North America. *Southeastern Archaeology* 4(2):93–106.

Zierden, Martha A., and Jeanne A. Calhoun

1984   *An Archaeological Investigation Plan for Charleston, South Carolina.* Archaeological Contributions 8. The Charleston Museum, Charleston.

1986   Urban Adaptations in Charleston, South Carolina, 1730–1820. *Historical Archaeology* 20(1):29–43.

1989   Approaches to Archaeological Investigation of Charleston, South Carolina. In *Studies in South Carolina Archaeology,* edited by Albert C. Goodyear, III and Glen T. Hansen, pp. 207–224. Anthropological Studies 9, Occasional Papers of the South Carolina Institute of Archaeology and Anthropology, The University of South Carolina, Columbia.

Index